# SOULSIDE

ULF HANNERZ

# SOULSIDE

INQUIRIES INTO ghetto culture AND community

THE UNIVERSITY OF CHICAGO CHICAGO + LONDON

The University of Chicago Press, Chicago 60637
The University of Chicago Press, Ltd., London

Printed in the United States of America

13 12 11 10 09 08 07 06 05 04     1 2 3 4 5

ISBN: 0-226-31576-2 (paper)

Library of Congress Cataloging-in-Publication Data

Hannerz, Ulf.
    Soulside : inquiries into ghetto culture and community /
Ulf Hannerz.
        p.  cm.
    Originally published: New York : Columbia University Press,
1969.
    Includes bibliographical references and index.
    ISBN 0-226-31576-2 (alk. paper)
        1. African Americans—Washington (D.C.)—Social condi-
    tions—20th century.  2. African Americans—Washington
    (D.C.)—Social life and customs—20th century.  3. Inner
    cities—Washington (D.C.)—History—20th century.  4. Com-
    munity life—Washington (D.C.)—History—20th century.
    5. Washington (D.C.)—Race relations.  6. Washington (D.C.)
    —Social conditions—20th century.  I. Title.

    F205.N4H3 2004
    305.896′0730753—dc22
                                                    2004044094

♾ The paper used in this publication meets the minimum re-
quirements of the American National Standard for Information
Sciences—Permanence of Paper for Printed Library Materials,
ANSI Z39.48-1992.

It is a peculiar sensation, this double-consciousness, this sense of always looking at one's self through the eyes of others, of measuring one's soul by the tape of a world that looks on in amused contempt and pity. One ever feels his twoness,—an American, a Negro; two souls, two thoughts, two unreconciled strivings; two warring ideals in one dark body, whose dogged strength keeps it from being torn asunder.

W. E. B. DuBois, *The Souls of Black Folk*

# Acknowledgments

Americans have a long tradition of hospitality toward visitors interested in their society. The present volume bears witness to the continued strength of this tradition. It is based on field work particularly in the Winston Street neighborhood of Washington, D.C., from August, 1966, to July, 1968, in conjunction with the Urban Language Study of the Center for Applied Linguistics; it was made possible in part by funds granted to that project by the Carnegie Corporation of New York. The University of Stockholm has provided further assistance in the form of a research fellowship as well as an additional minor grant which facilitated the completion of the manuscript. The financial support of these institutions is gratefully acknowledged. Of course, they bear no responsibility for any statements made or any views expressed on the following pages.

A considerable number of people have been helpful in other ways. Dr. Peter B. Hammond has supported my interest in black American life since I was a student of his at Indiana University; he also assisted in providing me with the opportunity to make this study. Colleagues at the Urban Language Study provided a stimulating intellectual environment in Washington, D.C., and gave generously from their knowledge of various facets of Washington life. I am particularly indebted to Mr. William A. Stewart, a consistent source of unorthodox insights into black culture and history; to Mrs. Anita Friedman, who before my arrival had conducted an interview survey of the Winston Street population and assembled other valuable background information; and to Mr. John Lewis, whose articulate views combined with a black community background did much to further my understanding of ghetto life during his stay as an Urban Language Study research assistant. At the University of Stockholm my friends and colleagues at the Institute of Ethnography have continued to stimulate my work. The head of the Institute, Professor Sigvald Linné, has my special thanks for his interest throughout the period of my study.

Some of the interpretations offered in the pages which follow have benefited from discussions of earlier versions, and I am grateful to those colleagues who made helpful suggestions on such occasions. I have drawn on the present chapters 4—6 in a paper presented at the annual meeting of the American Anthropological Association in Washington, D.C., in December, 1967, as well as in seminars arranged by the Departments of Anthropology of the University of Pittsburgh and the University of Minnesota. At the latter university I also had the opportunity of airing some of the views expressed in chapter 9. Some of the contents of chapters 1 and 4 were also discussed in a paper presented at the annual meeting of the Central States' Anthropological Society in Detroit in May, 1968.

I am also indebted to Mrs. Addie A. Allen, Mrs. Sibylla Haasum, Miss Mary Pat Hough, Mrs. Barbara Lancaster, and Mrs. Yara Romani who have all at various times courageously gone to work at typing parts of the manuscript; to at least one of them I am also obligated for prodding me into improving my handwriting.

Mr. Ralph Ellison and the William Morris Agency kindly gave me permission to use the quotation which appears on page 14.

Finally, it is obvious that I owe nobody as much as I owe to the people of Winston Street and their circles. For no very good reason, they offered me hospitality, friendship, and forbearance. Since they want to remain anonymous, I cannot even thank my closest friends in the neighborhood by name. Winston Street, of course, is a pseudonym, like other names for streets in the neighborhood as used in the text, and like all personal names except those of ghetto public figures. Various other insignificant descriptive details have also been altered. Thus I doubt that the neighborhood or any of its people can be identified on the basis of this book. However, I owe them thanks for the memories.

ULF HANNERZ

*Stockholm*
*March, 1969*

# Contents

# Introduction

The title of this volume is *Soulside: Inquiries into Ghetto Culture and Community*. Discussing what is in this title may be a way of starting to say something about the book, its perspective and its contents.

"Soul" is black. The black people of America's inner cities (a popular contemporary euphemism for slums, but often a less appropriate term, as the areas are often more rundown than centrally located) are soul brothers and soul sisters, listen to soul music, and eat soul food at least occasionally. "Soul" is said to be the essence of their blackness, shaped by their experience and expressed in their everyday life. "Soulside", then, may be as good a name as any for the black side of town.

"Ghetto" is commonly used as an anti-euphemism for the same area in a Northern U.S. city which some prefer to call "inner city" and others still call "slum". But while the former is only a term of location, sometimes wrong and sometimes right, and the latter tells us that the area is rundown and poor, "ghetto" tells us more about the nature of the community and its relationship to the outside world. A sociological definition of "ghetto" might say that a ghetto is resided in by people who share a social characteristic of outstanding salience which results in their living together. Getting down from the heights of sociologese, we can simply note that hardly any social characteristic is today as important in American society as pigmentation, and that consequently, we seldom hear about any other ghettos than black ones nowadays. Of course, "ghetto" is now a term of social rhetoric, and some people for that reason prefer to stay away from it. But even if the definition suggested above is stultified, it may say as much about the fundamental nature of this community as the definition of any alternative term, or more. If it is added that another salient characteristic, shared by most ghetto dwellers and closely connected with the color of their skin, is a low income, the term "ghetto" says just about all that is contained in "slum", without its pejorative connotations.

It should be noted that the reason why ethnic identity is important as a basis for membership is not necessarily the same in the black ghetto as in some of its American predecessors. In them, living in a ghetto was a good deal more likely to be voluntary than it is today. Those who grew away from the homogeneous way of life of the community then were often able to pack up and leave, as Louis Wirth (1928) showed in his classical study of the Jewish ghetto. With formal and informal devices of segregation, the white outside world today makes it difficult for many black people to venture outside the ghetto in search for dwellings. Thus the ghetto keeps on accumulating members who would rather not be there. Behind the signs of homogeneity which are blackness and at least relative poverty, there is much heterogeneity of a rather uneasy kind. If there is a "ghetto way of life", it consists of a web of inter-twining but different individual and group life styles.

When we talk of ghetto culture, we imply that in the segregated ghetto environment, there are ways of thinking and acting evolved and maintained which are communicated (as well as communicated about) between ghetto dwellers. These together constitute ghetto culture. If this sounds self-evident, we may hasten to note that some observers have felt that the culture concept has little utility for understanding the black ghetto. Thus one major problem turns out to be exactly what kind of culture the ghetto has, what makes it or does not make it a culture. We will deal with this question at length.

On to "community": it is convenient to refer to the ghetto as a community, but it is obvious to anyone accustomed to thinking in social anthropological terms that it is a community in some ways but less so in others. Like other communities the ghetto has a territory and a rather clearly defined population, the low-income black people who reside in the territory and a minority of somewhat better-off but equally black people who also live there. In social-structural terms, however, the definition of the community meets with more problems. The economic and political self-sufficiency of the ghetto is severely limited. Ghetto people support themselves through relationships with outsiders and are dominated by them. Every morning brings white non-residents into ghetto territory and black people out of it, for a day's work. Considering the impact of the wider environment, the ghetto is only a part-community, as most overarching social institutions are not its own. Considering how their working lives put many ghetto dwellers in touch with outsiders away from home rather than with each other, the ghetto, with its territory and its population, is a part-time community for many of its members.

What, then, beside shared external characteristics which outsiders regard as important, makes the ghetto a community? To start with, its own conscious-ness of kind which, among blacks as well as among whites, allows for little confusion about who belongs and who has "outsider" written all over his face. This categorization is an almost perfect guide to who can do what with whom. On the one hand there are the white people with whom the ghetto dweller has only impersonal relationships—the shopkeeper, the supervisor, the police-man, the social worker, the customer at the lunch counter downtown; on the other hand, there are the black people of the ghetto, the pool from which his partner in marriage, his intimate friends and enemies, his nextdoor neighbor are all drawn. Ghetto dwellers do not only share a position with regard to the outside and experiences with it, they are also actual or potential participants in close personal relationships with one another.

So if the outside society has, in its own way, integrated the ghetto with itself politically and economically, then family life, leisure life, and just plain neighborship remain largely separated. These are the spheres in which a com-munity social structure peopled only by ghetto dwellers is built up. It is serviced also by a few professions so attuned to ghetto life that an outsider hardly could or would take them on, at least not in that layer of the professio-nal hierarchy which deals directly with the ghetto dweller: the preacher, the gospel singer, the rock-and-roll group, the disc jockey on the black radio station, the numbers runner, the bootlegger, the prostitute, the dope pusher.

Not all ghetto dwellers approve of all of them, but that is beside the point. The incumbents can make some kind of living, and they are in the only service occupations to which recruitment is almost as exclusively along ghetto lines as it is for the more personal relationships. The reasons for this exclusiveness may vary. In some cases, *esprit de corps* and shared perspectives are fundamental; in others, inconspicuousness and accessibility at odd hours are requirements that call for a black incumbent, a ghetto resident.

This is as far as the title takes us. But there are other questions to be raised about the intellectual niche in which this volume takes its place.

We have said that it is largely concerned with the ghetto community—with the ghetto dwellers interacting with each other. For better or for worse, it is in the anthropological tradition of trying to get close to small-scale social structures. An anthropologist may feel out of place doing anything else; as ghetto dwellers sometimes put it, you "do what you know". But this approach may set limits to the relevance of the study. In recent years, anthropologists from Steward (1950:22) to Gough (1968:18) have criticized the tradition of their discipline on this point; parts of a larger whole must not be seen as isolates. In the study of black ghetto life this is particularly obvious. It is generally recognized that much of what should concern us about ghetto life has its ultimate determinants in much larger structures, beyond the reach of ghetto dwellers. Poverty and discrimination, and everything which follows with them, are caused, first of all, by white America, we were told in 1968 even in a bestselling report from a presidential commission of inquiry—which, of course, hardly said anything new and surprising.

I hope that despite its focus within the ghetto community, this book will not in any way serve as an example of neglect of such macrostructural determinants. On the contrary, I hope to have made quite clear the continuous impact of the constraints imposed on the ghetto dwellers by the wider society. A study of a depressed group is obviously doomed to failure if it is not informed by such an ecological perspective. Furthermore, I have endeavored to take adequate note of the nature of the cultural influences from the outside, rather than only economic and political pressures; this is clearly important in inquiries into ghetto culture. Yet these external influences are seen from within the ghetto community as delineated above.

Perhaps an anthropologist with social responsibility and a belief that his research ought to matter should go beyond this and either retrain himself somehow to study the large-scale structures where the real action is or at least direct his microsociological curiosity to those institutions whereby white America takes care of ghetto dwellers—the police, the welfare system, the hospitals, the schools—as for instance Paul Jacobs has done, from the perspective of a social critic, in *Prelude to Riot* (1966). But one may nurture a suspicion that more such applied (or, at least, applicable) research will merely take its place among a large number of other studies which for political, rather than scientific, reasons have not been acted upon. Review articles—by Drake (1957) and Smythe and Chase (1958)—show that social-problems approaches have in fact dominated among the studies of life in black America. No doubt studies focusing directly on the victimization of the ghetto dwellers are those which need most desperately to be applied. But when it does not happen, many of the social scientists who start out again on these well-trodden paths only seem to be participants in a therapeutic ritual serving to affirm their own democratic and egalitarian values, in the face of lingering racism.

Possibly, however, an anthropologist going about his work in his usual way can accomplish something else, simply by depicting everyday ghetto life. Black nationalists and intellectuals—who are not necessarily nationalists—often say that much of the attention showered upon the ghetto by social scientists is degrading and dehumanizing. This, for example, is the view often expressed by Ralph Ellison, the author of *Invisible Man,* who recently said this about life in Harlem:

"I don't deny that these sociological formulas are drawn from life, but I do deny that they define the complexity of Harlem. They only abstract it and reduce it to proportions which the sociologists can manage. I simply don't recognize Harlem in them. And I certainly don't recognize the people of Harlem whom I know. Which is by no means to deny the ruggedness of life there, nor the hardship, the poverty, the sordidness, the filth. But there is something else in Harlem, something subjective, willful, and complexly and compellingly human. It is 'that something else' that challenges the sociologists who ignore it, and the society which would deny its existence. It is that 'something else' which makes for our strength, which makes for our endurance and our promise. This is the proper subject for the Negro American writer. Hell, he doesn't have to spend all the tedious time required to write novels simply to repeat what the sociologists and certain white intellectuals are broadcasting like a zoo full of parrots . . ." (Ellison 1967)

It is certainly true that we have tended to go to the novels and autobiographies of black writers—Langston Hughes, James Baldwin, Claude Brown—rather than to social scientists for a picture of the real style of life in the ghetto. Of course, there are things these writers can do which no social scientist can get away with. In a way, Ellison is criticizing sociologists for being sociologists; it is the sociologist's business to make abstractions. Yet perhaps the problem is not so much that he makes abstractions, but what abstractions he makes. In much social science writing, ghetto dwellers have only been "cases"—of crime, juvenile delinquency, mental disorder, public assistance. As much as it has been made clear that these are caused by victimization, the image of the ghetto dweller becomes one of failure and impotence. It tells us little about how he goes about life from day to day, coping with the people around him and with the problems on his mind.

Perhaps anthropology can give a more insightful picture of this human side to the ghetto condition than other social sciences do. The willfulness, endurance, strength and humanity of which Ellison speaks—which is obviously close to what is now called soul—can be understood only within the grassroots context, and anthropology as a form of consciousness may be better able to inquire into these personal terms of life while at the same time remaining more systematic than the literary view of the black experience. When Malinowski sat down at the Trobriand mythmaker's elbow, when Redfield saw a Mexican village becoming modern, and when West followed the loafing and gossiping on the Plainville town square, they exemplified this anthropological tradition; in recent years it has been represented in black ghetto studies by Abrahams' *Deep Down in the Jungle,* Keil's *Urban Blues,* and Liebow's *Tally's Corner.* I will try to draw on this tradition here in presenting a view of some facets of the life of the ordinary men, women, and children of the

14

ghetto. It is necessarily *one* anthropologist's view rather than *the* anthropological view. As Clyde Kluckhohn once said, no two anthropologists will ever see life in a community in identical terms any more than one can step twice into the same river. They will be exposed to different events, and they will go about the problem of making an orderly interpretation of the slightly disorderly complexities of human life in different ways—unless they are willing to become fettered by certain rigidities of method which will blind them to much of the human experience.

The anthropological approach to ghetto life which I will take here is necessarily based on certain priorities. Some of these seem to be permissible simply because this is a field where so many students of different kinds are involved that some division of labor can be taken for granted. We do not have to cover ghetto problems which are seen in a clearer light from other perspectives than ours. Certainly anthropologists and sociologists of other inclinations, economists, political scientists, physicians and others have their own ways of looking at the ghetto, and we need only touch on their concerns rather lightly at times, in order to establish contact but not in order to preempt the fields which they can treat more adequately. Neither do we have to replicate at great length the common concern with particular instants of crisis or with those political cadres to which news media give so much attention and which many outsiders meet either with feelings of horror or with sympathy and perhaps understanding. The insurrections about which more or less sophisticated journalists turn out one book after another are seen here not so much as events in their own right but as an outgrowth of everyday ghetto life, reflecting experiences, expectations, concerns, relationships and cleavages within the community. The fact about the power of the ghetto with which we will become most acquainted is that most ghetto dwellers neither have any nor are actively working to acquire any at present. We must not underestimate the ability of individuals and small groups to make history at later points of their careers, but whatever wishes one may hold for the future of organized black militant politics, it did not at this time occupy much space in the lives of the people we meet in the pages which follow. Since these lives are what we try to understand here, we must let the tightly knit groups of politically motivated men remain somewhat distant most of the time.

Nor am I attempting in this volume to provide an inventory of ghetto social relations, modes of action, and ideas. Black culture in the United States is often referred to as a subculture of the general American culture. Perhaps we do not find the subculture concept very incisive as an analytical term, but at least it gives the idea that much of what any black American would do is the same as any American would do, while differences from the mainstream culture occur only in certain areas of life.

These essays dwell above all on such areas; the general question here is, "What is different about ghetto living?" This also means that all ghetto dwellers will not get equal time here. There are many who are in the ghetto but not of the ghetto in the sense of exhibiting much of a life style peculiar to the community. (In some ways, of course, everybody in the ghetto has special problems to cope with by virtue of his residence there.) There are people in the ghetto who have good, stable jobs, help their children with their home work, eat dinner together at a fixed hour, make payments on the car, and spend their Saturday night watching Lawrence Welk on TV—to their largely mainstream way of life we will devote rather little attention. This neglect may distress those who profess their friendship for the people of the ghetto, yet feel that conformity to mainstream standards is a prerequisite for full citizenship. For my "bias of exoticism"—which is perhaps typical of anthropologists (cf. Naroll and Naroll 1963)—they might want to substitute a bias of togetherness, an emphasis on the ways in which ghetto dwellers in general, and some of them in particular, are "just like white folks". Perhaps those who feel this way are motivated by an understanding of what may be the culturally authoritarian demands of the American majority. To this the only answer is that some differences cannot be swept under the rug and that it has always been one of the duties of anthropology to show that whether a way of life is like your own or not, it is a reasonable and understandable combination of common human themes with the experiences of a unique past and present.

The selective treatment of only certain facets of ghetto life to some extent gives this volume the shape of a collection of rather separate inquiries, not that of an integrated monograph. This form is also preferable because of the field work situation. In a complex social and cultural situation it is difficult for an observer to be present everywhere to an adequate extent, because of natural restrictions in time and space as well as because of his ascribed or achieved social attributes. This volume therefore deals with topics which can be handled from a reasonably unified field worker role. The approach taken— and to some extent bestowed—was one of informal participant observation (see Appendix, *In the Field*). This undoubtedly influences what is said and what is not said in the following chapters, as well as how it is said.

If these foundations for our inquiries make this a less than holistic study, perhaps some unity may yet be detected, aside from that of the general anthropological perspective. First of all, it draws continuously on field work in the same setting, centering in a neighborhood of the Washington, D.C., ghetto. The Winston Street scene keeps appearing, and so do some of the people of the neighborhood, as actors or commentators. Furthermore, an observer is perhaps likely to interpret human conduct in similar terms wherever he sees it, so that everybody brings his own personal baggage of concerns, experiences, and tools of analysis to the community he is to study. But other major interests certainly emerge from the nature of that community and force the observer to get hold of some new analytic equipment. Both these sources of continuous themes are probably visible in the chapters which follow.

In conclusion, it may be useful to preview the contents of these chapters, in order to sum up what they are hoped to accomplish and what are the major problems raised in them.

Chapter 1, *The Setting*, is an attempt to visualize the general context of the life of people at Winston Street, and to present some of the characteristics of the people themselves. Gulick (1963:455) suggests that it can be one of the urban anthropologist's particular contributions to the study of cities to portray quite concretely the sights and sounds of urban life. Perhaps this chapter can convey this kind of picture of ghetto life, as well as some understanding of how the people of the community themselves see it. Of course, some of the questions which are only intimated in this rounded view of the ghetto will be raised again in later chapters.

Chapter 2, *Life Styles,* surveys the heterogeneity of the ghetto population. After a brief discussion of how to categorize ways of life and the problems it involves, it is suggested that four life style types can be delineated in the ghetto which appear relatively congruent with the clustering of social relations in the community. These types, mainstreamers, swingers, street families, and streetcorner men, are described.

Chapter 3, *Walking My Walk and Talking My Talk,* continues the discussion of life styles with a delineation of how life styles relate to each other, both diachronically and synchronically. The possible influences which can lead an individual to take on a particular life style are also given some attention.

Chapter 4, *Male and Female,* is the first of three chapters on various facets of ghetto sex roles. This chapter gives a general outline of the structural and cultural influences at work in making the relationship between the sexes rather problematic for many ghetto dwellers.

Chapter 5, *Streetcorner Mythmaking,* is a more specialized discussion of the ways in which many ghetto men work together toward making the burdens of their role lighter, by establishing a more satisfying collective definition of manliness.

Chapter 6, *Growing Up Male,* is a critical examination of that common view of sex role socialization for boys in matrifocal families according to which this kind of domestic environment results in role confusion and extreme compensatory masculinity. A more "normal" mode of role socialization is suggested as an alternative explanation of much ghetto male behavior.

Chapter 7, *Things in Common,* points to the kinds of common experiences and orientations which contribute to community integration in the ghetto despite its diversity. Thus there is a discussion of such institutions, practices, and modes of outlook as bootlegging, the numbers game, black religion, the soul concept, and ghetto radio stations. Of course, there is no attempt to deal in detail with all facets of these phenomena—the emphasis is continuously on their functioning as ingredients of a shared perspective.

Chapter 8, *Waiting for the Burning to Begin,* may give some insight into how ghetto dwellers define their discontent with their relationships to the outside world, how they react to the prospects of turmoil, and how they view the insurrection when it finally comes. This is certainly not a complete account of the facts involved in ghetto unrest. Rather, the purpose of this chapter is to see this unrest in the context of everyday life, expressed in common social relationships and in a variety of incidents which both build up to a rising and discourage people from it.

Chapter 9, *Mainstream and Ghetto in Culture,* is a theoretical discussion of what is cultural about typical ghetto modes of action. Its point of departure is the controversy over the idea of a culture of poverty; its emphasis is on the social organization of culture, and it is concluded with a brief discussion of the strategy and prospects of black cultural nationalism.

The appendix *In the Field,* finally, provides a view of the conduct of the field work on which this volume is based. Some readers may prefer to read this first, in order to get a clearer understanding of the background of reporting and interpretation in the preceding chapters.

# 1
# The Setting

At one end of Winston Street is a yellow wall with a number of graffiti—a list of boys, *Jimmy, Norman, Eddie, Marvin, Robert,* and a list of girls next to it, *Barbie, Debbie, Sarah, Peaches, Janice.* There is a secretive *Leroy loves somebody,* and a couple of four-letter words scrawled by an uncertain hand. A little to the side, the message is that *Your mother drink wild irish rose,* with the reply *So do your cat.* Wild Irish Rose is the drink of the winos, "wineheads" or "juiceheads" in ghetto parlance.

Winston Street, Washington, D.C., is a narrow, one-way ghetto street, one block long and lined by brick row houses, two or three stories high and in varying states of repair. In the windows of some of them are flower pots, bright curtains or even venetian blinds. Others have broken blinds, dirty plastic sheets, or nothing at all. Sometimes a house is condemned as unfit to live in, and its doors and windows are covered with boards. It is largely a residential street, and since it is not really a thoroughfare, its pedestrian and auto traffic is largely confined to the street's own residents and their visitors. At the corners of Winston Street and the surrounding streets are small business establishments: groceries, liquor stores, carry-out food shops, variety stores, laundromats, shoeshine shops, barber shops, beauty salons; all very modest in appearance. These are the establishments which cater to the day-to-day needs, and supply the few luxuries, of ghetto living. The consumption of liquor is considerable. The carry-outs find most of their customers among the many single men who cannot prepare food in their rented rooms, as well as among the children and adolescents who spend much of whatever money they can get on extra food and goodies. Variety stores sell candy, school equipment, cheap toys, and a variety of other inexpensive odds and ends. The carry-outs, the barber shops, and the shoeshine shops serve not only their manifest function but are also the hangouts, the centers of sociability, of teenagers and adult men. To serve as locales of leisure, they add some more items to their furnishings: newspapers, vending machines for cigarettes and soft drinks, a pinball machine, a juke box, a public telephone. No one establishment would have them all, some would have none of this, but many have some of it. So this becomes the place of small talk, perhaps sweet talk with the girl behind the carry-out counter.

Much of this leisurely interaction takes place on the street itself, however, where people stand at the corner or sit on the high staircases in front of houses. During the cold months there are few people out, although there are usually some men at the corners. But in March and April when the early spring sun shines through from the south end of Winston Street, there will already be people sitting on the front steps and children playing in the street, and through the hot and humid summer months the street scene is a lively one until late at night. Many men and some women stand or sit around talking, children throw balls, hula-hoop, ride bikes, push each other in carts, or skip rope. Sometimes, the fire hydrant at the end of the street is switched on, and the children shower in the water spray and bathe in the gutter. People go back and forth to the laundromat or to Mr. Rubin's grocery store at the corner, doing the shopping for the day or just picking up a soda or an onion. A young man in sunglasses comes up the street carrying a transistor radio and listening to the soul music of station WOL. Two teenage girls, walking elbow to elbow, exchange news about boys. "And then I told him, 'Child, I couldn't care less if you come or not'!" The old man who goes from door to door on his mission for the Jehovah's Witnesses walks by, eyes fixed on the ground and with a brown briefcase in his hand. Since the people on the staircases know most of the passers-by, they greet them and sometimes stop them for a chat. Some, of course, avoid greeting each other, for there is animosity between them. And there are also the people who have not lived very long on the block and who are thus not very well known. On the other hand, some of the long-time watchers of the Winston Street scene actually reside somewhere else, on some neighboring street, just coming down regularly to the street to spend their free time there. And of course, in the same way some of the people of Winston Street have their regular hangouts on other streets.

The street has its regular events. In the evening, the word is spread about what is the winning number in the numbers game, one of the ghetto's illegal but nonetheless central institutions. Now and then a fortunate player may collect some money from a nearby agent, but most of the time there is no luck. "758? I was two off again. I had 742." During the warmer months of the year, the ice cream vendor's car also comes around in the evening, drawing the children's attention with its jingling bell.

The adult streetcorner men want other refreshments. Just talking, playing a game of cards, or shooting dice, they usually get around to pooling their money for something to drink, and one of them goes to the liquor store—or to a bootlegger, if it is Sunday, or too late on a weekday evening—to get some gin, of the kind which is $1.10 a half-pint at the cheapest store, or wine, of the kind that is 35 cents a half-pint (a higher price from the bootlegger). When he comes back, they try to share their drink somewhere out of the public view, as it is illegal to drink in public places. They go into a house or into the back alley, where they may not be seen, although of course it is no more lawful to drink there. The alley has a few trees, a rose bush, overflowing garbage cans, and lots of trash on the ground, including empty and broken bottles. Here and there is a clothesline. Some children play there, dogs guard the back yards, and there are heavy-weight rats running around. Some of the men also go there to "take a leak" if there is no toilet within reach.

There are slums which are more like villages and others which are more like jungles.[1] At times one would look down Winston Street, see only the neighborliness and tranquility, and place this neighborhood close to the village end of the spectrum. But the people who live there know that it also has some attributes of the urban jungle. Some people and places mean trouble, and there is danger in the dark and the unknown. There is the mentally disturbed woman who shouts at the men loafing below her window: "Get away from down there

20

or I'll pour lye over you all." There is the young man who is shunned by the girls and the younger women because of his reputation:

"That boy Chuck is crazy about sex. He goes to a bar and picks up a girl and brings her home and then he locks her up and screws her, and when he has to go out to work he locks her up and won't leave food or cigarettes or anything for her, and then he comes home and goes right on screwing her again. And that nice old mother of his don't say a word, I guess she don't dare, so she just acts as if she knows nothing about it. I've seen girls come out of there, and he keeps them in there for weeks locked up, and they look pretty near dead when they get out. Everybody is afraid of him and the girls around here won't go near him."

There is also Winston Street's own major trouble spot, the corner where the rougher streetcorner men hang out. Fights are rather common there, and the men occasionally show up with fresh knife wounds. True, most of the fights are within the group, and most of the people who have lived in the neighborhood for some time know the men well and are reasonably friendly with them; even so they warn newcomers and visitors about this corner. Yet, it is not so bad there, Winston Street people feel, as on the neighboring street where tough teenage boys hang out and are a menace to everybody who passes by. And the nearby playground is also worse. Some young men go there only to play basketball and table tennis, of course, but there is also a rougher clique which is held responsible for the fact that some people who have passed by have been "yoked"—robbed. Thus the playground is a place to stay away from, particularly after dark, according to neighborhood consensus. And if some young man whom one should happen to know begins to be seen with this clique, one points out the dangers of such company. As one young man was given a jail sentence for his participation in a holdup, an older acquaintance of his commented:

"It had to happen sooner or later, you know. He used to work as some kind of an instructor for the kids up there on the playground, and then when he lost that job he should have stayed away from there from then on, but no, he kept on hanging out there with those no-good fellows, gorillas, that's what they are, all of them. So he got mixed up in this holdup in this liquor store, and they ain't going to let him out for a while. I guess he thinks about what we all told him now."

Potential trouble spots such as those just described can, of course, be reasonably well avoided. But sometimes it is quite difficult. The people who could cause trouble may have their recurrent gatherings on the front staircase of a house which for some reason is well placed for the purpose while they are not necessarily on terms of personal friendship with the occupants of the house—or at least not with all the occupants. Sometimes the friends of one household occupy the whole front stairs leading to several apartments, thus making entry difficult. At times their conversation gets loud and boisterous, disturbing the people inside the house, and it may erupt into a fight. The empty bottles, paper bags, cigarette packets and other things which assemble during the gatherings are often left behind littering the sidewalk, the gutter, or the little patch of grass—or bare earth—which is in front of some buildings. Some residents who want to avoid trouble do not give any expression of their resentment to the people on the staircase, only occasionally voicing it in private to others—"They should have more sense." If they are on better terms with the loiterers, and in particular if the latter are not "gorillas" but more peaceful streetcorner men, they may occasionally reprimand them for the intrusion into other people's rights, or make a gesture of mild annoyance now and then.

Thus the people of the ghetto maintain a working knowledge of the potential for trouble in their environment. This knowledge undergoes constant revision, of course; and the concern with danger may also fluctuate, although it seems generally to be rather strong.[2] At Winston Street people seem to be a little extra worried during the weeks before Christmas, when it is widely held that robberies and holdups increase in number—"People are desperate for money then, you know, to have something extra." (Besides, the victims may also carry more money, and it gets dark rather early.) One man who had been robbed of his pay envelope a few days before the holiday and woke up to find himself in a police car on the way to the hospital said the following day:

"I'm just gonna go over and get myself some wine and something to eat, you know, so I got something in the frigidaire for the next few days, 'cause I'm not going to go out if I don't have to the next few days, and I won't let my old lady go out either."

Some periods generally defined as troubled times are of a more idiosyncratic nature. For a while during early 1967, people in the Winston Street neighborhood felt that the general mood was "kind of tense". A number of factors seemed to contribute. Some long-standing conflicts between families who had been in the neighborhood for many years reached a stage where one observer said, "Bricks could start flying any time now." The reason for the intensification never became particularly clear; some quarrels apparently made the tension more acute. Second, there were some unexpected and undesired pregnancies among teenage girls, and as one neighbor put it, "Their fathers may never have been very good fathers, but that only makes them more upset about this thing, so they need a scape-goat." Furthermore, a group of tough teenage boys from another part of the Washington ghetto started hanging out in the neighborhood and were responsible for two assaults within a few days. A couple of adult men with a reputation for violence also came back after a period of absence, and this was seen as an ominous sign. Another factor, not directly involving interpersonal violence in the neighborhood but yet contributing to the general gloom, was the state of the national politics of black-white relations. In the preceding summer black power had made its debut, and there was much talk of a "white backlash". The Vietnam war overshadowed the war on poverty, and cutbacks in funds for the latter were predicted. A more conservative congress was elected. These facts were described and commented on extensively in the newspapers, and there was also frequent mention of them on the radio. Ghetto dwellers read, heard, and commented to each other about this, and the expressed view was that it was going badly for black people. During this period which lasted about a month and then gradually expired, some of the people who generally contribute most to the village atmosphere of Winston Street life—by standing about, going around visiting, and being generally present in public places—felt that it was wiser to spend more time in the haven of their homes.

It can certainly be helpful for the people of the ghetto to map the trouble potential of their environment in these ways. When it comes to going about their daily life, however, they must necessarily compromise between safety and freedom of movement, for trouble remains very unpredictable, and to try to avoid every possible danger would be intolerably constraining. So the only possible general rule is that "you better be on the alert when you're walking on those streets." This is particularly important at night when it is easy for an attacker to hide in the dark and when the streets are empty. If a group of men have been drinking together and someone has a long way to go home, he may agree with the host to stay overnight rather than try to make his way home intoxicated, an easy prey for yoking. But certainly one cannot always be so cautious, and some day one may have to face the consequences. This is what one middle-aged man said when encountered at a street corner near Winston Street after he had been absent for some time:

"No, I sure ain't seen you for a long time, not since I was yoked—yes, just across the street from here. Remember last time I saw you, over at the Robinsons' house? Yeah, I was worried about you going home that night—remember how I told you to watch out? And then I was yoked, and I left just after you! If I lost anything? I damn near lost my life! And I was in hospital for six weeks, and all my teeth was knocked out, and I got to pay the dentist five hundred bucks. Yeah, I got a pretty good idea who they was, I've seen them outside that bar up the street—actually, don't look now, but that's one of them going into the liquor store behind me right now. I ain't going to no court, probably wouldn't do any good, and I got to think of my family. I got a wife and daughter, you know, and I don't want them to get into trouble. If I was alone it might have been another thing. Well, anyway, that's why you don't see me around so much any more, 'cause I don't want to go out of the house too much."

But despite the dangers people in the Winston Street neighborhood still face, many of those who have been acquainted with the street for the last few decades say that in some ways it has calmed down. One man who has been there on and off for seventeen years said that "this used to be the baddest damn street I've seen in my life." There was a time, it is claimed, when a stranger could be happy if he managed to get from one end of the street to the other alive, and he certainly would not have a whole lot of money left. There were signs which the natives used between one another to show if the person going down the sidewalk was fair game. In those days, Winston Street also had a great number of bootleggers, some of whom made their own whiskey, and people came from all over town to buy from them. The bootleggers then spent a great deal of their money gambling with each other. That way, one man said, "it all stayed in the family". Sonny, a former jazz saxophonist who lives off the street but spends most of his day on it, says that when he arrived in Washington from Florida some thirty years ago, his mother placed Winston Street off limits for him. But there was always some way of sneaking up there to watch the action.

These were also the times of organized gang conflicts among adolescents. The men who are now in their thirties have memories of this warfare at its height, but now such gangs, with names, offices, and all their *West Side Story* paraphernalia, are few in Washington.

The recollections of Winston Street in the past are most likely exaggerated. Probably they should be seen as interesting pieces of jungle imagery rather than as good historical evidence. Yet there is a notable unanimity among various informants, and there can hardly be a doubt that the street had a reputation as a stronghold of shady activities. Since then, some of the people who engaged in them moved to other parts of the ghetto without changing their way of life much. Among the hustlers at the corner of Seventh and T Streets there are some who can describe in detail the social organization of illegal activities at Winston Street in the old days. Others have moved on up and out, to more respectable jobs and better dwellings in other parts of the city. Then there are those who remain on the street but have undergone a similar change there. One man who used to make whiskey in his Winston Street home is now a janitor in an apartment house. His sons, growing up in the old days, have taken different paths. One is an office clerk, another is an apartment house receptionist, two are on-and-off construction workers one of whom still occasionally makes a handsome profit from gambling while the other is an alcoholic. A few people have remained in business while a couple of newcomers have taken over where someone left off, but they manage their affairs discreetly. Of course, since their activities are illegal, they may sometimes go out of business at least temporarily. Occasionally a bootlegger gets raided. One raid which caused many hearty laughs in the neighborhood was described by one young man:

"You know up the corner of Piedmont Street where there are bootleggers in three houses in a row? Somebody had tipped off the man about one of them, so they came with a search warrant with this person's name on it. But they got the wrong house number, you see, so they went to his next-door neighbor, and when he saw that they had a search warrant he didn't look closer at it 'cause he just thought his whole thing was over. So they went in and found all those half-pints, and only when they were on their way out did they find out they got the wrong guy. But then of course the fellow next door had seen there was a raid going on, so he had got all his stuff into the car and drove off. And of course they didn't know that they could have gone to any one of these three places and caught someone."

Today's bootleggers in the area do not make their own liquor but buy it at a discount and sell it at higher prices—something like 25 per cent higher than regular store prices—when the legitimate liquor stores are closed.

But of course, the large majority of people, whether remaining from the past or more recent arrivals on the street, hold ordinary jobs or are unemployed, and their contact with illegal activities may be non-existent or confined to their positions as customers and, now and then, victims.

What kind of people are those who live at Winston Street now? Like other people in the black ghettos of Northern cities, they are part of what is in a way an immigrant community. Certainly, their ancestry has been American longer than that of many groups which have been assimilated more quickly into mainstream American society. But black people do have a "back home" of their own. The trails from the rural South to the big cities are well established. Washington, D.C., has not been the goal of most migrants from the Deepest South—Alabama, Mississippi—who have usually gone more directly north. The majority of the black migrants have come from the states of the

Southeastern seaboard, and this is mirrored in the Winston Street population. Among the adults there, about a fourth were born in South Carolina, and a similar proportion in North Carolina. Smaller numbers came from Virginia and Maryland, the neighboring states. A few came from other states, and about a third were born in the District of Columbia. But many of those who are from outside the District came there while they were young, brought by their parents, and most of the children and younger people are native Washingtonians. Yet now and then a new family arrives from the South and moves into the neighborhood, and among those who are less recent arrivals many maintain contacts "down country" by visiting relatives there during holidays or sending the children to spend a part of their summer vacation with cousins.

However, the second generation of Northern city dwellers, and even more the following generations, often have only a more general idea of the South and know less about their specific ties to kinsmen and towns. There remains a more general sense of the South as the origin of the ghetto dwellers or their ancestors, and as a place where life was worse than it is in the city—here the news media seem to contribute as much to knowledge as the ghetto oral tradition, although they can complement and support each other in their effects. As ghetto dwellers see governor Wallace on TV a few unappreciative comments are exchanged between them, and when the cottonfield scene comes on in the Sidney Poitier movie, *In the Heat of the Night,* the audience in the U Street movie house howls and murmurs. The King David Carry-Out at the corner of Winston Street and many others like it proclaim that its specialty is "Southern Home Cooking", and streetcorner groceries advertise chitterlings, greens and other Southern foods on their window posters.

In their economic situations, a certain diversity emerges among the Winston Street people. As a ghetto street, it has a majority of low-income people, but there are some who stay on although they achieve a higher income. Their reasons for remaining may vary. The additional cost and the extra difficulties which still appear for black people trying to find a home outside the ghetto keep many from ever trying to move out. "Sure, the suburbs are nice, you know. But I don't particularly want to go where nobody wants me although I know they are wrong and I'm right." Others are reasonably satisfied with the ghetto and know that they would leave most of their friends behind if they moved. A few have vested interests in the ghetto which are best served by remaining there. Businesses, legal or illegal, provide one reason for staying even when it would be possible to move out. Especially among some younger people, a motive occasionally offered for remaining in the ghetto is racial solidarity. Leaving less fortunate "brothers" behind is "copping out". The ghetto can be defined in both racial and economic terms, but there is a conscious emphasis on the racial dimension.

Despite all this, some of those who have reached an economic threshold do indeed trickle out of the ghetto. If they have some kind of attachment to their old neighborhood they may come to visit friends occasionally, but on the whole the ghetto remains in many ways a community to itself without extensive ties of personal friendship with people in other parts of the city.

But most people have no choice of whether to stay in the ghetto or not. Although they may have jobs, they cannot afford to live anywhere else. It is difficult to establish exactly what proportion of the people in the Winston

Street neighborhood are employed. Clearly, at any given point in time, a majority of the adult males hold jobs. They are in a strong majority among those who are functioning husbands and fathers in childrearing households. The problem in arriving at more exact figures stems primarily from two sources; there is a variable employment situation over time, and the number of men who should be seen as inhabitants of the neighborhood can only be decided with difficulty, and then in a rather arbitrary manner. Many men drift in and out of jobs, with or without prolonged periods of unemployment between. Some are in occupations which have periods of unemployment, such as the many construction workers in the neighborhood who are laid off during the winter. As for the instability in the neighborhood population of adult men, it is particularly the rather regularly unemployed men who are sometimes in the neighborhood, sometimes out of it; now they live there, next they sleep somewhere else but spend their free time at Winston Street, later again they are completely out of the picture only to turn up again a few months later, resuming their old place.[3]

Most of the employed men are in unskilled or at best semiskilled occupations: general laborers, construction workers, garbage men, janitors, messengers, gas station attendants, truck drivers, etc. There is a bartender, a cook, a baker and a railroad trackman. But there are also a few white-collar workers; clerks in low-level government service or other offices, the receptionist in a downtown apartment building mentioned before, a drugstore clerk. One man operates his own business, a furniture refinishing shop. Obviously, most of the men make their living outside the ghetto.

Among the adult women who are not aged, those who have employment and those who do not are about equal in number. In those childrearing households where no adult male is present in the husband-father role, somewhat more women hold jobs outside the home than in the two-parent families where the male is usually employed. Women are usually in service occupations; a great many are domestic workers for white families, often in the suburbs. There are also hotel maids, laundresses, waitresses in cafeterias and at luncheon counters. A few are secretaries and clerks in minor positions.

Most inhabitants of the neighborhood, then, are in low-income occupations, and this is of course to some extent (that is, apart from discrimination in the labor market and some other factors) due to their limited formal education. One younger man in the neighborhood holds a degree from a Negro college and now works for the city's recreation department, but he takes little part in neighborhood interaction. The overwhelming majority of the inhabitants of the neighborhood have only a high school education, and most of them a rather poor one. Many dropped out of school before graduating, and whether they went to school in the South or in Washington, they usually went to segregated schools of low standard. Some of the adults have less than five years of schooling and are functionally illiterate. Of course, the Washington D.C., public school system is officially integrated, but residential *de facto* segregation has resulted in overwhelmingly segregated schools. Thus the generation now growing up in the ghetto continues to be poorly prepared for social mobility—although it may be argued that segregation in schools need not in itself cause poor education, it is generally agreed that ghetto schools are in fact ill-equipped for their purpose.[4]

How much do the Winston Street people earn on their jobs? The majority
is definitely at a low-income level. The greater number of the households
earn between $2,000 and $5,000 with about an equal number below and above
$3,000.[5] Some make even less (usually one-person households or elderly
people), some make more. A few households state their income as more than
$10,000 per year, but some qualifications and additional information need
then be given. Some would earn that much if employment were steady. This
is not always true, either because of shifts in the labor market or because of
personal matters; one skilled worker with a potentially high income earns
substantially less because he is a chronic alcoholic, working only irregularly.
Secondly, in most cases when a household income reaches higher figures, it
is the consequence only of many household members holding jobs. In the
three cases on Winston Street where household incomes above $10,000 are
earned at legitimate jobs, three members have steady employment—a car
inspector, a domestic worker, and a hotel maid; a skilled construction worker,
a hotel maid, and a recreation specialist (the young college graduate mentioned
above); and a truck driver, a laundress, and a typist. Of course, there are also
households of lower income where more than one member are employed and
contribute to the household economy, and a few individuals increase their
incomes by holding two jobs.

For many of the households at the lowest income levels, earnings from
employment are only a part or none at all of the income. A number of Winston
Street households derive some of or their entire means of living from public
welfare payments, particularly from the programs concerned with aid to
families with dependent children (AFDC) and old-age assistance. Among the
men, some who were disabled in recent wars draw veterans' pensions, and
others qualify for unemployment compensation.

* * *

The Winston Street neighborhood is not a world to itself. As a neighborhood,
it has its own web of social relations, but it is also a part of larger entities. As
far as trouble is concerned, it is in "number seventeen", an all-ghetto police
precinct. The small children of the neighborhood start at the nearby Elijah M.
Poole Elementary School, but as they get older they go to junior high schools
and high schools further away, where they come into contact with children
from much wider areas of the ghetto. And the adults also have their interests
spread out over the ghetto. They may have lived somewhere else in it before,
and they have friends and kinsmen scattered over it with whom they get
together more or less frequently. They also make use of a number of ghetto
locales which are outside their own neighborhood. The setting for their life in
the community is thus wider than just the few blocks closest to home.

The ghetto has many streets like Winston Street, with the same kinds of
row houses, occasionally a larger apartment house, and many of the small
businesses—the groceries, the barber shops, the liquor stores. There is a rather
high turnover among these, as many of them are rather unsuccessful operations,
and there are often vacant premises. Some of these become the homes of
storefront churches which advertise their services and Sunday school programs
in the erstwhile shop windows, most of which are white painted or covered by

self-adhesive plastic imitations of stained glass. The diversity of their names— *The Full Speed Gospel Church of God in Christ, The Peaceway Temple, The Miracle Temple of Truth, The Christian Home Penecostal* (sic) *Holiness Church of God of the Americans, The Maranatha Gospel Hall, The Solid Rock Church of God in Christ, The Way Back to Pentecost Church, The Full Gospel Tabernacle Church of the Living God* and a multitude of other combinations—is one pointer to their independence of old, large and well-established churches. These storefront churches, "Spiritual", "Holiness", or "Sanctified", have small congregations of perhaps a couple of dozen members and are led by preachers who may be male or female but are more often male. The tiny congregations usually have little or no connection with any other church. On a Sunday one may hear through the open door a preacher's staccato sermon, shout-singing and tambourines, or a slow and peaceful hymn, in the weak and cracking voices of older women. On the staircase of the house next door sit a few men who could have been their one-time husbands. A fragrance of pork chops hangs in the air as a message about someone's Sunday dinner, and one of the men may jokingly suggest that they track it down to the source.

The ghetto also has its main arteries. Some of them are the thoroughfares of the people of the suburbs and outer city who get a glimpse of the ghetto on their way to and from the downtown business area and its office buildings. There are also commercial establishments which cater as much to a white as to a black public, or more—gas stations, car dealers, repair shops, warehouses, small industries, and the like—spilling out into the ghetto from the downtown area. In a motley arrangement with the homes of ghetto dwellers, with their variety of shapes, sizes, colors, and states of upkeep, and empty lots covered with litter, these establishments give the ghetto a very cluttered look. It also appears rather spacious. Most buildings are not very tall, and the street plan of the nation's capital, with the streets and wide avenues lined by trees, also encompasses the ghetto. During the summer when the trees are green, the ghetto may even look idyllic; but from fall to spring, when cold winds shake the trees and envelop the loafers who huddle together in their aging worn-out overcoats, the view is a bleak one.

The ghetto main streets, however, are not only thoroughfares but also lifelines of the ghetto community. Seventh Street, Fourteenth Street, and U Street in Northwest Washington, and H Street in the Northeast section, cater to the ghetto public in many ways.[6] There are the large chain supermarkets, competing with the small streetcorner groceries; there are bars and restaurants, pool halls and a few movie theaters showing the same movies as the downtown theaters, usually only slightly later and at lower prices; record stores and big churches; clothing and furniture stores, for both new and used merchandise; employment agencies, drug stores, occult advisors, and funeral homes. Interspersed among them are more of the same kinds of small businesses as cluster at the street corners in the Winston Street neighborhood. But the barber shops and carry-outs which are routine hangouts for rather stable groups in the neighborhood take on much more urban anonymity on the main streets. There may be fleeting sociability among customers as well as between them and the staff, but there is more reason to "watch out" as one cannot be quite sure what kind of person one is dealing with. One middle-aged white-collar worker, also involved in numbers running and with rather moderate political opinions, commented on the increasingly militant mood among some ghetto dwellers:

"You know, nowadays if I see somebody in the barber shop I don't know I keep my mouth shut if somebody starts talking about politics. You never can tell if there's a Muslim or one of those black power people in there and they might jump you if you say something they don't like. I keep my mouth shut."

The larger establishments on the ghetto main streets are seldom owned by black people, although some of the ghetto dwellers may find employment in them. However, some of the smaller or medium-sized businesses are black owned and operated. They are the ones which have "soul brother" written on their windows when the Washington ghetto erupts into violence, as it did after Martin Luther King's death in April, 1968. Thus they hope to establish themselves as a part of the ghetto moral community, an effort which has more often than not been successful.

The intersections of the main streets are among the landmarks of the ghetto. Where U Street crosses Fourteenth Street, and where it meets Florida Avenue near the corner of Seventh Street, there are always people on the move, as well as people not on the move but just looking. These corners are where beggars, prostitutes, and dope pushers do some of their best business. One block south of the corner of Seventh and Florida is Seventh and T, already mentioned as a home of hustlers—pimps, gamblers, narcotics pushers and others—as well as plain "gorillas", men who, if the situation is propitious, are quick to use their fists and to jump on a passer-by who might have money. These, at least, are the terms in which ghetto dwellers speak of Seventh and T. If any one place in the ghetto sums up the imagery of an urban jungle, it is this corner, with its many bars and pool rooms. This, perhaps, is also the opinion of the preacher who sometimes takes a place on the sidewalk there, speaking out against all this sin in a stentorian voice to which the passers-by and loafers seem to pay scant attention.

But of course most people passing by Seventh and T go unharmed and unnoticed, including the audience at the Howard Theatre. The Howard has been a major entertainment spot in the ghetto for many decades, and a lot of black stage personalities who have since turned to large white audiences have played the Howard at earlier points in their career. Nowadays, the Howard usually alternates between rock-and-roll shows, with jazz and an occasional comedian thrown in now and then, and third-rate movies. The stage shows draw audiences ranging from small children to adults in their early middle age. The Sunday matinees have very youthful audiences crying out when their favorites come on, singing along and dancing in the rows and aisles; the evening shows, and particularly the Saturday midnight shows, draw more mature crowds. The emcees, usually disc jockeys from local black radio stations, adjust to these differences and spice their remarks more heavily as the afternoon yields to evening and night. This is one place where the ghetto public meets its stars alive—singers such as James Brown, Joe Tex, Wilson Pickett, soul groups like the Marvelettes, the Impressions, the Flamingoes, and comedians like Moms Mabley and Clay Tyson. Some young white people from nearby colleges occasionally drop in, but on the whole, the Howard is a ghetto institution *par preference*.

It is a rather small theater, however, and some big stars would rather play a one-nighter for a large audience than stay a week at the Howard. So when some of the big names turn up in Washington, they are billed at the top of a show held at some place with a larger capacity. The Coliseum, also used for a variety of sports events, has been a frequently used setting for this kind of shows, but after a minor riot at a Temptations show, its management has been more reluctant to book such events. Weeknight boxing and the roller-skating rink are also there as great attractions. The latter, however, is not the only one of its kind in the ghetto.

A few bowling alleys and a great number of pool halls are among the other foci of leisure life in the ghetto. The pool halls have an imagery of wickedness attached to them; they are all-male institutions where the air is heavy with smoke and where small-time hustlers in flashy outfits mingle with laborers on their way home from work. They are also places where one may lose a good deal of money. This is Sonny, the former saxophonist, reminiscing again about a couple of his friends:

"Bee Jay shoots a pretty good game of pool, but he loses his cool. You know, one or two shots go wrong and he goes to pieces. I remember once he was playing Henry, and you know Henry is a very cool player and so he is very good although he is close to seventy years old. So Bee Jay was playing him, and Henry won something like thirty dollars, and Bee Jay was sure he'd win everything back in the end, so he went and got his hundred and twenty-five dollar suit and took it to the pawn shop, and then they went on playing. But Bee Jay was all excited, so Henry got that money too."

The bowling alleys, on the other hand, have men as well as women among their patrons (although the men are more numerous), and generally you do not play for money there. The women are usually in their twenties or possibly late teens, the men have a somewhat wider age range from the late teens to the middle forties. Presumably, the women stop bowling when they become tied down by their families, while the men cease to go when they feel too old. During the week business at the bowling alley is rather slow, but it picks up during the weekend, particularly on Saturday nights when the teams compete in leagues. The teams may be of one sex or both; since leagues are sex-integrated the games can be too, even when the teams are sex-segregated. Thus the bowling alley is a possible arena for making new contacts with the opposite sex. Girls do not stop bowling as soon as the adumbrations of family life occur; many unmarried pregnant girls continue to hold their place on the team, and later they may appear at the alley with a child with whom they play between their turns and who is passed over to someone else when their turn comes to bowl.

Except for the lanes, the alley usually frequented by people from Winston Street also houses pinball machines, soft drink vending machines, and a snack bar, with the ordinary hamburgers and hot dogs as well as some Southern specialties. The snack bar also serves beer; the players sometimes bring in stronger beverages in secret.

The persons present on a Saturday night are not only the regular members of the teams but also friends who come to see the games or people who just drop in to look around, have a snack, and perhaps work the pinball machines. Since some team member may fail to show up, there is always a chance that one of these extra persons will be asked to play instead. Occasionally members of the staff at the alley are asked to fill a vacant position for the night.

Bars are also locales for leisure. However, there is more drinking going on away from bars than in them, and most visits to them also have other purposes than just drinking. The middle-aged men who drink in the back alley and in their rooms during the week go to the beer garden on Friday night, because that is when they want a good time. They go from one table to another, exchanging greetings, pleasantries, reminiscences, and occasionally hot arguments with friends and acquaintances. Although the poster on the wall expressly forbids dancing, some men take a few steps to the music of the juke box, alone or with one of the few middle-aged women, usually of more or less explicit prostitute status, who also frequent these establishments. Sometimes a fight develops; now and then someone is too drunk to stand up. In both cases, the management and the other patrons make efforts to get the delinquents to either shut up or get out.

The younger public usually prefers bars or "clubs" with some form of entertainment, usually live music or go-go girls. They are often at least somewhat more elegant than the beer gardens of the older men. More women come into them, and one important reason for visiting them is meeting persons of the opposite sex. Put more bluntly, they are often pick-up places. Since these bars are accepted as such by generally shared definition, any party made up of members from one sex only which enters the place leaves itself open to approaches from others. Although men usually take the first step, this is not always the case. A number of the women in these places are prostitutes or semi-prostitutes, both among visitors and waitresses, and it is sometimes open to question who picks up whom.

Freddy, Fats, and Big Jimmy were standing at the corner of Piedmont Street, trying to collect money for a half-pint of gin and talking about the waitresses in the beer garden down the street. Fats said he was talking "real sweet" to one of them, the yellow-skinned girl with the high hairdo, trying to convince her to take him home with her that night when she handed him an envelope full of nudie pictures of herself out of her handbag. "Ain't that a bitch," said Freddy, and they all chuckled.

Other bars have become established in the public knowledge as hangouts for more specialized clienteles: gamblers, "gorillas", homosexuals. Those ghetto dwellers who do not belong to such categories will usually avoid such places. There grows up an identification between people and the places where they hang out, and nobody would want to get an unearned stigma attached to himself. Besides, it is again a question of the mapping of trouble. If one spends time around a setting of trouble, one may run an immediate risk of violence, and in the long run there is the possible influence of bad company. Mr. Robinson, a 62-year old janitor, walks past a bar with a clientele of "young hoodlums"—as people in the area describe them—who are not only inside but who also stand around in front of the bar; he sees his 19-year old nephew among them. Afterwards, he comments to his own son:

"You know who I saw outside the Crystal Bar? Frank. That boy sure ain't got no sense. You know how worried his mother is he'll get into trouble, and there he is with all them gorillas outside the Crystal. I bet you he'll get himself into a mess one of these days."

\*    \*    \*

The people of the Washington ghetto obviously find some of the satisfactions of life in their own black community. It is also the source of some of their troubles: But the ghetto is also a part of the Washington whole; we have already seen how its inhabitants are integrated into the economy of the wider community. In politics, too, the ghetto is a dependency.

The black ghetto in Washington, D.C., has grown much over the last decades. In the late nineteen-fifties, black people became a majority of the city's population. It was the first large American city where this occurred, but it is only one of many urban centers in the nation where large low-income black populations stay in the inner city while there is an exodus of white people to the suburbs. Thus much of what are now parts of Washington's black ghetto were white or at least more mixed until the forties and fifties. (Winston Street, however, has always been a home of poor black people.)

The ghettoization trend has continued in Washington. In the late sixties, about two thirds of the population of the District of Columbia are black people. But the situation is naturally a different one in the metropolitan area as a whole, including the suburbs in Virginia and Maryland, and this makes black dominance in Washington largely a chimera. In this larger area, the whites are about three quarters of the total population. About eighty percent of them live in the suburbs, while only some fifteen percent of the black people are suburbanites. The whites who reside within the boundaries of the District of Columbia are to a disproportionate extent unmarried or at least childless. The childrearing white families have gone to the suburbs.[7]

The development of numerical dominance of black people within the District of Columbia has not made a great difference in their status, and their situation is largely the same as that of black people in a number of other large American cities. Their employers, their landlords, their rulers are ultimately white outsiders. Even though most of them are poor, the black people of the District of Columbia should be able to have more political power by virtue of their being in majority; but the District, as the nation's capital, does not have home rule.[8] It has only been allowed to participate in presidential elections since the 1964 election. Executive power for the District of Columbia is vested in a local government appointed by the President of the United States. Legislation for the District is handled by two standing congressional committees, one of the Senate and one of the House of Representatives, and bills concerning the District must be passed by them before they are sent to Congress for general debate and vote. The committees have often been dominated by conservatives from rural areas, and these have frequently had little understanding of the problems peculiar to cities. Thus there is a chronic conflict between the government and much of the District's population, and many of the ghetto dwellers who are most politically aware feel that they live under a colonial type of government. Although the loss of a form of self-government occurred already in 1874 and was caused primarily by economic mismanagement, the role of race relations in the continuation of federal rule into the present is not easily denied. To a great many white Americans with representatives in Congress, the view of black people governing the nation's capital is apparently distasteful. A change to home rule may come sooner or later, and the issue has certainly been in the focus of interest of political and civil rights groups in the District during recent years. Yet it has so far been impossible to get Congress to approve of such a change.

Without general participation in elections, political activity in the ghetto is rather limited. Although most ghetto dwellers are certainly in favor of increasing their citizens' rights, their active articulation of such demands has so far been largely missing. Local political organizations and civil rights groups— and branches of national ones—have been relatively small. The new black power groups have apparently not yet extended their organizations significantly beyond the cadre, although their influence is certainly growing. The leaders of the older organizations, and most of their active members, belong to the sizeable black middle class, which usually lives out of the low-income ghetto in either integrated areas or black areas of a higher standing. Their interest in ghetto problems may arise from civic concern, from involvement with the ghetto through business or as professional employees of government or civil rights organizations, or from church work (as usual, there are many black ministers in the leadership), and not necessarily from a grass roots ghetto origin. Thus many of them are a kind of caretakers, defining and articulating the problems of the ghetto. But their everyday channels of communication to large segments of the people of the ghetto are not always very wide. Thus the ghetto dwellers are in one way a "people without politics", in that their personal voices are rarely heard in the political community to which they are assigned. The widest setting of the ghetto dweller, the polity and economy of Washington, D.C., and the United States, is one where there is little black power and much white.

# 2
# Life Styles

Since ghetto dwellers are not much involved with one another in relationships of power and livelihood, the social structure of the ghetto community is made up primarily of a multitude of connecting personal networks of kinsmen, peers, and neighbors. Overarching institutions under community control are lacking. The networks, of course, cannot provide the ghetto with a particularly "tight" structure. Neighborship, mutual acquaintances, place of work, and other unpredictable contingencies influence which ghetto dwellers gain access to each other. Functional differentiation in stable social relationships is limited to age and sex roles, peer roles and kinship roles. However, there is another important kind of differentiation which we may refer to as a diversity of life styles. "Life style" is admittedly a vague term; this may be one of its advantages, at least for a while, in that it does not commit us to some well-established form of analysis which may be less suitable for this particular case. Preliminarily, we may view a life style as the involvement of an individual with a particular set of modes of action, social relationships, and contexts. It goes beyond any more formal definition of a single role, although as we shall see later, ghetto life styles as understood here are not wholly independent of the basic roles of age and sex.[1]

The diversity of life styles has a great impact on the ordering of ghetto social relations. People of different life styles have different kinds of networks, and the difference influences the quantity and quality of interaction between them. Thus there are noticeable social cleavages between people following different walks of life, although one must also note that there are instances when life styles complement one another. To get an overview of ghetto social structure, then, we may attempt to delineate typical social relations within and between life styles.

*Two styles—a ghetto view*

The people of Winston Street often describe themselves and their neighbors in the community as comprising two categories distinguished according to way of life. However, they do not stand quite united in their choice of terms. Some refer to one category—in which they then usually include themselves— as "respectable", "good people", or, more rarely and somewhat facetiously, as "model citizens". More seldom do they refer to this category as "middle class", in this case apparently more a reference to a life style ideal than to socioeconomic status, although some of them would qualify as lower-middle class in terms of income and occupation. They use these labels to distinguish themselves from what they conceive of as their opposites, people they describe as "undesirables", "no good", "the rowdy bunch", "bums" or "trash", as well as in other similar terms. The "undesirables", or whatever label is used, are felt by the self-named "respectables" to be characterized collectively by drinking and drunkenness in public, spontaneous brawls, unwillingness to work, sexual licence, and occasional trouble with the police. The "respectables", then, impute to themselves an absence of such character blemishes, or stated in more positive terms, an allegiance to American mainstream morality.

There is, of course, a category of people who in some ways conform to the "respectable's" description of the "undesirables". Among them the consumption of liquor is high and sometimes beyond the manners and away from the places prescribed by mainstream norms. They engage in occasional violence (which together with drinking and drunkenness is the main source of conflict with the law). Their concern with sexual activity is certainly noticeable. The unemployment rate is high, although this, of course, need not be interpreted as general reluctance toward work as some "respectables" understand it.

How do these people describe themselves and their opposites? In fact, they do not use any corresponding labels very frequently, probably because they are not as concerned with the maintenance of the boundary between themselves and others as the "respectables" are. The most common self-references among these people at Winston Street are simply such vague expressions as "people like us..." or "us brothers down here...". These can sometimes refer to ghetto dwellers in general, while at other times they are used in opposition to the more mainstream-oriented members of the community. These may be described occasionally as "stuck up", as people who "think they're really something" or, in a different set of terms, as "house niggers", "handkerchief heads" and "Toms" (or in the more complete form, "Uncle Toms"). These latter terms, of course, imply servility toward white rulers. A "house nigger" during slavery was the personal servant of the white master whose close relationship to the latter brought a somewhat better life and greater sophistication than those of the ordinary plantation slave or "field nigger" but sometimes also some reputation as a renegade. The tied headcloth imputed to a "handkerchief head" is similarly symbolic of the lowly black servant woman's status in the Old South, and "Uncle Tom", of course, is the stereotype of the docile servant of whites. This kind of label, naturally, implies that those who view themselves as "respectable" can somehow be seen as disloyal to the more dispossessed members of the ghetto community. True, the self-styled "respectables" often have closer contacts with whites, in particular at work, and have more confidence in whites than those people have whose most intensive contacts with whites may involve the welfare people, the police, and the arrogant owner of the liquor store. However, the perceived disloyalty of the "respectables" which makes them susceptible to such labeling need not necessarily involve interaction with whites as much as moral alignment with them. In accepting the mainstream morality of most white Americans, the "respectables" also pass judgment on the "undesirable" behavior of other ghetto dwellers and thus commit an infraction against the solidarity of ghetto dwellers. This, perhaps, is the most significant way in which a "respectable" is a renegade. However, we must remember again that those who show less inclination toward mainstream "respectability" do not continuously refer to the mainstream-oriented as "house niggers"—terms of this kind only crop up in conversations now and then. Also, they are occasionally used to refer to other people as well.

The sharp division of ways of life suggested by the use of such terms implies that the ghetto community is clearly divided into two large groups, opposed to each other but internally rather homogeneous. However, a closer look at the actual lives and group formations of people at Winston Street suggests that the picture is not quite so neat. This folk model of social cleavage is not a particularly accurate description of what real lives are like, or of how they are intertwined. Above all, even if there are some people who live rather consist- ently "respectable" lives, and some whom these people quite consistently view as "no good", these two categories are only the opposite poles of a rather complex continuum. It is much too easy, judging by the native terms, to see these two categories as residual in relation to one another—whoever is not a typical "respectable" is not therefore a typical "no good".

It seems wiser to see the dichotomy as one of elements of behavior con- cerning which ghetto dwellers have a well-developed vocabulary of social and moral designations. This vocabulary need not be applied consistently and unambiguously to specific persons. Rather, it is an image bank from which one draws as the situation calls for it and as it befits one's own position. Some people are thus more given to such labeling, and some people are more liable to be labeled. Naturally, however, others find themselves in more of an in- between position with respect to such terms or change between different posi- tions over time. These latter tend to disappear into the dark corners of the picture as ghetto dwellers and outside observers alike point out the most clear- cut examples which fit the moral vocabulary, for maximal contrast.

This point may need to be emphasized because the simple dichotomy seems often to emerge from social science writing, about poor black people or the lower classes in general, as well—perhaps because the observers have simply accepted the moral taxonomy of the natives as an acceptable way of ordering descriptions of the community, or because a similar dichotomy fits the outsider's moral precepts, or his concern for "social problems".[2] In the latter case, the least "respectable" people become the "multi-problem families" or the "hard- to-reach poor"—terms which may lend themselves well to the professional outlook of social workers or persons in similar positions but are not necessarily relevant or adequate for ghetto ethnography. Yet they are no worse than labels such as "respectable" and "nonrespectable" as adopted by social scientists to denote people's total life styles. This often leads rather absurdly to the extension of apparently moral judgments to such life style items as unemploy- ment, intensive peer group life, and flexible household composition, all of which tend to occur together with the original "nonrespectability": drinking, loose sexual liaisons, and interpersonal violence. Yet if such items tend to occur together, it may be convenient to have a label for them, useful in a sociocultural analysis of the ghetto community, yet distinct from those occurring in the dichotomous conscious model of ghetto dwellers.[3] The category suggested for this purpose is "ghetto-specific" modes of action, as opposed to "main- stream-oriented" modes of action. Mainstream-oriented acts are those held appropriate, acceptable or normal by most Americans of the wider society, while ghetto-specific acts occur more frequently in the ghetto than outside it. This, of course, does not necessarily mean that the latter are all unique to the black ghetto, nor that they occur there with greater frequency than mainstream-oriented acts. Although the distinction is probably not one of great precision, it may still function reasonably satisfactorily.

The argument for this distinction, of course, should not rest simply in the interest of a separate ghetto trait list. The modes of behavior identified as ghetto-specific need also be understood in relation to each other and to the background and the peculiar social niche of the ghetto dwellers. Certainly these factors will be at work particularly strongly on some people, so that these will have an entire life style more ghetto-specific than that of other people in the community. Yet for a number of reasons we will largely avoid making this new dichotomy the only basis of a classification of life styles and people. Even the people whose behavior is most ghetto-specific are mainstream-oriented in some ways; furthermore, as we have noted, it is not possible to distinguish clearly between two categories in the ghetto on the basis of this criterion in such a way as to include everybody in either one or the other. Finally, other criteria than ghetto-specificity and mainstream orientation are influential in life style differentiation.

A slightly more complex categorization of people into four main life styles seems to suit at least the realities of the Winston Street neighborhood better: we will call them mainstreamers, swingers, street families, and streetcorner men. The scheme is not perfect. The four categories are still only "ideal types", approximations of a reality which is hard to depict with any reasonable economy of conceptual equipment and descriptive detail. While it is possible to see the population at least of the Winston Street neighborhood as composed largely of four nuclei around these life styles, there are many individuals who are less clearly oriented toward any one of them. They are, from our point of view, life style straddlers. A major difficulty rests in the fact that a life style in this case is to a great extent an orientation toward participation in a certain social context in which given modes of action tend to prevail; since individuals usually do not participate exclusively in that context, there are necessarily instances when their behavior differs from that which we will consider typical of their life style as a whole. The streetcorner men, for instance, are seen here as oriented particularly toward the peer group context, but a great many of them are also more or less attached to street families. To an extent which varies from one man to another, they are thus involved in a second life style. The more the men become oriented toward the domestic context, however, the more do they remove themselves from the life style of the streetcorner man; and the street family life style, in its most clearcut form one which involves women more than men and which is complementary to that of streetcorner men, then begins to approach the mainstreamer life style.

Another problem is that the life style concept to some may seem to presume an independence of more basic criteria of social differentiation such as age, sex, and marital status; as we shall see in both this chapter and in the following one, there is no total independence of this kind. The swingers are an age category, the streetcorner men are men, the mainstreamers are usually married. But there is no strict determinism, for the swingers do not include all people of the given age, the streetcorner men not all the men, and the mainstreamers not all the married people. The life styles are thus not simply direct expressions of these orders of differentiation, although influenced by them in certain ways.

As we shall see, one of the things which distinguishes our four-way differentiation of life styles from a simple dichotomy of the type discussed above is the joint attention to such basic role criteria and the ghetto-specific / mainstream-oriented distinction.

When we noted above that the categorization of life styles attempted here seems to coincide reasonably well with the nuclei of people discernible in the Winston Street neighborhood, we did not simply mean that this appears to be a realistic way of classifying individuals. It also has sociological correlates, as there tends to be more interaction between people leading similar lives than between those who do not share life style. However, since there are certain complementary, largely instrumental relationships between people of different age and sex—factors which also involve life style differences—it may be added that the choice of companions with a similar life style is most visible in sociable interaction. It should also be pointed out that the designations for life styles used here are not native ghetto terms, as the ghetto vocabulary lacks clear-cut, stable, and frequently used terms of this kind. However, they seem to be reasonably informative capsule characterizations of the respective life styles.[4]

*The mainstreamers*

The people we will call mainstreamers are, of course, those who conform most closely to mainstream American assumptions about the "normal" life. Consequently, they are also those who are most apt to refer to themselves as "respectable" or by similar terms. Most of those at Winston Street who own the houses they live in belong to this category. However, there are also quite a few mainstreamers who rent apartments in the neighborhood. Some of the latter are younger families who expect to be able to move out of the area later, either by way of some social mobility with accompanying higher economic standards or by way of accumulated savings. One man in his early thirties who had lived in the Winston Street neighborhood most of his life said, as he packed up his belongings to take his family to another apartment in an area of town generally regarded as "better":

"We want to get to a place where it isn't so noisy, and where people aren't so rowdy. Sometimes when summer comes you just can't sleep around here, you know, 'cause there is so much noise. In this place we're going to now you don't have to have anything to do with neighbors if you don't want to. This new place isn't much bigger, though. Next time I hope it'll be a house, out of town somewhere."

The fact that the mainstreamers are home owners or have strong hope of social and concomitant spatial mobility implies that many of them are among the better-off members of the ghetto community. There is hardly any unemployment in this category. While almost all the males in white-collar jobs in the neighborhood who are functioning fathers and husbands—not a very large number—are mainstreamers, most of the membership of this category is made up of relatively stable working-class people. In many families both husband and wife are employed, thus pushing the economic standard considerably higher. The members of the category—we are only talking about the adults here—are usually in ages between the upper twenties and the fifties, that is,

38

in childrearing ages. In fact, most of them are married and live in nuclear families with a quite stable composition. Consensual unions, divorces, and separations are much more infrequent in this group than among the ghetto population in general. However, in some cases one or two of the children are those of only one of the spouses—almost always of the wife—in an earlier marriage or in premarital affairs. In a later stage of the household developmental cycle, a mainstreamer household may include the young children of daughters; the children may have been born out of wedlock or in a marriage which has broken up, and the young mother may either stay with her parents herself or she may have left her child or children in the care of her parents while she continues for some time to live a freer life. With such exceptions, there is only rarely anybody outside the nuclear family present in the household. When it happens, it is most likely to be the sole surviving parent of one of the spouses—usually this turns out to be the mother of one of them.

It is usually not very hard to detect from the outside which houses on Winston Street are the homes of mainstreamers. The new metal screen doors, the venetian blinds, and the flower pots in the windows are usually absent from other people's houses. Yet basically the small row houses in the neighborhood all look rather much alike, whether the dark bricks have a coat of paint or not, and thus it may be quite a surprise to enter a mainstreamer's home and find that behind the drab exterior there is often a home which looks quite out of place in a predominantly low-income neighborhood. One family on Winston Street has a living room set of imitated Italian antique furniture, bought at a price of about $1500 and encased in fitted clear plastic covers; in a couple of homes the occupant-owners have had their living rooms paneled. Some have modern although usually relatively inexpensive Scandinavian-style furniture, and there are many large table lamps, sometimes matched in pairs, one on each side of the couch. New TV and stereo sets are not unusual; although the record collections include a lot of black rock-and-roll and jazz, there is often also some white pop and, less frequently, some classical music. On the shelves there may be some vases and rather inexpensive china figurines, as well as framed graduation or wedding pictures of the inhabitants of the house or of close relatives. Similar pictures may be on the wall, perhaps sharing the space with some picture prints. There may be a picture or a color memorial plate of the late president Kennedy, whose memory is as greatly esteemed by many mainstreamers as by most other ghetto dwellers. This may be what the inside of the house looks like. During the warmer months one may see something of the mainstreamers' concern with contemporary comfort outside as well; while other people on the street sit on the stairs in front of the doors or make use of old chairs which are on their way to complete discardment, some of the mainstreamers take out new aluminum garden chairs and set them up on the sidewalk for an early evening look at the newspaper. A couple of people in the group even have small barbecue sets in their tiny back yards.

The mainstreamers are clearly very concerned with the style and comfort of their homes. This is visible in their reading habits as well. Not only are they the people on Winston Street who most regularly read newspapers—some of them take both the morning *Washington Post* and one of the evening papers, the *Evening Star* or the more popular *Daily News*—they also hold by far the greater number of subscriptions to periodicals in the neighborhood, and most of these are to publications oriented toward home and family such as *Better Homes and Gardens, the American Home, Ladies' Home Journal* and *Mc-Call's*. However, some also take such magazines as *Life, Look, Reader's Digest* and the Negro picture magazine *Ebony*. The latter, of course, is strongly oriented toward mainstream concerns and occupational achievement, although it also has articles about the problems of the black proletariat.

Book reading is certainly less frequent although not absent. There are many more mainstreamers than other people on Winston Street who have public library cards, but those who most frequently visit the branch office of the library—which is rather far away—are the children, in their pre-teens or lower teens, and many mainstreamers certainly never go there at all.

If one gets a good idea of the typical concerns of mainstreamers just by seeing their homes, they are certainly even more visible in everyday household life. "A nice home", "a good family" and "taking good care of the family" are things mainstreamers often mention as important things in life, and as moral imperatives when they talk about other ghetto dwellers whom they think are not overly concerned with such matters. In mainstreamer households, there is a set dinner hour for all members of the household, if this is made possible at all by working hours and other factors. If there are school-age children in the house, parents try to see to it that home work gets done and that the children can do it somewhere where it is possible to study uninterruptedly. The men take more part in work "around the house" than most ghetto men, take their children on walks and rides (many mainstreamers have cars of late models), and generally spend much time at home. The spouses are together a great deal during their leisure hours, whether they are alone or in the company of relatives or common friends—as we shall see, in some ghetto families the husband and the wife often both interact very little with people close to the other spouse, but this is more seldom the case with mainstreamers.[5]

The distribution of authority in mainstreamer families is somewhat variable. There is hardly ever any doubt that the husband and father is regarded as the head of the household, with the greatest influence on those household affairs in which he wants to have a say—much day-to-day management of the household is of course delegated to the wife. However, while in some families it is quite clear that the husband can make rather independent decisions and enforce them, there are many among the younger couples in particular which have a more companionate type of marital relationship with a greater amount of joint decision-making.

The mainstreamer families on Winston Street are in most cases close only to a few similarly oriented families in the neighborhood. Most of their friends are scattered over town—particularly in the ghetto, of course, but some friends have also moved to somewhat more affluent areas. Many households maintain contacts with friends, and in particular with kin, in the South or in other Northeastern cities, and on occasional weekends and holidays the family may drive for example to New York or Philadelphia for a visit, or receive visitors from such cities. During summer weekends many also drive to the Maryland and Virginia beaches.

The majority of the mainstreamers are not members of any voluntary associations. The parent-teachers associations at the children's schools may be an exception, as their meetings may be seen as a part of the concern with family life. The times seem to have passed when practically all "respectable" black people were active supporters of a church and regular participants in its services.[6] Most mainstreamers on Winston Street go to church only very occasionally, and in particular in connection with the great ceremonies of life, although a great many of them send their children to Sunday school. Perhaps their lack of active church participation has something to do with the fact that most mainstreamers in the Winston Street neighborhood, and perhaps generally, are not migrants from the South, where the black church seems to be a stronger institution, but are born and bred in the city. One of the few mainstreamers in the neighborhood who has moved with his family from the South to Washington very recently is quite active, with his wife and children, in a neighborhood storefront church. When this man sat on the front step of his house one evening, talking to one of the middle-aged alcoholics who hang out in the vicinity, he commented on the religious habits of the people in his new surroundings.

"I've never been in a place where so many people don't go to church as on this street. It's a funny thing, you know. Now, let me tell it to you this way. I know you drink, and you like a drink now and then, 'cause you're used to it. I mean, it's like that. Now, I take a drink myself sometimes. Not all the time, I mean, but I'm no saint. Anyway, so if you don't drink, you won't like drinking that much. You may want to sample it, but it's no big thing with you, like it is when it's a habit. Now me, I've got the church habit, you see. I feel there's something wrong if I don't get to church, 'cause I'm so used to going every Sunday morning, and I wouldn't want to miss it. See what I mean? So if you ain't used to going to church, you might think up lots of reasons for not going, like your clothes ain't right, or your shoes ain't clean, or something like that. But that's only 'cause you don't want to go in the first place, and that's 'cause you ain't got that habit."

It may well be that this man and his family are just still in the churchgoing "habit". Most of the other mainstreamers in the neighborhood are clearly out of it, and they certainly do not need the kind of excuses he suggests to stay home on a Sunday morning. But clearly there are still many enough people in the ghetto, and many of them are undoubtedly mainstreamers, who flock on Sunday morning to fill a considerable number of churches.

Despite their lack of participation in church life one organizational venture of some mainstreamers in the neighborhood recently had a relationship to the church. A small, predominantly white middle-class church group in Washington wanted to sponsor community activities in the neighborhood and made its entry into it through contacts with a storefront church. Most of the activities were aimed at children for whom various programs were run for a period, largely under the supervision of the preacher at the storefront church. The white volunteers also became friendly with some adult mainstreamers, however, and together with these they opened a Friday night open house to which everybody in the neighborhood was welcome for coffee, donuts and ice cream at cost—"so we can all get to know each other". As it turned out, the idea apparently did not appeal to very many. A few young swingers dropped in together very occasionally and usually briefly, some streetcorner men made it a Friday evening habit for a while, and some pre-teens dropped in now and then, but often the black and white organizers were a majority of those present.

White wellwishers from the sponsoring congregation drove up "to see how things were going" quite frequently in the beginning, but their presence seems above all to have scared neighborhood people away. Too high dress standards for just a coffee hour was mentioned by some of them as a reason for not going, and some who went were irritated by the condescending attitude they felt in the behavior of some white visitors. Others complained that the taped music was not soul music but some classical music which one of the mainstreamer organizers preferred—he mentioned at one time that "some better music can't hurt". Quite a few, finally, felt that Friday night is the big night when you really "let your hair down", not a night for sitting around politely sipping coffee. Randy, who came to the coffee house once or twice, seemed to find the right words to express the unnaturalness he sensed there, as he explained mockingly to an acquaintance: "It's very nice, you can come there and converse with people on different subjects."

Thus the open house did not accomplish what the sponsors had wanted it to—the goals were never very clearly defined but they had something to do with more neighborliness, perhaps in pursuit of neighborhood improvement of some kind, and possibly with giving neighborhood people a more wholesome setting for their Friday night sociability. Giving up their efforts, the mainstreamer organizers just said that the same people had to do the work all the time and that nobody else seemed to care. By then the white church group was not directly concerned with the neighborhood any more.

### The swingers

The people we may call swingers are somewhat younger on the average than the mainstreamers, and many of them have brothers and sisters or parents who are mainstreamers. In due course, some of them will become mainstreamers, because it is hard to be a swinger when one gets older. However, some remain swingers longer than others, and many swingers later take another road than the mainstreamer one.

Swingers are usually somewhere between the late teens and the middle thirties in age. This means that many of them have not yet married and started families on their own, so that familial obligations would naturally be less demanding in terms of time, money, and emotional investments. But there are many swingers who are married and have children and who even so are not family-oriented. Of course, married men are more able to take part in the swinger life than are married women, as they can leave children and household affairs more readily in the hands of their spouses. However, some women manage to continue as swingers by leaving young children with the grandparents, as we noted in describing the mainstreamers. Also, quite a few marriages are broken as one or both spouses prefer to continue the swinger's life.

Swingers typically spend relatively little of their free time just sitting around at home alone or with the family. Weekday nights and particularly weekends are often spent going visiting, whether one travels alone—by private car, taxi, or bus—or in the company of a few friends. The spontaneous gatherings are not complete without some gin, whiskey, or beer, and the talk involves joking, banter, reminiscences of past shared experiences, and exchanges about the trivia of the day such as football results, forecasts of coming boxing bouts, and local grapevine items.

Of course, girl friends also visit boy friends and vice versa, for a few hours or over night. If the girl has a child or two, she might take them along if no babysitter in the form of a mother or sister is available, and on weekends they may all go windowshopping, to the Zoo, or to the movie theater together. Some of the young men are thus on close terms with their girl friends' children.

Friday and Saturday nights are the great nights for parties, with a lot of music and the latest dances, and many swingers manage to take in quite a few if they would not rather stay all the time at one party. After one New Year's Eve, a particularly big party night, one young bachelor on Winston Street announced that he had been to nine parties, none of which was in his own neighborhood and a few of which were in widely separated parts of the Washington ghetto. And Marvin, 22, reminisces about one evening a couple of years earlier:

"This was a Friday, and I had just got paid, and so I was going out with Geraldine. So we went to one party after another, and we were in and out of taxis all the time, and were going drinking at different places. And then I woke up the next morning and I had to go to work, and I put my hand in my pocket, and there was only two dollars! Two dollars left of all that money! I felt so bad I went right back to sleep."

Other nights when one does not go visiting, one may spend time at the bowling alley or in a pool room, at a bar, at the movies, or at the Howard Theatre. There may be a lot of driving around for no particular reason, or a group may drive over to nearby Baltimore—approximately a 45 minute ride—for a visit to its ghetto entertainment establishments which enjoy a more lively reputation than those in Washington. But all evenings cannot be spent like this, of course, and quite a few evenings most swingers can be found just passing time in front of a TV set. However, swingers, unlike mainstreamers, often talk of this as one of the dullest possible ways of spending one's time.

A rather small number of swingers, but more of them than of any other category in the ghetto, belong to voluntary associations of a rather purely sociable character. These are for men or for women but hardly ever mixed. On the other hand, the activities they organize are practically all occasions for meeting the other sex. Nobody at Winston Street is a member of such an organization, but a number of young men and women in the neighborhood are close friends of members of the Midcity Brotherhood Club, a kind of group with many counterparts in the city. When this club organizes an event, many of the neighborhood swingers will thus be present. Some of them also attend the events organized by other clubs they might hear of through friends and neighbors. As one young man said, "There's always something on somewhere you can go to. You hear about them through the nigger network, if you pardon the expression."

The Midcity Brotherhood Club, with a membership of about fifteen men, organizes a couple of "cabarets"—that is, dances with a band and some other entertainment—as well as a picnic annually, with the members as well as their friends selling tickets to friends, neighbors, and relatives. The dances are held at the premises of an old middle-class Negro fraternity lodge, and hardly anybody but swingers—perhaps a couple of hundred of so—is present. The ticket says B.Y.O.L., which means Bring Your Own Liquor. Potato chips, ice, and soft drinks for a mixer are supplied by the club. The summer picnic, on the other hand, is a family affair for those who have families, and there is a mixture largely of swingers and mainstreamers. The outing is in a Washington park with large picnic grounds, and the club members, all in the same kind of sports coat with the club name embroidered on the back, provide the visitors—usually two or three hundred—with hot dogs, hamburgers, corn-on-the-cob, and soft drinks. Park regulations forbid the serving of alcoholic beverages, but many visitors bring their own beer or perhaps something stronger. For the adults it is a good place to meet old friends for a few hours or make new ones, the teenagers do likewise or play a game of football, and the smaller children just follow their parents or try the swings. There is an age graded series of dance contests with records for prizes, where teenagers usually excel, and a raffle on the numbered tickets—first prize, a portable TV set, second, a case of whiskey, third, a transistor radio. The proceeds are donated to charitable organizations active in ghetto work.

Swingers thus lead lives full of company and spend much time away from home. This often means that a swinger who is married has friends relatively unknown to his (or her) family. In many cases, this means extramarital affairs, but often it is not a question of intentionally shielding the two spheres of life from one another. Sociability for swingers is simply an individual thing, not a sphere of activity where the couple is the "natural" unit.

It is possible to be a swinger on a variety of economic bases, although swingers have certain concerns which are hard to satisfy on a minimal income. It helps to have a car if one leads a mobile wide-ranging life, and many go to great efforts to keep abreast with fashion trends, for men as well as for women, as these are presented in certain downtown stores as well as on the ghetto main streets. Among the swingers on Winston Street and among their friends there is relatively little long-term unemployment but somewhat more periodical unemployment. A few of the men who are regularly without jobs earn money living off the incomes of women or through illegal pursuits such as robbery, burglary, or gambling. Most of the others in the category frown upon these activities and wonder how long the people in question can get away with it, but they usually do not break altogether with people they may have grown up with or may be closely related to.

A fact partially related to periodical unemployment is that of a rather high rate of job changes. These contribute to the swingers' widening social circles, as they accumulate new friends from among their work mates. Other friends remain from childhood and school days, and yet others are people you met at parties or in the company of other friends and took a liking to. Some acquaintances do not last very long, of course; "It's just a hi and bye thing, you meet and then you see a lot of each other for a while, and then somehow you don't see each other too much, and that's the end of it," as one young woman said.

Yet one more factor in the wide and shifting friendship networks of many swingers is their residential mobility, but this is one which they share with many other ghetto dwellers. When ghetto buildings are condemned as unsanitary, or torn down in urban renewal, the residents have to move; poor people are often expelled when they cannot pay rent; and it is natural that with little money to spare for extra space as a luxury, ghetto dwellers often adjust the size of their quarters to the minimum necessary for the household at its particular point in the developmental cycle—which means that as a family grows larger, there is a continuous pressure for more space.

The swingers' particular reasons for moving may have to do with these, or they may be of other kinds. Since swingers break up old marital and consensual alliances or form new ones rather often compared to other groups, this may influence the question of residence now and then. Other swingers on the move just say that they didn't like the neighborhood they were in—at times because some neighbors seem to feel that swingers should extend the same hospitality and sociability to them as they do to other swingers.

All factors taken together, with their investment of time and effort in sociability and entertainment, their mobility, and their living in a large metropolis where people's paths need not often cross accidentally, the swingers are in a position to make a great number of friendships and acquaintances, but these also easily come to an end if not pursued actively. Stated in somewhat more exact structural terms, the many more or less fluctuating relationships may be seen as making up networks in which large segments are relatively loose-knit and where there is a relatively low frequency of interaction as well as a low degree of permanence in many of the relationships.[7] "Loose-knit", in this case, means that a person's friends and acquaintances are not in direct relationships with each other, independently of their indirect contact through that person. Thus he knows a great many persons unknown to any particular one of his friends and acquaintances and is on the other hand as ignorant of parts of their social circles. Furthermore, and just as significant, even in segments of the network which are close-knit in the sense that persons who know each other also know of mutual friends and acquaintances, people are not always constantly in touch with one another. The often low frequency of interaction and low degree of permanency in sociable relationships mean that in part, the networks are only latently close-knit.

There are phenomena, however, which work toward the renewal of dormant relationships. Large-scale and widely known gatherings such as social club dances and picnics bring together many swingers who have not seen each other for a long time—indeed, this is frequently mentioned as an important reason for going to them. In a different way, mutual friends can prevent people from dropping completely out of one another's awareness. News of people whom one knows but seldom if ever sees are thus often received through intermediaries. Discussions of what is on the grapevine, we have already seen, are often on the agenda when swingers come together. This informative gossip may deal with who has a new job, who has moved, and where, who has married, or separated, whose little sister has grown up and is looking good, or who has got a new car.[8]

While mainstreamers in a way often encapsulate themselves in a few close relationships, many of which are with relatives, and enjoy the stable day-to-day life with home and family, the swingers' interests thus span out over the ghetto and seek variety and entertainment. The difference between them tends to be somewhat like that between "routine-seekers" and "action-seekers" which Gans describes from an Italian-American working-class and lower-class community in Boston (Gans 1962 b). In that case there was also a relationship

45

between age and life style, as well as between marital status and life style, but both among black ghetto dwellers and Italian-Americans there is less than a perfect fit, in that there is a period in one's life when one can live either way irrespective of marital status. When that period is over, however, a swinger has to become something else.

### The street families[9]

Some of the swingers then become members of street families, as many of them were when they were children. They are called street families here simply because they are conspicuous in the open-air life of ghetto street corners and sidewalks. Probably it is their way of life, and the complementary life style of streetcorner men, which most closely correspond to an outsider's image of typical ghetto life. It is often the members of street families who are conspicuously engaging in affairs with the other sex outside marriage, whose children are born out of wedlock and engage in juvenile delinquency as they grow up, and who drink and fight in public. Although not all street families, or all members of street families, engage in such behavior, and hardly anybody does so all the time, it is to them and their way of life their mainstreamer neighbors occasionally voice moral objections. (It may be added immediately that the members of the street families are not much given to idealizing the life style either.) Little attention is then given to the fact that some members of such families, in particular middle-aged and older women, may attend church quite regularly, and express quite puritanical views about what goes on around them. Of course, there are also women who only go to church on weekday evenings, to play bingo.

The street families are childrearing households. This means that there is practically always an adult woman in the household who is the mother of all, most, or at least some of the children there, and whose age is somewhere between the upper twenties and the fifties in the great majority of cases. (This, of course, means that this category is parallel to the mainstreamers agewise.) The women may or may not have a husband who is a member of the household—among the street families on Winston Street, between one-third and one-half are headed by women without husbands.[10] In the majority of these cases, however, the woman has been married previously.

A childrearing couple in a street family seldom has anybody from an ascending generation present in the household. A single woman with children, on the other hand, often shares her home with her mother. In a very few cases in the Winston Street neighborhood a woman has both her husband and her mother under the same roof, but these households have intensive mother-in-law troubles, and in other cases where this arrangement had been tried, it did not last very long. Thus, in general, street families are either two or three generation conjugal union[11] households, with husband, wife, and one or two descending generations (as young daughters' children may be included in the household), or two to four generation husbandless households, with an adult woman, sometimes with her mother and/or one or more brothers and sisters, and with the same one or two descending generations as those of conjugal union households. In both cases, of course, the younger daughter whose small child or children are in the household may be of the swinger set, just as the young women who leave their children with mainstreamer grandparents.

Naturally, this is only an outline of what may be seen as the two major types of household composition. Particular households with a large number of members of many generations and with age divergencies between members of the same generation can turn out to be quite complex. In the Winston Street neighborhood, for example, one older woman lives with three children—two daughters, one of whom is considerably older than the other, and a son. The elder daughter has nine children, and her oldest teenage daughter in turn has a son. The older woman's other daughter has one child. As a fifteen person household, this is one of the largest in the neighborhood. Those which compete with it in size and complexity are also husbandless. This is hardly surprising, as they are made up primarily of a combination of mother-and-child units with a common grandmother. Such combinations with husbands present in the procreating generation are not apt to occur.

Another aspect of the apparent complexity of households similar to the one just mentioned has to do with the relatively low ages at which many women first give birth and their relatively long periods of childbearing. Most teenage pregnancies in the Winston Street neighborhood occur among the street families, and many women who bear their first children early proceed to get quite large families. This means that generation spans are short, and the age difference between the oldest and youngest children of the same mother may be considerable. The consequence of this is often that a woman and her oldest daughter (or daughters) are childbearers and childrearers at the same time. In a number of households, then, children grow up in the company of uncles and aunts not much older, and sometimes younger, than they are themselves. Also, of course, if childrearing sisters share a household, cousins are raised under the same roof. However, there is no established pattern of etiquette between cousins or between aunts and uncles on the one hand and nieces and nephews on the other when they are of similar age and raised in the same household, so they function as close playmates and almost siblings— each child is aware, of course, that among the adult women of the household, he has a particular relationship to his own mother. Occasionally, in play such as wrestling, an uncle may playfully demand deference from his nephew, but otherwise their exact kinship status with respect to each other is of little importance.

As far as the mothers in a household like this are concerned, they tend to duplicate a mother and household manager role in that they usually all take some part in child care, cooking, cleaning and so forth. There are some dangers of conflict in an ambiguous arrangement like this, of course, over for example individual responsibilities or the proper way of handling a matter (particularly as the young woman either begins to take on her mother role or neglects to do so). On the other hand, it gives a certain flexibility for the participants in the work pool, as people with similar competences can substitute for each other. For one thing, it may permit at least one of the women to hold a job some of the time; for another, a young woman who wants more leisure time to spend in the company of friends can leave her children in the care of her mother.

Such an arrangement necessarily also means that an aunt or grandmother is somewhat like a mother to her sister's or daughter's children. This leads her to take on more authority as a disciplinarian toward these than an aunt or grandmother usually does. The indulgence which particularly a grandmother normally showers over grandchildren is thus circumscribed to the extent that she is behaviorally also like the children's mother.

Thus far it may have seemed here as if the husbandless households among the street families are completely without adult male members. However, this is not necessarily the case, as the case of the fifteen person household mentioned above shows. Relatively often the presence of the older woman also brings the brother of the childrearing woman into the household. The brother may be unmarried, separated, or divorced—if he does not have a home of his own, moving home to mother is a common solution, and in this case it brings him into the household of his sister. Usually, however, a brother of this kind has a very tenuous position in the household, as he is linked to it primarily through the oldest member who might not live much longer and because an unattached man of this kind often behaves in ways which are discomforting to other members of the household. On Winston Street, Reinhardt Ross, 45, is a good example of this.

Reinhardt lives with his 39-year old sister Grace, her eight children and her first grandchild, and his and Grace's 72-year old mother. Reinhardt is unemployed except for occasional day work (several years ago he worked regularly in a streetcorner grocery store), and he spends most of his time together with some other unemployed men at the street corner or in the back alley. However, he also frequently brings the other men into the house at practically any hour, and just like outside, they drink and get drunk there. Although Grace is on reasonably good terms with most of the men she would rather not have them around so much and at such inconvenient times, partially because she thinks they are a bad influence on the children. Besides, she wants more privacy. As it is, an evening in the Ross house is frequently like this:

The front room is crowded. One of Reinhardt's friends is asleep under a blanket on one of the two decrepit couches, while two of Grace's youngest children sit on the edge of it. Reinhardt and two other men are on the other couch, with another of Grace's sons between them. There are three tables. One has two TV sets on it, one of which is broken, while the other set shows a Western to which the smaller children are tuned in. The two other tables, on the other side of an oil burner, have heaps of clothes on them, as closet space in the house is very limited. Occasionally a roach runs up a table leg and disappears among the clothes. The edges of one of the tables are kept free so that some can take their meals there while others eat in the adjoining kitchen and the rest wait for their turn and watch TV meanwhile. After the meal, the women clean up carefully, the smaller children are asked to go upstairs, while the older ones go out or hang around. Reinhardt and his friends are sharing a drink—one of them just returned from the liquor store. Grace's 17-year old son David is inconspicuously leafing through a pornographic magazine. When Grace sees it, she snatches it from him and says, "You know you're not allowed to read that kind of trash. Didn't I raise you better than that?" A little later, David goes out. Now only the adults are left downstairs. Grace and her mother work in the kitchen and talk to each other while Grace's sister who is visiting sits half asleep in the front room. The men are also still there. They try to draw her into the conversation but she says nothing. One of them looks appreciatively at her and says, "You know, you're a fine-looking woman, big fat legs, good color, a mouthful on each side ..." Grace's sister still says nothing but smiles with half-closed eyes. Later, when Reinhardt and his friends are still there but the older woman and the children have gone to bed, Grace and her sister leave the house to go and play cards at a friend's house.

It is this kind of presence of Reinhardt's friends, as well as Reinhardt's own unruliness and untrustworthiness, which Grace objects to, and which generates much conflict between her and her brother. Both Grace's children and Reinhardt's friends say that Reinhardt only lasts in the house as long as his mother is there. Grace sometimes threatens, in harsh words, to put him out even earlier—"I'll have to get that nigger's ass out of here."

In cases such as this, it is clear that the man included in the household of his mother has little or no household authority. On the other hand, he also has very little responsibility and is hardly at all under the control of anybody in the household. Thus he does not alter the functioning of the household to any significant extent by his presence, except perhaps by being an irritant.

Another frequently occurring type of extra member in the households of street families—both those including a husband and the husbandless ones—is the boarder, taken in to give some additional income, but sometimes also or even primarily because someone in the household pities him. He, too, is usually an unattached male who cannot afford his own apartment and who has no relatives or is simply not accepted into the home of his kinsmen. In some cases, of course, he does not want to stay with relatives either. In many cases, the boarder in a street family is like a member of it, in that he eats with the family, uses its living room, and is an intimate of the people in the house. On the other hand, of course, he has no particular responsibilities in the organization of household life, and no authority except perhaps to a minor degree over the children, in the absence of their adult guardians. In some cases, boarders stay with the same household for many years, but many shift homes frequently because of failure to pay rent, because the landlord dislikes the boarder's behavior—drunkenness etc.—or because of other quarrels between them.

Finally, more frequently than other ghetto households, those of street families include additional children, usually related to household members but not directly descended from them, who stay there for longer or shorter periods. These are present only in a small number of the households, yet frequently enough to deserve mention. Sometimes, one gets no other reason for the presence of such a child than such explanations as "my sister and I thought Eric (the sister's son) ought to get to know his cousins a little better, so he'll stay with us for a while", but at other times, and more often, it is a question of an adaptive response to particular circumstances. If there is a severe lack of space, for instance, it may be seen as a good idea to let one or two children stay with relatives with more room, and if an older child does not get along with a stepfather it may be a solution to let it stay with an aunt or an uncle. Other reasons may be more complicated; a divorced man's former wife is becoming an alcoholic, and since he cannot himself take care of the children he asks a brother or sister with a family to do so.

All this goes to show that the household composition of street families is quite variable, both between households and in a single household over time. To a certain extent, this is undoubtedly due to strains arising from external

49

pressures—the many separations and divorces, for instance, which result in husbandless households, and the economic pressure which makes it more or less a necessity to take boarders even when there is hardly any extra space to spare. But one should also see the variability as an adaptive flexibility, as in the pooling of resources of adult husbandless sisters or an old mother and her adult daughter with children. Perhaps it is the habituation to this kind of flexibility in household arrangements, and to the adaptive relaxation of mainstream rules of household composition, that makes it easier to accept boarders even if the economic benefit is doubtful, or additional children even when it is not an absolute necessity. A streetcorner man throws the point into relief with this statement:

"I bet if you couldn't pay your rent and you were evicted from your place you couldn't just go to any of your white people and expect they'd take you in, they'd just be thinking of all the trouble. But you could come over here and stay with somebody 'cause we're used to helping each other out."

It can perhaps be said, then, that it is in the style of life of street families to maintain relatively open household membership boundaries. The mainstream American notion of the composition of a household is that it ought to be stable and coincide with the nuclear family in some stage of its development. Ghetto households often diverge considerably from this type. If we allow ourselves the luxury of making the point a little too strongly for the sake of contrast, they are more in the nature of temporary coalitions of persons relating to the household core in a variety of kinship, friendship, and landlord-boarder ties, for whom sharing residence is expedient even if it may only be for a short period.

Street families clearly have looser internal relationships than mainstreamer families. Compared to the latter, a person's relationships to the other household members have a lower salience and those to outside persons considerably higher. This means that whoever is the manager of the household (usually a woman or a team of women) has less influence on the lives of household members. The whole household is less often united for meals (something which may often also be made difficult by the large number of household members), and there is less control over children's home work. Attempts to steer the lives of household members often fail. In some households this results in recurrent open conflict. Children are given verbal thrashings, a lash with a leather belt, or a sentence of confinement to their rooms, but the disagreements continue. Some children are threatened with reform school by their mothers and regard it as a real possibility that they will be sent there at the initiative of their own family, although it is actually much more likely to be the result of outside intervention. Managing the male-female relationship in the street family where a husband is present may be no easier as he is frequently drawn to his friends at the hangout and perhaps to some outside sexual affair. There may be continuous and sometimes physically violent quarrels over this, and one can notice how many men ignore household hours when these come into conflict with peer group life.

The ghetto-specific bases, shapes and courses of conjugal relationships as they occur in street families will be discussed in some detail in chapter 4. For that reason we will take note here only of some factors involving household composition and embedding in the ghetto social structure.

Husbands are included in some street families, while others are husbandless. However, most adult women without a man in the house have been married. Usually they are divorced or simply separated—a legal divorce takes more trouble and some expenses to get, and therefore many only become interested in getting a divorce when a new marriage is to follow. When people who have been married contract new unions, however, these often remain common-law unions. A great many men and women enter new relationships of one kind or other, and as these result in children, the offspring of more than one union will often live together in one household, generally that of the children's common mother. As the children are usually given the last name of their father—sometimes even when they are the result of a short-term extraresidential union—they often have different last names, a fact which adds to the complexity of many street families. However, it happens that as a consensual relationship is broken and the father loses contact with the household his children are in, the last name of the mother also comes to be used for her children out of wedlock. Apparently, no particular usage is very definitely established for children's last names under these circumstances.

Obviously "having husband" and "not having husband" are neither very stable nor very clearcut as attributes of women in street families. One may have a more or less close male companion within or outside the household without being married to him, and the position of such a male partner in household affairs may be quite variable. Whether or not a woman is equipped with a husband or a male partner at one point in time, this is not necessarily her lasting status. A number of the marriages which exist at any given time are likely to split sooner or later.

Most husbands and wives in street families are not very close to each other. One may well characterize their relationships as segregated.[12] They spend most of their leisure time apart. The women (who have less leisure time, being in charge of most household affairs) tend to spend their time with an intimate circle of close kin—mother, sisters and daughters if these live close enough— and a few neighbor women. The men on the other hand, spend their time with a somewhat larger peer group of more fluctuating composition, in which male relatives may or may not be included. A great number of the men have rather marginal involvements with family life, and apart from these their life style is that of the streetcorner men described below. Others, however, are somewhat more oriented toward home and family, which means that their family relationships are a little closer to those typical of mainstreamer families.

The segregation of relationships between man and wife means that they may know little of each other's company, and in particular that the wife hardly knows the wives and girl friends of her husband's friends at all, while the husband is as unfamiliar with the male company of his wife's female friends— unless these are her close kin, of course. Patricia Jones, a Winston Street woman, sees a great deal of some of her husband Harry's friends, as they often assemble on the front staircase of the Jones house, and sometimes in the Jones living room—it is an "open house" to a greater extent than most—but their wives and girl friends are usually unknown to her except by name and sometimes by sight, as they have been pointed out to her on the street. The following incident, involving Harry Jones' friend Sylvester's relationship to his girl friend Diane, shows some of this. Sylvester is a liquor store messenger and a boarder in "Miss Gladys' house" down the street.

Harry, Sylvester, Sonny, and Wes are sharing a pint of whiskey in the Joneses' parlor. As Patricia comes in from the kitchen to get a drink, Sylvester starts making a little show of leaving the group to go over to Diane, ostensibly to stay over night. The other men tease him, as they often do, about the risk of finding some other man with Diane. Patricia says the risk must be small. If Diane thinks Sylvester is good enough for her, she must be an ugly old hag without a tooth in her mouth. The other men laugh as Sylvester indignantly says that she is not like that at all. Patricia keeps on deriding Diane, claiming that she has heard from somebody who had seen Sylvester and Diane together on the street that she was the ugliest thing she ever saw. Sylvester asks who said so, and Patricia finally laughs and says she was just kidding. Actually the only thing she knows about Diane is what Sylvester says, but then that is probably not very reliable either, Patricia says.

More than mainstreamers or swingers, the street families have their leisure lives rooted in a rather small area around the neighborhood. A greater number of relatively close neighbors become engaged in sociable interaction, while one sees less of friends in other parts of town. No doubt, this is partially due to the fact that compared to mainstreamers, many of whom have cars, the members of street families cannot move around so easily. But it seems, too, that the members of street families are less reluctant to engage in interaction with people they have met by chance, such as through repeated encounters in the neighborhood.

It should also be added here that Winston Street has a nucleus of street families who have lived a long time in this area. Some of them have even been present on this street for two or three decades, although they may have moved from one house to another on it as better houses have become available or as eviction notices have forced a move. These families, of course, are well acquainted, and in some cases temporary alliances have been formed between their members and children have resulted from them, as boys and girls have grown up together or as some woman's unattached brother has cast eyes on the divorcee next door.

The participation in street life may cause strains on domestic organization; however, it also has its rosy sides. The informal communications passing between friends may be useful social capital. If a man knows of a job opening at his place of work, he may tell an unemployed neighbor about it in a street-corner conversation; if there is some day work anywhere in the area—moving, painting, cleaning, or carpentry, for instance—the men who are in the midst of street life are apt to hear about it first.

Furthermore, in a society where life on a small income is a continuously unfolding series of instant crises, the small informal loans and services granted between neighbors may ease the burden by channeling resources each moment to the point where there is a current need. This may be a problem for a person who is repeatedly called upon to help but who is seldom in need of assistance himself; but to the extent that these relationships really work out as balanced reciprocity, they are helpful to all involved. The case which follows provides a picture of how a man with good contacts in the Winston Street neighborhood engages in a series of small transactions of this kind in the course of a couple of hours.

I met George about 4.30 p.m. outside Rubin's grocery. Mrs. Dunham just passed by. She was in a hurry to get to her job and borrowed a quarter from George—his last—for her bus fare. Since George is usually at work at this hour, I asked him how it came that he was off, and he said he had been changed to a new shift, from 5 a.m. to 1 p.m. Since he works in Virginia, I said it was a good thing he had just gotten a car; he had paid 200 dollars for it.

"Yeah, but I tore that thing up yesterday," he said. "I wrapped it around a tree."

It turned out he had been working two shifts in a row to get into his new shift, and afterwards he had been out drinking with a work mate. On his way home he had obviously been a little drunk and more than a little tired, so he had probably fallen asleep.

"So I called Lewis, you know, he works at this garage, so he got a buddy from over there to come and tow my car back here."

After we had taken a look at the car which was in uncertain condition, George asked if he owed me any money, and I replied I was afraid he did not.

"Could you stand for a half pint?" he asked. We got one and finished it on our way to Sonny's place, but Sonny was not at home, so we went to look for him and Sylvester at Diane's place—Diane is Sylvester's girl friend. They were not there either, however, so we went back to Winston Street, first to Albert McNeill, a truck driver and amateur but expert auto mechanic who promised to take a look at George's car "first thing in the morning". George had the next day off and would not have to show up at his job again until the day after. Of course, if the car was not running by then he might be in trouble, since there was no public transport to his job in Virginia between midnight and 6 a.m. But another neighbor knew someone who also started work somewhere out there at an early hour, so perhaps he could arrange a ride.

We then went on to Mr. Clark, and George told him about the car, and Mr. Clark thought it was a shame. But the visit failed as far as its real purpose was concerned. Since George's wife was away he would not get dinner at home, so he needed some money to go to the carry-out. Mr. Clark could not help; he pulled out the lining of his pockets to show that they were empty. So we continued to Mr. Lewis, the man at the garage who had helped George get his car towed the night before. George borrowed a dollar there and went to the carry-out to get a barbecued rib sandwich which he brought back to his friend Harry Jones' house. Harry was asleep, but his wife Patricia was getting ready to go to a church to play bingo. She asked George to come along, so he went across the street to another neighbor to borrow money so that he could play, too.

Street families have a lower average income than mainstreamer families, and a great number of them fall below the poverty line.[13] Many of the men in street families are in unskilled manual work, and a number of them are at least periodically unemployed. The women with jobs are also in unskilled work— many are domestics and cleaning women. A number of the husbandless households receive welfare payments. There is clearly a relationship between low income and elements of the street family organization; we have touched on some of them here. We will return to such problems of economic constraints and adaptations in chapters 4 and 9.

*The streetcorner men*[14]

Our sketch of the street families dwelt particularly on the life of women and children—even when there are men in these households, they are often peripheral to domestic life. To give a view of the life of men, we must direct our attention to the peer group life of men, much of which takes place at street corners but also in other settings such as some people's houses—at the Ross house and the Jones house on Winston Street, for instance, as described above —carry-out shops, back alleys, or pool halls. Some streetcorner men, we have found, are members of street families, but others are unattached and live as boarders, have their own apartments, or just drift around staying for a while with anybody willing to put them up. In the latter cases contacts with kin may be minimal or altogether absent. This became tragically clear when Rufus, a long-time resident of the Winston Street neighborhood who had been boarding with Patricia and Harry Jones for a couple of years, suddenly died of a heart attack. His friends among the streetcorner men tried to locate his closest relatives—only at this time did some of his peers find out what his last name was. It was impossible to trace any brothers or sisters at all, however, although Rufus had mentioned their existence now and then. The men also knew that Rufus had been married once and had also had a common-law union of some longevity, but they only found his first wife after several days' work. She said bitterly that she had not seen Rufus for years and that since he had contributed nothing to the care of their children for so many years, she did not think it mattered one way or the other if he was dead. Thus she saw no reason to contribute to meeting funeral costs. Nobody else could or would raise the money either, so Rufus was finally cremated at public expense. His friends were quite upset but could not do anything about it.

We mentioned above that male members of street families usually hold low-paying, unskilled jobs and are sometimes unemployed. The unattached men are even more likely to be unemployed for long periods or even permanently. They have often dropped out of school early, and many of them are relatively recent migrants from the rural South.

The streetcorner men usually return day after day to the same hangout. There they talk and drink, play cards and shoot crap, or just do nothing. Some go home to eat, others get something from the carry-out or the streetcorner grocer—some bread and cold cuts, perhaps, things they can eat while they are standing at the corner. There is continuous drinking—a lot of gin and somewhat less whiskey, while some men drink only cheap wine. If they are not already alcoholics, they are well on their way. Many of them have had attacks of *delirium tremens*; the symptoms of "deetee" are familiar to most ghetto dwellers. Now and then somebody at the corner mentions that yet another friend has got cirrhosis of the liver, and everybody knows of friends and acquaintances who have died from ailments caused by their drinking. Quite a few men have attended rehabilitation classes for alcoholics, but these are usually seen as a farce.

"Those classes are a lot of bullshit. Lot of niggers bring their bottles right into class, and then there's one of these fellows standing up there telling you about how he stopped drinking, and you can see he's half drunk right up there, and he's gonna get more drunk as soon as he gets out of there."

There is not much beer drinking except during the summer. This is also the season of most beer commercials on the black radio stations.

Collections for liquor are taken among the streetcorner men themselves, but there is also a lot of begging from people who pass by. Most of it is quite friendly—from neighbors whom the streetcorner men know quite well—but some men can also behave in rather threatening ways or engage in robbery. Many of the men have some kind of police record. In the case of a relative few the record is serious and may include housebreaking, robbery, and aggravated assault. These are the people known in the ghetto as "gorillas". In other cases there are charges for minor assaults or petty larceny such as shoplifting and purse snatching. Most of the men's records, however, involve drinking and drunkenness in public places, and in some streetcorner groups the members are much more law-abiding than in others.

Some of the unattached men may have extraresidential relationships to women in street families. However, others rely largely on prostitutes for meeting their sexual needs, which is one reason for the spread of venereal disease among them. A couple of single women in the Winston Street neighborhood eke out a meager living as prostitutes catering to the desires of the streetcorner men who hang out there. One of them, a sickly woman named Ruby, occasionally lives with one man or another for a while, but these unions do not last very long. Her one-room apartment is also used as a kind of lounge by some of the men, particularly during the winter when it is too cold to be outside much. One evening at Ruby's place may be like this.

The one room has a concrete floor and is partially below the street level. There is a couch and a few small tables, a couple of old upholstered chairs into which cigarettes have burned many holes over the years (usually as drunken smokers have fallen asleep) and a couple of kitchen chairs. There is no rug. Of the three holders in the ceiling only one holds a bare lightbulb, while the other two are empty. On one of the tables there is a porcelain lamp in the shape of a half-naked woman. Its shade is broken. On this day neither lamp is lighted, since Ruby has failed to pay the electricity bill so that the current has been switched off. Instead, there are a few candles. The walls are adorned by one picture of president Kennedy, three of Jesus Christ, one of a group of black rock-and-roll artists, and one print of a landscape with a beer advertisement pasted on the frame. There are also a plastic wall clock advertising another beer brand (a type of clock usually found in cheap beer taverns) and a calendar from a nearby liquor store. Roaches are running all over the walls and the furniture.

As the men begin to gather this evening Ruby is not yet there. There is an elderly man, Nathan, who talks about his hunting and fishing trips down South; there is Jimmy Wilson, Percy, and Reinhardt; and there is Joshua who came up from North Carolina some eight months ago and has been talking about getting a job since then but has not succeeded so far. Joshua wants to impress people as one who knows his way around and as a smart dresser. His flat, smallbrimmed hat, his coat and his tie are all in matching colors, but by now they are all very dirty, and his coat is torn here and there. His baggy, dirty pants and muddy shoes also fail to contribute toward the image he wants to promote.

The men pool their resources for a pint of gin and a bottle of soda for a chaser. Old Nathan provides most of the funds. He has a job right now, and besides he is on his way home to his wife and wants a taste before he leaves. Percy goes to the liquor store to get it. He has a fresh knife wound on his cheek after Bee Jay cut him the night before. When he returns, Dennis, the man who has been living with Ruby for several months, is with him. Percy mentions that Lorraine, the 14-year old girl across the street, is pregnant. "Those fellows had better watch out", Dennis says. "You don't go around knocking off young broads like that. That's statutory rape, and the judge won't pay it no mind if she wanted to or not." There are some reminiscences of other early pregnancies, about men who got away with it and about men who did not. Then Ruby comes in. "Lord have mercy," she says. "You all here, and you got a taste, too." Then she tells Dennis she is tired of him, so he will have to go. Dennis is silent, but Jimmy Wilson says Dennis will soon find another woman. Nathan leaves to go home. Joshua takes his harmonica out of his pocket and starts playing old country blues. He is not particularly good. Reinhardt and Percy have become more and more drowsy after the gin; now they both sleep on their chairs. Ruby, Dennis, and Jimmy Wilson ask for tunes, and Joshua tries to play them. Even if he is not very successful they are all enjoying themselves. Jimmy Wilson, a jet black man with processed hair and a very hoarse voice, stands up to sing to Joshua's accompaniment. He stands in front of Ruby and leans over her as he sings. "You ain't good looking, but you're my kind of woman . . ." Ruby smiles, and after Jimmy stops singing she stands up and dances with him on the small space which is free in the middle of the floor. They clench each other tightly and move slowly. Joshua laughs and plays his harmonica, and Dennis looks on. Reinhardt and Percy still sleep, their heads hanging down toward their chests. After a while the men who are awake leave to go and try to find something to eat, and Ruby is left alone with her two sleeping guests.

When the members of a streetcorner men's peer group describe themselves, they lay much emphasis on solidarity. Sometimes, this is a general solidarity among all the members; "When they drink wine, I drink wine; when they drink gin, I drink gin; when they drink whiskey, I drink whiskey." More often, however, the solidarity refers to bonds between one man and another. "Dennis is my main man. If he gets into trouble, I'll be right there with him." Many streetcorner men, like Joshua, and like many younger swingers, are acutely conscious of male clothing fashion, although they can usually ill afford to do anything about it. It is another fitting expression of friendship, then, when Fats says, "Freddy can use anything in my closet, and he'd let me use anything in his." And Percy remembers how Lonnie helped pour wine down his thirsty throat when Percy himself had the shakes so badly that he could not hold the bottle.

But all is not peace and friendship in the circle of streetcorner men, and there is much to show that the rosy view of close relationships lasting through thick and thin is considerably exaggerated.[15] The speech style of streetcorner sociability is often tough and scornful, and hospitality is not always liberally extended. If a collection is taken for a half pint of gin and one man has no money, he cannot be too sure to get anything to drink. Fats specifically denies Reinhardt a drink out of his bottle because "That damn motherfucker never brushes his teeth. I ain't gonna let him get close to my bottle with his dirty mouth." In this case Reinhardt says nothing, but at other times a man might be less happy to accept abusive comments on his appearance, behavior, or intelligence. While streetcorner peer groups vary when it comes to the members' reaction to slights upon their honor, there are some where a challenge often leads not only to a heated argument but on to a violent fight (see chapter 4). It happens that knives, bottles or other objects are used, which is one explanation for the scars on the faces and bodies of many streetcorner men. Sometimes, such quarrels lead to lasting animosity, and people who are good friends one day may be bitter enemies from the next day and on. And the conflicts are easily expressed in violence again, as the two enemies continue to hang out at the same place and with peers they have in common.

Violence also easily erupts in the streetcorner men's relationships with women as some men are no more ready to take insults from these than from other men. Besides, the fast-changing and by no means clearly defined relationships between streetcorner men and the women they interact with easily breed disagreement and distrust about sexual faithfulness, and violence occasionally erupts over such matters as well. Although some women are quite ready to defend themselves with a knife or a razor, many would rather call the police. This, of course, adds to the police records of some men.

It might seem from what has been said that the life of streetcorner men presents a lurid picture of sex, drinking, and violence. This may be true to the extent that the men show much and continuous concern with getting "a taste" and "a piece of pussy", and in that they are undoubtedly well acquainted with violence. But after all, fights occur only now and then, and many men have so limited access to sexual relationships that they must turn to prostitutes. Most days in the life of a streetcorner man, then, are filled with the same faces, the same hangout, the same struggle for money for food and drink, the same kind of talk—in short, the same routine.

\*  \*  \*

Naturally, some people do not quite fit into anyone of these categories. Some of the old people, for instance, living alone outside childrearing households and without much interaction with neighbors or anybody else, cannot easily be placed in a category, although they may still lean toward the street family, streetcorner man, or mainstreamer orientations which were theirs during their more active lives. A few unattached women without significant household obligations are a kind of female counterparts of the streetcorner men with whom they interact rather intensively. Some of them, like Ruby who was mentioned above, make some money from prostitution but are hardly professionals; rather, they "turn a trick" when an opportunity presents itself, but mostly with friends and acquaintances as customers, people they may often "do it" with anyway. Other people are not so much left out of the four categories as they are left between them. It is not difficult to see that it is possible to follow a middle course between mainstreamer and street family, between swinger and mainstreamer, between swinger and street family, or between swinger and streetcorner man. A curious case of such straddling is that of some households in the Winston Street neighborhood which are well established in illegal businesses —bootlegging and the numbers game. Except for these means of income, the households seem to lead mainstreamer lives. Their houses are well kept, the families keep largely to themselves, although they are friendly with their neighbors and well liked by most people, and they sometimes voice concern with the improvement of the neighborhood. Other people are aware of the incongruity between on the one hand the respectable front and the mainstreamer life, on the other hand the kind of business they engage in. As one mainstreamer neighbor said about one of the men involved: "Of course Jimmy Thompson is a crook, but he is a good man." Other people in illicit businesses may be more aligned with other life styles. Many bootleggers, dope pushers, pimps, and other hustlers are in street families, and some of the more successful ones are well-known "men about town" swingers—very well dressed, with expensive cars, and well known in those ghetto bars which are the main settings of the fast life. Illegal activities can thus be combined with a variety of life styles.

In this chapter we have taken the ghetto population apart, sketching how it is divided according to styles of life. In the next chapter we will try to make a whole of the parts again.

# 3

# Walking My Walk
# and Talking My Talk

The ghetto community is obviously heterogeneous. However, after delineating the different life styles and noting the border cases, we must go beyond this conclusion. There is also an organization of diversity. People of different life styles interact with one another or at least take note of each other in ordering their actions, and they are not ascribed to the same life style throughout their lives. It is with these phenomena of accommodation and change we will be concerned here, as we continue our inquiry into the complexity of the ghetto social order. We will first approach them by taking a look at life careers.[1]

*Careers and life styles*

The ghetto life styles are not equally well represented in both sexes and in all age groups. There are no old swingers; the streetcorner men are obviously male. On the one hand, then, there is reason to look at sex differences in life style; on the other hand, we should follow the movement through the life cycle in order to see if there are patterned sequences of life styles, and how these relate to the individual's position in the social structure.

Young adults naturally start out unmarried. This, of course, is the state most conducive to the life of a swinger, and many of them will follow this life style for a considerable length of time. Others, however, turn to other ways of life rather soon, whether they marry or not. Some younger men are much closer to the life of streetcorner men already to begin with, some young women turn more to household affairs at an early stage and are thus never really in the swinger stage. But the possibilities for being a swinger are relatively good for many, and a great number make use of them. There is no expectation that the single young man or woman should hurry to invest all time and emotions into any one relationship. The claims of the family of orientation have been attenuated. Whatever is the size of the income, and often it is no lower at this stage than later in the kinds of jobs ghetto dwellers hold, there are no claims for providing for spouse and children. Thus the swinger quite possibly has more left than he ever will for his leisure life. Likewise, there are no great demands of time for home life. Resources for intensive and rather wide-ranging sociability are thus available to a reasonable extent. Sooner or later, of course, most swingers get married. This may be a definitive step away from the swinger set, but it happens that it is not. We will come back to this. On the other hand, since swinging often involves short-term sexual relationships without serious intentions of marriage, quite a few conceptions out of wedlock occur. In some cases, these unexpected pregnancies lead to marriage, but often they do not, and in these latter cases, the young fathers have few or no obligations toward the children. At least, this is the way it often turns out. This means that there is frequently more pressure on the young unmarried mother's resources than there is on the unmarried father's. She has a child to take care of, which takes time and money. The female swinger thus easily drifts out of the life style sooner than does the male swinger.

However, childbearing and childrearing do not automatically bring with them the end of swinging. As we have seen, a young girl with one or two children may be able to leave them in her own mother's or parents' home for some of the time or practically all of it, if this generation is available, in shape, and cooperative. This may well mean a deferment of heavier household duties for the young woman, and an extension of the swinger life. Whether she lives in her parents' household—where she takes some part in household work, but not very much—or has her own apartment, domestic obligations take less time and effort than they would if she had her own household together with her child or children.

If she continues to bear children, however, the situation will most likely have to change. The resources of the grandparental family—in terms of income, time and stamina—are hardly so elastic that it can take care of many grandchildren. Their mother might then either marry, ending up with a family of either the mainstreamer or the street family type, or she may remain unmarried, in which case it seems that she is quite likely to find herself at the center of a street family.[2] With only one or two children, however, her continued career need not yet have been decided. Not even the mainstreamer segment of the community, or more exactly, the young males who are likely to become mainstreamers when they settle down, are as intolerant as to attach significant stigma to the unmarried mother of one or possibly two children.

It may be added here that the fact that a young man does not marry the mother of his child either before its birth or soon after does not necessarily mean that he will not do so at some future point. Certainly a pregnancy involves some heightened consideration of the possibility of marriage, in that those who are ready to settle down may feel that this is the time to do so. But if the two parties are not yet inclined to enter married life—it is more often the man who hesitates than the woman—they may continue an extraresidential relationship with the explicit intention to marry later on. For example, Marvin Taylor, a 22-year old man on Winston Street who occasionally does construction work but who makes part of his living from robbery, has a girl friend, Thelma, who lives with their 2-year old daughter in another part of the ghetto. Marvin visits them regularly (and is visited by them), sometimes stays with them for a few days at a time, and says he intends to marry Thelma in a couple of years or so, but first he wants to have a good time and enjoy his bachelor days for a while longer. He also makes it clear that when he marries there will have to be an end to his "street work".

What follows in a man's or a woman's life after marriage is obviously not a certainty. Some couples are ready to become mainstreamers, with a close husband-wife relationship and relatively limited outside sociability. In other couples, we have pointed out, particularly the male remains a free spirit with considerable independence of action from spouse and children, thus further postponing his farewell to swinging. Some turn to a more mainstreamer-like way of life only when they reach the approximate upper age limit for a swinger, while others then become more or less streetcorner men. In the latter case, of course, they can extend the emphasis on outside sociability with concomitant limited household participation indefinitely, although the pattern of outside sociability naturally changes. This path, of course, is also the most likely one for men who are unmarried, separated, or divorced.

In summary, males and females can have similar or different life style careers. However, their career contingencies—the factors on which mobility from one style to another depends—tend to differ, leaving women with less of a choice of what road to follow and how to time changes. Whether she is married or not, a young woman who has a child finds herself more committed to home and family than the child's father, with a concomitant decrease in the opportunities for swinging. Her circumstances can become less constraining only if she has access to kin (usually her own mother) who is ready to assist her in childrearing, but this is only a temporary solution in most cases. Sooner or later, most ghetto women, regardless of their marital status and whether they are in mainstreamer or street families, will find their time taken up to a great extent by household work and child care, chores which may leave few hours easily set aside for leisure—particularly if they also hold outside jobs.

A man, on the other hand, can conceivably remain a swinger until he passes the upper age limit, whether he is a father or not and whether he is married or not. And even as he gets older he has the two possibilities of a life oriented toward his household, more or less in the mainstreamer manner, and a life oriented toward outside sociability, as in the case of a streetcorner man. But this is not to say that these possibilities are always open to him, or that men choose according to some rational calculus of what they consider is the best available life. A streetcorner man who has failed in a marriage or is too undesirable a partner cannot easily choose a life style oriented toward home and family for his future, and certainly few men can trace the steps that led them to the lives they lead now, or explain what made them take the steps. Rather, they have drifted into their life styles by way of a series of contingencies only some of which are easy to discover. Yet the fact remains that there is more variability of ways of life among men than among women in the ghetto, and that men's life style careers are therefore less predictable.

*Drifting between life styles*

"Career" sounds like something rather orderly, a sequence of changes depending on rather few factors. So far, we have also used the concept to discuss those changes between life styles which are typical courses relying mainly on such clearcut contingencies as sex, age, accessible family resources, marital status, and parental status. But we have noted that in particular the ghetto males are not strongly constrained by this set of factors in arriving at a life style. We might also look at a couple of other factors which might be life style correlates, and discuss what influence they might have.

For one thing, we have noted that the income of mainstreamer households

61

averages higher than that of households in other categories. It seems quite likely that good earnings may lead to a stronger orientation toward home and family life. One has more to spend on furnishings and similar wants, and a satisfactory economy undoubtedly increases marital harmony. One does not have to pool resources with peers to get food and drink, and so one is less liable to get involved in improper conduct on streets and in other public places while one is hanging out with them. It certainly appears that income influences life style.

On the other hand, however, the influence is not absolutely decisive. A great many men hold a satisfactory economy as a premise for continued swinging; as long as the family's immediate needs are met, nobody can complain if a man has "a good time". One man with two children who is a clerk in a government office and moonlights as a taxi driver some weeknights and whose wife is an elementary school teacher—which clearly makes the couple one of the better situated in the ghetto—has this to say:

"I earn good money, you know, with those two jobs, and my old lady earns a lot on her job, so actually I don't have to leave too much money at home 'cause she takes care of much of that. So this means I got a lot to spend just fucking up."

This man has an outside affair with a young woman on Winston Street. The woman is unmarried but has two children. These are often in the care of her mother or aunt in the same household as she is still very much a swinger. This is a part of her account of the relationship with the man:

"He's very nice with gifts and things. He makes quite a lot of money, you know, and he's also had a couple of hits on the numbers, one for ten dollars and one for twenty dollars. He doesn't support his family too well, I suppose, but his wife works, too. So when he came up for twenty dollars, he left all the money to his wife because he had messed up a lot at home then, but when he came up for ten dollars he said, 'No, this is for my baby', and that's me. And he gives me gifts, like dresses and slips and brassieres—and you know, he comes with a slip for eight dollars and I say, 'Honey, I could get three slips for that price.' And yesterday when it was my oldest boy's birthday he came with a cake almost as large as this table! I gave some cake to this other girl's kids and then I took the rest over to my other aunt's house, 'cause otherwise we'd have had to let everybody in. And another time he took me to this social affair downtown which was fourteen dollars per couple just for the food, and people came around to our table, and at eleven-thirty we had a bill of twelve seventy-five for drinks and at two-thirty when we left it was sixty-three fifty! And I was sure everybody was looking at me, you know, I had this long green dress with slits coming up the sides like this, and it came down, down like this from the shoulder, and I had this long green and black cigarette holder. I got a beautiful picture of myself taken, and it was such a good picture people tried to steal it from me, but I said I'd send it to my boy friend in Vietnam."

In the case of this man, continued swinging is probably still a prelude to a later mainstream life. There is no question of his family splitting up, his wife certainly keeps the household on a mainstreamer track, and the man himself functions successfully and happily in a mainstreamer style between his escapades. He also talks about "settling down" some time in the future. In some cases, however, middle-aged married men with reasonably satisfactory incomes also spend a great deal of their spare time with friends at the hangout or with

62

another woman, away from home, wife, and children. This is the view put forward by one of these men, as he leans over the fence of his back yard where his mixed-breed dog is lying on guard:

"I earn pretty good money, and I spend a lot of it, too. Usually I come out here and have a taste with those other cats, you know, they're pretty good buddies. I don't mind spending more than they do, I mean I wouldn't say no when I got money and they don't, 'cause you never know, some day maybe you'll have to go to them and ask them for something. I could probably save some, too, but look—I'm fifty-five, on the fifty-sixth, and if I couldn't save nothing before now, it ain't much sense starting now. So I just spend it on myself and on my dog. I really love that dog. I love it much more than my woman, 'cause she treats me like dirt and the dog don't."

These men, of course, are streetcorner men rather than swingers; they interact with fewer people (but more intensively), do less traveling around town and less partying, and are more likely to get into violent situations. Their main-streamer neighbors, some of whom earn less than they do, are aware of the fact that poverty is often taken to explain the "undesirable" behavior of street-corner men, and they specifically point out that this is not an excuse for the way of life of these particular men.

The state of one's economy may thus contribute to determining a person's life style in that better resources give more choice, but people can still use the same resources in different ways. There is also the possibility that the life style determines one's economy to some extent. It is clear that children growing up in a mainstreamer household more often do well in school and get a decent education (at least by not dropping out of school so early), and this in turn makes it possible for them to get a better job later. Staying home with the family may mean that one keeps in better shape for work than one would standing at the hangout and becoming an alcoholic, and a mainstreamer may be able to save a lot of money which flows through the streetcorner man's hands for liquor, gambling, and outside sexual affairs. (The latter factor, of course, involves expenses rather than income.) Apparently there is a two-way flow between life style and economy. We must also consider the possibility that people simply return as adults to the life style prevalent in the household where they grew up, and that they may tend to do so in whatever economic circumstances they find themselves. This is clearly a kind of cultural deter-minist proposition, and since the nature and dynamics of ghetto culture will be examined more intensively in the last chapter we will only discuss it briefly and in a preliminary way here.

Clearly there is some continuity of life styles between generations in many families. Those who grew up in mainstreamer families often establish such families themselves as they marry, and those who spent their childhood in a street family and interacted much with streetcorner males may frequently later take on the same life styles. The fact that they all often lead rather similar lives as swingers during an intermediary period may be partly due to that peculiar transitional situation of the young unmarried person which they all share. It must also be kept in mind that swinging tolerates some variation and some choice of peers, so those who come from different backgrounds and are due to follow different paths do not necessarily all participate in the same circles and are not always swingers in exactly the same manner. One may notice that some groups are more like mainstreamers and some more like street people. But there is clearly more interaction between people of different backgrounds in the swinger stage than there is later.

If there is continuity of life styles between generations in many cases, however, there is still no lack of examples of how children come to lead lives quite different from that of their parents, or of how brothers or sisters have quite different life styles. One young mainstreamer man who grew up in the Winston Street neighborhood and now lives there with his wife and children throws light on his change as he says: "That lady down at the corner still don't say hallo to me, 'cause she remembers my family from when I grew up and she thought we were no good." Thus the influence of childhood background does not always seem to be decisive either. This does not mean that the influence of cultural transmission has an equally limited effect. With the heterogeneous environment of the ghetto in mind, one cannot be sure that the life style which dominates a person's family of orientation is the one which is most effectively transmitted to him. We have noted that peer group life is important in the ghetto community. It is more important for some people than for others, but particularly from adolescence to young adulthood, hardly anyone is outside its influence. Life style socialization clearly goes on here as well. The question of which life style one is most strongly exposed to thus becomes a rather unpredictable career contingency. It may depend on what neighborhood one lives in, what school and work mates one has, and so forth. For that matter, it may also depend on what kind of person one is married to, as particularly a close marital relationship can be an extremely effective agent of cultural transmission and stabilization.[3]

The point which is emerging is that the boundaries between life styles and between the groups formed around them are rather permeable, and that one can cross over from one to another at many points in one's life if circumstances should happen to call for it. Many ghetto dwellers are in a state of life style drift, a condition midway between freedom and control.[4] Contingencies work together or at cross purposes to effect a change or to prevent it, with the individual responding now to one of their demands, next to another. While some ghetto dwellers remain relatively stable in life style orientation except to the extent that change is practically inherent in the life cycle, others go through changes which are much less predictable. One son of a mainstreamer couple becomes an army officer; his younger brother gets some friends from a different way of life, starts "hanging out at the wrong places", and is jailed for robbery. Carl Jones, a streetcorner man, promises his wife to mend his ways as his drinking leads to a serious ailment and the recovery takes a long time; since then he spends much more time with the family and much less with his peers at the corner. Bee Jay, a middle-aged bachelor, had a good job at the post office and participated very little in street life as long as he lived with his grandmother who had raised him. Since she died he has become intensively involved with a tough, hard-drinking group of streetcorner men and now suffers from chronic health problems connected with his alcoholism. One man is involved in crime but never gets caught and finally stops participating in illegal activities; somebody else gets a jail sentence, meets others in the same situation in the inmate community, and is denied a job as he gets out because he has a police record, all of which makes it more likely that he will turn to crime again. Obviously, while ghetto life style careers for some people only involve the expected passages, there are other people who go through much unforeseeable drifting.[5]

*Managing co-existence*

Life styles relate to one another not only because they are stages or alternatives in individual careers or because there are certain regular relationships across life style boundaries, such as between the streetcorner man and the street family or between the young female swinger and her mother who helps her with child care. The co-existence of life styles in a community is also a question of how its segments more generally manage their social traffic with each other, how they look at each other, and how they influence each other.

Since interaction between members of different households is largely limited to sociability and the fleeting encounters of neighborship, there is not much of a necessity for intensive social contacts between people with clearly different life styles. Mainstreamers do not usually seek out streetcorner men and vice versa. Thus it is possible for people with different life styles to maintain largely separate networks side by side, although individuals straddling between life styles usually have contacts on both sides and many people retain contact with relatives who have somehow ended up with a different life style.

However, people vary in the extent to which they are actively trying to disengage themselves from contacts with individuals of other life styles. Moral judgments are obviously a part of the reason for this; we have seen how the mainstreamers, the "respectable" people, are most ready to condemn the behavior of other ghetto dwellers. Closely related to the moral question is the pragmatic question of trouble. In chapter 1 we noted that this is a strong concern in the ghetto community. The danger certainly rests particularly in the activities of some of the swingers and streetcorner men, and they are by no means confined to contacts between them and the representatives of other life styles—the streetcorner men are themselves probably more liable than anyone to be the victims of stabbings, shootings, robbery, and theft, and husband-wife fights occur more frequently in street families (with a streetcorner man as the male party) than in mainstreamer families. But trouble is a part of the scene for all ghetto dwellers, and they must all try to avoid undesirable confrontations. In this way, if no other, every ghetto dweller must be a member of the ghetto community as a whole and orient his actions with reference to the conduct of all its members, as he shares ghetto space with them. Proximity as such is no social relationship, of course, but the process of taking note of it and acting upon it in one way or other establishes a relationship of a kind—if only an asymmetrical avoidance relationship. A major technique for coping with the ghetto environment is to stay away from those who could cause trouble and not to meddle with their lives. As one man put it as he found he was getting involved in an argument, "Look, I ain't gonna do nothing for you, I ain't gonna do nothing to you, so just don't mess with me." Less directly and more proverbially, "I walk my walk and talk my talk" is a ghetto phrase for minding one's own business. Frequently, too, preachers in ghetto churches dwell in their sermons on the importance of not meddling, as a matter of both righteousness and cautiousness.

Since the mainstreamers have few of the problems and the concerns which can make people cause trouble, they are involved with it largely as potential victims. Thus they pursue a strategy of trouble minimization more consistently than most of their neighbors, trying to insulate their families from many of the characteristics of street life. The parents keep an eye on whose children their own are playing with on the street and declare some of them out of bounds. They also make attempts to keep the children happy and busy at home to keep them from playing on the street and in the neighborhood at all hours. But the street remains a center of activity for children, with age mates for all, and it is practically unavoidable that children from all segments of the ghetto community will mix there. Just as unavoidably they will sometimes get into fights, and if parents intervene this may lead to friction between households, although these are certainly not always of different life styles. By the time the children are teenagers their parents usually have little control over their choice of friends.

Although swingers also tend above all to keep to themselves for sociability they are more likely to have good contacts also in other segments of the community, among mainstreamers as well as among street families and streetcorner men. They are particularly open to contacts, of course; they also count among themselves people from different backgrounds and do not always give the appearance of final commitment to a life style. This fact probably has some influence in making them acceptable to a wider range of partners in sociability. In a way one may look at them as life style straddlers of a particular kind.

Even with the existing limitations on interaction, neighborship provides a basis for some friendly contacts between people leading different lives on Winston Street. Fleeting encounters are usually personal and amiable if the persons involved have lived in the same neighborhood for a longer period of time. While mainstreamers may despise and condemn the life style of street-corner men in general, without offering any explanations to excuse them, they quite often draw a line between the way of life as a whole and particular streetcorner men they have become familiar with. In these cases, they may say "it's a shame" that the man in question should lead this kind of life, under-standingly accounting for it in terms of "bad company", "lost his job", or "his wife died". Some such personal relationships thus involve a degree of suspension of the moral judgment exercised against the category as a whole. Yet for all their informality, these contacts continue to involve the maintenance of some distance and are not actively pursued. The informality itself may in fact be somewhat formalized: ghetto dwellers have their own joking relationships whereby overt conflict is avoided.[6] Humor is often used to affirm friendliness while at the same time it maintains distance. As you pass a streetcorner man you know and he asks you for a quarter which is obviously intended for liquor you can either give it to him, which you would rather not, or you can refuse, which is unfriendly. But if you say, "Too late, you can't take it to the bank today anyhow", you have at least corrupted the definition of the situation and thereby contributed to the fun. The same is true of the man who is asked, "What have you got for me today?" and answers, "I can give you my blessing", raising his hand. Or to give another example, when a mainstreamer with a reasonably comfortable standard of living finally succeeds in getting his car into an empty space at the curb, his unemployed neighbor calls out to him, "No, don't take that space, my chauffeur is bringing my limousine around any time now, so he'll need it."

Thus relationships are kept going because encounters are put on the lighter side. One evades issues which could either intensify the relationships or make them deteriorate; when the jokes are roundabout comments on the differences between the parties, this becomes a matter to laugh at rather than something possibly serious.

If working friendships across life style boundaries are thus kept going at just the right comfortable distance, they are nonetheless real. The streetcorner men are sometimes openly protective of people from their own neighborhood. Mainstreamers point out that it is good to know some of the people who hang out at strategically located places in the area, and women who otherwise have to go on some errand alone are sometimes happy to accept an offer of escort. When for example Francine Ellison, the swinger daughter of a mainstreamer couple at Winston Street, has to walk over to Seventh and T to look up her boy friend at a pool hall, the 50-year old alcoholic Wilson who has known her parents for years and herself from her childhood offers to come along, although it is quite far away—"Seventh and T is no place for you alone."

The streetcorner men are often particularly close to the generation growing up, whoever the parents may be, as children and adolescents, with streets and alleys for playgrounds and hangouts, share their territory. Again and again the men intervene when play brings the children too close to dangerous traffic; sometimes they seek out the parents to tell them to take better care of their children. On the other hand, the streetcorner men may be a socializing influence on the children which parents do not always find very desirable.

It is a part of peaceful co-existence in the ghetto that mainstreamers usually do not voice opposition to a person's way of life directly to his face. Straight and sustained criticism occurs most frequently in relationships where the critic's credentials of good will are in no doubt. Such discussions may take place when a mainstreamer and a streetcorner man have known each other long as friendly and generally tolerant neighbors, but in particular they occur between family members with different life styles. The conversation related below reveals how people more or less oriented toward a mainstreamer life feel about the ways of streetcorner men. Leroy, a white-collar clerk and a swinger but undoubtedly heading toward a mainstreamer life, has a couple of friends visiting on a Saturday afternoon as his older brother Percy, a neighborhood alcoholic and habitually unemployed, comes visiting. Leroy criticizes Percy's behavior and is assisted by Warren, one of the visitors who lives in the neighborhood, knows Percy well, and himself straddles between a street family life and that of a mainstreamer.

As usual on his rather few visits, Percy asks Leroy to loan him some money. His younger brother replies, "Blood ties us together, Percy, but wallets don't." Leroy's friends, well acquainted with the situation, laugh at the reply and slap each other's hands to show appreciation of Leroy's point. Leroy then looks at his brother silently for a moment, then asks, "How old are you, Percy?" Percy answers, "Thirty-three." Leroy feigns a surprised look and says, "Thirty-three! I thought you were older than daddy, you sure look older." Warren falls in: "Yeah, Percy, the way you live it's just right you look like sixty. You better change your way of life, man, stop hanging out up there at the corner with all those no-good fellows, 'cause they ain't gonna do nothing for you. Yeah, you got money one day and you're all big and everybody gets wasted on your money, and next day you're broke and you're out panhandling again, and when Leroy and I pass by on our way from work you all stand out there and do nothing. Ain't that right, Leroy? And you drinks just anything you can lay your hands on, any time. Now I mean, look at me, I don't say I don't ever taste liquor, I get together with buddies like Leroy on a weekend and we drink together, and now and then maybe we get tore up, but I got a wife and six kids to take care of, so I knows I just got to keep straight most of the time. And if you really get yourself set on something like that, you can control yourself, so you only drinks on Friday night and Saturday and maybe Sunday morning. And you don't drink just anything, you don't just pour gin, whiskey, beer, and wine down your throat one after another. And don't tell me you can't get a job, Percy. There ain't nothing wrong with you. Your head ain't fucked up, you got a good vocabulary, you could look pretty good if you tried."

Percy, who has been sitting quietly, occasionally nodding and a few times trying to reply only to be interrupted immediately, points to his chest to indicate a long scar from a streetcorner fight with Reinhardt and says, "But you know about this, I can't climb or anything, the doctor said so. So what kind of job do you all think I can get? Supervisor or something?" (Obviously he has construction work in mind; he has been in it occasionally before, and another brother is a construction worker.)

"Hell, who says you have to be climbing places?" Leroy says, and Warren nods his agreement. "Warren's a plumber, he don't climb things. I don't climb nothing where I work, and Huff here's kind of working and he don't climb nothing, so don't tell me that. And besides, that's just a skin wound you got there. That don't stop you from nothing, just like it don't stop you from fighting." Warren gets ready to leave to drive his wife across town for a visit to her sister, and the conversation breaks up. "Yeah, I guess I ought to go straight", Percy says, as he has said many times before. "Soon as I find a good woman I'm gonna marry her. And it won't be no common-law marriage either." "Aw man, why don't you get a job first and get married later," Leroy chuckles.

Leroy and Percy do not interact very much. Percy calls at Leroy's place in search of a drink, a free meal, a place to sleep, or money, but usually tries to get them somewhere else. Leroy hardly ever seeks out his brother. Brothers or sisters usually seem to be more close to each other if they live similar kinds of life, but even if they are quite different ties are seldom totally severed if the people involved are otherwise reasonably accessible to one another. It does not appear to reflect on a mainstreamer's reputation very much if a brother or sister is less "respectable"; of course, it is much more likely to be a brother, as men considerably more often behave in openly "undesirable" ways. Such life differences occur too frequently for anybody to be very surprised at them, and the principle that everybody is responsible only for his own life is so well established that little damage can be done to anybody's social standing by them.

It is clear from such criticisms as those directed toward Percy and the moral vocabulary concerning life styles which was discussed at the beginning of the preceding chapter that mainstreamers tend to see streetcorner men and many of the street families as "a lower class of people", and themselves at least by implication as a kind of ghetto elite. They are the ones who talk most about uncooperative neighbors and think up and take active part in schemes for neighborhood betterment such as the neighborhood open house described earlier. However, the street families and the streetcorner men pay little attention to mainstreamer efforts at leadership and do not accept the mainstreamer's higher status with symbolic shows of deference. They often show noticeable irritation when people from outside their circle try to exert influence on them —"I'm just tired of being pushed around, that's all." Thus the mainstreamers' idea of social stratification has no particular effect on community organization.

This does not mean that there are no people who could not at least potentially be more influential than others. It is likely that some of the older swingers, with good contacts in all categories among adults as well as among older teenagers, more than others have the ear of the whole community. Some people in neighborhood businesses, like barbers or one of the "respectable" bootleggers referred to above, are also in close touch with all segments of the neighborhood population; it is well known in the Winston Street neighborhood that many customers take time out to listen to what the latter man has to say. However, such centers of communication are seldom used to influence ghetto public opinion more consciously, although the Muslims operate some ghetto barber shops with a reputation as propaganda centrals. Instead, to the extent that there is a demand from the outside for ghetto "grass roots leaders" beside the ordinary largely middle-class Negro leadership, these positions are frequently filled by people appointing themselves—some mainstreamers, preachers in the churches of the respective neighborhoods, some professional community organizers. This is at least the case in the ghetto area where Winston Street is located. Occasionally, neighborhood people express suspicions of the forces propelling people who engage in such work. A cynical view of the divergence between public and private motives of the high and mighty is a part of many ghetto dwellers' picture of society. But there is no real resentment against these spokesmen, even when they make no particular effort of finding out their constituents' personal views, as long as they voice ghetto grievances as competently as anyone could.

# 4

# Male and Female

Many buildings along the main street of the Washington ghetto had just been burned, and many of its white-owned stores had been raided by black people embittered by the assassination of Martin Luther King, as a streetcorner man on a Winston Street sidewalk talked about the nature of society.

"There ain't more than two kinds of people," he said. "And it ain't white people and black people, color don't make no difference. It's men and women."

The concern with the characteristics of male and female and with the relationship between the sexes is widespread and deep in the ghetto. As poor black people and as Americans, many of the men and women of this community are in a peculiar dilemma. Living in the United States, they are exposed much like other Americans to the mainstream images, meanings, values and slogans set forth by what C. Wright Mills (1963:405 ff.) called "the cultural apparatus"—the institutions and channels whereby authoritative interpretations and evaluations are fed to the general public in a society. The apparatus reaches the ghetto through schools and the welfare establishment, through newspapers, TV, and radio (with the possible exception of some aspects of the programming of black radio stations which are not completely mainstream-oriented). Hayakawa (1968) and McLuhan (1965:5) have both suggested that the exposure to television has heightened black Americans' awareness of the dominant values, customs, and standards of living in the society and thus socialized the present generation into rebellion and rejection of their own traditionally assigned place in the scheme of things. Whatever the case may be, these same channels transmit a mainstream model of family life with which ghetto dwellers are also made familiar in personal contacts with whites, and even in contacts with the mainstreamer members of the ghetto community. This mainstream model, of course, need not be altogether true to life; whatever are the actual characteristics of most families, the authoritative family model has the character of what Birdwhistell (1966) has called a "sentimental model", a particular ideal people should try to "live up to"—or at least they ought to appear to do so—and in terms of which they think and feel about family life in general. As far as marriage is concerned, this model shows a strong, emotionally exclusive relationship, not to be dissolved, with the partners joined in concerted action for common purposes. There is a traditional division of labor. The man has a job and thus brings home resources, to be converted into goods and services for family consumption. The wife is largely in charge of domestic activities such as housekeeping, cooking, and childrearing. Since status is something one gets by one's work "out there" in the wider social structure, it is the man who is assigned a place in the ranking system, and his status reflects on his family. The other family members thus depend on him for both livelihood and social position, and by implication they should be grateful for what they get—this usually causes no great strain in a middle-class family. Since the man is usually felt to be more knowledgeable about the outside world than anybody else in the family, he interprets it authoritatively to the others and is in charge of many of the family's outside contacts. This adds up to a position of male dominance in the family which is considered right and natural; much as a husband and father should be loving and considerate, there should be no doubt that he is the head of the household.

The ghetto dwellers know all this. But as the sections in chapter 2 on street families, streetcorner men, and to some extent swingers showed, many ghetto dwellers live rather far from this model. The other side of their dilemma as far as marriage and sex roles are concerned is expressed for instance in the fact that about a quarter of those households on Winston Street in which children are growing up are headed by single women.[1] Most of them have been married before, or are still legally married, but they and their husbands have parted ways. A few mothers, included in this number, were never married; another number of women, not included, have remarried, but their earlier unions can be added to those which somehow ended in disruption.

Such raw facts point out that there is something specific to the ghetto about the relationship between the sexes in this community. On the one hand, there is the idealization of the mainstream model of marriage. People get married and hope to make a go of it largely along its lines. On the other hand, there is an awareness among ghetto dwellers that they may be literally "taking a chance on love". The opinion among young adults seems well summarized by a young unmarried man:

"Yeah, I guess we all know you take a chance when you get married and sometimes it won't work out, you get into fights or one of you cuts out or something. But it's like there's something missing in your life if you don't know what it's like to be married. And I mean really married, not just shacking up with somebody 'cause that's not the same thing, you ain't got each other really if you ain't got the papers, I don't think."

*Interpreting black family forms*

Divorces and separations, female-headed households, and shifting unions are thus more common in the ghetto than they are among Americans of the white mainstream. But the same or similar phenomena can be found also in other black communities in the New World. Over many years, but in particular over the last couple of decades, a great number of anthropologists and sociologists have taken an interest in these facts, and a body of scholarship concerned with black marriage and family life has grown up.[2] Some of it has been largely of academic nature—especially the sophisticated studies made in the Caribbean —while particularly in later years the writings on the black family in the United States have often taken a social-problems perspective. For better or for worse, the single most influential statement is probably the "Moynihan Report", a U.S. government document which pointed to the "deterioration of the Negro family"—that is, the allegedly increasing number of husbandless households—and purported to show that this was the source of a ghetto "tangle of pathologies" including juvenile delinquency, poor school performance, and ghetto violence. The report set various interests on fire; by the time the controversy subsided, much light had been thrown on its ambiguities and much doubt on some of its conclusions.[3]

The question which has aroused most of the curiosity about black marriage and family life is what are the determinants of their forms. There are some contingencies, of course, which could be particularly influential in some New World black communities but are likely to be less important in others. Large-scale male migration and the specifics of land tenure among agricultural populations are obviously likely to have an impact only in particular cases, such as on some West Indian islands.[4] On the other hand, there are background factors shared by New World black communities. The African background, the history of plantation slavery, and low and insecure economic status are among them. These three have become the bases of the dominant schools of interpretation of black family forms.

The guru of the Africanist school was Melville J. Herskovits.[5] Noting the strong bond between mother and children in black American households, and the weak and marginal relationship of the husband and father to this household nucleus, Herskovits related this to West African polygyny where he held that the male naturally was somewhat peripheral to each group of mother and children. West African women are also traditionally rather independent economically, a fact which could contribute to keeping the husband-wife relationship rather weak. West Africans, Herskovits thus felt, had an idea of the conjugal relationship as relatively weak, and when taken into slavery in the Americas they brought this idea along.

A problem here is that this traditional West African marriage ideology is postulated—albeit with reasonable logic—rather than really known. The criticisms of the Herskovits theory, however, have also focused on some points where it is actually more sophisticated than it is made out to be. For one thing, it has been claimed that all elements of West African social organization were destroyed by the slave trade and slavery, as all existing social relationships were broken, in trading and selling in which no thought was given to pre-existing bonds. In a way, this is beside the point as far as marriage is concerned—while specific marriages were broken up, the conscious models of and for marriage could well remain and influence the form of union adopted under new circumstances. Another part of that garbled version of Herskovits' theory which has become a part of anthropology's oral tradition—and which sometimes has made it a fashionable straw man to knock down—has it that Herskovits totally neglected the social structure into which black people were brought in the New World. While Herskovits was perhaps not particularly strong on this side, he was certainly well aware of it. When slavery made uncertain the permanent unions of men and women, as men were sold away from female partners and children, this reinforced the West African idea of the separateness of the male on the one hand and the female with children on the other, Herskovits wrote. In this sense, slavery may in a sense have promoted cultural continuity. Against this it may be argued that slavery would have caused a relationship of this kind whatever was the cultural heritage of the slaves. On this point it seems hard to be absolutely certain. Although slave sales surely forced many separations of men and women, we do not seem to know enough about the absolute constraining influence slavery and the plantation social system had on ordering the relationships among the slaves. Anyway, what could have functioned in slavery must have been a very diluted African model of marriage, and although it still stands as a possibility that this could have been among the original construction materials of the black American marriage forms which have continued until today, this would be difficult to show.

We have practically already stated the case of the slavery school of inter-pretation. E. Franklin Frazier, its grand old man, emphasized how slavery undermined marital stability (Frazier 1934; 1939; 1949). Undoubtedly it tended to break up unions in a great many cases. However, a weakness in Frazier's reasoning is that he wonders little about what the husbandless household is an adaptation away from. Considering Frazier's old-fashioned American puritanism and cultural absolutism (attested to by Glazer 1966 and Valentine 1968) one may suspect that he felt the mainstream model was both the natural and the ideal state of a family. What slaves were forced away from, he thus implies, was the mainstream model of marriage. Although this may be the ideal of black people today, as they are under the pressure of the mainstream cultural apparatus with its never-equalled efficiency, it seems questionable that it was also the ideal of recently displaced Africans.

This, however, is a question of the culture and structure of the old plantation rather than of the ghetto now. If it is claimed that slavery continues to be the cause of shifting unions and husbandless households in the black urban com-munity today, one must wonder how. Frazier is conspicuously ambiguous on this point. He was no great social or cultural theoretician, and so for an analy-tical statement he substitutes the prejudices of early evolutionism and some romantic imagery about simple peasant folk. In Frazier's view, slavery does not seem to have created a model for male-female unions; it broke one down (whatever it was), and the poor cultureless blacks seem to have been rambling on ever since, reverted to that conjectured low evolutionary stage of human history when marriage hardly existed.

Frazier saw a strengthening of the marriage institution among rural freed-men but another weakening in the ghettos of the North. It is in his view of the latter we should be particularly interested. Here he foreshadows the third major analytical perspective in noticing that economic insecurity may have a role, but this insight is dimmed by his image of urban life. Perhaps he was influenced in unfortunate ways by his contemporaries in the Chicago school of sociology, as he saw mostly evils in the big city: anonymity, disorganization, lack of social supports and controls. Urban life again permitted the non-culture of slavery; instead of structural influences on family life, there were the in-fluences of nonstructure toward total permissiveness and promiscuity.

If Frazier's theoretical understandings seem remarkably limited for a scholar so celebrated even in the present, this need not cast a shadow on other writers who have found the explanation of certain contemporary types of male-female relationships in slavery. The leading contemporary anthropologist holding this view, M. G. Smith (1962), makes it clear that models of such unions parti-cularly adapted to plantation slavery were established in the West Indies and have continued to exist as cultural definitions of mating patterns since then, side by side with new forms of unions more like what we here call the mainstream model. Here Smith suggests that there has been continued cultural transmission of a heritage originated in slavery; this, from the point of view of today's anthropology, seems to be a much more tenable position than Frazier's transmission of nothing.

The third school of thought is macrostructural rather than cultural. Probably its major paradigm is R. T. Smith's *The Negro Family in British Guiana* (1956). In some ways this school is like the original hard-nosed slavery school, in that it explains mating forms as forced adaptations to the contemporary constraints of an ungenerous social structure, without much reference to cultural ideas.[6] An application of this perspective to the ghetto situation could go as follows, with some innovations in conceptualization and added detail.

Among ghetto dwellers we find rather variable relationships to the wider socio-economic structure of American society. There are some families in the ghetto whose external conditions reasonably well match those delineated for the mainstream model. The husbands and fathers in these families, with stable working-class or even lower-middle class jobs, can provide rather satisfactorily for their families, and while their status in the system of social stratification of the entire society may not be high, these families usually consider themselves of higher rank than at least many other ghetto dwellers. Such families, of course, make up the core of the category described as mainstreamers in the preceding chapters. On the other hand, there are those whose relationship to the socio-economic structure of the society is quite incongruous with the mainstream model. These are the people whose social position we refer to here as ghetto-specific. The structure of the society does not provide an adequate niche for all ghetto men to be satisfactory breadwinners for their families, as there is widespread unemployment as well as poor pay for unskilled labor.[7] This fact alone means that many ghetto men's position according to the family division of labor is not that prescribed in the mainstream model, or at least that this position is undermined. Furthermore, when the man is without a job or has a kind of job generally held in low esteem throughout the society, the family may find little satisfaction in the status reflected on them. As the wife of a periodically unemployed construction worker on Winston Street puts it:

"So my husband says to me, 'You ought to be happy you got a man.' What's so great about being married to an old construction worker?"

It may be added that the men tend to concur with this low evaluation of their jobs.[8]

The ghetto male's access to resources and status within the socio-economic system is thus often unsatisfactory in absolute terms when compared to the mainstream model. However, we must also look to the characteristics of his niche as compared to the ghetto female's access to similar resources. According to the mainstream model the wife tends to depend on her husband as a provider, and he is the family's anchor in the wider society. However, as we noted in discussing the characteristics of income and employment among the people of Winston Street (in chapter 1), a rather large number of women in the ghetto are employed, while many of the men are not. This does not mean that more women than men have employment, but in comparison with the wider American society, the job distribution of the ghetto involves relatively more women and fewer men. Thus the contribution to the family of the husband and father as a breadwinner is not only absolutely smaller than it ought to be according to the mainstream model. It is also relatively smaller compared to the contribution of the wife and mother.

There are other factors which contribute to this situation. One which emphasizes the economic weakness of the male in a dramatic way is the setup of the public welfare system. Families with insufficient income can be assisted through the Aid to Families with Dependent Children, but social workers deal with mothers rather than with fathers, thereby giving the woman an independent source of income. Furthermore, in many areas, including the District of Columbia, a "man in the house rule" excludes families with an employable male from AFDC, although that male may not be able to find employment (or at least not employment which would give a satisfactory income). The point is sometimes made that this rule in fact forces men to desert their families, or at least hide their presence in a way not conducive to a normal family life, in order to make it possible for the rest of the family to qualify for welfare payments. The rule, based on mainstream assumptions about the family provider role but not on ghetto economic realities, may not have been the direct cause of any greater proportion of the desertions on the part of husbands or expulsions of husbands by their wives. However, the fact that it can contribute to the alienation of men from their families is well known to ghetto dwellers who often cite it in support of their animosity to meddling "welfare people".

What has been said here so far about the differentiation of male and female niches for ghetto dwellers within the wider socio-economic system refers only to access to status and economic resources. It seems useful also to take note of the differentiation of exposure to mainstream culture built into typical male and female jobs. Male jobs tend to emphasize physical prowess rather than the subtleties and niceties of mainstream culture and social organization. Men such as general laborers and construction workers get little exposure to carriers of mainstream culture; they may have occupational contacts with white lower-class or working-class men, but such contacts are unlikely to lead to much learning of mainstream culture. Female jobholders are more likely to find employment involving mainstream skills and values. Working as waitresses, domestics, or hotel maids, they are apt to get a stronger exposure to white middle-class or upper-class people and thus learn some of the skills necessary for unimpaired functioning in a society dominated by them. It is also likely that such exposure leads to increasing attachment to mainstream values.

Thus it seems that the ghetto woman on the average is more at ease with Standard English, while many of the men are more tied to the black dialect. In a more general way, she knows the mainstream interaction idiom better and thus gives the appearance of more poise in situations where it has to be used. This gives her an advantage over many ghetto men in institutional and organizational activities relating to mainstream culture. While the mainstream family model has the husband as the external affairs specialist, the ghetto woman is often more qualified to handle such things as relationships to public agencies and institutions. It is often she rather than her husband who is in charge of rent payments, bills, and other offical business. When the elegantly attired insurance agent makes his Friday evening round on Winston Street, he often transacts his business with the wives. If the parent-teachers association meetings at the children's schools are much more regularly attended by mothers than by fathers this may not be particularly unique to ghetto dwellers, although there may be a difference of degree from middle-class whites. The great influence of women in ghetto community groups and church organizations, however, can perhaps be attributed to the greater female competence in and orientation toward activities in which mainstream skills are held important. This certainly does not mean that a great many women are active in organizations, only that female participation is often conspicuous in such organizations as exist. Thus ghetto women also to some degree preempt the "external affairs" sphere of activities which the mainstream model largely assigns to the man in the house.

This is the kind of stuff from which the macrostructural kind of interpretation is built. The underlying assumption is that the marriage corporation has its form determined by internal transactions. The allocation of authority and prestige is negotiated between the partners on the basis of an assessment of the relative value of their respective contributions. The mainstream model is the result of negotiations typical of the contributions the majority of American men and women make to marriages. With different contributions determined by the wider socio-economic structure, ghetto men and women easily arrive at a different settlement, if it deserves to be so called as both partners continue to see it as unfavorable. The male placed in ghetto-specific circumstances may make unsatisfactory contributions as a provider; his ability to manage family business is small; and his wife remains in charge of domestic organization, so he does not compensate by taking over any of those contributions to household functioning which are at the basis of the mainstream wife's reasonably high status in the household. The female, on the other hand, may increase her share of the total contributions made to household functioning, and even if she does not, at least she makes largely the same contribution that a mainstream wife makes. Thus it is not correct to talk loosely, as some commentators on ghetto family life have done, of a family role reversal. It is rather a question of male role deprivation and, sometimes at least, of female role expansion. The result is what has been termed matrifocality, loosely defined as *de facto* leadership by the woman (or women) in the household, with the man taking on a more marginal domestic role or absenting himself altogether. The extreme form, of course, is the husbandless—that is, consanguineal—household, but there seems to be little reason to confine the term "matrifocality" to such a compositional definition.[9]

\* \* \*

The three analytical perspectives we have sketched—africanist, slavery, and macrostructural—each tells us something and fails to tell us something. Some categories of analysis suggest themselves by being there as ready-made pigeon holes; others only by presenting themselves as more or less conspicuous gaps. Before turning back to the men and women of Winston Street and its environs, we may do well to ponder what lessons we have learned.

The slavery perspective, applied to its own day, and the contemporary macrostructural perspective, are both strong on pointing to structural constraints and the need for adaptation. They make it clear that the conjugal relationship is sensitive to its surroundings. No marriage is an island. It is difficult to remain unconvinced of the strength of this argument. At the same time, these interpretations are relatively non-cultural. If the marriage form, in its presence or absence, is a mechanical adaptation to constraints, then we may legitimately wonder what people think, feel, and say about the relationship between male and female, as it is and as it ought to be. When one's circumstances are as depressed as they were during slavery and as they are in the ghetto, one may expect people not only to adapt but also to have feelings about it. We have already seen that ghetto dwellers are influenced by the mainstream cultural apparatus toward a model of marriage which the wider matrix of their existence does not provide for. They are made fully aware that the "normal", valued pattern includes a husband with a good, stable job who is a good provider for his family and whose relationship to the family is close. Thus ghetto dwellers living under ghetto-specific conditions do not have the cultural autonomy to negotiate their family structure only according to environmental structural constraints. There is a continuous conflict between the particularizing premises of the socio-economic structure and the generalizing demands of the mainstream cultural apparatus, and the relationship between the sexes in the ghetto may be strongly although ambiguously influenced by these two external influences. Both of them must be seen as logically prior to ghetto adaptations in that they are environmental constants, showing little responsiveness to the life of the ghetto.[10] "Father knows best" on TV pays as little heed to the realities of family life among black viewers as the job market does to their ideals.

Even so we have not said enough, for to macrostructure we have only added mainstream culture. What happens inside the ghetto community is still left largely out of the picture; it is made to look as if every couple were left on its own to work out anew a solution to problems which have confronted many of both their predecessors and their contemporaries in the black community. In an oft-cited statement Albert Cohen has pointed out that new cultural forms tend to emerge rather easily when a number of people with similar problems of adjustment are in effective interaction with each other. Innovations are suggested in exploratory gestures which may elicit reactions of receptivity and acceptance from others; in such cases, innovations proceed in a cumulative manner through mutual exploration and joint elaboration (Cohen 1955:59—61).

It is certainly not likely that black people in America have adapted to circumstances as boxed-in individuals or couples. With a structurally segregated and rather uniformly depressed group such as this, it seems more likely that there has been a hothouse atmosphere for new collective adaptations. This means that there is good reason to look out for internal cultural developments in the ghetto community, as well as for those social processes inside it which work in conjunction with the external constraints to shape ghetto dwellers' lives.

So much for "structural constraint" theories. The africanist theory, as well as the slavery-as-heritage perspective, are both diachronic cultural points of view, and as such they may be strong on points where we found the others somewhat remiss. When it is suggested that matrifocality and conjugal instability even today can be derived from West African culture or from slavery—and when this is not in the latter case a Frazierian deculturation hypothesis—this must necessarily imply that from either one of those origins there came forth an idea of the male-female union as a relationship with rather weak corporate aspects and a large potential for dissolution which has been transmitted as a mental model in the black population continuously since its inception. Such a perspective matches rather well the proposition just stated that we should take a greater interest in cultural developments and social processes within the black community. But in this form the perspective is largely programmatic, for in fact little or no explicit attention has been paid to the mechanisms whereby such a model may have been transmitted, although certainly this type of cultural explanation is noticeably incomplete without a discussion of the dynamics of communication. Perhaps the channels of transmission have been taken as self-evident and thus not worthy of further attention, but Frazier's example makes one suspect that everybody does not have such clear notions. Perhaps the writers in this field simply have not come out of a research tradition where such matters as communication and socialization are of much concern; when some of them affirm that there is a "heritage from slavery", they base this opinion simply on the fact that contemporary unions between men and women in the ghetto show some similarity to the mating patterns of plantation slaves.[11]

Even when such transmission can be shown to occur, however, one may be wise not to place all one's eggs in the cultural basket. We must continue to be aware that macrostructural stability or change will have an influence on the possibility and relevance of cultural transmission. It is this interplay between culture and social structure, and between the ghetto and American society, which we must keep in mind in interpreting life at Winston Street. Only so can we hope to avoid the ambiguities, the stereotypes, and the myths of the Negro present which seem so easily created in discussions of life in the ghetto.

*A masculine alternative*

The macrostructural perspective shows us that many ghetto men will have a hard time to succeed when measured against the tape of the mainstream model of male behavior. A relative few can use their position in the ghetto community, or ghetto-specific cultural resources, as an alternative basis of economic success—some of those engaged in illicit activities, for instance, and those whose unusual skills in ghetto-specific concerns can be converted into occupational virtues. Talents in music, fast talk, and physical prowess are efficiently socialized in the ghetto and may lead on to careers in show business and sports.[12] Celebrated as a few persons of ghetto background may become on the public arena, however, most men have to stay in the severely compressed niche assigned to them in the regular socio-economic structure of American society.

This fact is certainly important enough for the men's relationship to women and family life. But the macrostructural picture of what a man can do seems to list only components with negative valences; it says little about what men are really like. Its variables are those defined as important in the mainstream model, and in this way it is potentially biased. It is definitely not irrelevant, for ghetto dwellers are influenced by mainstream standards. However, it largely leaves out the creative responses the black community has made to its circumstances. The male-female relationship in its ghetto-specific forms is influenced not only by what the male cannot do but also by what he does instead. An alternative avenue of masculine expression is less constrained by the macrostructural matrix, and the existence of a ghetto-specific male role formed along its lines is an important part of the picture of ghetto sex roles and male-female relations.

The major construction materials of the ghetto-specific male alternative, to which particularly swingers and streetcorner men are attracted, can be listed as strong overt concerns with sexual exploits, toughness and ability to command respect, personal appearance with an emphasis on male clothing fashions, liquor consumption, and verbal ability.[13] These can be combined in various ways and with different emphases but still tend to occur as a cluster. One might note that while it is ghetto-specific in that it finds unusually strong expression in the ghetto community, some components of this male role are certainly also part of a lively although slightly subterranean masculine tradition in mainstream culture as well—probably nobody would deny that toughness, hard drinking, and freely roaming sexuality are more typically regarded as male than as female characteristics.[14] At least on this point mainstream culture does not contradict the expressions of masculinity of many ghetto men.

Various facets of the concern with sexual activity are discussed at other points in this volume, so only one of them will be dealt with here. It was stated somewhat obliquely above that a typical expression of masculinity is a "concern" with sex. This is not quite the same as sexual activity itself—rather, sex is an area in which ghetto men express an intensive interest in one way or other, but at least as much through conversation and gestures as through the real thing. For instance, it comes up constantly as a topic for talk at the street corner:

Freddy, Bee Jay, and Alvin are standing outside the shoeshine shop as a young woman passes by.
  "Good evening, darling," Freddy says, and she smiles back.
  "Who's she?" Alvin asks.
  "She just moved in down the street," Freddy replies.
  "I like her, maybe she's something for me," Alvin says, and Freddy adds some more information.
  "She works, too, nine to five."
  "Good, that's the best kind of woman, the kind who got bread."
  Bee Jay asks Alvin about his old girl friend.
  "What happened to Carla, she had a job, didn't she?"
  "Yeah, but she got nothing for me no more, and I'm a pimp, you know, I'm an old pimp."

Alvin was claiming to be a pimp in the wider sense of the ghetto—a man supported by a woman "'cause she loves him so". What really seemed to have happened was that Carla put him out after he lost his job. They got along well enough while he worked, but a pimp she would have none of. Yet it was an existence Alvin fancied, and the encounter outside the shoeshine shop provided an opportunity for setting forth a claim to it. Of course, there are indeed men who receive more help from their girl friends than they offer in return. But there are more men who like to imagine themselves as pimps than who actually make much of a living from love, and more generally, a great many men are intent on giving the appearance of more intensive and successful dealings with women than they actually have. This by no means denies the fact that the men are constantly looking for sexual opportunities and that many also find them; but as we noted in the section on streetcorner men in chapter 2, there are many who are unattractive as partners. Thus what is common to the men is the intensive concern with sex, rather than intensive sexual life, and this means that the overt expressions of the concern are based not only on solid fact but also to a high degree on impression management.[15]

With toughness it is not altogether different. Some men get involved in trouble frequently enough, and at such times they may show if they are indeed "good with their hands". But there are also some, although fewer than in the case of sex, who are strongly involved in talking and symbolizing a toughness which may be poorly founded in reality. These men reminisce again and again about fights they claim to have been in but which sometimes never took place and in other cases were very different from the way in which they are described. Some men are keen on demonstrating their knives and other weapons; others make shows of their aptitude in karate. Yet they may be known to at least a few of their associates as rather unsuccessful in fights. Again, the concern with toughness may be more widespread than the toughness itself.

Toughness is shown both on one's own initiative and in response to others. "Selling wolf tickets", that is, threatening or showing readiness for violence, occurs both between longstanding acquaintances and in more accidental encounters. You are not respected if you do not show some toughness; if people can step all over you and you do nothing about it, you are nothing but a punk.[16] Of course, some people are more hot-headed than others, more apt to find injuries to their honor. As one streetcorner man commented on another:

"Jimmy is always getting into trouble 'cause he blows his cool whenever somebody does something. You know, 'they can't do that to me, I'm a man' and all that shit."

Men like Jimmy cause much of the instantaneous violence in the ghetto—indeed, Jimmy has been going back and forth between the Winston Street neighborhood and short jail terms for streetcorner fights. Their quarrels do not need much provocation for quick escalation.

Fats and a few other men are sharing a half pint of whiskey at the corner of Winston Street as Joshua comes up and asks for a taste. He gets one, and then holds out the bottle as if to place it in the breast pocket of Fats' old army coat. "If you put it in that pocket I'll knock you over your head with it," Fats says. Joshua does exactly that, and Fats promptly takes the bottle out of the pocket and brings it down squarely on Joshua's head. Fats' friends move over so as not to get directly involved in the fight they expect. However, no further blows are exchanged this time, as Joshua, already drunk to start with, stumbles dizzily away.

But there is also more premeditated violence on the part of those who feel there are still accounts to settle. A recollection by another man in the neighborhood presents a vivid picture; it was caused one winter evening by a grape-vine news item about one of his antagonists of long standing, Ribs, a one-eyed man with a long criminal record.

"Sonny told me they took Ribs to the hospital this morning, seems he had another fit. I told Sonny as far as I am concerned they could have took him to the morgue. I hate that man! You know, he just standing there at the corner demanding money from people, and you know how he looks, six feet three or something, and he just stands there and says, 'Gimme a dollar, motherfucker.' Now he ain't got no business calling nobody that kind of name. But with him looking like that, you know, a lot of people get scared and just give him the money. Like Sonny, Ribs took four dollars right out of his pocket and Sonny only laughed 'cause he figured there was nothing he could do about it. Hell, he couldn't treat me like that! If he fucks with me I'd just go for his good eye and beat that out, and then they could give him a dog and a bucket, and he could go right on begging for money up and down the street, and I'd drop a penny in it now and then. That's how much I think of him! You know how he lost his other eye, don't you? He was giving this little fellow a hard time about his money, and this little fellow could be happy if he was five feet tall, so he couldn't get away too easily. So he dropped a dollar on the ground, and Ribs bent down to pick it up, and this other cat just kicked and kicked and kicked! So that's how Ribs lost his eye. And I don't think this little fellow should have been sent to jail for that, 'cause he just wanted to get away and kick out Ribs so he could take his dollar back. And Ribs deserved that, you know, anyway.

But Ribs wouldn't mess with me now, not since we had our fight. I gave him seventy-five stitches! You know, he cut me up for no reason at all, so they had to take me to the hospital and give me a whole lot of treatment and stuff, and then they told me to go straight home and sleep. But as soon as I got home, I took that bandage off and took a shower to get rid of all this blood, and then I put on some dark pants like those I got on now and a dark blue shirt with high collar, and I got my knife and a half pint of whiskey, and I went to this place where I knew that Ribs always used to come and I sat down there in the dark and had my whiskey. And at four or something Ribs' girl friend came, and then Ribs came, and he asked her if the police had been around looking for him. So she asked him why, and he said, 'I cut myself a nigger tonight'. And so I finished the whiskey and got my knife out, and that was a real good knife, man! A real good knife! It was only this long, and I could have used it to shave with! So I came up behind him, and I said, 'Here I am, Ribs!' And I cut him all over, in his neck, in his back, over his ass, in his face, everywhere! I really tried to kill him, I hated him so! But he started running, of course, and I figured it was enough, so I went straight home and went to bed. But of course I knew the police would come, 'cause he couldn't go nowhere except to hos-pital in that condition, and they would ask a whole lot of questions, and he would tell them it was me. So sure enough next morning the police came knocking on the door, and I was staying with my wife and mother-in-law then, and my mother-in-law is downstairs, and she opens the door. But she didn't hear me go out again last night, so she figures after I came back from the hospital like that I'd gone straight to bed, 'cause I was in no shape for anything else. And of course my wife knew, but she wouldn't squeal. So my mother-in-law opens, and the police comes in and she says the whole thing must be a mistake, 'cause she knows her son-in-law hadn't been out-side since he got out of the hospital. So they come upstairs and knock, and there we are in bed, and I act like I just woke up and is half drunk anyway, so it's clear I'm in no shape for running around cutting up people! And I says, 'What's the big hurry? I know who cut me'—this is about when Ribs cut me the first time, you know—'so I can come down to the precinct and make a statement later.' But the policeman says, 'well, lieutenant so-and-so'—I've forgotten the name—'lieutenant so-and-so wanted you to come down.' And I know all the time this is about my cutting up Ribs. So I stagger around and put on my clothes, and then when the policemen go outside, I tell my wife to call bondsman Pratt right away, so he's at the precinct when we get there. And sure, there he is leaning over the desk when we come into the station! So this lieutenant Alfred Brown charges me, you know, and I tell him my story about being in bad shape when I got out of the hospital, so I couldn't possibly have gone out after I got home. And of course when Ribs cut me everybody was watching, but nobody saw it was me cutting up Ribs except Ribs, 'cause his girl friend was already running! So I said, 'you ain't got a thing on me, and that's my statement right there', but he wanted to charge me anyway, so bondsman Pratt bails me out, and so I am out again. And so when we go to court they ain't got a thing on me they can prove, so the case is dismissed, and then Ribs got six months for cutting me! And that serves him right, and he ain't doing nothing but going in and out of jail anyway. He ain't but forty-six years old or something, and he has been in jail for everything! For everything! He's been in jail twenty years or something! In and out! But he ain't messing with me since then, 'cause he knows I'm going to get him sooner or later. Don't nobody mess with me, cause I tell them I'm not going to stand for any shit. Like Fats up the street, he was always hitting me like this on my shoulder, you know—Wham! Wham!—when I passed by, so I said, 'Fats, if you do that one more time I'm gonna get you!' But the next time I come by, you know, there he goes again —'Wham!'—So I go straight home and get this old jungle knife out, as long as my arm or something. And then I go out and look for Fats. And when I find him, he gets scared and starts running, and I chase him for three blocks or something. And then I'm tired, so I let him go, but he sure don't mess with me any more. You know, I think if somebody is minding his own business nobody should try to fuck with him, and if they do and something goes wrong it's their fault."

There is a rather widespread belief that much of the violence is planned and based on old animosities. One man in his late twenties, a resident of the Winston Street neighborhood for over ten years, stated it as follows:

"Quarrels go on for ever here. If these people have been in a fight or something, they never forget it. Sure, they meet each other in the street and say, 'Hey, how're you doin' and all that stuff, and they seem to be the best of friends and everything. But watch out if you come home at night and you're a little high, 'cause they'll be waiting for you all the time, and when they get a chance like that they'll beat the shit out of you."

But despite such assertions, it seems that most of the violence which occurs has the form of brawls following arguments. Meddling, scorn, and condescending manners come into conflict with the men's feeling for autonomy. "He's a man, and I'm a man, and I don't take no shit like that," is how streetcorner men tend to defend or explain their fighting responses. But some of the men who are not themselves inclined to take anything from anybody repeatedly get themselves into trouble by provoking violent reactions. Jimmy, for instance, mentioned before as one whose temper is quick to explode, has a rather condescending manner which occasionally makes his peers furious. He explains it as attempting to "get those fellows to act right". One of those to whom he offered his advice was Ribs:

"He's always going around cussing, and I try to make him stop it, you know, and I tell him every time, 'Stop that cussing, Ribs!' But he say, 'I can't stop, Jimmy. That's my way of talking!' So I say, 'Was you born cussing?' And first he says, 'Yeah, that's the way I was born!' And then I say, 'Oh no, you wasn't'. So he says, 'No I wasn't born cussing, but I got the habit, and that's the way I am now, so don't you pay it no mind'!"

The instance Jimmy described did not result in more than a rather violent argument, but sometimes Jimmy has landed himself in more serious trouble in such encounters, and occasionally the fights have become transformed into more lasting feuds. After he repeatedly told Dennis to "stop cussing" and scorned him for "not knowing better", Dennis got his knife out and cut Jimmy across the chest—apparently it was a half-miss as Jimmy did not need much treatment for it, except a considerable number of stitches. The day after the fight the other men with whom Jimmy and Dennis had been drinking at the time of the incident all took Dennis' side and asked Jimmy to stay away, or else. However, Jimmy continued to hang around and for a while got into one more fight after another, interspersed with shouting matches. During this period he often mentioned the risk of being shot or knifed in the back by someone of the others, sometimes adding that he was "only trying to help them".

The third characteristic of ghetto-specific masculinity we mentioned above was the concern with appearance, particularly with clothing. It is held important that colors match; ideally, one should not wear more than two colors. A man who ignores this rule too conspicuously, appearing in clothes of many bright colors not considered matching, may be branded a "bama"; the word is derived from "Alabama" and denotes an ignorant rustic. (It should be added that there are quite a few such "bamas", so tastes vary.) There is also considerable awareness of prices and brands. A man in a boasting mood talks of his pairs of "forty-dollar shoes" and his "thirty-dollar hat", all of expensive brands of some renown—a renown of which ghetto men may be more aware than most people. As young ghetto males ransacked Washington stores during the violent days after the assassination of Martin Luther King, it was conspicuous that the downtown stores which particularly attracted their attention were the male fashion stores, and such establishments were also prominent among those raided on the ghetto main streets. The interest in appearance, too, occasionally involves exaggerated claims. One middle-aged man, very aware of fashion himself, had a comment on this:

"You see, these guys can't afford a real good pair of shoes, so what they do instead is they go and get some decent shoes they can afford, and then they go to one of the real good shoe stores, and they talk to one of the colored salesmen there, you see. So they ask him for a box with one of the brand names on it, and then they put their cheap shoes in it and march around town for hours with the box under the arm or they hang around at the corner all afternoon, so everybody can see they got a new pair of shoes of that name brand."

Concern with clothing is not necessarily apparent in everyday dressing habits. Some men are conspicuously shabbily dressed and may actually seem less concerned with appearances than most mainstream-oriented men. Of course, there are ghetto men who share in most ghetto-specific male concerns but who are not particularly involved in this one. But once more we must remind ourselves that a concern is not always something with which one is completely successful.

The lack of money certainly prevents many ghetto men from acquiring the wardrobe they desire, although a few prestige objects are usually within the range of real possibilities. Also, the men dress to fit the occasion. For hanging out at the street corner one can as well use an old army coat and dirty boots, leaving the expensive coat and the forty-dollar shoes at home in the closet as treasures which may be proudly displayed to a visitor and used on more special occasions.

As far as liquor consumption as an expression of masculinity is concerned, it is considered "natural" for men to like liquor, and the opinion may be expressed on occasion that it is an index of masculine strength not to want to dilute the liquor with too much soda. A noteworthy corresponding folk belief which appears common among men is that "liquor makes hair grow on your chest". This is taken literally; beard growth is allegedly also affected.

Finally, the skill of talking well and easily is widely appreciated among ghetto men; although it is hardly itself a sign of masculinity, it can be very helpful in realizing one's wishes. "Rapping", persuasive speech, can be used to manipulate others to one's own advantage. A good line can attract the attention of a woman who passes by in the street and open the way to a new conquest, while at the same time it may impress other men with one's way with women:

"What's this, recess in heaven? Angel!"

"Hey darling, pray for me, will you?"

Verbal manipulation is also important in acquiring new resources. One man who had taken his girl friend's five-year old son to see Santa Claus at a downtown department store recognized the theme of this verbal game as he recounted what had happened:

"Santa asked him what he wanted for Christmas, and Floyd knew exactly, of course. Some kind of car, and a miniature pool table, and a train, and a lot of stuff I don't remember. Oh man, did that boy rap to Santa! I'm sure he thought he could make Santa give him the stuff right there!"

Later on in life streetcorner men may use their verbal skills to relieve others of petty cash, for carfare, a hot dog, or something to drink. Although there are some "gorillas" among them, most men eschew violence for such purposes. True, some of the begging can be rather aggressive in tone, but this is largely tactic; if it works, fine, if it does not, try the next person to pass by. But much of the game involves a friendlier strategy. With a joke or with conspicuous friendliness, the man in need of funds defines his interaction with the other so that a refusal would be a hostile disruption of the situation. The lines of action need not be very complex. It is more a question of striking the right note and using charm.

It is a cold evening in January as Fats and Bee Jay are working their game. Between dashes out to talk to somebody they keep out of the winter wind in the corner between the house wall and the protruding window of the liquor store. A middle-aged man comes by; Bee Jay steps out and greets him.

"Hey, brother Wilkins, how are you doing? Heard you been sick a few days. Yeah, don't work too hard now, we want to keep you around here. Oh, say, can you spare sixty cents?"

Brother Wilkins gives Bee Jay a quarter and adds a useful bit of information— Clarence, a man who lives up the street, hit the numbers today and is due back any time now with his money. Brother Wilkins met him as he was going to collect it.

"And that ought to be a half-pint right there," he says.

"Thank you, Jesus," Fats says mockingly, imitating a storefront church preacher. Fats himself is inclined toward the Muslims.

After a while Clarence does indeed come by. Fats is suddenly walking next to him. "Clarence, I got news for you!" he calls out, and continues confidingly after a moment's pause which heightens Clarence's curiosity, "We're thirsty." Of course, this can be no news at all to anybody who passes by this corner as often as Clarence does, so Clarence bursts into laughter, and a dollar changes hands. Fats returns to the nook behind the liquor store window. Dennis and Randy cross the street and join Fats and Bee Jay. They have spent a while at another corner on the same errand.

"We tried to do some business but there was no action."

Fats tells them about Clarence's hit on 363—"Clarence really in power tonight." Randy returns home, while Dennis stays with the other two, sheltered from the wind. As some younger men pass by, Fats and Bee Jay go futilely to work on them. The men just laugh them off. Dennis nods toward the neon-lit store sign above him.

"See that? L-I-Q-U-O-R. I don't know what it means, but I think it stands for Come One, Come All, Everybody Welcome to Buy. Seems like a cold and dry night, though."

Bee Jay and Fats give up their attempt and return to the corner. Finally a woman from the block approaches, with a shopping bag from the super market in each hand. Fats walks up to her, puts his arm around her shoulder, and speaks softly.

"Ain't this Pearl, my main girl?"

She shrugs her shoulders with a smile, then gives him some small change out of her coat pocket. Just in time before the liquor store closes at nine, there is now enough money for a half pint of gin and a can of grape-fruit juice for a chaser, and Dennis is sent into the store to get it. Bee Jay does not like the man in there, and Fats is not allowed in.

"He say I steal all the time," Fats explains, laughing.

Thus a good verbal style in encounters is recognized as a useful tool in the business of life, and those men who like Fats are known as skilled manipulators of interpersonal transactions gain some prestige from it among their peers. Besides, talking well is useful in cutting losses as well as in making gains. By "jiving" and "shucking", ghetto concepts with the partial denotation of warding off punishment or retribution through tall stories, feigned innocence, demeaning talk about oneself, or other misleading statements, a man may avoid the undesirable consequences of his own misdemeanors. Reminiscences of talking one's way out of trouble with the police or with the irate husband of a paramour provide some of the entertainment of streetcorner gatherings.

However, all prestige accrued from being a good talker does not have to do with the strictly utilitarian aspect. A man with good stories well told and with a quick repartee in arguments is certain to be appreciated for his entertainment value, and those men who can talk about the high and mighty, people and places, and the state of the world, may stake claims to a reputation of being "heavy upstairs". Some men are given to embellishing their prose with euphemisms; a marijuana cigarette becomes "one of those cigarettes with no name on it", dice "the little cubes you take chances with". Such talk is perhaps above all a kind of dramatization of one's self—it attracts the attention of others, even if this attention does not seem to be immediately convertible into tangible profit.

The dramatic character of this kind of male behavior has in fact not gone without notice by other writers.[17] A general explanation of such behavior, aside from the point that it has now become a normative routine of masculinity, may be that recreational activities and concerns such as these may express, and to some extent solve, personal conflicts induced by social experience.[18] Accustomed to being at the bottom of the heap, at work or out of it, and sometimes even at home, the men seek a heightened awareness of individual excellence, and if this can be strengthened through the responses of other persons, so much the better. This pleasurable awareness, of course, may be found in drinking as well as in marijuana smoking—which most men in this category use occasionally and some regularly—and in harder drugs, used by a relative few. The thrill of possible triumph and dominance is found not only in successful shows of toughness and in sexual conquests but also in pool, card, and dice games.

In these matters, of course, each man is not on his own. If such motivations are behind men's actions, they will also influence modes of interaction, as men seek recognition from others and triumph over others in their surroundings. Because interaction within the male peer group seems to be defined as a kind of zero-sum game in which one man's triumph is another man's loss, many interaction sequences take on an intensively competitive character, expressed in heated arguments. The strong involvement in debates over minor questions of little direct import to anyone of the men is probably best understood in the light of this contest character. Disagreements over facts often result in a proposition that a bet be made; although this is not often carried out literally, it implies that something is at stake which the men want to show themselves ready to defend. The following exchange between Sylvester and Sonny, occasioned by a news item about the Kremlin in the afternoon newspaper, is an example of this idiom of debate.

"Khrushchev is dead 'cause he knew too much," Sylvester commented.

"No," Sonny said, "Khrushchev is alive. He was deposed and lives in a villa somewhere."

"I tell you! Khrushchev had to die, 'cause they thought maybe he'd go over to this country and tell us all he knew."

"You don't know nothing about this, don't show your ignorance. They just deposed him as a premier. They said, 'Get out, we don't dig you no more, man.' That's all. Like, ain't Truman alive?"

"That's different . . ." Sylvester started saying.

"Now, do you believe all that propaganda? It ain't that bad behind the Iron Curtain. I know Khrushchev is alive."

"How do you know? Have you seen him? No, he's dead, I tell you. He ain't alive. Wanna bet? I got ten sixty-five, that's more than you have."

As the argument proceeds, the men become progressively less inclined to wait for each other's statements without interruption, and their voices get louder and more high-pitched.

86

The same interaction idiom of contest appears in a readiness to express doubts about other men's claims about themselves. The following conversation occurred in a carry-out, as one of the two men said he had 250 dollars in the bank. The other man responds:

"Shit! You ain't got nothing in the bank or in your pocket or nowhere!"

"Yeah, I got 250 dollars in the bank, that bank down by the circle."

"Do you know what—what do they call it, the interest rate—do you know what the interest rate is?"

"It's . . . It's five per cent."

"Shit, they don't give you no five per cent. How often do they add the interest? How often do they add the interest?"

"Eh . . . I don't remember. But I know I get it."

"You're bulljiving, man. You ain't got nothing in the bank. When is the bank open? What hours is it open?"

"Every day 'cept Saturday. It's open when I go there."

"You don't know nothing about banks. You ain't got no money."

Thus claiming and debunking become important ingredients in the ghetto-specific mode of interaction between peers, and loud verbal contests are a recurrent part of those social occasions during which the men regard themselves as "having a good time". Although we have seen that the arguments at times result in violence—particularly when one or both participants are somewhat intoxicated—this happens comparatively seldom. Most exchanges dissolve at the point where one of the participants begins to emerge as a clear winner and carries his line no further, leaving well enough alone. Fleeting contests like these leave no trace in the continued relationship between peers which seems elastically enough defined to allow such momentary shows of aggression.[19] It is more likely the continuously overbearing manners of men like Jimmy, discussed above, that cause lasting conflict.

It is obvious that ghetto-specific masculinity brings its own problems. The allocation of resources favored by this model of man, with comparatively heavy spending on liquor and clothing, appears not to match the objective facts of life in poverty. Violence and alcoholism may be by-products of the male identity which ghetto men have shaped from the limited possibilities open to them. Particularly for older men ghetto-specific masculinity is difficult; if a man has not by then managed to make the transition to a more mainstream-like male role, middle age may meet him well on the road downhill to alcoholism, isolation, and poor health, while his ability to live up to his role, with sex, toughness, and all, becomes progressively more impaired. Several of the men hanging out in the Winston Street neighborhood are obviously near death.

Yet it seems that in some ways, and for men in younger years, the ghetto-specific male role cannot be seen as only dysfunctional. In the crisis life which many men live, short-run strategies must be adopted just in order to "make it", economically and otherwise, and we can see that some of these concerns may come in quite handy. A good talker with just the right degree of dominance at the street corner may be better able than somebody without such attributes to find someone consenting to be relieved of some money; and the charming, good-looking rogue is often more likely to find a woman, perhaps with some independent means of income, who is willing to enter into a relationship involving not only romance but perhaps also finance. Nobody who has seen a dance at a ghetto school or has been in one of the bars where dude meets chick can fail to note the successes of the sharp dressers and fast talkers, and of the men who are not too timid. In some ways, the expressions of ghetto-specific masculinity are apparently quite instrumental.[20]


*The diversity of conjugal forms*[21]

Obviously many ghetto men bring into their relationships with women not only the limited resources assigned to them in the wider socio-economic system but also some of the ghetto-specific male role baggage just described. This can result in male-female unions of a variety of kinds. In many unions conflicts occur continuously; most frequently, it appears, because the wife is dissatisfied with her husband's performance. Taking the mainstream model for her reference point, she nags about his inability to provide adequately for the family. When bills cannot be paid, or when there is no money around for groceries or for clothes for the children, the setting is provided for quarrels. The situation is not improved, of course, when the male often spends his money on activities relating to peer group life which from his wife's point of view are quite unnecessary, such as drinking, gambling, and highly uncertain loans to friends. Many wives see a threat to their marriages and family lives in the men's active involvement in peer groups; not only are resources lost for the family, but the husband who ought to be spending his time at home with wife and children is only there a little, and when he comes he may be drunk, so he goes straight to sleep if he does not start trouble first. There is also the danger that the peer group life involves the man in fights, outside sexual affairs, and illicit activities which may cause interruptions in family life. Marital disagreements over the husband's behavior can thus span over a rather wide field, as the following incident shows.

Randy Ballard left his streetcorner hangout at about 9.15 pm and went to his apartment on Charlotte Street a couple of blocks away. He was obviously a little high. As he came in he asked his wife who was ironing in the kitchen what there was to eat.

"Ain't nothing there for you to eat now", she replied curtly. "The kids finished it, and there wasn't much anyway. I figured you wouldn't be in."

"Ain't that a bitch," Randy said. "I give her money for food, and I don't get nothing myself. Nothing in my own house!"

"Listen, nigger," his wife said. "You didn't hardly give me nothing, not compared to what you ought to have given me. And if you hadn't spent the money you kept drinking out there with those hoodlum friends of yours, I could have had more and you could have had your dinner. So hush your mouth."

"You hush your mouth," Randy shouted. "You ain't talking to me like that."

"I sure do when you come home drunk and think you can act any goddam way around here when you ain't got a nickel to spend on your own family. I'm sick and tired of taking all that crap."

"I'm a man," Randy said. "I ain't gonna take that from nobody. You better watch out."

There was a moment of silence. His wife went about her work, and Randy abruptly turned around and walked out again.

Conflicts like this are based primarily on the characteristics of the male's performance. The husband is not a successful breadwinner, and he participates too little in domestic life. There are occasional conflicts which have to do with female performance, however, in that some men are dissatisfied when their wives make family decisions without consulting the husbands—because they have little confidence in his judgment, perhaps, or because they are using their own income and thus feel it is within their rights to act independently. In such cases, the men may be just as prone to call on the mainstream model for support as the women may be when the males do not conform to it.

"Shit, a woman ain't supposed to be like that. If she got a dude at home he's the master of the house, ain't he? I mean, I ain't against her having her say once in a while, you know, a good man would allow that, but sure if he wants one thing and she wants another thing, he decides what to do and she just shuts her mouth and goes along with the program, right? That's the way a family is supposed to be."

Of course, since female independence of this kind is often directly related to male underperformance—compared to the mainstream model—the two bases of discord often occur together. Thus the conflicts arise because the rights and duties prescribed in the mainstream model are applied to the situation so that facts of limited access to resources are transformed into ambiguities and deviations in the definition of the conjugal relationship.

We see that in such cases the influence of the mainstream model prevents a stable settlement on the basis of ghetto-specific macrostructural conditions. Beside the conflicts this gives rise to, infidelity is undoubtedly the greatest source of disruption in marriages. Although it is not absent on the female side, it occurs more often among the men. Wide-ranging sexual activity, we have said, is a dominant concern in the ghetto-specific male role, and this is noticeable among married men as well. But again, the marriage ideal is the mainstream model with its emphasis on exclusive sexual rights for spouses. Thus that male role which can be seen to be adapted to the ghetto-specific niche and which may even be understood as a compensation for male household marginality itself contributes to alienating the male even further from the mainstream model.

There are certainly degrees of infidelity and of marital conflict over it. When a man or a woman is flagrantly unfaithful, and especially when this is combined with faulty domestic performance—in providing or housekeeping—it is quite likely that discord becomes serious. Although the marriage may continue bickering goes on; wife and older children may shun the husband and father who is a "fooling around", while he feels "treated like dirt" and continues to find little satisfaction in family life. Ghetto dwellers also regard it as a rather common occurrence that jealousy is expressed in violence, by the wife as well as by the husband.

However, the opinion is widespread that one ought to allow a certain range of tolerance for minor and more occasional outside affairs, particularly on the part of the men. As long as they are good providers and reasonably tactful toward their wives, the men feel they have a right to "play around a little". One middle-aged man made this point as he reminisced about his own childhood:

"There was twelve of us in the family, but I tell you, we had a good home and my mother and my father stayed together till they died. Now, I know my father had a few outside women, but that didn't do a thing to our home, and he didn't let it hurt my mother."

Although the women certainly feel that total faithfulness is the ideal, many of them are ready to pass over such minor infidelity on the part of their husbands rather quietly. "Mama and I have kind of an understanding when it comes to things like that," as one man tells his friends. No doubt many ghetto women have a certain preparedness for male infidelity, having grown up to see it among neighbors, relatives, and even in their own families. Men are simply felt to be like that, and if they "cut out" only occasionally and reasonably discreetly, it could be worse.

Coming to terms with ghetto-specific circumstances and ghetto-specific behavior, couples may thus still manage to establish an implicit consensus on a working order. Through his demeanor, a man may collect credits for the undisputed position of household head although he is not a fully satisfactory breadwinner. He may give high priority to family life, stay away from the streetcorner world, and generally behave "respectably". In such a case, the couple may manage to lead largely a mainstreamer life as far as the internal organization of the household is concerned.

There are others who also establish a working relationship, not particularly conflict-ridden, by paying somewhat less attention to the mainstream model and making a pragmatic adjustment to the ghetto-specific niche. These are the cases in which the women achieve a relatively uncontested dominance— the most clearly matrifocal families of those where the husband is still present. These women have accepted the fact that their spouses are not going to act like mainstream model husbands, while the men are reasonably content to leave a great many decisions, and the highest prestige in the household, to their wives—possibly because interests outside the household domain give them certain other satisfactions. Marriages which started out more conflict-ridden seem sometimes to arrive at a kind of equilibrium this way, as this statement by a streetcorner man shows:

"I used to quarrel like hell with my old lady, but then you know, I figured most of what she did actually made sense, and I couldn't really handle those things better myself, so I thought, OK, why raise hell about it all the time? So now I leave most of what I take home with her, usually I do, anyway, and let her handle things. I respect her, you know, and she don't fuss as much as she used to about what I do, when I go out and things like that."

There are ways, obviously, in which this rational adaptation to male and female ghetto-specific niches may be rather satisfactory. Expectations of gratification from marriage may not have been set very high; both men and women get emotional satisfaction from relationships with kinsmen, peers, and others, and can accept that they may not be very close to each other. While a husband may not be a particularly good provider, whatever he makes—together with the possible earnings of his wife—is still relatively often better than what she could do alone. A marriage may thus give some economic security even if this is not great. Furthermore, marriage itself gives some respectability to both men and women, and many feel it is important to stay together "through thick and thin" for the sake of the children, as these ought to have both parents in the house. For such reasons, women sometimes feel that almost any marriage is better than none, and so they try to keep their somewhat marginal husbands from drifting away from the family. Patricia Jones of Winston Street, who has been married for some fifteen years and who clearly dominates her husband Harry and the rest of the household of five children and a grandchild, has this to say about her own marriage:

"I gotta be strong. Maybe that's why me and Harry are still hanging on when so many people don't. Somebody gotta be strong, and Harry ain't strong at all."

So Patricia Jones sees to it that her husband stays home with his family at least occasionally, although his peers are tempting him from the outside, and makes it clear to him that it is his family as well. Although she may not succeed in bringing him into the middle of household life, she at least seems to manage to give him some sense of family roots.

Even when female-dominated households are not torn by direct and acute conflict about marital rights and duties, however, they tend not to reach the stability and security of the mainstream model. First of all, of course, its premises are not the same. The resources of the man and the woman taken together are still likely to be a poor economic basis for family life. While women in mainstreamer and street families tend to be less different in behavior than the men, it is also natural that a woman who marries a man more oriented toward the ghetto-specific male role is also more likely to behave in ghetto-specific ways herself. Here marriage partners tend to be similar rather than complementary, and thus some women who end up dominant in their marriage have views similar to those of their husbands about the good and natural things in life. If they are less convinced than mainstreamer women that permanent marriage and sexual fidelity are absolute moral imperatives, then it is easier to make and break relationships. However, the women certainly differ on this point. Maternal toughness, while sometimes contributing to domestic control, may distress other family members, and a few women's household functioning is made somewhat erratic by drinking. An episode from a household where Annie Patterson, the wife, strongly dominates the others, including her husband Richard, shows some of this. She is a domestic worker, he is a janitor.

Annie Patterson returned from her job rather late Saturday night. Richard Patterson and a few streetcorner friends of his were watching television. When she knocked at the door, her 9-year old son Robert exclaimed "Mama!" and rushed to let her in. She went into the dining room with him and her two other sons, and in the adjoining living room one could hear nothing from them until Annie raised her voice at one of the boys—"... you do the work I tell you to do or I will break your fucking neck." Soon after that she went upstairs, and probably to bed.

The following day she stayed in bed until late in the afternoon, apparently drinking meanwhile. When she came downstairs, a friend of her husband's was playing cards with Willette, the 16-year old daughter, while some other men watched and commented on the game. Annie Patterson cheerfully commented, "I bet none of you have brushed your teeth today," noticed that Willette had prepared dinner for the boys, and gave her a smacking kiss on the cheek. Then she went into the living room, found her pack of cigarettes empty, and said to her husband who was sitting on the couch, "Richard, I bought two packs yesterday and now there ain't nothing left. You got to give me money for a new pack." As Richard Patterson tried to laugh it off, she grabbed his shirt and shook him.

She went back to the kitchen for a while, then came back into the living room as Willette, Richard, and Slim, the boarder of the house, were watching a bowling tournament on television. Annie jumped into her husband's lap, petted him, and asked for sixty-five cents which he owed her and which she needed to go to the bootlegger. Willette said, "Daddy, don't give it to her, then she won't make it to work tomorrow."

Despite such episodes, Annie Patterson manages her family rather successfully. She gets much help from the children in household work, particularly from her daughter who seems to have about as much authority with the younger children as the father. When limitations on Annie Patterson's dominance become visible, this occurs in a couple of areas where they can be noted also in other female-dominated households where the husband and father is present. First of all, *de facto* dominance may be only hesitatingly expressed in public behavior; the dominant wife sometimes feels called upon to assert that her husband is "really" the head of the family, or at least that "we decide things together", even when this is clearly not the case. The husband, taunted by his peers, also occasionally makes a show of dominance. Some discord may still occur as the husband or the children occasionally neglect the woman's commands, although they may avoid flaunting such disobedience in her face and thus do not protest against her authority in principle. This leads us to take note again of the fact mentioned in chapter 2 that when a woman is in control of household activities, it often means no more than exactly that. As household members move out of the domestic domain, she has little influence on their activities. Richard Patterson, spending much of his spare time away from home with his peers, is often outside his wife's sphere of dominance. Although she may be the stronger party when actual interaction is going on, this does not mean that he or other men in a similar situation are Caspar Milquetoasts ready to accede to their wives' wishes twenty-four hours a day. The difference between this kind of marital relationship and relative male dominance according to the mainstream model is clear. While in the latter case the husband dominates a family life to which his spouse is strongly committed, the dominant ghetto wife is in control of domestic life to which her husband attributes much less weight. It should be added that the husband's commitment to his married life is often low not only in terms of time invested in it. Many men in such marriages also engage in outside affairs with other women, and these sometimes lead to separation or divorce.

To the questions of who dominates and to what extent, and whether there is consensus or conflict about decision-making and management, rights and duties, ghetto marriages obviously provide a variety of answers. Even though female dominance occurs rather often, matrifocality does not emerge as a particularly neat and homogeneous category of classification. It becomes even less so when to the cases where female dominance is a quality of an ongoing marital relationship are added those where the husband and father is absent. The marriage may never have taken place, or there was simply too much nagging, quarreling, and fighting, or one of the spouses found a new and in some way more attractive partner. More often it seems to be the man who leaves, but the opposite occurs as well. In one case on Winston Street a man came home to his apartment to find his wife gone, with all the children. Another man return-ed to his house after a quarrel to find his belongings packed in cardboard boxes and paper bags standing outside the door, while his wife refused to let him in.

When marriages break up, women are almost always left in charge of the children. Yet many men remain in contact with their offspring. They visit them and are visited by them, they give them money, gifts, and clothes if possible, and they take them for walks, rides, and occasional outings.[22] In some cases the father who comes to visit his children continues to be close to their mother. He may become the father of more children with her, although in an extra-residential union, and occasionally it happens that such a father joins the household again after a period of separation. More often, however, meetings may become few and far between, until sometimes the man loses contact altogether with wife and children.

Thus most of the husbandless households come into existence. Concepts such as "broken families" conjure up an image of something shattered beyond redemption, but this does not always fit with reality. True, most of these households are still very poor and many worse off than ever. It is also a fact that the household may continue to be poorly integrated; its younger members may still be under little control of household elders. But there may be little difference in these facts from conditions before the marriage came to an end as an ongoing relationship, and as far as domestic functioning is concerned, some women with stormy marriages behind them feel that they are better off alone. A relationship which is largely one of conflict makes little positive contri-bution to the household, and it appears that there is sometimes more order in the husbandless household than in the "intact" one, as this mother explains.

"You know, before my husband took off we used to be fighting all the time, I mean, arguing usually, but sometimes fighting too. And I couldn't trust him, and he really messed up a lot, drinking and just throwing away a lot of money and bringing a lot of bums to the place we had then. And I guess it disturbed the kids, sometimes I guess they just didn't know what to do, and they got mad or scared and started hollering, and sometimes the older ones just stayed away. So I think it's really much calmer now."

Of course, all the people who have had one marriage disrupted do not stay single—a great many of them enter into new unions of one kind or other. Some remarry; but as we noted before, many get no formal divorce from their first spouse, and therefore many of the later relationships are consensual unions. These may become much like other ghetto marriages—with all their variability —but there is a tendency to keep these unions less close, and many of them are not very stable. The point is made now and then that there is a difference in what you have a right to expect from a partner in a regular marriage and in a common-law union. "Cutting out" is more acceptable in the latter, and you cannot expect the same degree of pooling of resources. Of course, as far as actual behavior is concerned, some marriages are not very unlike consensual unions in these respects.

Consensual unions are also less likely to be fully incorporated into ongoing domestic organizations. Women with children may have their new male friends staying in their households on a rather stable basis, but the men tend to have little authority in the home and do not necessarily assume much of a father role toward the woman's earlier children. (However, there are certainly instances when this happens.) Of course, if children are born into the new union the man is likely to be closer to these.

The tendency to segregate new unions from household life certainly has something to do particularly with the woman's experience in previous unions. But they are also aware that by the time they have one or more unions behind them the men who are available are even less likely to be ideal husbands than those in the pool they could draw from the first time around—those who remain now also have failed unions behind them, unless they have for some reason never been married. While these men may be good company as sociable and sexual partners, and may sometimes be able to "help out" economically, they are best kept out of household business. Later relationships therefore often become extraresidential unions, often of short duration, or at most the kind of functionally segregated residential union sketched before. While they may be seen to fall short of the mainstream marriage ideal, they seem to be rational adaptations to ghetto-specific conditions. It makes strategical sense, then, when one streetcorner man says, "The women I meet never want to marry, they just want to play around."

## Male and female in public imagery

Like other people, the men and women of the ghetto do not only react and adapt on the basis of the conditions assigned to them. They also observe one another, mull over what they see, and communicate about it to each other. Thus ghetto dwellers acquire their own ideas of ghetto life, based not only on their individual experiences but also on the interpretations their associates make for them. These verbal exchanges of opinions, however, do not deal equally with all the experiences of ghetto dwellers; certain topics are singled out for intensive treatment, while others are relatively neglected. It is around those former topics that a rich and intricate web of public imagery—collective representations—is spun, an imagery which is constantly replenished at the same time as its basic postulates are stabilized because they are given informal social support. The group thus evolves and maintains a motif collection into which individual experiences are fitted, but it may be, too, that this becomes a screen through which impressions are sifted, as individuals become trained to take particular note of those phenomena which match or can be brought to match public images.[23] This becomes the culture of common sense—common sense because the facts of life actually seem to be in line with the images, culture because this is the way of looking at the facts of life one is socialized into through interaction with others.

We have seen that ghetto men and women form a heterogeneous mass as far as the kinds of life they lead are concerned, and each individual life is a complex structure of premises, reactions, and adaptations. However, the public imagery about male, female, and male-female relationships in the ghetto does not give equal attention to all these facets; diversity in the real system is glossed over in a simplified public imagery.[24] What ghetto dwellers express particularly strong concern about in their public imagery is the moral aspect of male and female ghetto-specific behavior. Possibly this has something to do with the practical problems which arise out of deviating from the code which dominates the wider society. It seems more likely, however, that this concern arises out of the intellectual strain of having such strong involvements in modes of action which go against the mainstream morality to which one is strongly exposed and which one in large measure accepts as ideal.

As the kind of involvement varies which one has with ghetto-specific behavior, so does one's perspective toward it. Among the people directly touched by ghetto-specific modes of action, it is rather natural, considering the differences in premises and adaptations discussed above, that men and women should look at things somewhat differently. Furthermore, we have noted that among those ghetto dwellers living most clearly under ghetto-specific conditions, sociability is to a large measure sex-segregated. Thus the conversations in which imagery about male and female qualities occurs can often be carried on without the intrusion of anyone with a different perspective. This may go some way toward explaining why men and women have evolved and maintained somewhat different imageries.

While a woman's life in the ghetto is certainly far from easy, at least she has the satisfaction of living up to her mother role—defined the mainstream way—rather fully. Under the circumstances she has to face, it sometimes comes easy for her to define the ghetto woman as a heroine—or as a martyr when things go wrong. This self-typing is shared and talked about among women; between mother and daughter, talking in the kitchen while preparing dinner, as well as among friends and neighbors. One mother, now living alone with her children, describes her notion of it this way:

"A mother just got to fight for her children. It's hard if you ain't got no money and your man steps out on you, it's real hard. But you got to struggle, no matter what, 'cause they need you. So you got to be sure they got something to eat and something to put on and don't get into no trouble, and you make them understand that no matter what they can always come to mama. And you know, that's hard on you when you ain't got nobody to go to, when there ain't nobody to help you out, so you got to earn some money and raise a family, too, like when Abbie was sick with a fever, and I had to go out and go to work and I just had to leave her home and I was worrying about her all the time, that was a couple of weeks ago. And I sure wished I could just have stayed home and sat next to her bed and taken care of her. But then, you know, when you've worked all day long and you've taken care of the kids and they're in bed and you can just sit down or maybe go over to some neighbor for a game of whist or something, then you really feel good, 'cause you know whatever you've done, you've done your best."

Women also tend to comment favorably on one another, and in their sociable conversations there is frequently a tone of relaxed sweetness, sometimes bordering on the saccharine, which contrasts sharply with the heated arguments of the male peer group. Such positive typing of ghetto femininity also influences the woman's behavior toward her own children. Her daughter, most able to validate her role as a little woman in the household, also meets with the most positive expectations for her future. When the daughter performs household tasks, the mother sees in it a premonition of experiences of mother-hood similar to hers in the following generation. So a little girl helping her mother may hear comments such as, "She knows how to act right, just like a little mother." Annie Patterson has this comment on her daughter Willette, as Willette combs her mother's hair:

"You know, Willette and I, we're such good friends, and she knows as much about this house as I do. I've told her about keeping house ever since she was little, and she's very good. Ain't nothing gonna be wrong with her house when she gets one, she's gonna be a good mother. I give her credit for it, but I guess I've been a good mother, too."

The image of the woman as the pillar of strength and high morals in the family leaning toward matrifocality is communicated to the younger generation in diverse ways, sometimes conspicuous and at other times minute. When a girl goes to school, her mother often appears to expect better results from her. Many mothers voice a preference for girls over boys, whether for themselves or their daughters, while the opposite preference seems to be less often stated. The point is also made now and then as a woman upbraids a boy for a mis-demeanor—"I wish I'd had another girl!" It is the women who complain most frequently about the disorderliness of specific individuals or of their neighbor-hood in general, thus implying that they uphold conventional—that is, main-stream—morality. They may also indulge in a little backbiting gossip which carries the same message about the speaker's concern with morals. When children go to church, they will usually find that the active congregation has a great majority of women—particularly in the small Holiness churches—and preachers often dwell on the theme of these women's problems with no-good men.

The concern of the women with the image of respectability stands in a sharper relief because the difference between male and female in the women's public imagery tends to be more pronounced than the difference in actual behavior. As we noted before, the women who engage in relationships with men tending toward ghetto-specific behavior often show somewhat similar tendencies themselves—Annie Patterson, who commented on her daughter Willette's abilities above, was our example. Even so, they participate in keeping the public imagery about the "good woman" going by speaking favorably about female behavior and morals more often than not, and by finding excuses for female infractions of mainstream norms when confronted with evidence more often than they do for men. Thus when a woman engages in sexual affairs outside marriage, it is often said that the men are taking advantage of her; women "fall for" men, but the real responsibility for such behavior appears to be placed on the males. Only a few women seem to have little concern for this image. Wanda Logan, a young unmarried woman with three small children, is an interesting example in that she seemed in many ways to take pleasure in negating the women's usual self-imagery. While she lived on Winston Street she was more likely to seek the company of men than of women among her neighbors, and she quite openly engaged in sexual relationships with a few men at the same time; they seemed to be more her peers than anything else. She expresses her opinion as follows:

"You know, I despise those girls who come into a beer garden and let somebody buy them a drink, and then they play a game with the poor guy and won't give him a thing before he gives them everything, and play hard to get and all that stuff. If I can afford a beer I'll buy it myself, and if I like a guy I'll tell him I like him."

Wanda asserts that women like liquor just as much as men do; in many ways she is probably like her mother whom she lived with until the older woman died of cirrhosis of the liver. The mother was also rather indulgent sexually, according to some of the male neighbors; in discussing her childhood, Wanda recited this verse, undoubtedly with some poetic exaggeration:

> I was raised in a whorehouse,
> I was born in a cave
> and all I know
> is to fuck and to rave.

Wanda was well liked by most people in the neighborhood. However, it was generally but affectionately acknowledged that "she's a little crazy". This, of course, can well be seen as a "deviant" label for her. Since her behavior was asserted to be idiosyncratic, it had little bearing on the moral view of female character.

The women's view of men is more complex. On the one hand, they talk about a "good man", the kind who generally conforms to the mainstream model of holding a steady job, providing for the family, staying home, and getting into no trouble. They recognize that there are quite a few of these in the ghetto, but not enough to go around. On the other hand, then, many of the women in street families, with experiences of trouble in past or present unions, tend to emphasize the "no-good" side of men—the "facts" that men do not work, or do not take care to keep the jobs they have, that they are habitually unfaithful, that they drink, and that they get into trouble with one another and sometimes with the law. These characterizations certainly do not always come up together as integral parts of a fixed imagery, but alone or in one combination or other, they occur in a great many statements of what males are like. It may be noted that the male-female tensions which are made apparent in the imagery are clearly generated above all in marital or similar relationships, but images pertain to the sexes generally rather than to people in specified role-relationships. Some spontaneous statements on men by women, generalized but occasioned by different incidents, are those which follow. The first one is by Randy's mother-in-law, visiting with her daughter.

"Men talk too much and drink too much and work too little, that's what I think. Look at all those good-for-nothings Randolph brings up here! They ain't good company for him or for anybody. Always spending their last quarter on liquor and playing around and that sort of thing."

"Those men always get into trouble the way they act, or they get somebody else into trouble. Always something bad on their minds. Talking sweet to women, and then they don't do a thing for them when they're in trouble."

"If you think a man will help you out you're dead wrong. Sure they're all sweet to start with, and you have a good time together, but then they start spending your money and running around with other women the moment you turn your back. You hear people say every man has a dog in him? That ain't no joke, you know."

97

The kinds of behavior the image of the "no-good man" refers to are obviously those relating to the ghetto-specific niche and to the ghetto-specific male role adapted to it. Yet as we have already noted there are also some elements of that role which are rather attractive to women—the man who dresses with a certain flair, talks with charm, and evinces the right degree of toughness may be "no good", but he is also a "real man". This makes for some ambivalence in the evaluation of different types of men. Some "good men" are not particularly exciting, while a "bad cat" can really be quite desirable, for a male friend if not for a husband. Thus in some contexts "bad" becomes a term for certain masculine qualities, a particular manner of man, rather than for a low evaluation of character, and it may indeed express admiration rather than contempt—"Robert is a ba-a-ad man." As Keil notes in his book *Urban Blues* (1966), many of the stars of black music have the "no-good man" as a significant part of their stage personality; when artists such as Wilson Pickett and Bobby Bland present themselves as such men during their performances at the Howard Theatre the enthusiasm of the female audience is audibly and visibly expressed. (In this context we may note the concept of the "bad motherfucker", used more often by men in largely appreciative statements on this kind of counter-mainstream supermasculinity. The emcees at the Howard use a euphemism, the "bad motorcycle".)

When the men talk about themselves their imagery is not altogether different from that used by women, although there are variations in nuances. The men who tend more or less strongly to act in terms of the ghetto-specific male role also distinguish between a "good man" type and the one they consider more average. They idealize the former, but they also draw attention to the instances in which they themselves are or claim to be propelled by motives of mainstream culture, not to say chivalry or puritanism. Elijah Williamson, who has worked irregularly during his fifty-some years and who has spent some time in jail, gives only occasional support to his former wife and children. Yet when he returned from Philadelphia where he had gone to live it up after a hit on numbers (see chapter 7), he had this to say:

"I was just worrying and worrying all the time for my kids. Even if you ain't going with the woman you want to be close to your kids, you know—to fix them up and things like that when they need someone. So I thought, well, I got this money, but I could just as well fuck up in D.C. as in Philly, and be near them."

And when Freddy, Fats and a couple of other men were sitting in a back alley one night, Freddy upbraided Fats for using foul language when he had visited Freddy and his "old lady" (in this case common-law wife, although it could also mean legal wife) the night before. Explaining to the others in a side note, Freddy said:

"He was saying 'fuck them' and 'goddam motherfucker' and all that shit right in front of her, so I say, I won't let him in again if he don't promise to act right. I wasn't brought up like that, my mother told me how to act in front of women."

In different contexts the men thus apply the imagery concerning both the "good man" (mainstream) and the ghetto-specific male role to themselves. We have already noted some of the ways they state claims to the latter, as we delineated that role. Chapter 5 focuses on the maintenance of that image, of males, for males, by males. Like the women, the men tend to regard it as natural for men to be in some ways "bad"; although a man should try to be "good", it is difficult to control his essential masculinity, and so he shows his "no good" characteristics.

"Men have a little bit of dog in them, you know. That's why they can't leave women alone."

"You know liquor makes your beard grow, so maybe men and liquor were made for each other."

On this point there is some agreement between men's and women's views; it comes naturally to a man to be "bad". But the men tend to see this as an excuse, while women see in it a reason for passing unfavorable judgments on men.[25]

The men's public imagery concerning women also shows some similarities to the women's stated view of themselves; women should be "good" and actually tend to be so. However, just as the female conception of "no-good men" is somewhat ambivalent, so is the male picture of the "good women". Yet it is not quite the same kind of ambivalence. The women's imagery expresses the opinion that "no-good men" are indeed "real men"—sometimes and in some ways, at least—and thus in a sense good. On the other hand, the men hold that "good women" are certainly good if they really stick to the ideal in their behavior, but they nourish doubts about female sincerity. The suspicions are generally of two types; those concerned with infractions of norms which would make the halo fit less perfectly, such as infidelity and drinking, and those which involve showing off positive characteristics at the men's expense. Like the contests between men described earlier, the latter in a way takes on the character of a zero-sum game; the men intimate that by running the families rather single-handedly because "somebody must do it" and by reproaching men about their behavior, women monopolize goodness and power, thus helping to deprive men of their mainstream role and in a way to emasculate them. One young man offered an etymology of the slang term for heroin, "white lady", relating to this theme:

"It's called 'white' because the stuff is white. 'Lady' is because it's strong, you know, powerful, just like a woman."

Of course, this interpretation is not the only one possible, but the truth is less important here than the fact that a native of the ghetto found it an acceptable explanation.

Men thus see women as perhaps in some ways a little too concerned with showing off their good character, and in other ways sometimes less good than they are supposed to be. The latter is seen in particular in the area of sexual behavior. As we have said, while women's behavior averages closer to the mainstream model, and while the female niche is a better basis for such a performance, there are women who drink, form loose unions, and "carry on" generally. We have also seen that staying clear of more permanent and close attachments may indeed be adaptive for many women with children. Such women are often branded "gypsies" or "whores" by the men; the streetcorner men who affirm their own natural tendency toward promiscuity often talk about whatever they see as female infidelity in moral terms. "That bitch is a gypsy, that's all she is."

So arises the pessimistic theme about women seeming to be good who are actually bad.[26] "We're all battle-scarred," as one middle-aged streetcorner man said. Men become suspicious of the reliability of the women around them, and other men are often ready to support their doubts. This is Fats asking his friend Freddy for advice about his girl friend who wants to give him the key to her apartment.

"Yeah, she said, 'Darling, I want you to come to me whenever you feel like it.' Now, that sounds good, don't it? But I'm not sure it is so good. What if she ain't there when I come?"

"Yeah, you know, sometimes when you get a key from a chick and you get there you might end up alone for two or three nights in a row, and you know she ain't staying with that mother of hers. So if you don't want to be hurt, don't take that key. Now, if you don't worry too much about it you could take it, 'cause then if she ain't there you can just say, 'What the hell', and then you go somewhere else. Now ain't that right?"

The belief that women cannot really be trusted is also expressed in more humorous ways in men's conversations. The following exchange about Sylvester's relationship to Diane took place on the steps outside Harry Jones' house where a few streetcorner men were assembled. They had been drinking together, and Sylvester, the liquor store messenger, adjusted his collar and appeared ready to leave.

"I'm going over to Diane," he said. "I want some love."

"You think you can come this late?" one of the other men asked. "You think she'll let you in?"

"Yeah, she'll let him in," a third man said with a smile. "She'd let me in, too."

"Oh, no, she wouldn't," Sylvester replied. "You don't even know Diane, you don't even know where she lives."

"Oh yes I do. She lives on Blackman Street."

"You know that only 'cause you heard me say so." Sylvester looked a little angry while the others seemed to try to hold back their smiles.

"Yeah, I was just kidding. Take it easy now, we'll see you tomorrow. Hope Diane don't have no other company when you get there."

The others laughed, and as Sylvester left, he said, "I told you you don't know Diane."

Beliefs about men and women are easily transformed into beliefs about unions between them. If it is believed that men are by nature always on the make and that women, although not innately promiscuous in the same way, can be expected to succumb to temptation, then it easily follows that new sexual contacts are sought continuously. Sexual accessibility as a culturally constructed expectation tends to become a self-fulfilling prophecy. When men hold both that a "real man" is like a dog, always pursuing the other sex, and that there "ain't no pussy you can't get", then they are likely to be more sexually active than they would if such action were not a basic fact in their self-image and if they held that most women are unaccessible.

The understanding that men are promiscuous and women at least tempting and tempted are not only directly acted upon. There is often a suspicion that the pursuit of sexual activity is a hidden motive behind actions which one cannot place otherwise. Jake, about 40, comments spontaneously after a stranger he meets in the street asks him for the time:

"Now, why should I give him the time? He might want to keep an appointment with some girl, could be my own daughter, you know, and they go to a bar and he gets her drunk and they have an affair and she becomes pregnant, and then he leaves town or goes to jail or something, and where does that leave me? Then I'll have to take care of my daughter and her child, and I don't know nothing about the father—could as well have been the insurance man who knocked her up or somebody."

And this is Elijah Williamson pointing to a woman on the sidewalk across one of the busy intersections in the neighborhood:

"See that woman over there? That's my old woman. She lives over in Southwest now. You know, she used to be walking back and forth in front of my old lady's house, and nobody said nothing, but finally my old lady got wind of the whole thing, and so she asks me, 'Is that your old girl friend walking up and down the street over there?' So I says, 'Yeah,' and so she gets out there and they start screaming and hollering at each other, and that gypsy ain't been around here since."

To other strains in the male-female relationship are thus added those resulting from the ghetto dwellers' beliefs about their partners' trustworthiness; there are suspicions of infidelity or at least premonitions that a relationship might not last. Here there emerges again some public imagery on how to look at one's broken or to-be-broken unions. It may be "a hurting thing" when relationships are dissolved into which one has made large emotional investments, but one should try to take it in the stride—it is "no big thing". Since it is an experience shared by so many of one's contemporaries, a broken relationship is not a very significant fact in one's public biography, and one should be ready to accept that it happens all the time. This is Freddy, 36, frequently unemployed construction worker, commenting on an earlier union of his:

"I used to have a place up there on Blackman Street, and I had a beautiful brown-skinned baby, and I loved her so. She sang in a club, and she was really a fine-looking woman. So one day when I came home—I was working on one of those big apartment houses on Connecticut Avenue then, we were remodeling it—so when I came home, I asked, 'Where's my dinner, baby?' And she said, 'It ain't ready.' And I didn't like the way she said it, so I said, 'Look Jane, if you don't love me no more, why don't you leave?' So she got her things together and moved out. And I felt bad about it for a long time, 'cause I still loved her, but I figured it was better that way. If you don't have a good time together no more, just don't stay together."

Apparently Freddy telescoped a more continuous friction in the career of the relationship into this final crisis, but what is important in the statement is its moral. One should be ready to accept the breakup of a relationship. Certainly many people may find it hard to accept this privately, as there is not necessarily any lack of personal feeling. It is also true that people hardly discuss their own relationships in such terms until the breakup is clearly approaching or already a fact. But at that point, at least, personal sentiments are not compounded by significant changes in one's outward self as understood by one's peers. Breakups tend to be discussed in the public vocabulary as if they had not much disturbed the person involved personally. For instance, Lester and Beatrice had been going together for some time but had been quarreling lately, and it was rather clear that their relationship would not last much longer. Beatrice nagged about one thing or other, and Lester tried to make up but had not done so to her satisfaction. The morning after the break, Lester appeared quite cool and laughed off suggestions that he had been thrown out.

"So I said goodbye to her, and there she was, crying like a baby, but I just didn't want no more of her, you know, it's all over, Casanova. Just think, next Saturday I won't have to buy drinks for nobody, I can just lie back and drink champagne by myself."

The incongruous reference to Casanova is a quotation—"It's all over, Casanova" was a rock-and-roll hit by Ruby Andrews on the top sixteen at the time.

The "no big thing", shouldershrugging imagery is not consistently applied. We have seen in other quotations that sentiments of personal injury are expressed now and then, and it has been a major motif in black music. Yet when disruptions and shifting liaisons occur so frequently in a community it is advantageous for its members not to appear too vulnerable to the effects of such occurrences, and this imagery is at least a resource for one's continued social functioning.

*Structure and culture*

We have reached the end of our exposition of pertinent facts about ghetto men, women, and their relationships with one another. A couple of more specific facets of this complex will be dealt with in the following two chapters. At this point, however, it may be possible to return to the problems of interpretation we discussed earlier in this chapter. What do we understand now about macrostructural and cultural determinants of male and female behavior?

First of all it seems clear that contemporary structural constraints in the form of a depressed niche in the socio-economic structure of the wider society are a major determinant of the form of male-female unions in today's ghetto, just as they appear to have been at every stage of the social history of black people in America so far. This condition contributes strongly to marital conflict, female dominance, and the incidence of husbandless households, because social, economic, and cultural resources derived from participation in the wider structure are distributed so as to favor such social forms. The conflict element in the male-female union is probably particularly dependent on the fact that unions of ghetto-specific forms are continuously compared, if only implicitly, to the mainstream model of marriage for which the ghetto-specific ascribed resources are a poor basis. No ghetto-specific model for a male-female union has anything close to the normative validity which the mainstream model enjoys in the ghetto as well as outside it, and this makes it hard for couples to find a state of the union which is as morally satisfying to them. To put it another way, while a great many white Americans—with a culturally authoritarian outlook—might see it as a saving grace of black people that they also hold the mainstream ideal, the ideal creates a dilemma for the black people themselves.

So far the macrostructural influences seem overwhelming, as they may well be. We may wonder, then, what has become of the cultural influences. The answer appears to be that they are first of all of an interstitial character. Within the space left by the constraints of the socio-economic niche and the mainstream cultural apparatus, it has been left to social and cultural processes internal to the ghetto to work out some of the details.

One of the factors involved is obviously the simple one of the co-presence of a great number of people in a situation where adaptations are needed and where they do occur. The tendencies to female dominance and to marital conflict and disruption could occur in families in a macrostructural position similar to that of ghetto dwellers even if the family were isolated from others in such a position, but when these occur in a community where such social forms have already become common, the striving to avoid them may be blunted because of their obvious statistical normality. This kind of perception is the basis of a ghetto-specific common sense. The ghetto community has its own native categories of probability; its members are aware of what kinds of behavior occur frequently and react by prophesying that these will continue to occur. A statistical fact thus becomes a state of affairs seen as normal and expected to be recurrent. There is an individual preparedness to meet the modes of behavior directly which he has noticed as an observer throughout his life. We can apply this argument to a point we have raised before. In discussing the slavery and africanist schools of black marriage and family interpretation, we pointed out that these at best implied the transmission of a mental image of a weak marital relationship. In its most primitive form, the simple perception of such relationships in one generation after another would lead to continuous re-creation of this image among black men and women, To this extent, one may well feel that such transmission goes on in the black community now, as it probably has for a long time.

But this is not all, for ghetto dwellers are no more isolated as observers of ghetto life than they are as adaptors to their macrostructural niche. Individual experiences are strengthened or modified by participation in the social processes in which public imagery emerges. Here expectations and interpretations are stated and agreements worked out through which one's "common sense" is given a more authoritative character. By finding out "what everybody knows", one becomes equipped with ways of dealing with one's surroundings. In the domain we are concerned with here, one learns for instance how the other sex works and how to deal with it. Since public imageries are generally rather unfavorable here, one becomes introduced to an opinion that men should beware of trusting women wholeheartedly and vice versa. To the extent that male-female interaction in the ghetto is a "battle of the sexes", this is provided for not only by the macrostructural niche but also in transmitted ghetto-specific common sense.

From public interpretation the step is not very far to public evaluation. Earlier we noted Cohen's (1955) point about group solutions to problems of adjustment—not only do group members suggest modes of behavior to one another, but they also put them up for approval. Acceptance, or at least lack of punishment, is needed if the kind of behavior is to continue. How do ghetto dwellers evaluate ghetto-specific forms of behavior?

We have seen that in this domain the mainstream model usually takes precedence as an ideal. There is no equally valued ghetto-specific alternative;

in this sense cultural influences on male-female unions from inside the ghetto and peculiar to it do not seem strong. Nobody says that infidelity, broken unions, and premarital or postmarital sex are "good", that is, morally valuable in their own right. But on a lower level, there may be a kind of ghetto-specific cultural influence, in that the community seems to have evolved a certain measure of tolerance for a certain non-conformity as compared to the main-stream ideal. One should not make too much of this, for it is not consistently applied, and some of the apparent tolerance may be due to the lack of means of punishment; here, at least, Frazier had some point in speaking of the lack of social control. But the public imagery does indeed openly provide some basis for greater permissiveness. It is "in a man" to drink and hunt women, so to some extent he can be excused. A little infidelity is "no big thing", a broken relationship likewise. Perhaps it may be said, then, that ghetto-specific culture provides some degree of socially recognized release from certain mainstream norms.[27]

In one area, however, ghetto-specific cultural evaluation goes a little beyond this. The male role seems to be the major case in the domain of sex role and familial behavior where a ghetto-specific complex of modes of action has at least some normative basis of its own, and with some right it may thus be posed as a cultural alternative to the mainstream male role. (As we have seen, female deviations from the mainstream sex role do not at all have the same kind of ideological underpinnings.) Granted, men idealize the mainstream male role, to which they have little opportunity to conform, and for many the ghetto-specific behavior can thus be seen in some ways as a forced adaptation. It is also true that men are often criticized by people with whose interests their behavior clashes, for instance by wives, sisters, and mothers. Yet the ghetto-specific male role provides some particular ideals to "live up to"; these are accepted by a large number of men, and there is also some attraction on the part of many women toward men striving toward these ideal characteristics. If there is any normative cultural phenomenon in the ghetto community which contributes to making the mainstream model of marriage hard to achieve there, it is not some alternative ghetto-specific model of marriage but the ghetto-specific male role which comes into conflict with the mainstream male family role, by substituting satisfactions outside the area of family life for those ideally found inside it. (Yet stable marriage and ghetto-specific male role behavior are not entirely incompatible; by striking a bargain between them, some men manage to bring off the act of pleasing everybody.) It seems hard to deny that the ghetto-specific male role under the present conditions enjoys some stability of its own, albeit precarious; the next two chapters are discussions of some of the social and cultural dynamics involved in its maintenance.

# 5

# Streetcorner
# Mythmaking

Many streetcorner men, and quite a few swingers, spend a great deal of their time in clusters with other men at street corners or on the front staircases of the rundown houses. If it is too cold or if it rains, they may gather instead in someone's home, in a barber shop or at some other indoor hangout. Many of the men join the gatherings only in their spare time before or after work. Others belong to the spurious leisure class of the unemployed and spend a great part of their days, and sometimes a part of their nights, in the gatherings. There are usually some men who form a core membership of such a clique, participating in its get-togethers one day after another. Other men take part more occasionally, and now and then somebody joins the circle only for a single encounter as he happens to be on the scene in the company of one of the more regular participants. Almost never is a woman present. Possibly she may sit in (without contributing more than sporadic comments) if she is married to the man at whose house the gathering takes place, but most women prefer not to. The gathering begins and ends elastically as the men drift in and out of it, coming from home or from work, going to see a woman, or to a pool hall, or to a bowling alley. Although all this is usually referred to as peer group life, it is clearly more a question of *ad hoc* gatherings than of well-delineated groups.

What happens in these gatherings? Not much, it may seem. "You just get together and try to be sociable, that's all," one man puts it. Somewhat less charitably, another man says: "You just sit there and let your mouth run."

Obviously the men do not hold this interaction to be something of great import. As analysts of leisure the ghetto dwellers follow George Simmel, the sociological pioneer in the field; sociability is interaction for interaction's own sake, without a purpose other than enjoyment of the moment and without consequences beyond the encounter itself (cf. Simmel 1950:45).

Yet this conception may tell us too little about what is really going on. What is it that makes men feel good about getting together? What are the things they enjoy about "running their mouths"? Are there values realized, or problems solved, in a togetherness of streetcorner men? Can this sociability really be understood apart from the wider social world in which the men participate?

Of course, the answer to such questions must come out of knowledge about what the men do together, by listening to what the men say instead of dismissing it as idle talk. Do the conversations linger on at random, or are there consistent patterns?

Certainly the gatherings are not all the same. There are times when the men at the corner stand around without talking much, just watching what goes on around them. Sometimes they may play cards or shoot crap, and hardly anything is said that does not have to do with the game. If somebody, player or spectator, tries to get a conversation started then, at least some players will brusquely ask him to shut up. At yet other times, conversations become contests, such as those detailed in the preceding chapter. But here we will be particularly interested in the more peaceful small talk.

This is not all confined to one or two topics. Clearly some men are more given to talking than others, and they may have their idiosyncracies. Sonny, the former saxophonist, appears to have been downwardly mobile and has an unusual although uneven stock of knowledge; with a visitor from outside the ghetto—like an anthropologist—he may discuss Allen Ginsberg, Rabelais, Swedenborg, and Indian mysticism. Among his streetcorner peers he often talks about past engagements and famous colleagues. When he speak of the mutual appreciation between himself and Charlie "Bird" Parker, few of his peers may wholeheartedly believe him, but the mass of reminiscences about the jazz community in the years before rock-and-roll have established for him a special niche in the Winston Street neighborhood as a man of past professional status.[1] Similarly, Bee Jay, middle-aged, usually unemployed, and in poor health from too heavy drinking, speaks of the years he claims to have spent at an Ivy League college, casually drops in garbled quotes from Socrates, Oscar Wilde and assorted other notables, and repeatedly returns to the topic of his hunting trip to Africa as Ernest Hemingway's valet. This, plus an astounding vocabulary, certainly make many of his friends and neighbors recognize him as an intellectual, just like Sonny. Yet just about everybody has strong doubts about the truth of some of their stories.

More ordinary streetcorner talk may take off from the afternoon newspaper. Its human-interest stories have a broad appeal, and the South American woman who had quintuplets, the latest boastful interview with Cassius Clay, alias Muhammed Ali, or the most recent murder-with-passion among rich people in Florida are all good for a moment of conversation. Sometimes there is indeed something tangibly practical in the exchanges, as when somebody knows of a job one of his peers might get. But most of the talk is entertainment. There are the daydreams about sitting on a cloud high up in the sky, or landing on the moon, or there is somebody who has learned something he wants to pass on about the world. Most of it, of course, is reasonably well-informed. Occasionally, it becomes very clear that at least the adult generation of ghetto dwellers, many of them of Southern country origin, do not share the stock of knowledge which is taken for granted by most of their countrymen.

At the street corner, around the lamp, one evening in November, Wes was talking about a book he had read the other night, "about biologists and all sorts of people from all over the world who say they can prove it wasn't God who made man, they say we all came out of the sea... Actually, they say they can show the origin for every animal except two, the rat and the fly. I think they called it cre-ation... No, it wasn't cre-ation... Evolution, that's what they called it." Most of the other men accepted Wes' statement without much comment, while Sonny said it was true but that it was actually more complicated than that.

For all the diversity of the conversation, however, one area which the men return to again and again is personal reminiscences. Many of these exchanges take place over a drink—much less frequently a marijuana cigarette is passed around and shared—as the participants contribute their narratives. Some of the men have more to tell than others, but generally one man after another has something to say, and each does so spontaneously. No one is called upon by the others to tell a story; this kind of acknowledgment of narrative skill is lacking although some of the men are recognized as better performers and more likely to have a good story. There is much laughter, now and then someone inserts a comment, and as a particularly good point is made a man slaps the palm of another's outstretched hand to show appreciation.

Some men are gathered in the evening at Harry Jones' house. His children are out playing, his wife Patricia has not yet returned from work. Sylvester, the liquor store messenger, is there; so is Sonny, George, and Harry's brother Carl, all unemployed. In an adjoining room are three other men; one of them is unemployed, one is a construction worker, the third one is a janitor. All the men are in their thirties or forties. They have had a series of card games going the whole afternoon. One of them has kept the scores which by now fill a whole sheet of paper. There has been a collection of money taken toward a half-gallon bottle of cheap wine, and one of the men went to the Price-Rite liquor store to get it, thereby saving 20 cents compared to the price in the more nearby stores—this concern for savings only intermittently overrides the consideration of walking distance. The TV is on, first for the news and later for Westerns and family comedies, but nobody really watches it. King, the Joneses' mixed breed dog, comes in through a hole in the wire-mesh door, grumbles, and lies down at Sonny's feet.

"That dog is so cool." Sonny comments. "Just like one of the fellows. Tries to mind his own business, but if somebody does something to him, he ain't gonna take it lying down. I bet he can take on any dog around here. And always looking for a piece of pussy, too. And last summer you know, it was funny. I think he knew every bootlegger around here. Wherever I went, he was running in front of me, seemed like he knew exactly where he was going. He likes wine, too. Remember when we gave him some, and he came begging for more? Yessir, that dog is really one of us."

The other men laugh. "Yeah, he really is." Sylvester says. The men who play cards come in now and then to fill their glasses. Later, when the talk turns to the world of sports, they come in and join the conversation. But before that, there are reminiscences and exchanges of opinion about drinking experiences.

"Did you see Jimmy is back?" Sonny asks. "I saw him today down at the corner. I guess his daddy bailed him out. That's a good precinct anyway, don't treat you too bad. Nothing like Eighteenth Precinct, they start hitting you over your head in no time. That's the meanest precinct in town, I tell you."

"Shi-it, Nineteenth is much worse. You don't have to be drunk for them to take you in, you just have to smell alcohol."

"Yeah, and they don't pay no mind if you're on your way home or not. I was in that area once and I was drunk, but not too drunk, and I was trying to go home when they came, and I told them, 'Look, I'm on my way home.' And they said, 'Yeah, you're on your way home, 'cause you're coming with us.' And then they took me to the judge, and he said, 'How many times have you been arrested this year?' And I didn't really know, so I said, 'Twice.' But they checked my record, and it said seven. But the record was wrong, 'cause I know it was more than that."

"Well gentlemen," says Carl, who has not participated in the preceding exchange. "I don't really know which precincts are good and which are bad, 'cause I have no dealings with any of them, and they have no dealings with me." Carl does not drink any more. He stopped after a serious disease caused by drinking and has undergone therapy for some time. He often emphasizes his redemption when in the company of drinkers. After doing so now he laughs, and the others smile.

Sylvester turns to George and says, "You remember when we were arrested on Foster Street? Some years ago? I was staying with my sister then, and she had taken George in too. And we were arrested and they put us in the same cell, and I went to sleep. And when I woke up George was gone! So the officer asked did I want to make a call, and I said no, 'cause if George was out he would be sure to tell my sister. But nobody came to get me out, so finally I asked to make a call, and my sister managed to get the money and so she came and got me. So I asked her about George, and she said, and she said yeah, George had come back, and when she asked where I was he said, 'Last time I saw him he was in jail.' And then he had fell asleep, and she couldn't get one more word out of him!"

Everybody laughs, and Harry Jones adds a recollection of his.

"I remember a summer some years ago, we were sitting in front of this house on S Street, and we had all been drinking, you know, going into this alley. And David was with us, you know, the fellow who was married to Esther then. We didn't know him too well. Anyway, the police car came and stopped at the corner and just stood there, and we didn't want them to come and look us over, with the breath of liquor we all had. So we all went into this house. But David left his other bottle behind on the stairs! So he said, 'One of you go out and get that bottle. I can't do it, 'cause I don't want them to see me. I'm out on parole'!"

The next two stories were told by Big Bill, a friendly alcoholic who has been in and out of the Winston Street neighborhood for many years, on a summer evening as men gathered on a front staircase while dusk fell. Big Bill is a talented story teller who keeps his audience enthralled with his choreography, facial expressions and abrupt voice changes, as he performs in front of them, standing before the staircase.

"Let me tell you fellows, I've been arrested for drunkenness more than two hundred times over the last few years, and I've used every name in the book. I remember once I told them I was Jasper Gonzales and then I forgot what I had told them, you know. So I was sitting there waiting, and they came in and called Jasper Gonzales, and nobody answered. I had forgotten that's what I said, and to tell you the truth, I didn't know how to spell it. So anyway, nobody answered and they were calling 'Jasper Gonzales! Jasper Gonzales!' So I thought that must be me, so I answered. But they had been calling a lot of times before that. So the judge said, 'Mr. Gonzales, are you of Spanish descent?' And I said, 'Yes, your honor, I came to this country thirty-four years ago!' And of course I was only thirty-five, but you see I had this beard then, and I looked pretty bad, dirty and everything you know, so I looked like sixty. And so he said, 'We don't have a record on you. This is the first time you have been arrested?' So I said, 'Yes, your honor, nothing like this happened to me before. But my wife was sick and then I lost my job you know, and I felt kind of bad. But it's the first time I ever got drunk.' So he said, 'Well, Mr. Gonzales, I'll let you go, 'cause you are not like the rest of them here. But let this be a warning to you.' So I said, 'Yes, your honor. Thank you, your honor.' And then I went out, and so I said to myself, 'I'll have to celebrate this.' So I went across the street from the court, and you know there are four liquor stores there and I got a pint of wine and next thing I was drunk as a pig."

"This other time I was just coming out of the whiskey store and I was in pretty bad shape you know, so I kind of stumbled out through the door with this fifth of wine in my hand when these two cops spotted me, and they said, 'Hey boy, hold it right there.' So I turned around halfway and said, 'Do I look like a boy to you?' And then I started running and this was at the corner of Ninth and S. So I ran and ran and ran, and I didn't hardly know where I was, and I'm sure that must have been a sight, me running like hell in that condition. Huh! Huh! Huh! And I heard these two fellows coming after me. So I ran to my sister's house which is at Eleventh and T, and I got in there, and they came and knocked on the door, and my sister opened, and they said, 'We want that fellow.' And so they took me to the precinct, and then on to court. And so I told the judge what happened, and he looked at these two men and said, 'Is that true?' So they said, 'Yes, your honor, that's true.' And then the judge said, 'You mean you couldn't catch up with a man who is as drunk as a dog in more than two blocks? Tell me, what had you been drinking?' And so he said to me, 'You get out of here. You can't have been as drunk as these two if you outran them like that'."

On the theme of drinking, another man who has a reputation as a winehead had this to tell a similar gathering.

"My little niece Jo Ann called me today, you know, and she said, 'Uncle Ollie, are you drunk?' And I said, 'No dear, I'm dead sober. So she said, 'I don't believe you 'cause I ain't seen you sober in twenty years. Anyway, if you stay sober I'll come and see you after church on Sunday.' 'That's fine, sweetheart,' I said. 'I won't have nothing to drink till then.' Of course I was so stoned I could hardly stand up. Then she said, 'Hey, you sound funny. You sure you ain't drunk?' So I said, 'No dear, I just had a couple of more teeth pulled out'."

A great number of the stories involve women:

"Mack asked me did I screw his daughter, so I asked, 'I don't know, what's her name?' And then when I heard that gal was his daughter all right, I says, 'Well Mack, I didn't really have to take it, 'cause it was given to me.' I thought Mack sounded like his daughter was some goddam white gal. But Mack says, 'Well, I just wanted to hear it from you.' Of course, I didn't know that was Mack's gal, 'cause she was married and had a kid, and so she had a different name. But then you know the day after when I was out there a car drove by, and somebody called my name from it, you know, 'Hi darling,' and that was her right there. So the fellow I was with says, 'Watch out, Buddy will shoot your ass off.' Buddy, that's her husband. So I says, 'Yeah, but he got to find me first'!"

"Were you here that time a couple of weeks ago when these three chicks from North Carolina were up here visiting Miss Gladys? They were really gorgeous, about 30—35. So Charlie says why don't they step by the house and he and Wes and Dee Kay can go out and buy them a drink. So they say they had to go and see this cousin first, but then they'd be back. But then Brenda (Charlie's wife) comes back before they do, and so these girls walk back and forth in front of the house, and Charlie can't do a thing about it, except hope they won't knock on his door. And then Dee Kay and Wes come and pick them up, and Rufus is also there, and the three of them go off with these chicks, and there is Charlie looking through his window, and there is Brenda looking at them too, and asking Charlie does he know who the chicks are."

"When I was down in South Carolina I went to see those people I knew from before, and when I was with them in their house I met this beautiful woman who ran an alteration shop—you know what an alteration shop is? Well, she was tall and brown-skinned and had a good shape and charcoal black eyes and big legs, and she lived there alone 'cause she was a widow. And she was doing real good. So when we sat there having drinks, you know, these other people left for awhile, and then she says, 'Mr. Jeffries, have you met any girls while you've been here?' And I says, 'No, I've been no closer to any woman than I am to you now, 'cause I haven't seen many women here, and what I saw I didn't like.' And so this gal says, 'Well, Mr. Jeffries, maybe somewhere along the line you and I may be able to comfort each other.' So we were together most of the time I was down there."

There are also times when men going for a joy ride in someone's car take women as the topic of conversation.

We went for a ride in Ted's new '68 Chrysler convertible, equipped with radio, air conditioning, and just about every other gadget you would want. (Ted is doing rather well, pimping and holding down a government job.) The model had just been released, and Ted was obviously proud to show it off, including a demonstration of acceleration on North Capitol Street, but Larry and Fats were more interested in driving slowly through the streets where they knew people.
"I know a big-legged bitch in that building over there, second floor."
"That building? I know a yellow-skinned chick in there, but she's on the fourth floor. She got her own place, you can get a piece of pussy there any time."
A few streets away:
"That's where Lucy Ann lives, the girl I used to go with. Wouldn't go anywhere near her now, though, with my old lady . . . Don't know what kind of shit that old bitch could start if they met."
And some more blocks away:
"Remember when I took Theresa home, Robert Smith's daughter? And I just let her off at her place, and didn't ask to come with her up to her place or for her number or anything? And she said I was the first nigger who didn't invite myself up or any of that shit. But I was so high 'cause I'd been smoking pot so I just didn't care. Might see her some other time, though."

At times, one may have good reason to suspect that the stories are somewhat less than completely truthful. Big Bill's encounters with the judge may well have been improved upon a little the way he described them, or they may even be fabricated, and some of the autobiographical statements of purportedly successful ladies' men are demonstrably untrue.

Mr. Simmons, in his fifties, janitor in an elegant apartment building downtown, told some of his friends about the receptionist in that building:
"You know, today this gal at the front desk said to me, 'You know, Mr. Simmons, I think a gal must be crazy if she don't fall in love with you.' And she's a beauty, brown-skinned, black hair coming down to here (indicating halfway down to the elbow), big legs . . ."
As the conversation was ebbing out a little later, Mr. Simmons suggested that I go with him to see the building. On our way in we passed a middle-aged, short-haired, not particularly good-looking woman at the reception desk; she answered Mr. Simmons' questions about requests from the residents rather curtly. I had already decided that the girl he had been talking about earlier must work another shift when he said, after we turned around the corner, "Yeah, that's the chick I was telling you-all about. Ain't she cute?"

\* \* \*

110

What is the place of narratives and mini-memories such as these in ghetto life? One might characterize them, of course, as the recounting of unique individual experiences, but in doing so, one may miss an important point. They are experiences of common interest, variations on themes relating to the typical traits of the ghetto-specific model of masculinity—hunting women, drinking, getting into trouble or somehow getting out of it. Since the men favor such topics over others, it obviously matters to them what is the content of sociability. We must go beyond Simmel's concern only with its form, in order to determine why the men draw on these specific conversational resources from the world outside the gathering, and why these topics can be handled to such particular satisfaction in this forum. This also means that we see streetcorner sociability as a phenomenon which cannot be discussed in isolation from a wider social context.

In looking for a better path to follow in the interpretation of sociable interaction we may begin with the notion of leisure as "free time". "Free", of course, in this case means free from work tasks. But as Bennett Berger points out in an essay on the sociology of leisure (1963), there is no really unconstrained time: the constraints which determine an individual's activities during his leisure hours are those which affect him as a moral and intellectual being and which make these activities rewarding enough in themselves, without material consequences. And the moral and intellectual problems to be acted upon in leisure may themselves be socially structured. Sociability, as social relationships in leisure, can thus be assumed to involve such moral and intellectual concerns which the individual can most satisfactorily deal with in interaction with others.

This reasoning ties up well with the work of some more recent students of sociability. These have directed their interest particularly to the analysis of American middle-class and upper-class gatherings (cf. Watson 1958; Riesman *et al.* 1960; Watson and Potter 1962). However, we may find it both pleasurable and useful to assume that there is little functional difference between the small talk at these parties, luncheons, and kaffee klatsches and that which goes on at the ghetto street corner.

According to these scholars, sociability is a kind of interaction in which definitions and evaluations of self, others, and the external world are developed, maintained, and displayed with greater intensity than in other interaction. Successful sociability is that where participants find satisfying understandings of the world and support for some reasonably high degree of self-esteem. An individual's vision of reality is often a precarious thing; we can find comfort in the knowledge that it is shared by others, thus acquiring social anchoring as an objective truth. And it is an old tenet of interactionist theory in sociology that a human being is particularly dependent on what he finds to be the view of significant others as he forms his conception of himself.[2] Yet it is not necessarily laborious, exhaustive, and literal statements of the truth as one sees it that constitute the best expression of shared understandings in sociability. In Erving Goffman's terms (1961: 26—34), the sociable gathering has transformation rules which determine what experiences from the outside world are to be utilized as resources for conversation as well as what form they will be given. First of all, there may be a strain toward definitions of reality which in some way support the participants' self-esteem. Conversations are also often more

111

rewarding when understandings are only alluded to in examples, exaggerations, half-truths, jokes and other indirect or inexact forms of reference whose relation to the consensually established reality can be taken for granted. Furthermore, it is important in sociability to avoid boredom. Thus it is better to bring new materials to bear on shared understandings and values than just to state these repeatedly in their pure form. Sociability is at best a dramatic experience for the participant.

Can these ideas about the nature of sociable interaction lead the way toward an interpretation of the ghetto conversations we have exemplified above? It appears that they can. The men seem preoccupied with creating and maintaining a definition of natural masculinity which they can all share. By seizing on individual experiences of kinds which they have all had, they "talk through" and thereby construct the social reality of the typical Ghetto Man, a fact of life larger than any one of them. This Ghetto Man is a bit of a hero, a bit of a villain, and a bit of a fool, yet none of them all the way. He is in fact a kind of a trickster—uncertainty personified, a creature fluctuating between competence and incompetence, success and failure, good and evil. He applies his mother wit or is plainly lucky some times, as Big Bill in front of the judge, and this helps him come out victorious or at least unscathed. But not all the time, for native wit and luck have their limits, for instance when David left his bottle behind and the police were watching, or when Brenda came home and prevented Charlie from sneaking out with the gorgeous chicks from North Carolina. Anyway, when Ghetto Man succeeds, he is a hero, considering his limited skills and powers in an environment full of adversaries; if he fails, it is natural because he was up to no good.

Why is it that this Ghetto Man so consistently is made the topic of street-corner sociability, out of all qualities of self and social reality which need to be defined? Of course, one part of the answer may be that he has become normatively established as an appropriate subject for discussion in the social context of the men's gathering; he is a conversational resource which it is always acceptable to draw on. But we may go beyond this understanding and ask what makes men involve themselves personally and find satisfaction in these story-telling sessions. We have said that leisure is the time for taking care of moral and intellectual business. The construction materials of the Ghetto Man certainly seem to derive from problems of this kind. We noted in the preceding chapter that there are two definitions of masculinity which co-exist, not altogether peacefully, in the ghetto community. Many men are prevented by macrostructural conditions from performing satisfactorily in the mainstream male role and therefore take on the ghetto-specific alternative; as we shall attempt to make clear in the next chapter, they are also socialized in some degree to the ghetto-specific role from childhood on. But they can never ignore the mainstream model of masculinity, for it is actively promulgated by the wider society in many of its contacts with the people of the ghetto, and many ghetto dwellers also voice the opinion that there is no other morally appropriate way of being a man. Those who are men in a more ghetto-specific way, then, are constantly morally and intellectually besieged; they have a common baggage of role ambivalence to deal with.[3] If they are to find support for the kind of masculinity they have achieved, they had better look for it among other men in the same situation.

Watson and Potter, in one of the analyses of sociability cited above (1962: 249—251), distinguish between "sharing" and "presenting" as types of sociable interaction. In presenting, the individual participant acts as a unique, separate entity; his self is exhibited as if unproblematic, so self-boundaries are kept intact, with each person responding to the façade established by the other.[4] Sharing, on the other hand, involves interaction over a common, more or less problematic identity which is developed clarified, modified, or simply maintained. It may be wise to see sharing and presenting as ideal types; there seem to be interactions where they occur mixed with one another.

In terms of this distinction, the corpus of streetcorner small talk offered above appears to involve a great deal of sharing. In doing so it exemplifies an important complex of ghetto cultural process whereby evaluations and definitions of what is typically masculine are formed. The never-ending series of narratives by different men taken together is a joint exploration of man's nature.

This cultural process, however, is notably lighthearted. One might suspect that this is a peculiarly efficient way of working with some of the problems it has to deal with. Mary Douglas, stating an anthropological approach to the understanding of humor, suggests that the joke is typically an anti-rite; contrary to the regular rite, it attacks the solemnity and unescapable power of the established order of meaning (Douglas 1968:370).[5] The mainstream definition of masculinity is a part of such an established order, and the ghetto men who do not conform with it are engaged in an off-and-on moral and intellectual battle against it. By withdrawing seriousness from breaches against mainstream morality as discussed in reminiscences, they imply that its relevance to their lives is limited; it is an adversary they can live with. As a consequence ghetto-specific masculinity gains in acceptability. There is a social anchoring for such a view, in that a man can note that this is also the opinion of his peers who may count among his most significant others. It helps, of course, if it is his particular emphasis of ghetto-specific masculinity which becomes defined as an altogether human rebellion against the established order. Thus it is natural that in those circles where drinking and drunkenness is common this becomes a frequent topic for sociable conversation, while in others sex and unfaithfulness draw more interest, and in yet others toughness and violence engage the attention most intensively.

The lightheartedness of the cultural construction work is maintained by giving it anecdotal form. The discussion of the ghetto-specific male role is hardly ever more than implied in the narratives. Very seldom is the characterization of the streetcorner man as explicit as in Sonny's description of the street-corner dog, King, and even then he was only stating the male image by indirection. The men are not laboring toward a brief and exact definition of masculinity to contrast with the mainstream conception—they heap example upon example, without coming out clear in saying what is being exemplified. The principle becomes obvious, yet it remains by and large unstated.

It may be in the interest of all the participants to keep it this way. First of all, it may keep interest high. It is more satisfying to hear novel and dramatic expressions of presumably shared understandings than to get "the same old thing" in terms of an intellectual analysis. It is also probable that such an analysis would actually cast doubt on the validity of ghetto-specific masculinity, as it is manifestly not taken for granted any more in such a case; it would increase rather than decrease the intellectual and moral problem on the part of the men. As it is, the men appear not to acknowledge that they are actually involved in sharing. They make it seem as if they are only presenting, while it seems reasonable to believe that they are actually doing both. On the one hand they delineate what interests and what kinds of experiences they have in common and arrive at an implicit consensus on its normalcy; on the other hand, each single recollection is an individual's presentation of a claim to a part of the collective identity. It may depend on the individual's personal state what facet is most important to him at a particular time, but whatever ambivalence he may feel privately is not made obvious to his associates. Thus the group is made to seem committed to the ways of behavior the talk is about.

The image of ghetto masculinity, recurring in statement after statement, takes on a considerable stability in its general outline. Uncertainty and the picture of man as good-bad, competent-incompetent appear to become ordered into a cultural template which can be used in generating new statements of a similar character; they turn into a screen through which events are seen and interpreted.[6] This view of the common characteristics of men is applied not only to the "I" and to the immediate "we". It is also a way of talking about the unknown people met in fleeting encounters in the ghetto, and in particular, it is often the manner in which men talk about small-scale crime. Certainly ghetto dwellers are worried about crime and violence in their environment— "This place is nothing but a jungle. Nothing but a jungle." Or as Sonny, the philosophically inclined musician, puts it, "Life is a sequence of incidents." But their view of "gorillas" and other occasional delinquents is a very human one; they do not consistently place them as enemies outside the moral community, nor are they seen as particularly skilled professionals. Rather, they are tragicomical rascals, incorrigible, but only "half smart" and rather inept. The streetcorner gatherings may entertain themselves with demonstrations of how neighborhood toughs fumble with their knives or their guns, dropping them in what should have been an impressive fast draw. If someone up the street is too ostentatiously cultivating an image of the classical movie gangster, the group assembled around drinks might enjoy itself with the imitations of the fellow who "thinks he's George Raft" but who is actually a rather bumbling rustic. And the anecdotes of encounters and observations also show the good-bad side of crime in the streets.

"Did you hear they robbed the Down Country Market this morning? I was sitting right here with Bee Jay, and I was looking over there 'cause Carl was in the whiskey store next door, and he had some of my money, and I saw this fellow coming running out of there. He must have been nervous though, ha-ha, he just held his pistol to that little baldheaded man in there and said, 'Gimme the bread,' and he didn't even notice he only got small change before he ran off! You know, it's dangerous with people like that. If they can't stay cool they might kill somebody, and then they'll find out they did it for 85 cents."

"I remember when I was going home once, it was pretty late one night and you know, the streets were empty and everything. So I was just going to cross the street when this fellow comes up to me out of nowhere with a gun and says, 'All right, gimme what you got.' So I give him three bucks, that's all I have. And then he asks,

'Got any cigarettes?' And I have this new pack almost sticking out of my pocket, so he takes that. But I need a smoke myself, so I say, 'Do you mind if I keep one?' And he smiles and says, 'Take two.' Big-hearted Nick!"

At this point we might find it interesting to remind ourselves that the trickster motif which we find so frequently expressed in the informal intellectual activity of the ghetto street corner has its traditional counterparts in black folklore. Long ago, Joel Chandler Harris collected Brer Rabbit tales in a series of books, and much has been written and said about trickster lore in black New World communities, as well as about its possible connections with the folklore of Africa and Europe.[7] It has been suggested that the trickster, as an underdog facing the overwhelming power of his opponent and yet sometimes emerging the victor thanks to his wit, would appeal to any group experiencing oppression. Thus whatever may be the origin of the trickster conceptions of black America, past and present circumstances of black people in the New World would maintain and perhaps strengthen such ideas in symbolic action.[8] Although Brer Rabbit is no longer very important, the traditions of today still deal in characters who in one way or other oppose, circumvent or ignore the order imposed on them. The "gorilla" type of ghetto man is idealized in long elaborate rhymes (known as "toasts") about legendary "bad niggers". One of the most notorious, variously known as Stagolee, Stackolee, and Stacker Lee, a constant troublemaker but also a great ladies' man, has also been a topic of black music.[9] Wilson Pickett—the "wicked Pickett" after the title of an LP album of his, and thus himself the bearer of a trickster image—had a rock-and-roll hit with "Stacker Lee" in late 1967. Other toasts still revolve around an animal trickster, the monkey, but he and his opponents, the elephant, the lion, and the baboon, live in a very urban jungle with pool rooms and card games, and the monkey is identified as a pimp, very concerned with male clothing fashion. The monkey works more with his brain, men like Stagolee with their brawn. This has led Roger Abrahams, whose *Deep Down in the Jungle* (1964) is the outstanding study of black ghetto folklore, to distinguish rather sharply between them as "trickster" and "badman" types, the former engaging in cunning indirection and the latter in violent face-to-face conflict. Yet it seems that such a distinction may be misleading, for smartness and toughness are only facets of a single if somewhat amorphous conception of ghetto-specific masculinity which both Stagolee and the monkey serve.[10] That is, most street-corner men would be able to recognize both of them as cultural models for their own role, although they may personally emphasize one or the other.

With such similarities between on the one hand the content of streetcorner sociability, on the other hand contemporary black folklore, one might contend that we should look at the small talk with all the seriousness which anthropological thinkers have customarily given traditional narrative. The notion we are entertaining is that reminiscences may be like myths, sociability a kind of mythmaking. Myths, we have often been told, are intellectual phenomena by way of which men reflect on their condition; on myths men ground their beliefs about what moves them and their world. Of course, streetcorner narratives are not in all ways like prototypical myths. They are not sacred tales; they do not deal with primeval times, or with men who are like gods. The time is yesterday or yesteryear, and the protagonist may be unemployed, separated, or perhaps most noted as someone who occasionally drinks too much. But ghetto men's reminiscences when added together may give the understanding of forces transcending the fate of any particular man, because these forces are the same regardless of who happens to be the narrator and temporary incumbent of that eternal protagonist's position which we have referred to as Ghetto Man. The forces act from the world surrounding him, but they also move him from within. By sharing experiences, the men establish the fact that a man can hardly help womanizing, drinking, and getting into trouble. It is all part of the sex ascribed to him, his most important identity. Whatever the followers of mainstream culture have to say about such activities, it seems he will have to be at peace with his nature.

But myths are not only instruments of reflection. Once intellectual dilemmas arising from past experiences can be regarded as resolved—for the moment at least—myth faces the other way, toward the future. It is programmatic; from Malinowski (1926) and on, it has been seen as a charter for social action. The man comes away from streetcorner mythmaking strengthened in his belief in ghetto-specific masculinity, but through an intimate connection between meaning and value it follows that once it is agreed that it is masculine to drink and to be attracted and attractive to women, one's claim to masculinity does less well without these. As far as continued participation in sociability is concerned, this means that one proceeds from sharing to presenting. The question is no longer what are the criteria for masculinity but whether one meets them or not. The stage has been reached when one uses an established myth in arguments to one's own advantage; in presenting reminiscences about the quality or quantity of one's girl friends, as some men did above, one attempts to impress the others and gain a response favorable to one's own identity. But one person may move quickly back and forth between sharing and presenting, and when somebody is presenting another person may be sharing, as he appropriates other people's experiences in fashioning his own identity and knowledge about the world.

Outside the sociable circle the belief that ghetto-specific expressions of masculinity are justifiable—not to say necessary and unavoidable—will lead the men to renewed such expressions and back to conflict with mainstream norms. Thus ambivalence is probably never completely resolved. There is a perpetual triangle of interacting phenomena for the streetcorner men: acting, occasionally at least, in line with the ghetto-specific model of masculinity; legitimizing such behavior "after the fact" by talking about it with peers who are in the same position, but at the same time programming such behavior for the future; and being exposed to criticisms of such behavior, made in conjunction with the statement of the mainstream model. To put it simply, it appears that the first two, acting and talking, tend to support each other, while the exposure to criticism, for someone who cannot easily "mend his ways", increases the need for the more satisfying definitions and evaluations of the peers. The nagging wife, for example, thus pushes her husband toward streetcorner sociability because it is only there he finds more understanding for that part of his identity which was largely developed in that setting. The peer group is the information storage unit from which the materials for the ghetto-specific male role and its validation can always be replenished.[11]

\*   \*   \*

In the section on "a masculine alternative" in the preceding chapter, we dwelt largely on the substance of ghetto-specific masculinity and also to some extent on how men present themselves as individuals in terms of the cultural definition of their sex role. With these notes on sociability, we may have developed a better understanding of culture building and cultural maintenance. The moral and intellectual situation in which a streetcorner man finds himself is not neat, consistent, or hospitable. In this situation he gets together with his peers in a cultural process where their shared problems are made the basis of shared understandings. Clyde Kluckhohn (1942), quoting the statement that "every culture has a type conflict and a type solution", saw in mythology a storehouse of supra-individual type solutions. For ghetto men, the contradictions of two kinds of masculinity are a type conflict. They may not easily be able really to get out of it, but their collective streetcorner mythmaking, whether in the form of fragmented recollections, long narratives, or a Stagolee toast, can at least momentarily ease the burden. This is why the men "running their mouths" under the street lamp, in the barber shop, or on the front staircase are doing something important.

# 6

# Growing up Male

In this final chapter on sex roles, and in particular on the male role, we will take a look at some social and cultural data concerning the life of ghetto boys as a context for raising anew a question to which some people apparently feel they already have a satisfactory answer. The question, in its most general form, is, "What is the character of sex role socialization for young lower-class black males in a community where matrifocality is common?" It seems important to point out that we are really only raising the question and examining it. To give a definite answer to it, for one thing, one would need a degree of psychological sophistication which is outside the area of competence of at least this social anthropologist. The reason for taking another look at this complex, then, is that some of the pronouncements on it have been somewhat deficient in their considerations of culture and social relations, and these are the facets which will be examined here.

Our point of departure is the commonly accepted opinion that a boy growing up in a household where the father is more or less absent comes to suffer from confusion over his sexual identity. First of all, the person with whom the boy ought to identify is missing, so the boy has no appropriate model for his sex role. The information about the nature of masculinity which a father would transmit unintentionally to his sons merely by going about his life at home is lacking. Furthermore, the adult who is available, the mother, is inappropriate as a role model for him; if he starts to identify with her, he will sooner or later find out that he has made a mistake. ("Identification" is here taken, perhaps somewhat simplistically, to stand for perception of real or desired similarity between model and observer, leading to the observer's acting in imitation of the model.) This misidentification with mother would lead the young males to become more feminine. Some commentators on black family structure do indeed cite examples of men out of matrifocal families of orientation inclined toward feminine behavior: Dai (1949:450) writes of a psychiatric patient who ever since early childhood had wished to be a girl and who acquired such feminine interests as playing with dolls, doing house work, and being his mother's helpmaid. Rohrer and Edmonson (1964: 165—167) describe more extensively the case of Roland who stayed with his mother until her death and devoted his life completely to caring for her. He took a "womanly pride", as the two authors put it, in the furnishings of his apartment and their care, and seemed to have little to do with other men. His psychological test responses showed confusion over his sex role, and it appeared that he had largely taken over his mother's position in the home and in the family.

Cases such as these would serve as examples of rather overt tendencies toward femininity among some men coming out of matrifocal families. Very casual observations in the ghetto also lead one to believe that male homosexuality is not particularly infrequent in the community. Small ghetto boys are well aware of what a "faggot" is (but also of what a "bulldagger"—lesbian— is; there are obviously sociopsychological forces propelling toward female homosexuality as well[1]). However, all sex role confusion does not take this course. Brody and his collaborators (Brody 1961; Derbyshire *et al.* 1963) mention such identification problems as a contributing cause of schizophrenia (sometimes occurring in conjunction with homosexuality) among black mental patients. Many more writers, however, see as the final consequence of this early misidentification and confusion a compulsively masculine reaction, in that males from matrifocal families of orientation come to embrace a very conspicuously male role definition—of the type we first delineated as a ghetto-specific male alternative in chapter 4.[2] In this view, the male peer group, as the locus of shows of anxious masculinity, has developed as a response to the male need for a forum where identity problems of this kind can be resolved. Walter B. Miller is one of those scholars who have pointed to such a relationship between matrifocality and the type of masculine expression we find in the black ghetto (1958:9; 1959:227). Roger D. Abrahams (1964:32 ff.) is another. Rohrer and Edmonson write that although the peer group is a necessary institution, it is only a poor substitute for family security and stability. Yet without the group, the self-doubts and insecurity of the male would be even stronger and more crippling; in the peer group they can be shared by the frightened and confused little boys and the tough but embattled "mama's men" they grow into (Rohrer and Edmonson 1964:167—168).

This is the kind of depiction of the process of growing up male in the ghetto which we will discuss here. It is rooted in an implicit or explicit microsociological notion of what goes on in domestic life under matrifocality. Restated in a perhaps somewhat extreme form, the interpretation is that there is a male model vacuum, and even a risk that the little boy will start striving to become more feminine like his mother. When he belatedly discovers his mistake—and this "discovery", of course, need not be on a high level of awareness—he strives hard to compensate by being extremely masculine, but traces of the identification with mother are hard to destroy, so the process of ostentatious male identity definition has to go on continuously, as a kind of rhetoric of behavior directed as much at oneself as at anybody else.

Are we to believe this?

In the face of a lot of evidence, this view of male identity development cannot easily be rejected altogether. There are points in the story, however, where modifications may be suggested, question marks inserted, and alternative interpretations proposed.

First of all one may want to point out that the problems of identification and re-identification are not qualitatively unique to the boy in the black ghetto matrifocal family. It is, of course, a commonplace and generally accepted tenet of psychoanalytic theory that infants first identify with the mother and that boys later have to change their identification to the father as the major available male. The necessity of some kind of change of identification for boys is thus far from peculiar to the ghetto; what is unusual, if we follow the interpretation summarized above, is the problem of finding someone to reidentify with. Furthermore, however, and more noteworthy, there have been claims set forth that precisely this kind of difficulty in finding a useful model is characteristic of white urban middle class in American society. Parsons points out that girls can be initiated into a female role from an early age because their mothers are usually continuously at home doing things which are tangible and meaningful to the children, while fathers do not work at home so that their role enactment remains to a large extent unobserved, inaccessible and relatively unknown. Girls can help their mothers with many domestic activities and thus get sex role training; the boys have little chance to emulate their fathers in action, partly because of the abstract and intangible nature of many middle class male tasks (Parsons 1942:605). Elsewhere Parsons views the peer groups of white middle class boys quite similarly to the way other commentators have looked at the peer groups of boys from black matrifocal families; these groups are seen as a focus of compulsive masculinity where boys reinforce one another's reaction formations (in Parsons and Bales 1955:116).

The gap between white mainstream and ghetto matrifocality thus appears to have narrowed down even more as far as the socialization experiences of boys are concerned. Yet the observers of matrifocal families cited above obviously consider this difference great enough for the boys involved to have particular problems in arriving at a satisfactory definition of their male identity. To give some opportunity for evaluating this view, we will take a look at the typical contexts of potential sex role socialization of ghetto boys from matrifocal families, starting by paying particular attention to that extreme case of matrifocality, the husbandless household.

*Socialization at home*

Several factors are obviously involved in determining what kind of sex role learning for young males goes on in the household. One of them is whether adult male role models are really as unavailable as they are presumed to be, although the father is absent. In previous chapters we have indicated that husbandless households need not be maleless—many of them have boarders, others include a mother's brother. In a great many cases, the boys' mothers have male friends who make regular visits; some households are not strictly husbandless in that the mother has a resident male friend, common-law husband or ordinary husband, who is not her children's father. Quite frequently, then, the adult male vacuum within the household is less than complete. It should be possible to some extent to use these men as role models, so that the boys can make some sense of what is "typically male" from their behavior. The question to what extent the boys really fashion their own behavior after these potential models cannot be conclusively answered here. As we have noted earlier, the relationship between these men and the children of the dominant woman (or women) in the household is not usually particularly close. (It may be added here too that in many cases the difference between such households and matrifocal families with a resident husband-father may not be great. In the household of Harry and Patricia Jones of Winston Street, the closest relationship is undoubtedly that of Patricia Jones and her teenage daughter. This is not at all balanced by Harry Jones' relationship to his sons, for as he readily admits, he seldom speaks to them except to ask them to run errands, keep quiet, or get out of his way. On the other hand, he is also quite attached to the teenage daughter, whom he often takes along when he goes for a car ride with a friend or when he goes bowling. The sons tend to turn to their mother or older sister for help or advice rather than to their father.) It may be that this relatively non-nurturant quality of the relationship of men to boys in matrifocal families makes it unlikely that it will be a basis for identification and role modeling, but there is also some evidence that in general, nurturance is not a necessary antecedent of imitative learning (cf. Bandura and Walters 1963:95). Other writers on identification, like Parsons (in Parsons and Bales 1955), have assumed that the person of power in the household is the major model for the children, everything else held equal. If this is valid for the ghetto matrifocal family, the mother may indeed be a more important model for the boys than any domestically peripheral male figure. Yet it should be noted here that the woman in a matrifocal household far from always is in a position of uncontested dominance over the adult males—husband, male friend, or brother in residence —and this could tend to blur her image of power for the children. In addition, we should remind ourselves that the degree of control a woman in a matrifocal household really has over members in the household oriented toward participation in street life is often quite limited. Thus even if there is no other adult in the household, the children may not become overawed by maternal powerfulness.

Burton and Whiting (1951) present another approach to the nature of identification in what they call the "status envy hypothesis", according to which identification consists of the covert practice, in fantasy or in play, of the role of an envied status. In a husbandless household, they see the mother as the person to be envied, as she controls the resources sometimes withheld from children—resources which are thus to be envied her. Burton and Whiting cite the studies of Miller and of Rohrer and Edmonson which were discussed above, and accepting the interpretations of compulsive masculinity in peer groups as made by these authors, they see this as evidence for the status envy hypothesis; obviously the boys must have overidentified with their mothers to arrive at such a strong reaction formation.

However, even here the evidence from ghetto matrifocality is not quite as clearcut as it may seem. Burton and Whiting point out that the Oedipal situation is only a special case of the status envy hypothesis, and if ghetto mothers have male friends on whom they spend some of their affection because they are, if nothing else, desirable company, then there is an Oedipal situation in which the boys' object of envy is another male—to be identified with according to the hypothesis. Again the necessity of identifying only with mother is not quite as obvious as it might have appeared at the outset.

Another issue which we will leave largely unresolved is whether the relatively asymmetrical character of a functioning father-son relationship, as in a mainstream American family, really provides the optimal conditions for a son to learn his male role. As the father assumes his leader and authority role, the son becomes assigned to a complementary dependent and submissive role. The central position of an adult male in the household could also conceivably lessen the boy's chance of practicing his male role by providing too stiff competition.[3] Yet it may be that we are introducing a red herring here. First of all, father-son relationships are not necessarily forced into a rigid mold of

121

dominance and submission; according to an early paper by Gregory Bateson (1942), there is a noticeable difference in this respect between English and American mainstream culture in that American children are encouraged by their parents toward independence and even a certain boastfulness. Furthermore, and at least as important, the child's imitation of the adult need not take place in the direct interaction with that adult. Rather, he may pick up the adult's behavior covertly in the process of role taking which goes on continuously in interaction, rehearse it to himself, and display it in quite different relationships. Even in a dominance-submission relationship can thus the submissive party learn to be dominant. Finally, as Parsons points out (in Parsons and Bales 1955:59), the socializing agent plays at least a dual role in relation to the socializee. In his direct relationship he may motivate the latter to take him for a model, but the modes of behavior he models may be taken out of quite different social contexts and relationships which the socializee may observe only as a non-participant or a participant not directly interacting with the model.

These points may lead us to doubt that the mainstream household is inferior to the matrifocal household as a male role socialization milieu as far as the influence of paternal presence is concerned. But neither can we state conclusively that the matrifocal household is devoid of potential role models, or that these potential models do not really function as such, even if circumstances are such that their modeling efficiency is probably not optimal.

Another major question is what kind of influence the mother (or any other adult woman in the household acting in some way like a mother) actually has on a boy. For one thing, there seems to be some danger here that those commentators who have most strongly drawn the attention toward the possibility of socialization into non-masculine behavior in a female-headed household have made too facile an inference from childrearing in female-headed households which are possibly quite different from those in the ghetto. Pettigrew, for instance, cites evidence from studies of white American boys whose fathers were absent from family life during World War II, and of Norwegian sailors' sons. These boys were reported as clearly more immature, submissive, dependent, and effeminate than other boys (Pettigrew 1964:18). But here the strong possibility must be noted that these boys had very different relationships to their mothers than many ghetto boys in matrifocal families have. A housewife with few children and relatively limited everyday contacts with other adults is likely to devote a great deal of time to nurturant interaction with the children, and her relationship to them is thus likely to become intensive and quite possibly overprotective. If the boys then turn out as described by Pettigrew there is little reason for surprise. Obviously there are instances of such mother-child relationships in the ghetto; the case of Roland described by Rohrer and Edmonson and cited above may well have been one of them. But those who worry about ghetto boys becoming more immature, submissive, dependent, and effeminate on account of mother's influence might have done well to give more heed to the comment on this topic in one of the pioneering anthropological studies of black Americans, Hortense Powdermaker's *After Freedom*. Writing of a Mississippi town, Powdermaker points out that the black mother in households where there is no father either works outside the home or is busy at home with her own work, thus having little spare time and energy to lavish on her children. Powdermaker also notes that the women have outside sexual contacts and thus do not make the children emotional substitutes for a mate (Powdermaker 1939:197).

The matrifocal households in the Winston Street neighborhood are in many ways like those described by Powdermaker. They often contain large numbers of children, and taking care of domestic chores for such large households—and with so limited resources—makes it rather difficult for the mother to engage actively in very intensive emotional relationships with the children. Furthermore, many of the mothers have—aside from possible male friends—female friends among relatives and neighbors with whom they tend to spend spare time. Thus the possibility that boys would continue to identify too strongly with the mother is somewhat weakened by the quality she gives—willingly or not—to her interaction with them.

Another facet of maternal influence on the identity of young males involves her actions in instructing them, knowingly or not, about masculinity. Cannot the mother, in her domestic behavior, get her distinction between her own sex category and that of her son across to him, and thereby contribute to having him choose other models? Of course she can, to some extent, and we have already in an earlier chapter noted that the ghetto-specific public imagery about sex roles tends to influence mothers in their behavior toward their children; for instance, they appear to prefer to have daughters, and they have other expectations for their sons' behavior than for that of their daughters. This is how one single mother of three boys and two girls expresses it:

"You know, you just got to act a little bit tougher with boys than with girls, 'cause they just ain't the same. Girls do what you tell them to do and don't get into no trouble, but you just can't be sure about boys. I mean, you think they're OK and next thing you find out they're playing hookey and drinking wine and maybe stealing things from cars and what not. There's just something bad about boys here, you know. But what can you say when many of them are just like their daddies? That's the man in them coming out. You can't really fight it, you know that's the way it is. They know, too. But you just got to be tougher."

So the women are tougher toward their sons, and they expect their sons to be tougher than their daughters. They feel this is as it should be; a boy who is not tough in his overt behavior may be ridiculed as a "sissy" not only by his peers but also by the women of his household, and his mother admonishes him to act like a boy.

This should not be taken to mean that women consciously and exclusively socialize their sons toward ghetto-specific masculinity. On the contrary, one may be quite certain that most of the instruction mothers are aware of giving is in line with mainstream norms. But even in the domestic context there is some ghetto-specific male role socialization because the women in the household—primarily the mother, but also a grandmother, an aunt, or sisters if they are present—have their behavior toward boys colored by the implicit or explicit notions of the typical characteristics of masculinity. As the socialization relationship in some ways comes to reflect the generalized relationship between men and women in the community, it is to a certain extent a question of an antagonistic socialization. The women are much more concerned to warn sons than daughters against drinking, stealing, staying away from school, and so

123

forth, as they perceive these as male activities; they warn both boys and girls against having too much to do with the other sex, but they make it perfectly clear that boys should refrain from initiatives, while girls need only be on guard against such initiatives. One may speculate that there is an element of self-fulfilling prophecy in such instruction, as the women thus make explicit to the boys what can be expected from a male. This suspicion would seem to have much less support if all mothers were quite consistently and unambiguously negative in their response when such behavior occurs. However, like their older counterparts, young ghetto males, correctly or not, seem rather often to perceive some ambivalence and contradictoriness in the views held by women concerning what males should be like. One may in fact occasionally discern an admiring undertone in complaints by mothers about their sons, just as in those by women about their male friends. One young man in his late teens, still living at home, made this comment about his mother:

"Sometimes my mother makes a big deal out of it when I have a taste and says I shouldn't drink and I'm turning into a bum and that kind of stuff, you know what I mean. And she acts real angry and says I shouldn't be running around so much, and one day I might get in trouble and all that stuff, you know. And then I hear her talking to all her old women friends about how I go out with all those girls and how I'm really going strong, and once she came and offered me a taste, big smile on her face you know, and then she said she found the bottle in my room a week ago! Shi-it, I'm sure I'm just the way she wants me to be. Women just want to make themselves look good, you know, so they keep fussing about you and showing off."

For an additional fragment of evidence that ghetto women's response to shows of ghetto-specific masculinity on the part of young males is not uniformly rejective one may turn again to ghetto entertainment; there is an enthusiastic reception from the female audience, adolescents and upwards, to youthful stage personalities showing such behavior. For instance, the child prodigy Little Dion—a song and dance boy—and the youngest member of the young rock-and-roll group Alvin Cash and the Registers, both sometime stars of that series of ghetto stages known as "the chitterling circuit", had a choreography with a heavy sexual load, entered into aggressive verbal contests with the emcees, and put on a *blasé* air about affairs with women, while the mothers in the audience rocked with laughter at this expression of masculinity.

There seems to be some indication, then, that ghetto mothers differentiate between the sexes in the socialization which goes on within the domestic domain; perhaps they do so more strongly than other mothers because the social cleavage between the sexes is so pronounced in the ghetto and is seen as a very fundamental social fact. This differentiated socialization can at least make it obvious to the boy that the mother is not an appropriate role model for him; to some extent it may, largely quite unintentionally, show the road to ghetto-specific masculinity. Rohrer and Edmonson note this (1964:161—162), but they attach little weight to it in their over-all view. Yet, all in all, the phenomena we have pointed to here may lead us to believe that the sex role vacuum for the socialization of males in the matrifocal family is considerably less than complete. This need not mean that a ghetto family of such a structure is just as efficient as the mainstream family in socializing males toward a culturally appropriate form of masculinity. But perhaps we may find it reasonable to doubt that the difference between them is as great as it is sometimes made out to be.

*Socialization in the street*

Anyway, these notes on what goes on in the matrifocal family as far as male role socialization is concerned are of somewhat marginal importance when compared to the point at which the absent-model view of male role development can be most strongly criticized. In an earlier chapter, we cited Bird-whistell's (1966) comment on what he called the "sentimental model" of family life; Birdwhistell pointed out that much thinking about the family, among social scientists as well as among the general public, is based on an idealized image which need not be a very accurate reflection of family life in reality. One of the characteristics of the "sentimental model" is that the family is depicted as relatively self-sufficient. It is implied that most of the members' psychological needs are met in interaction with other members.

Theoretical frameworks for socialization research seem often to be based on the unquestioned assumption that the "sentimental model" is a correct representation of reality—see for instance Kagan's review article (1964:145). This assumption may be reinforced by the strong influence that Freudian thinking has had on the study of family processes; it may be, of course, that this model was closer to real life in Freud's days, and in Freud's milieu, than it may be now, particularly in the ghetto community. According to the "sentimental model" it is natural that if the family does not socialize its boys to masculinity, nobody does. But as we have already pointed out, it is characteristic of many ghetto dwellers, in particular of that segment of the community where matrifocality occurs most frequently, that they participate intensively in the social life of the street, and they start to do so at an early age. And when young boys start taking part in street life, they are exposed to a great number of males, even if there is little by way of an adult male presence at home. As we have noted before, there is no lack of males in the ghetto community, although many of them are no more than loosely attached to any childrearing household. True, in seeing the behavior of their adult male neighbors, young boys get a number of potential role models who show great variability in behavior between themselves, as several life styles co-exist in the community. This may well contribute to variation, compromises, and drift in the boys' behavior. But the men showing ghetto-specific masculinity are in a majority among those who hang out at the street corner, in the alley, or at the carry-out. Thus there is a tendency for the boys to be more strongly exposed to this kind of masculinity than to any other as they start to spend much of their lives away from the household, in territory they share with these men. Again, of course, we come back to the question whether the interaction between the boys and the men is such that it will influence the boys significantly in ordering their behavior. Here we can only note that the men are at least no amorphous mass of anonymous individuals, seen once and then never again; many of them are known neighborhood residents whom the children see practically every day. The men are also familiar with the children. As we have said before, they often keep a watchful eye on the children's play; they tell the children not to play too close to the traffic, they serve as an audience for games, they break up a fight occasionally, and sometimes they give a little instruction for instance in boxing. Now and then they send a boy away on an errand to the store, for a nickel or a dime. Such interaction may lead the boys to experience these men as significant others and perhaps as role models. And in the context of the street corner, if nowhere else, these men—or some of them, at least—may have their share of power and success which might make them seem enviable persons.

## The company of peers

However, adult men are not the only role models ghetto boys may find in street life. The peer group is a highly influential phenomenon in the patterning of their existence, and its importance begins to be felt early in life. Mothers in ghetto families, both matrifocal and others, often have many children and much to do, so they frequently let older children take care of their younger siblings; particularly often, it seems, those of the same sex. This may mean that one older male whom a small boy may take as a role model is his older brother.[4] More generally, however, the boy is thus introduced at an early age to the all-male peer group. For other boys the link to such a group may be slightly more difficult to achieve so early, but even for them the initiation into the peer group context soon comes. Peer group life, of course, brings boys into contact with others of the same age, so that they can seek concerted solutions to common problems. However, the groups are not severely age graded; the members' ages span over a few years. Thus boys may participate both in groups where they are among the younger members and in groups where they are among the older, and a great many boys are in both positions at the same time, in relation to different groups.

In these groups, of course, there is intensive interaction between members. Much of the activity in the boys' groups may be viewed as "just ordinary children's play"—ball games, roller skating, and so forth. It is noticeable, however, that much of the behavior evinced in the peer group context is of the type we have described as ghetto-specific masculinity, typical of many adult men in the community. There is the concern with sex; already boys less than ten years old talk in the group context about "getting some pussy" (or "some leg" as boys in Washington started saying about 1967), and although there is undoubtedly the same kind of exaggeration in their claims of which one might suspect some of the older males, there is little question that many of the boys start sexual experimentation early, with the girls who form separate but somewhat more loosely knit groups parallel to those of the boys. Many boys also eagerly grasp for opportunities to taste liquor. A streetcorner man may let them have a little, but they may also manage to get it some other way, from somebody's house, from a parked car, or from some intoxicated streetcorner alcoholic who is in no shape to guard his belongings. There is fighting for fun or in all seriousness, and there are intensive involvements in verbal contests, as we shall discuss at greater length below. The interest in male clothing fashions is also there—this is the comment of a man in the Winston Street neighborhood on his young neighbors:

126

"These kids criticize your clothes even if their own clothes are the raggediest things you ever saw. Leroy kept talking about my shoes the other day, and there wasn't one thing right about them the way he carried on. And his own shoes hardly got soles underneath!"

The proponents of that view of male role socialization which emphasizes the lack of paternal role models at home interpret these masculine concerns in the peer group in a manner consistent with their over-all analysis, as we have already seen. Peer group formation is seen to be simply a response to the discovery that the identification with mother is all wrong; the boys get together to enhance their masculinity. According to the vocabulary in which this kind of interpretation is usually formulated, this is a reaction formation of compulsive masculinity. Rohrer's and Edmonson's delineation of the characteristics of peer group members were cited above; they couch it in such terms as "self-doubts", "insecurity", and "frightened and confused little boys". The peer group is seen as a "second-rate substitute" for family life.

There seems to be a certain weakness in this kind of view of peer group life, at least in its most clearcut form. First of all, one may wonder whether the "sentimental model" of the family is not rearing its head from below the surface of the analysis here. Is this model not a significant ideological underpinning for the judgment of the peer group's worth relative to that of the family? Despite the strength of the mainstream family model in the ghetto community, it is obvious that many of its male members, on the basis of their experience, turn the entire thing around and consider the family a poor substitute for the peer group as far as satisfactions are concerned. Furthermore, the interpretation exemplified by Rohrer and Edmonson seems to contain a fair amount of psychological reductionism in the explanation of the genesis of peer groups, and this reductionism may be open to some questioning. In this view of ghetto male behavior, it appears that the peer group is born again and again, like a Phoenix arising from those ashes of mother identification perhaps not completely burned to the end, out of a sheer psychological need for a place where masculinity can be celebrated. An alternative or at least complementary view of peer group functioning ought to be stated.

We may speculate that peer groups originally became an important component of the structure of the black community precisely because there was a need for them of this kind, and we can assume that they continue to meet such a need. It is very questionable, however, if it is an accurate representation of the continuity of the ghetto social structure to claim that peer groups emerge repeatedly independently of one another. As we pointed out above, small children are usually inducted into relationships with already existing groups of slightly older children, and there is constantly the idea of the peer groups as a natural context of children's life. Parents, neighbors, and older siblings contribute in making boys members of peer groups. The young males easily end up in these whatever are their families of origin and their psychological needs, and as ghetto-specific masculinity tends to be an idiom of interaction in the peer groups these serve as cultural equalizers for boys starting from different points and moving toward different goals. We have noted in an earlier chapter that generations of one family may show different life styles, and that peer groups may have an important influence in causing such changes; but even if boys later move toward mainstreamer lives, a great many of them have established some competence in ghetto-specific masculinity during their period of more intensive peer group participation. This may be helpful even for a mainstreamer member of the ghetto community, for instance in interaction with streetcorner men.

The craving for an arena for masculinity need thus not be *the* motive for entering into the first stage of that series of age graded groups which always exists in the ghetto. Any thoroughgoing psychological reductionism in accounting for the existence of male peer groups is, if not unfounded, at least too one-sided.

At this point one may also ask whether some of the psychological characterizations of peer group members are not couched in too strong terms in order to make them fit with the rest of the interpretation. The fact that children of large ghetto families are left to take care of their own entertainment, or in the company of an older sibling rather than in that of the mother, seems to constitute an independence training, intended or not, which seems quite successful in the case of most children in the Winston Street neighborhood. (It was an early impression in field work that the small children's way of life reminded one of the *Peanuts* comic strip. Later it was realized that this was probably because most of them seemed very independent and self-confident, and handled their interaction without much of the parental mediation which has a relatively large place in small middle-class white children's play.) Thus is seems hard to vouch for the general applicability of a description of small ghetto boys as "frightened" and "confused."

The other view of how boys come to participate in peer groups, as stated above, does not explain the intensity of masculine expression, as does the reaction formation view. It is necessary, therefore, to interpret this in some other way. The most obvious explanation is again that of role modeling. The older members of a peer group tend to be somewhat dominant to the younger ones, and it is thus likely that the older ones are perceived as role models; but at the same time these older boys participate as junior partners in relationship to boys older than them. It is likely, therefore, that adult concepts of masculinity are continuously trickling down through the age grades through a series of role model relationships where the boy who is the socializee in one relationship is the model in the next. At the same time, of course, there is the direct influence of adult role models.

We may also note that peer groups may take up the masculine theme and elaborate on it in their own way because their members can easily perceive that public imagery is preoccupied with the differences and the relationships between the sexes. There is probably a less significant discontinuity between childhood and adulthood in this regard in the ghetto than there is in mainstream society. While mainstream children are often somehow "protected" from knowledge of adult interest in matters of sex, ghetto children easily learn a great deal about this topic by listening to adult conversations. Even if the adults try to avoid this, the lack of privacy in ghetto homes makes it difficult to shield the children both from overhearing such exchanges and from witnessing sexual behavior of one type or another. Besides, ghetto children are intensively exposed to the broadcasts of black radio stations, blaring continuously in many households and often out on the sidewalks as well—one index of this exposure is that they often know the texts of the top tunes word for word. The rock-and-roll tunes as well as the disc jockeys' talk are primarily aimed at adults and older teenagers and have some rather obvious sexual content. In this way, too, the younger boys may learn their concern with masculinity and sex from age groups above them. Borrowing a concept from Cloward and Ohlin (1960), we may say that the ghetto community provides a relatively open learning structure for the ghetto-specific male role.

### Rituals of obscenity

We pointed out above that verbal contests occur among young males as well as among their adult counterparts. Here we will halt for a while to consider one of the forms these contests take, both because in its elaborateness it provides a conspicuous example of ghetto-specific culture and because it is of interest in illuminating our two alternative perspectives toward ghetto male role socialization. This is the phenomenon which has become most known as "the dozens", but it is also known as "sounding" and under some other local names. The term most often used in Washington, D.C., is "joning", which we will therefore use here.

Joning is an exchange of insults. It has been described earlier at some length by Dollard (1939) and Abrahams (1962); since the latter also includes a representative collection of the kind of statements involved, we need only give a few examples here, from the repertoire of boys in the Winston Street neighborhood. The boundaries of the concept are a little fuzzy; there is some tendency to view as joning any exchange of insults of a more or less jocular type in sociable interaction among children and adolescents. Joning is definitely closely associated with joking. For most smaller boys it seems to shade imperceptibly into the category of "cracking jokes", and when joning occurs in a peer group sociable session it is often preceded or followed by other kinds of jokes. These are also often exchanged in a manner resembling a contest, and some of them have a form and content somewhat similar to jones, as for instance these two show:

*Batman was flying in the air*
*when he lost his underwear*
*Batman said, I don't care*
*Robin, bring me another pair!*

— *What do you do when a girl ask you for something?*
— *?*
— *You tell her to lie down and then you give it to her!*

The type of joning which may be taken as the most central referent of the term, however, consists of disparaging statements about the opponent's family, most often its female members and particularly frequently the mother. Some of the statements are simple one-liners, such as the following:

*Your mother play baseball for the U.S. Navy*
*Your mother smoke a pipe*

129

*Anybody can get pussy from your mother*
*Your mother a prostitute*
*Your mother ate a cockroach sandwich with mayonnaise on it*
*Your sister live in a alley*
*Your sister a bulldagger*
*Your sister name Crazy leg Sally*

However, there are also quite elaborate rhymed jones such as the following:

*I fucked your mother on top of a wall*
*that woman had pussy like a basketball*

*I fucked your mother from house to house*
*she thought my dick was Mighty Mouse*

*I fucked your mother from tree to tree*
*The tree split*
*and she shit*
*I didn't get nothing but a little bit*

*I fucked your mother on a car*
*she said, Tim—you're going too far!*

*I fucked your mother in a Jeep*
*she said, Kenny—you're going too deep!*

*I fucked your mother on a red heater*
*I missed her pussy and burned my peter*

Quite similar in content to such jones are certain songs occasionally sung in the peer group context—either by a single boy or in unison—of which the following two may be regarded as representative. The first is quite short:

*Your mama ain't pretty*
*she got meatballs for her titties*
*she got scrambled eggs*
*between her legs*

The other song, like a few others, has many verses:

*A ha ha baby I know*
*you get'em from the peanut man*
*Ye Ye Ye Ye*
*ha ha baby I know*
*you get'em anywhere you can*

*See that girl*
*aha*

*in the pink*
*aha*
*I betcha five dollars your mother stink*
*A ha ha baby I know* . . .
(refrain repeated)

*See that man*
*aha*
*in the blue*
*aha*
*I betcha five dollars your mother sleep in a shoe*
*A ha ha baby I know* . . .
(refrain repeated)

*See that man*
*aha*
*in the white*
*aha*
*I betcha five dollars your mother smoke a pipe*
*A ha ha baby I know* . . .
(refrain repeated)

*See that man*
*aha*
*in the black*
*aha*
*I betcha five dollars your mother live in a shack*
*A ha ha baby I know* . . .
(refrain repeated)

*See that girl*
*aha*
*dressed in white*
*aha*
*I betcha five dollars your mother ride in a Cadillac*
*A ha ha baby I know* . . .
(refrain repeated)

*See that girl*
*aha*
*in the red*
*aha*
*I betcha five dollars your mother pee in bed*
*A ha ha baby I know* . . .
(refrain repeated)

*See that boy*
*aha*

*all in gray*
*aha*
*I betcha five dollars your mother sleep in the hay*
*A ha ha baby I know . . .*
(refrain repeated)

The latter song obviously allows for some variability in performance. One does not always run through the whole list of colors, and the colors are not always matched with the same persons—boy, girl, man, or woman. Sometimes there are mismatches; in the version transcribed above, "Cadillac" should probably rhyme with "black" rather than with "white". This also means that there are alternative rhymes for some colors, as "black" had already been rhymed with "shack".

These songs are noted here rather parenthetically, as another expressive form containing the themes encountered in joning. As far as the content of the regular jones is concerned, it is all more or less humiliating, in one way or other, to the person mentioned. Particularly the elaborate rhymed kind involves sex; jones are generally seen in the ghetto community as obscene, "nasty", and some boys are obviously too inhibited to become adept at joning. The rhymes are frequently of a rather nonsensical kind—rhyming takes precedence to making absolute sense—but are not always quite exact, although at least in some of these cases they may be understood to be exact in the ghetto dialect. The performer who claims to have had intercourse with his opponent's mother often depicts himself more or less as a sexual athlete, by indulging in sex in odd settings if in no other way. What is perhaps the most conspicuous feature of these jones, however, is that the mother involved—or sometimes the sister—is usually seen to be guilty of some kind of moral deviation from her idealized woman's role, and the deviation is of either of the two kinds often imputed to females in the public imagery of ghetto males, as described in a preceding chapter. She is not as "good" as she ought to be, in that she engages in sex with quite inappropriate partners, or she has taken over too much of the male sex role—smoking a pipe or playing baseball for the U.S. Navy, for instance. (Probably riding a Cadillac is also too masculine for a woman; there hardly seems to be anything else wrong with it from a ghetto dweller's point of view.) Other themes of joning are degradation (the cockroach sandwich) and ugliness (the sister named Crazy leg Sally); occasionally a jone appears to have more than one level of meaning, but one cannot at all be sure that the boys are aware of this.[5]

The practice of joning is quite prevalent among young ghetto dwellers, although not much talked about since it is considered "nasty".[6] There are many girls who are skilled at joning, but it is in particular a phenomenon of boys' peer group life. Men who can be made to reminisce about it usually say they were most involved in it when they were in junior high school, that is, in early adolescence. However, some of the boys in the Winston Street neighborhood who are best at joning are several years younger, but intensively engaged in peer group life. The exchanges can occur between two boys who are alone, and it is even possible for them to jone on some third absent person, usually one of their peers, but the typical situation involves a group of boys; while a series of exchanges may engage one pair of boys after another, most members of the crowd function as audience, inciters, and judges—laughing, commenting on the "scoring", and urging the participants on:

*He's talking about YOUR mother so bad*
*he's making ME mad*

Usually the joning just stops after a while, as the participants' repertoire has been used up, as no good new ideas about insults seem to be forthcoming, or as the contestants simply get tired of it. The boys in the Winston Street neighborhood appear to have rather similar repertoires (although some know more jones than others) which indicates that a great many of especially the more elaborate obscene rhymes have become traditional cultural artifacts. (However, if collected on a nation-wide basis, their number may turn out to be very large; none of those rhymed jones quoted above as examples is identical to anyone of those offered by Abrahams (1962), although the third represents only a minor variation from one of his, and the fifth and the sixth have a recurrent theme which can be found also in Abrahams' collection). This may explain why joners themselves are sometimes not sure of the meaning of the jones.

There are times when joning is transformed into fighting, but this happens relatively seldom. It should be added, too, that this is often only playful wrestling, only a slight escalation of the non-serious activity of joning. For after all, it is all a game. The insults are generally stereotyped, and there is relatively seldom any need for a boy to get very personally upset; some informants claim, however, that a boy whose mother is dead might get in an angry mood if someone should jone on her. All in all, it would seem that the boys' own interpretation of how an insult should be taken depends much on the social relationship within which it is uttered. An enemy who jones on you becomes a little more of an enemy, as your resentment grows, but a friend who is joning is a friend you are playing a game with.

As the boys become men they gradually cease to amuse themselves with joning. Although verbal aggression continues, it becomes less patterned; the insults contain hardly any references to mothers any more, and if a man, often by chance rather than intentionally, should say anything which could be construed as an abuse of another's mother, the latter might simply say, "I don't play that game no more."[7]

The question now emerges, how are we to understand joning in terms of either role modeling or masculine reaction formation? It is clear in this case that the boys are not modeling themselves closely on the pattern of adult males, as the latter have stopped rhyming about their mothers. Early adolescence, we have said, is the high point of joning. Role modeling can exist in this instance only in the sense that the boys have time to pick up their skills from slightly older boys, before these start getting out of practice. But the reason for the involvement with joning at this age cannot be just "reaching for the adult role", pure and simple—at least the locus of joning in this age grade must be accounted for in some other way.

On the other hand there appears to be a rather nice fit with the thesis of reaction formation. The boys have supposedly just found out that they have identified with the wrong person, the mother. Now they must do their utmost

133

to ridicule her and thus convince everybody and themselves—but particularly themselves—of their masculinity and independence. (Only since they are not yet daring enough to attack their own mothers, they attack somebody else's instead, thus setting the stage for him to go to work on their own.) Rohrer and Edmonson draw an analogy between joning—which they term "the dozens" but give only brief mention—and brainwashing (1964: 162), and Abrahams (1962) also makes a bow in the direction of seeing joning as a way of dealing with an unsatisfactory sense of sex identity.[8] By indulging in joning, the boys fashion for themselves a collective ritual cleansing in which they point out each other's weaknesses, so that they can finally all emerge as better males.

Again, we need not reject such a view altogether in order to suggest another perspective which is again more closely connected with the emphasis on role modeling. The reaction formation view seems to see joning as primarily a backward-looking ritual—in order to arrive at a "normal" male identity, the boys have to purge themselves of mistakes made in early childhood. One may consider the other possibility that the boys are looking forward, and seeing a community with a major social division between males and females whose relationships to each other are often characterized by conflicts and ambivalence. Up to the point of adolescence, their closest relationships to females have been to those at home, above all to the mother but also to sisters and possibly to others. These relationships, whatever they are like, are not relationships between potential sexual partners; however, that is the kind of relationship the boys envisage for themselves in the future, and which is at the basis of the generalized male-female relationship and the public imagery pertaining to it in the community. It is also at about this age that boys start using epithets such as "bitch", "gypsy", and "whore" in referring to females. It may not be an altogether improbable interpretation of joning, then, to see it as a rite of passage whereby boys train themselves for the particular adult relationship between the sexes which exists in the ghetto community, not only as one whereby they unlearn peculiarities picked up in matrifocality. As far as the relationship to the mother is concerned, we may add that she is also aware that her son is moving into the adult male category, and this contributes to making the mother-son relationship more tense than it has been at earlier points. This may well be another reason for boys to express hostility in joning. Perhaps one could express this in terms of identification and reaction formation, but there may be a danger of exaggerating the case if one does so.

Adolescence, then, may be an age in which male role socialization becomes intensified because the initiation into the final adult role is imminent, and this is why a particular cultural complex such as joning is stored in this transitional age grade. Making mothers and, to a lesser extent, other close female kin the topic of joning could thus serve the purpose of driving home the point that to a man, all women are alike in their characteristics. Of course, by claiming to be the sexual partner of a peer's mother or older sister, a boy also states a claim of more or less mature status while at the same time putting down his opponent who must then strive to come back to at least equality by answering in kind. At the same time, of course, joning may be seen as an attack on the collective family honor—not necessarily only that of the mother —which no real male can let pass.

Clearly the view sketched here and the reaction formation perspective toward joning are not mutually exclusive. However, we may now feel less sure that problems with the male identity arising out of matrifocality constitute the only reason why ghetto boys should indulge in joning. Another problem with such an explanation arises out of the fact that some girls take part in joning exchanges, as noted above, often in interaction with boys; the girls are not likely to have the problems with the male identity that boys have. Obviously this form of cultural expression has simply diffused to the girls. But if there can be such a diffusion process between the sexes, why not within the male sex? It is much more likely, of course, that boys who participate in the same peer groups should take on joning as an interaction idiom although they have no matrifocality problems, than that girls, interacting much less with boys in such contexts, should do so. Thus it is likely that although some of the boys who jone may have sex identity problems, others take part in the ritual simply because it is part of peer group culture, to be mastered if personal success in the group is to be ensured. (Unless, of course, they are motivated to jone by their perspective of the future.) Among the boys in the Winston Street neighborhood, some of the boys who are good at joning are not from husbandless households, or even from two-parent households dominated by the mother. On the other hand, they have central positions in their peer groups. This would indicate that household structure and peer group participation are variables relatively independent of one another, and that possibly the latter is at least as important as the former for a boy's involvement and skill in joning.

## The alternatives in review

This chapter has been openly partisan in order to point out what looks like weak points in a well-known view of the process of growing up male in the ghetto. We would not serve this purpose well by denying or passing over points in favor of that argument altogether; it should be noted, therefore, that many of the streetcorner men out of matrifocal families of orientation have a strong attachment to their mothers, although the relationship is not free from conflicts. Fats, unemployed, a heavy drinker, and a streetcorner strongman, claims he is a Muslim and is in constant conflict with his mother who is an old-fashioned Baptist. Yet he leaves the rent for his apartment for her to keep for him over the weekend before he goes out on Friday night; "So I can't take from it," he explains with a slightly embarrassed smile. Another Friday evening, the two Preston brothers were fighting and threatening each other, in the family's house and all the way down Winston Street. The neighbors explained it in terms of their mother's illness: "They never got along good, but they're very upset now 'cause their mother is in the hospital, and so they just break down you see." Both brothers are close to sixty years old and alcoholics. One may note, also, that when a marriage breaks up, it is often the man who moves home to mother; and many streetcorner men readily condemn their fathers who left their mothers alone, although they have behaved similarly themselves. Finally, we may observe with Abrahams (1964:261—262) that the word "motherfucker" and its derivatives are used in a curiously ambivalent way, sometimes in statements of admiration and at other times in a thoroughly pejorative sense.

In this context it should also be pointed out that there are expressions of a kind of fascination with sexual deviation. "Faggot" is in frequent use as a term of abuse among men, "sissy" and "punk" (with a less clear reference to homosexuality) more often among boys. The "Jewel Box Revue", a transvestite show, travels regularly on the chitterling circuit, including appearances at the Howard Theatre. Thus it can hardly be denied that there is an apparent concern with sex role problems in the ghetto.

It is questionable, however, whether they can all be laid at the door of matrifocality. It would seem rather likely that sex role deviations, and a concern with such deviations, could occur rather frequently in a community where ambivalent and conflict-ridden relationships between the sexes are understood to be prevalent, where one of the alternative male roles is difficult to live up to because of severe macrostructural constraints, and the other alternative is as personally demanding as the ghetto-specific role may be to some. If there is anything in the guess that such factors may also be at work, the influence of matrifocality may have been overestimated even in the shaping of those sexual deviations which ghetto dwellers themselves recognize.

The major goal of this chapter, however, is not to pose an alternative explanation of a "pathology", but to throw in doubt the existence of much of it. Fot it seems that the thesis which has been criticized throughout this chapter is one which constantly views the ghetto-specific male role as a kind of psychopathology; because the matrifocal family does not conform to the mainstream model and because the ghetto-specific male role does not either, one "deviation" is said to cause the other by way of first a lack of role models, then a compulsive masculine reaction continuing into adulthood. To reach this result one employs a framework of interpretation loaded with mainstream assumptions, about what a man should be like—a mainstream male, of course—and about the kind of relationship which sex role socialization needs if it is to occur—the father-son relationship, of course. In both cases, it seems likely that the normative bias makes the scheme of interpretation unfair to a community with a different social organization and different cultural norms. To a considerable extent, it seems to be a spurious claim that ghetto boys have no role models, and it seems quite possible that the ghetto-specific male role recurs in generation after generation in the manner sex roles are usually transmitted, through role modeling and in other ways. In the interpretive scheme of sex role confusion and compulsive male reaction formation, little or nothing is said about the ghetto-specific male role as a cultural entity in its own right, because adult males are largely absent from the picture until they appear as grown boys, embattled "mama's men"—the imagery here seems to have the child as the father of the man, as reaction formation seems to carry on into infinity. The existence of a ghetto-specific male pattern of behavior seems to be only a recurrent accident caused by matrifocality.

The alternative perspective set forth here and foreshadowed in preceding chapter holds that the ghetto-specific male role is dependent on macrostructural factors not just because these make males disappear from the arena where they should be role models, but because these factors have forced ghetto men to redefine their sex role in a ghetto-specific way. After this role has been defined in accordance with circumstances, however, the man may well be the father of the child, in a socializing sense—that is, the role modeling process is at work.

The criticisms made in this chapter may well have been shaped by the typical predilections of a social anthropologist, vaguely uneasy with a more complex use of psychological arguments in explaining social forms while at the same time ready to challenge any point of view which takes cultural invariance for granted and which assumes that a certain function, such as role modeling, can only be vested in a particular structure, such as the nuclear family. Obviously the ghetto is not the most clearcut possible example of cultural difference; the picture is complicated by the fact that the community has so little autonomy but is under pressure to idealize a set of cultural norms to which many of its members can hardly conform. Thus ghetto boys, according to this social anthropological perspective, are socialized not only into their ghetto-specific sex role—rather, they are biculturated.[9] At home and in school, and through diverse mass media, they are instructed in mainstream culture, with its attendant proper behavior for boys. There are also the ghetto's own mainstreamers who acquaint the boys with this cultural alternative by their sheer presence, and furthermore there is some personal contact with the surrounding society.[10] Yet this involvement with mainstream culture on the part of ghetto dwellers provides no excuse for ignoring the facts of life peculiar to the ghetto, or taking such a narrow view of which of them are relevant that possibly significant social and cultural relationships are left out. If the kind of argument about male growth which has been questioned here is carried too far, it lends itself to facile judgments about "solving the masculinity crisis" which are more than a little bizarre. It may be claimed, for instance, that since the father is not around, the model vacuum can be filled with male school teachers and social workers.[11] Whether ghetto boys would really be given to modeling themselves on the representatives of these two categories seems highly uncertain, and one may wonder why they should be able to beat all other men outside the family out of the competition. But it may well be that the commentators who suggest such solutions see in the mainstream manner of man not just the only proper model, but also the only possible model—persons differing from it are seen as "confused", and thus nobody would bother to take them as models.

The lack of awareness of the possibility of ghetto-specific culture can also be seen in attempts to measure the "femininity" of ghetto males with far from culture-free psychological instruments, according to which it is feminine to agree with such statements as "I think that I feel more intensely than most people do" and "I would like to be a singer" (cited by Pettigrew 1964:19). The first index ignores the fact that black people have simply had a great deal to feel intensely about, something they now identify quite consciously in their self-conception, as embodied in the vocabulary of "soul" (see chapter 7). The other takes no note of the general great concern with music in the black community, nor of the fact that singing is generally recognized as a road to success, more open to a black man than are many others.

There is no need to claim that all interpretations of ghetto masculinity in terms of misidentification with mother, followed by compulsive masculinity, are so culturally naive. As we have pointed out above, facts remain which favor such an interpretation. We must also be aware that boys from matrifocal families may have quite different experiences, and that individuals may evince the same behavior and participate in the same institutions for quite different reasons. It may well be that neither the thesis criticized here nor the one outlined as an alternative can alone provide an understanding of how ghetto boys become ghetto men; they, and perhaps other interpretations as well, may be needed as complementary perspectives rather than as alternatives.[12] But even so—or perhaps particularly in such a case—it is necessary to point out exactly how far one single mode of interpretation may go, and what are its weaknesses. This is particularly necessary when the correctness and completeness of one of them become taken for granted, and when there is a tendency to pursue it to extreme and untenable positions, as seems to have happened in this case.

# 7
# Things in Common

All communities are in some ways differentiated and in others undifferentiated. In preceding chapters we have seen how the people of the ghetto are ordered along lines of age and sex, in terms of peer group and family alignments, according to their economic relationships to the wider society, and on the basis of variations in life styles which to some extent accompany these other variables. On the other hand, there are things ghetto dwellers tend to have in common—things we will look at here as a shared perspective toward the ghetto condition.

Not all ghetto dwellers are equally involved with this perspective, since their individual experiences and concerns differ. We have seen that ghetto-specific circumstances and modes of behavior are unevenly distributed among the population of the community. Yet it is hardly possible for anybody to remain unaware of what is "typical" of the ghetto and how its people define their experiences. A mainstreamer has neighbors, relatives, and perhaps friends in other ghetto life styles, and his own past may have involved him more directly with facts of life unique to the ghetto than his current way of life lets on; in an earlier chapter we dwelt on how ghetto dwellers move between life styles. All members of the community will thus in one way or another, and to one degree or another, come to witness the same things. Furthermore, they are aware of the fact that they have these shared experiences. They communicate about them and thereby influence one another's views. We have already noted how such cultural construction and maintenance goes on in the area of sex roles. A set of conventional understandings of ghetto life is developed, and it is generally recognized to be the property of the entire community. This alone gives the ghetto dwellers a kind of Durkheimian mechanical solidarity.[1] Since they realize that their common perspective is not shared with the world outside their community, it also marks them off from the surrounding society in their self-definition. This contributes to making the ghetto in some ways a united community. If it does not have overarching institutions of control which are its own, at least it has an overarching perspective.[2]

## Bootlegging and the community

The ghetto institution of bootlegging provides a simple example of how the members of the community tend to arrive at a shared view which both unites them and marks the contrast to the outside world. We have seen before that bootleggers are community members who function in the neighborhoods where they live and whose life styles vary. Potential customers thus get to know the bootleggers as neighbors and more or less as "whole persons"—they are not as likely as people outside the community to form a stereotype of the "typical bootlegger" as some kind of despicable character, even though their own sense of respectability may prohibit them from engaging in such illegal enterprise themselves. For a while when the major bootlegger in the Winston Street neighborhood went out of business a lot of people started dabbling in the trade, and one streetcorner man commented that it was indeed in a sorry state when even the lesbian alcoholic hanging out with his group could be found at the corner with a half pint of gin in a paper bag, ready for a sale; but more often the bootlegger is a long-time resident of the neighborhood who runs the business from his home. (We use masculine pronouns here to refer to the bootlegger, but there are a number of housewives in the trade as well.) Thus the bootlegger is as stable a neighborhood institution as the streetcorner grocery.[3] Since he cannot compete pricewise with legitimate liquor dealers but is open for business only when these are closed—in Washington, D.C., weekday nights after nine, but above all on Sundays—he caters only to immediate needs. Many of the customers are streetcorner men who have taken up a collection or done some successful panhandling and who are unlikely to have liquor acquired during legal sales hours standing around for later consumption. But others, including mainstreamers, are also among the customers, for much of the sociable drinking takes place as people go on spontaneous visits to each other, and these visits quite frequently occur during hours when liquor stores are closed. Few ghetto dwellers regularly have a supply of liquor at home for such unexpected gatherings, and nobody feels that a host has an obligation to supply refreshments. Instead, the guests pool their money with his so that he can go to the neighborhood bootlegger—it may be noted that although this brings a higher shared cost for the liquor, it is more advantageous to both host and guests than it would be for one of them to take on the entire cost alone by stocking up at a legitimate liquor store in advance. This means that ghetto dwellers are fairly united in viewing bootlegging as a convenient institution. Yet they are aware that while they find it both useful and morally acceptable, the wider society generally condemns it and tries to put an end to it. For fear of plainclothes detectives, many bootleggers refuse to deal with customers they do not know personally or have not been introduced to by a trustworthy person—such a suspiciousness, of course, is only possible in a business where relationships to the regular patrons are close. For such reasons, a neighborhood, and the community in general, is fairly protective of its bootleggers. Anybody who spends enough time in a neighborhood would be able to spot which household does business on Sunday, as the customers' comings and goings can hardly be hidden, but if they are aware that their actions could reveal the identity of a bootlegger to outsiders, most ghetto dwellers would attempt to be loyal to him, and thus in a sense to the community. Even storefront church preachers, forever railing against the evils of drinking, seem usually to prefer not to report bootleggers in their neighborhoods, even when there can be no doubt that they are personally against the practice.

*The concern with numbers*

In a minor way, then, the common perspective toward bootlegging may make ghetto dwellers aware of their unity by setting them off against the official

view of the practice held by the outside world.[4] Another illegal ghetto institution, the numbers game, promotes such unity even more intensively; there is
the same suspiciousness and protectiveness (although numbers agents seem to
suffer less from interventions from the agents of law than bootleggers do), the
same feeling that nothing very objectionable is really involved, but also an
additional factor in that it provides a topic for talk which readily brings
members of different segments of the community into interaction. When the
winning number of the day is spread informally by word of mouth along the
streets throughout the ghetto, the mainstreamer housewife who is irritated at
the wineheads lounging on her front steps may still find out the number from
them and exchange a few comments on it. The game is a concern above
segmental conflicts.

The origin of the numbers game is obscure; it has been claimed that is was
brought to the United States and introduced into the black community by
Cuban immigrants at the beginning of the century, but there actually seem
to have been several games of a similar kind from the late nineteenth century
and on.[5] The traditions surrounding the game in any particular black ghetto
today are likely to draw on a number of these games as they have existed at
different times and in different places. The current version in Washington,
D.C., derives "the number", a three-digit figure, in a rather complex manner
(with which ghetto dwellers are usually no more than faintly familiar) from
the payoff figures of certain daily horse races. "Numbers" is thus a game of
chance. As the digits become known one by one, the last one becomes known
in the ghetto late in the afternoon. One may bet one's money on one, two, or
all three of them. It is easier to get a hit with a single digit, of course, but one
cannot expect to get a big one. The three-digit hit can involve a large sum
of money, but the conditions are rather unfavorable. One's chance of hitting
is one in a thousand, but the payoff is only six hundred to one or less, minus
handling charge, thus leaving a handsome profit to those who run the game.
"Numbers" has a rather complex business hierarchy; in Washington, D.C., its
higher echelons are reputedly dominated by whites, as in most other large
cities. The customers in the ghetto have no personal contact with these numbers
bankers. The agents who deal directly with them are usually ghetto dwellers
themselves. Many of these numbers runners are known to be available at
certain hours at given places, such as at certain street corners or bars. However,
there are also many agents, often women, who take up bets at home, so that
the players in the neighborhood can seek them out there. Thus numbers, at
least on the lowest level of the organization, may be a neighborhood institution
much like the bootlegger.

The bets can be very small. Ten-cent bets are fairly common, but many are
considerably larger. However, the agent may be reluctant to accept too large a
bet. It also happens that a certain number becomes very popular, so that a hit
on that number would cause the bankers a serious loss. To prevent this, the
agent may declare that the number has to be "cut"—this would bring down
the payoff on a hit yet further.

To explain why any one number would be more popular than another, one
must note the ways in which ghetto dwellers decide what number to play.
Sometimes it is a question of idiosyncratic attachments. Somebody born on
March 3 may play 303, others try the street number of the building they are

in or their apartment number. One young man says that for the last week he has played the apartment number of a girl he has been dreaming about. But there are also other ways of finding a number which could make many people choose the same. Many stores in the ghetto sell "dream books", in which authorities on the occult science of numerology give advise on lucky numbers; many of the "readers", "spiritualists", and "psychic advisors" who offer ghetto dwellers their services on such problems as love, sickness, and magic also serve as experts on numbers.[6] Furthermore, there is some oral tradition on the meaning of numbers derived from numerology. Paul Oliver, in *Screening the Blues* (1968:128—147), has shown that many old blues text contain references to such numbers. However, it does not seem that today's numbers players, in Washington, D.C., at least, are usually very strongly influenced by such traditions or even very knowledgeable about them. Rather, if factors outside their personal lives influence what numbers they choose to play, they may involve considerations of what numbers had hits on the same day in previous years, or significant current events. According to a story circulating in the Washington ghetto, a lot of people in Harlem had noted the birth weight when president Johnson's daughter Luci gave birth to a son, and the number they derived from it had a hit. This caused severe strain on the numbers bankers who apparently had not had the number cut so as to bring down the payoff sufficiently.

Such lore provides a topic of conversation in which ghetto dwellers have a shared interest—everybody is familiar with the game, and most adults are either playing it or have done so in the past. There are also stories about spectacular hits, such as this one:

"I heard about a man in Baltimore, he was a hustler, so he already had a Fleetwood (Cadillac) and a ring with a stone as big as this bottle-cap here. And then he hit it for $100.000! And he got it all, too, 'cause the banker didn't take the whole thing himself, it was too much, you know, so he had other bankers share the risk, and that way they could pay."

In addition, one can exchange reminiscences about one's own hits—at least if one plays "single action", that is, one digit, one can get small hits easily enough—and those of acquaintances, about what one did with the money, about near misses, as when one was only one digit off or when one did not play a winning number one had thought of or had been playing before, and so forth. And when in a neighborhood such as that around Winston Street somebody has a big hit, a lot of people take an intensive interest in it, both because of a sense of excitement in general and because it may touch on their lives too, as these notes show:

There were an unusual number of people standing around on Winston Street for a late dusky winter afternoon, but anyone who had been in the neighborhood the previous evening would know what it was all about. Elijah Williamson had had a big hit—it was estimated that he should get about fourteen hundred dollars. There was a complication in this case, however: Elijah, drifting around from household to household and between different women, had been living lately with the woman who took numbers around the corner, and since he had no job but ate and drank on her money, he had been rather expensive for her. Thus she felt that a part of his big hit rightly belonged to her, and there had been repeated arguments about this throughout the day. This had delayed the payment which is otherwise usually made around noon. Thus as darkness arrived, Elijah Williamson still had not appeared with his money.

Bee Jay and Annie Patterson were standing outside the Patterson house. "He'd better be around soon", Bee Jay said. "I need a drink so bad."

A little further down the street, Annie Patterson's husband Richard sat with a couple of friends in a removal truck, watching the street and swapping numbers stories as well as other anecdotes. A few younger men passed them by and asked, "You ain't seen him yet?"

In Carl Jones' house, Carl, Sylvester, Sonny, and Randy had been playing cards all day, pinochles most of the time, watching the street through the window and waiting for Elijah Williamson to emerge. Although they were not usually very close to him, they were very interested in his hit. When he finally passed by, they stopped playing and left the house to catch up with him. In the meantime, Elijah reached Annie Patterson and Bee Jay and dug into his pocket for some money so that they could get a drink. He brought out a handful of assorted bills but refused to tell them how much he had finally received. Later, as people started talking about how much he seemed to have, most estimates were between five hundred and seven hundred dollars, although some felt there was more. Annie Patterson got a few one dollar bills, handed out with a nonchalant gesture. A boy passed by slowly on his bike and called out, "Mr. Williamson, could I have some?"

Elijah Williamson continued his walk, now accompanied by Sonny and Carl. They talked excitedly for a while outside the grocery at the street corner, then turned back to go to the house of the numbers agent. She had agreed to give him some of the money, but at the same time she had told Elijah to get out of her house, so he had left his belongings in a suitcase outside the door. The three men now went to get it. Then they walked up the street again, but Carl had to return home as he had promised his wife to babysit. Sylvester joined him, while Sonny went with Elijah Williamson, saying that he would help him to the bus station. Elijah was going to a sister in Philadelphia whom he had not seen for a long time. This was obviously the time for a trip; it would also let things calm down in the neighborhood, so everybody would not be asking him for money.

As the two passed by the grocery again, they met two other men who were hanging out there as usual. After a quick conversation they got two dollars. One of them shook his head as Elijah and Sonny walked on. "Someone gonna follow him and pick up all that money." One of the younger mainstreamer men in the neighborhood came out of the store and said to the two, "You all still figuring on how to spend Elijah's money?" They all laughed, and the two men remaining outside the store wondered whether Elijah would really get to Philadelphia. After a while they got started on a medley of Supremes hits, tapping the sidewalk with their feet and shuddering a little in the cold air.

I went back to Carl's house where Sylvester and Carl were also talking about what Elijah and Sonny might be doing. Since they recognized that Sonny could really be a very persuasive person, they figured that he was probably helping Elijah to spend some money on drinks before moving on to the bus station. So they thought they could as well enjoy a little more of the action. Hoping that Carl's wife would not return before we were back, we took off for the Price-rite liquor store where they expected to find the lucky winner and his escort. This was a miscalculation, however. Sylvester got some gin anyway, and we returned to Carl's house, where his brother Harry joined us. Everybody sat down at the kitchen table, but since Carl did not touch liquor after his ailment, the others did the drinking. Carl's children were dancing upstairs to the music of a black radio station. Carl himself urged his visitors to finish the gin as quickly as possible, before his wife would come back; she disliked drinking sessions in her home. He then took the bottle outside to the trash can at the end of the street.

Sonny returned before Carl's wife. He said he had finally left Elijah at the bus station, but only after he had taken him to a trustworthy woman who had agreed to keep some of the money until Elijah returned. When the other men smiled and Sylvester wondered out aloud whether it was to Elijah or Sonny the woman was trustworthy, Sonny realized that while he was absent the image of disinterested intellectual observer of ghetto life which he had been cultivating toward me had probably suffered from the others' comments. He told them indignantly that he was willing to bet that Elijah would get all his money back from her; Sylvester asked where he got the money for the bet. Sonny then observed to me that as I could see this was a very interesting kind of life, like a novel in a way.

In the next couple of days people mentioned Elijah Williamson and his hit now and then, wondering whether he was squandering his money in Philadelphia. As he returned there did not seem to be much left of it, nor was it talked about so often very much longer. But the people of the neighborhood added the case of Elijah Williamson and the circumstances surrounding his hit to their repertoire of anecdotes, and when the topic of numbers came up in conversations from then on, his name was occasionally mentioned.

Bootlegging and numbers contribute to a common perspective for ghetto dwellers on two levels. In a neighborhood like that around Winston Street, at least, they provide localized foci of attention, in that the neighborhood is more or less the territory of particular bootleggers and numbers agents who are known personally to the people in the area and recognized as providing services shared by them. Furthermore, as Elijah Williamson's case shows, a hit also tends to give a neighborhood some sense of cohesion, and it may also be added to a common body of neighborhood tradition.

But beyond their impact in giving a neighborhood things in common, these institutions are known to exist and function in the same way all over the ghetto community, so ghetto dwellers can assume that a general knowledge of such things is among their shared understandings. It is particularly in this sense that numbers and bootlegging are paradigms of the common ghetto perspective. But the perspective encompasses a lot more, and phenomena which are much more pervasive in their influence on black life than are these two institutions. Since they are of many kinds, the perspective may seem rather fragmentary. Yet this also means that what is held in common seems next to all-encompassing, in a sociological sense diffuse, to the ghetto dwellers.

*Soul: concept and content*

It is to this broadly inclusive perspective that the concept of soul has come to be applied in recent years. One might say that this is a black folk conception of the "national character" of black people in America—to have soul or to be a soulful person is to share in the conventional understandings unique to black people and to be able to appreciate them and express them in action. Since such knowledge and ability are felt to be almost ascribed characteristics of black people, they need not qualify individually for the designations soul brothers and soul sisters. That such a self-conscious concern with what is typically black has emerged in the community at this point in black history may have to do with the increasingly efficient exposure to mainstream culture; it is probably also due to the ambiguities and contradictions in the status of black people which are at present probably more apparent than ever before. These uncertainties are present, of course, in the lives of rather divergent groups of black people, although in different ways, and so the soul concept has come to be employed by the black middle class and by black jazz musicians as well as by ghetto dwellers to define their identity. No doubt people in all these categories have a number of similar experiences in the United States because they are all black. However, they are obviously not entirely alike, so the implicit referents of the soul concept are probably somewhat different for each group. Yet there is clearly no need to specify what one means by soul every time one uses the term. Thus when people who might have different conceptions of it engage in interaction, soul may still serve as an umbrella for the *esprit de corps* of them all together.[7]

Here we are concerned specifically with the kinds of understandings of life which ghetto dwellers communicate about and which they formulate more or less explicitly into a notion of soul. There is no reason to believe that even within this community an absolute consensus could easily be reached about what to include and what to emphasize.[8] Essentially, the ghetto concept of soul involves an affirmation of the black experience. One should "tell it like it is" instead of making pretenses of being different from others; one should value earthiness, the "nitty gritty" of black life. Soul is not only acceptance but an assertion of empathy with the typical experiences and actions of ghetto dwellers—even when it is only a gently mocking empathy with human weakness. But these are general and abstract terms. To become more specific and concrete, one must turn to contexts where the understandings of soul may be affirmed.

There is the rather recent history of most ghetto dwellers as Southern country people. Many are certainly of two minds about this; as we have noted before, recent arrivals from down South are typed as simpletons, "bamas". Yet it cannot be denied that this is part of the common ghetto identity. As the comedienne Moms Mabley put it in front of a black audience in Washington, D.C.:

"... I said to my old man, 'I'm going to the country for the weekend. Do you know anything about the country?' He says, 'Sure, I know all about the country. I used to live in the country when I was a boy.' I says, 'When you was a boy everybody lived in the country'."

Thus there is a "home country" not too many generations back, and ghetto dwellers recognize that they are still marked by it in many ways. They know that they are not only black people surrounded by whites but also Southerners in a Northern city.[9] The ghetto dialect may be referred to as "big feet talk"— poor people down South got big feet because they could not afford shoes. From a Southern background the ghetto dwellers have also derived one of the domains of most intense soul symbolism. The things poor Southern country folk ate, most of the time or as circumstances sometimes permitted, have been transplanted into ghetto kitchens: greens of various kinds—collard, mustard, turnips, and kale—blackeyed peas, chitterlings, ham hocks, neck bones, hog maw, barbecued ribs, pork chops, fried chicken, fried pig skins, grits, corn bread, sweet potato pies, water melon, and so forth. These are the things redefined as soul food. Although many groceries and carry-outs still advertise them as "Southern", more and more of these businesses turn to the soul vocabulary. And so do the storefront churches when advertising take-away meals, prepared and sold by members to earn money for church activities. Thus a very tangible component of the Southern heritage has become understood as a part of what it means to be black.[10]

Soul also means perseverance. To be black is to be poor and oppressed and to suffer, and most likely to be marked by this, but to keep on struggling, successfully or not. Having to cope with adverse conditions is generally recognized as a common ghetto experience; in one way or another, it is a part of most ghetto dwellers' definitions of soul. It also has correlates. One of them is the feeling of lack of control over the circumstances which influence one's life. A lot of things can happen both within the ghetto milieu and in the wider environment to give one's life a new and unexpected turn, often for the worse. Since one's possibilities to protect oneself are limited, a ghetto dweller can only try to keep on his toes to be aware of what is going on. One understanding involved in this centers on the possibility that things are not what they seem to be. Life is a game, and a lot of people are working their personal games in situations where this is not readily apparent; they are corrupting contexts and relationships which should not ordinarily be looked at in terms of profit. Sonny summed up the ghetto perspective toward gaming, the concern with "figuring out an angle", with an irony well appreciated by his listeners as he commented on the amount of drinking at a recent funeral reception in the neighborhood:

"Some of the greatest throats in town were there. Ooh! I wish I had had the ice cube concession."

On the night of Halloween, as the children had been going trick-or-treating up and down Winston Street, one of the men in the neighborhood had a similar idea:

"Why don't we go trick-or-treating now, to all them bootleggers? And we tell them we don't want no candy either."

Another facet of the common ghetto perspective often mentioned in the soul context is the experience of the ambivalent relationship between the sexes. We have already noted that there is a shared public imagery concerning male and female characteristics and the problems men and women have with one another. What is covered by the imagery is also held to be common personal experience; ghetto dwellers may vary in the intensity of this experience, but they assume that they share the knowledge of what it means to be "hurt" by the opposite sex. However, this is not all that has to do with soul as far as sex is concerned. Soul also involves the open expression of appreciation of sex; this is one of the points where one should "tell it like it is" rather than feign a lack of interest. One man makes the point this way:

"When white people see a good-looking chick go by, you know, they pretend they ain't interested, almost like they were looking the other way. They don't think it's *nice* to look. Did you ever see any of the brothers up here pretend they didn't see nothing? Did you? They're looking them all over, and then they tell them what they look like. That's soul brothers."

146

The term  soul itself points to another ingredient in the ghetto perspective. Soul, the essence of a human being, is a religious term, and fundamentalist religion continues to be an influence on the ghetto dwellers even as the institutional grip of black churches on them is loosening. There are still lots of churches in the community, and a great many people have had some kind of religious education, if not in Sunday school perhaps in a less organized and conscious way by female kin—mothers, grandmothers, or aunts. Phrases such as "a soul-stirring revival meeting" are still common in the public relations sheets distributed by ghetto churches, and the vocabulary of even quite secularized ghetto dwellers contain such exclamations as "God, have mercy!" or "God almighty!" Freddy, a streetcorner man, reminisces about a chance encounter:

"I was downtown about 2 a.m. one night, and a girl, really wild one, you know, comes up to me. So she says, 'Don't you recognize me, Freddy?' Last time I'd seen her she'd been going to church and everything. The devil had certainly got hold of her."

Jimmy, another streetcorner man whom we have already encountered as one who often gets into fights, says about his life:

"But I don't worry, you know, 'cause I know He's up there taking care of us all."

Such unsolicited remarks show that religion is still a a part of the ghetto perspective, even for those whom the regular church goers consider most obviously lost to the flock; it is something ghetto dwellers can more or less count on having in common. But many have skeptical words to say about God's representatives on earth, and in particular about those in the ghetto. The unofficial image of the ghetto preacher borrows much from the notion that some people always turn human affairs into a game. For all his pious words on Sunday and in quite a few weeknight meetings, the preacher is seen by many ghetto dwellers as a con man in a silk suit and with a long white Cadillac, forever fooling around with the sisters in his congregation, and every preacher risks having his own actions interpreted in this ready-made fashion.[11] There were those in the Winston Street neighborhood who suspected a preacher in a nearby storefront church of being both a moonshiner and a slumlord, although there was actually nothing to substantiate this. One of the preachers who hold forth on black radio stations on Sundays made a point in one of his broadcasts of denying the rumor that he had lost his ghetto church because he had used the rent money of his congregation to buy a new car. But even though ghetto dwellers may at times exaggerate the shady sides of the persons who are supposed to be their spiritual leaders, there are certainly examples among the preachers of people with conspicuously worldly interests. Many of them, of course, are among those storefront church ministers and freelance prophets who are entirely self-made men or women as religious leaders and who operate free of the shackles of any larger established organization. The following account of a Sunday night blessing service, a "special event" not related to any particular church, may just possibly give a somewhat extreme view of one kind of such enterprise—one which was in this case not entirely successful. In any case, it may contribute to our understanding of the cynicism with which some ghetto dwellers regard the hold of religion on some of their compatriots.

The blessing service is well under way; it is held at WUST Radio Music Hall at 9th and V Streets, at the heart of the ghetto. Tickets are $2.00 in advance, $2.25 at the door, and some 170 persons have paid their way in. As you came into the hall you passed a large waterfilled plastic bowl into which the persons entering dropped coins, nothing less than dimes. You could also buy a record by one of the gospel groups to appear during the service (at a price higher than that of the record stores). The service started at about 8.30, about a half-hour after the time advertised, but people continued to enter even later. There has been an opening prayer by a visiting minister, the congregation has done some half-hearted singing, and the minister has asked its members to return to the plastic bowl at the entrance to put a silver coin in it, "and I don't want no nickels now". They should do this "'cause this will do something for you, and you'll feel better when you get back to your seats." Visiting ministers have stood up to present themselves—about five or ten of them—and about thirty visitors from Baltimore have been introduced; there has been a charter bus tour arranged. After testifying service two gospel groups have made short appearances, and now the emcee, the man who presents station WUST's religious broadcasts, introduces Prophet Isaiah Jones, "a man who has done *so* much for *so* many here in Washington". Prophet Isaiah seems to be between thirty-five and forty years old and claims to have been a prophet for some twenty years. He hails from Birmingham, Alabama, and now has his church in a basement on S Street. Tonight he is dressed in a blue flowing brocade gown. He takes up a hymn and gets the congregation to join in. Then he starts talking about his blessing—"Yeah, I'm still in the blessing business." Will everybody please line up in the right aisle to receive a candle and a piece of paper, in order to receive a large sum of money before Wednesday? About half the people in the congregation, most of them women, do and step forward to the prophet one by one to receive the blessed candle and the paper at a price of $2.00. As the line has passed him Prophet Isaiah affirms that by Wednesday night when people begin to receive all the money, he will be the talk of the town. He points out that those who did not get his blessing are foolish, but he will give them another chance. However, nobody else stands up. Prophet Isaiah's style of speech is typical of storefront and travelling preachers, a constant alternation between aggressiveness toward the congregation and assurance of future successes.

As the prophet is through with his part of the service he gives the stage to a middle-aged woman in a clownish red costume with white dots who is introduced as Dr. Henson. She claims to be of German, West Indian, Cherokee, and "good old Negro blood", a combination which might perhaps imply that she has unique powers. She says she has travelled all over the world and just returned from working in Mexico; she is now Prophet Isaiah's collaborator at his church. Her offer goes beyond the prophet's. At the limited cost of $5.00, she will put you in touch with the spirit of one of your deceased relatives who will write a check which will take all your money troubles away. (No details are given on what banks will cash the heavenly check.) Dr. Henson uses the same aggressive style as Prophet Isaiah to make people step forward, but the members of the congregation may either be running out of funds or doubt that it is a good proposition. In any case, only one woman comes up to her. Dr. Henson does not hide her irritation but says she will need at least fifty people if this transmission is to work. If they change their minds they are welcome to the church on S Street on Monday, but in the meantime she has no plans to go home empty-handed, she says. So will those who want to be anointed with her special oil for $1.00 stand up and get into the line? About forty do so, again mainly women. As she is through with the line, Dr. Henson points out once more that she and Prophet Isaiah will both be available at the church tomorrow for further blessings. She then leaves the stage, and a gospel group from Birmingham, Alabama, closes the evening.

The South, poverty, oppression, suffering, and lack of control over one's destiny are thus part of the ghetto dwellers' shared perspective, as are the battle of the sexes, the old-time religion, and a certain irreverence toward man's motives. Last but not least, soul is in black music.[12] If a belief that all black people have a good sense of rhythm is a part of the stereotype white people believe in, it is also a part of the ghetto dwellers' collective self-conception. "Clap your hands and show you got soul", the emcee at the Howard Theatre tells his audience. Soul music is the area where the current concept of soul may have its strongest roots. James Brown is "soul brother number one", Aretha Franklin "soul sister number one", according to record liners, black disc jockeys, and the emcees of black stage shows. Although jazz has had its own soul tradition, soul music is now above all the term for what has otherwise been known as rhythm and blues or the black variety of rock and roll, the popular music of the ghetto.

The characterization of soul music in musicological terms will not concern us here. Instead we will note that soul is not only in the name of this music, but also in the song texts: Sam and Dave had a hit with "Soul Man" in the fall of 1967, and the Bar-Kays' "Soulfinger" was popular the summer of that year. Wilson Pickett has recorded "Soul Dance No. 3", Shirley Ellis "Soultime", Arthur Conley "Sweet Soul Music", the Coasters "Soul Pad", Smokey Robinson and the Miracles "The Soulful Shack", and so forth. Thus ghetto popular music often emphasizes its blackness in words by way of the soul vocabulary. The common black perspective is also affirmed in frequent references to soul food. King Curtis gives the recipe for his orchestration in "Memphis Soul Stew"—half a teaspoon of bass, a pound of fatback drum, etc. —the Joe Cuba Sextet's "Bang! Bang!" has the refrain "corn bread, hog maw, and chitterling", and the Soul Runners have recorded both "Grits And Cornbread" and "Chitterling Salad". The soul emphasis on down to earth sincerity is expressed by Solomon Burke in "Take Me Just As I Am" and by Aaron Neville in "Tell It Like It Is". Endurance in the face of trials and tribulations is another soul value; there are songs like "Just Keep Holding On" by Sam and Dave and "Keep Pushing" by the Impressions to celebrate it. (The latter contains the line "I know I can make it with just a little bit of soul".) And even though soul music like white popular tunes tends to deal predominantly with men, women, and love, it often gives its own nuances to the subject. There is the male way of taking a good look at women in Wilson Pickett's "She's Looking Good!" and in the less charitable "Skinny Legs And All" by Joe Tex. There is the sometimes frenzied sensuality better expressed by Aretha Franklin and James Brown than by anybody else, and there is the old story of relationships breaking up, as in the Impressions' "I Loved And I Lost", in Lou Rawls' "Yes It Hurts, Doesn't It", or in Jimmy Ruffin's "I've Passed This Way Before". Certainly soul music today has a lower average of such content than did the old blues; the record companies aim much of it at a younger audience, partly white, and for this group the downward course and breakup of existing relationships may not be a particularly important motif.[13] Yet there is still some of the same old worry over how one's love is going to fare. The man who usually sang the blues was one who had found in love only pain and disappointment, Samuel Charters wrote in *The Poetry of the Blues* (1963:8), and many of the soul singers and their listeners today have had similar experiences. We have noted before that as deeply as individuals may feel about their breakups, in public morality such happenings "ain't no big thing". The vicarious participation in soul music, then, may be a safety valve for private emotions; the music is making a hit with what is hard to say. To "tell it like it is" and like it cannot otherwise be told may be one of the most soulful things about soul music.

We see that soul music is not only one of the parts of the soul perspective. By serving also as a running commentary on the other parts, it serves to integrate this thing of shreds and patches into a whole. It gives expression to a great many of the shared understandings of the ghetto, and by giving them an impersonal form—while yet involving intensely personal concerns—soul music also gives them a more official standing as community ideology, above the level of particular personal relationships. But in so stabilizing the ghetto perspective, soul music does not work alone.

## The soulful apparatus

What we have just said is that music is not only an ingredient of the shared perspective but also a vehicle of it. It objectivates the public imagery which we have otherwise found expressed only in the everyday face-to-face interaction of ghetto dwellers.[14] It is also distributed through channels of a more institutional character than personal relationships. We will now turn to these community institutions which promote the ghetto understandings discussed above: church, radio, entertainment business. While these institutions have no authority over the community as such, they engage in symbolic action aimed at the entire ghetto, and in this sense they come as close to overarching institutions as anything in the community. Ghetto dwellers can expose themselves to the institutions at will, but most people tend to be reached by their messages in one way or other. Thus they form a kind of ghetto-specific cultural apparatus which is at work beside the mainstream apparatus of school, TV, newspapers, and so forth, which we have discussed before.[15]

Like soul music, ghetto churches are not only involved as a part of the shared understandings but also in spreading the word about them. Particularly the smaller and more independent churches are active in this way. While their theology may be derived to a great extent from outside sources, their anthropology is soul. Storefront church preachers dwell on the evils of drinking and gambling, on the dangers of the streets, on the hardships of poverty, and the road to salvation from all this—"Hallelujah Avenue", as one travelling preacher called it. Since these churches have a considerable female predominance in the congregation, both male and female ministers tend to emphasize the trouble no-good men cause for their women, thus adopting a woman's perspective toward trouble between the sexes. Even so, the conflict is acknowledged as a commonplace occurrence, and so is the fact that there are strong women. A female preacher made this anecdote a part of her sermon, showing one of the advantages of being a good church member:

150

"I want to make you feel so good you can go home tonight and take just anything. I'll tell you about this woman, she was married and she had a mean left, so she used to knock her old man to the floor every time. And he didn't dare do nothing, he wouldn't even cash his own check. So she came to church once, and she was taken by the Holy Spirit, and when she came home that night she was just like a lamb, and she said to her old man, 'Look, there will be no more fighting in this house.' And all week she kept her peace, so her husband started to shape up. And next Friday when he got his check he went out and cashed it, and then he had a taste, he had many, and then he went on home and said to the woman, 'Look, I cashed my check, and I've been drinking, and don't you say nothing about it.' And she just stood there real sweet and said, 'Darling, I have your dinner ready, will you eat now please so I can get down to the church in time for the service tonight.' So the man said, 'Something must have happened to her. I'd better get down to that church and see what's going on down there.' And you see, if she hadn't been so holy after she'd been to church, if she'd gone right on beating him up, ain't nobody seen him in church."

Ghetto preachers thus work with the collection of motifs which they expect to be familiar to the members of their congregations, as a way of establishing a relationship to them. The more secular components of the ghetto cultural apparatus work in the same way. The black radio stations—three in Washington, D.C., WOL, WOOK, and WUST—have hit music, almost all soul, on their programs more or less around the clock, interspersed with newscasts; Sunday programming is largely occupied by religious broadcasts (mostly services from ghetto churches) and community service programs. The radio stations are thus the major channels of soul music into the community and thereby contribute to strengthening the shared perspective of the ghetto dwellers. But beyond this, the disc jockeys—who are the leading radio personalities of the community—have their commentaries revolving around soulful motifs. The WOL disc jockeys have the collective label "the Soul Brothers", and WOOK and WUST have followed suit with "the Soul Men" and "the Soul Bandits". WOL, the leading station in recent years, has had a superman parody serial named "Captain Soul", and one of the disc jockeys had a white friend of his elected "honorary Negro", with the privilege of burning water melons on white people's front lawns—an inversion of Ku Klux Klan cross-burning which a ghetto dweller hardly fails to appreciate. The disc jockeys express their soulful enjoyment of music in cries, shouts, and comments interjected into it, they address themselves to the subject of women, and they make references to soul food in their running commentaries. After one record during which he had loudly proclaimed his appreciation, a disc jockey commented, "Whoo-ee, I ain't had this much fun since Lurleen Wallace got sick," Lurleen Wallace being the then governor of Alabama. While the comment might seem in bad taste and would probably strike most ghetto dwellers as a little *risqué*, there can be no doubt that it could strike a black refugee from the South as rather funny.

Stage entertainment in the ghetto is strongly linked to radio programming. The soul artists and groups in strongest demand for appearances at the Howard Theatre or other places such as the occasional shows at the Washington Coliseum are those with frequent or at least recent recordings on the hit list of black radio stations. While stage shows may be emceed by such travelling celebrities as King Coleman or Georgeous George, nationally known in America's black ghettos, or by a freelancing local talent such as Petey Green, most often the master of ceremonies is a local disc jockey. Thus what occurs on stage has some similarity to what black radio stations broadcast, with the same emphasis on what ghetto dwellers have in common. In the old days the performers at the Howard Theatre sometimes announced the winning number of the day on the late afternoon show, as they could find out about it in the alley next to the theater before going on stage. Perhaps they do not do so anymore because with the current style of shows the audience at that time of day tends to be too young to be numbers enthusiasts. But the emcees continue to ask now and then if there is anybody from Alabama or from Georgia or from South Carolina in the audience, getting more and more response as they name states close to Washington. Of course, many are too shy to stand up, for no particular reason or because it is a little awkward to admit to being "from the country". King Coleman comments on this as he makes his entry on the Howard stage to emcee the Wilson Pickett Show:

"It's good to see the same old faces I've been seeing here the last thirty years . . . Yeah, I see some are making their first visit to the Howard. Some of them come from down home, you see. They won't say so, though, 'cause they think there's something wrong about being from down home. Folks, there ain't nothing wrong about that. It's being down home that's bad."

Soul music, of course, is the major ingredient of a Howard Theatre show. A ghetto hero like James Brown has no problem packing the house for two shows a night for a week as he brings his show to Washington; at other times the quality of the performers is more varied and the reception considerably cooler. As a supplement to the music there is sometimes a black comedian. Someone with the reputation of a Moms Mabley may well headline a show; Moms Mabley is a versatile woman in her upper middle age who typifies the lowly, bitchy old lady who after all has a lot of common sense and a good heart. Dressed in a flowerpot-model hat, clothes with bright flower patterns carefully chosen to clash wildly, and gym shoes, she speaks her mind in her husky voice while continuously chewing gum, commenting on poverty, crime, the South, and the state of the nation. Other comedians usually get less prominent positions in a show. Some of them, like Pigmeat Markham, are masters of the old-fashioned vaudeville, others like Clay Tyson and Irwin C. Watson are standup comedians, while some such as Slappy White are somewhere between such categories or move over a wider field of expression. A great deal of what most of them do, however, involves the shared understandings of the ghetto which we have discussed above. Sex and food are topics they share with soul music; poverty and the South are subjects which are more often dealt with by the comedians. The jokes about the South often involve the Ku Klux Klan:

"There was a real nice story in the paper this morning. Two hundred Klansmen were choked to death 'cause somebody had sold them plastic sheets."

"Down where I'm from the Klan is so bad they put a cross on your front yard and then they come and ask you for a match."

"My old lady is running around with a member of the Ku Klux Klan. She says he's a wizard under the sheet."

The poverty jokes often take the form of reminiscences from childhood:

"Remember how you felt when your mama greeted you with a Western sandwich—two slices of bread with wide open space in between? Or when the rats came in and looked around and said, 'Ain't no use staying here, we'll starve to death.' Or the running water—from the front door to the back door when it rained?"

"We were so poor our daddy couldn't afford even the thinnest slice of cheese for the mouse trap, so he put a picture of a cheese in it. Next morning there was a picture of a mouse in the trap."

"We were so poor our daddy invented the limbo when he tried to enter a pay toilet."

A short skit may be a final example of joking about poverty:

"This new place of mine is a boss place. You really got to come and see it some time. It's ninety by fifteen by thirty."
  "Uhuh . . . Hey, what does that mean—ninety by fifteen by thirty?"
  "It means if I don't pay ninety by the fifteenth, I'm out by the thirtieth."

\* \* \*

Preachers, disc jockeys, soul singers, emcees, and comedians all celebrate the cultural integration of the ghetto community. In the introductory chapter of this book, we noted that this community is only loosely structured; its population constitutes a pool from which a ghetto dweller draws the participants in his personal network, but with most of the constituents he never interacts directly. As partners they remain potentialities. However, the persons who enact the roles of the ghetto cultural apparatus show that this pool of people is indeed a collectivity set apart from the rest of the society, not only because it is excluded from effective mainstream participation but because shared understandings form a basis for communication within the collectivity. Ghetto preachers, disc jockeys, and stage personalities are not engaging in anything resembling symmetrical relationships with their audiences, even if there is a perceptible response from these. They are not familiar with the personal characteristics of audience members but establish the same simple categorical relationship to each one of them, ignoring individual variation.[16] As expert communicators within the ghetto perspective, they can assume that the cultural homogeneity of their audiences is great enough for them to enter into a kind of we-relationship on the basis of understandings they all have in common. Functioning in such a way, the ghetto cultural apparatus also assures the members of the audience that their personal troubles are only reflections of the public issues of the community. It gives the conventional understandings a more enduring public standing in the community than they would have if their relevance to the individual ghetto dweller depended only on the personal experiences of his immediate social circle.

153

On the whole the ghetto community obviously responds rather favorably to the dramatization of its concerns by the cultural apparatus, and it seems to have a certain effect in strengthening community integration not only in asserting the common ghetto perspective but also in serving as a set of institutional foci of attention for the community. These institutions are not under community control, however, but privately managed and responsible only to themselves or outside interests for their exploitation of their ghetto niches. They must rely on the purely voluntary support of the ghetto dwellers in order to gain for themselves a sufficient piece of the action. Thus preachers must constantly try to win over new members to their congregations and keep the old ones active and in line; collections and offerings of various kinds take up much time during services, and the ministers complain about those unsatisfactory Christians who stay home and watch TV instead of coming to weeknight meetings. And, one of them wonders out aloud in her sermon, why do so few people think of bringing the preacher a gift basket some time? There can be little doubt that the precarious economy of many storefront church leaders forces them to pursue financial questions so openly as to make other ghetto dwellers wonder if they have any other motives at all. The black radio stations, too, are in competition with each other to guarantee potential advertisers as large a slice as possible of the ghetto market as listeners to their commercials. In a situation like that of Washington, D.C., with three ghetto-oriented stations as well as a host of others which ghetto dwellers may also choose from, a successful station may need to engage in some vigorous self-promotion.[17] WOL, the newest and most successful station in Washington, D.C.—"the station that brought the nitty-gritty to the Capital City"—is a good example of a station which works hard to become the ghetto dweller's choice. Although relatively little and rather poor programming time is devoted to the social problems of the ghetto, WOL has been militant enough in this area to win the approval even of radical black spokesmen. Its weekly hit lists are distributed through all ghetto record stores, with pictures of its disc jockeys on them, and are useful to those who are out shopping for records. The station also promotes itself by making its staff members ghetto celebrities.

"The World-Wide Gospel Singarama for Peace and Youth Fellowship Crusade", in November, 1966, seems to be staged by WOL to a great extent to build up the public stature of Madame Lucille Banks Robinson who runs its Sunday morning religious broadcasts. Mrs. Robinson celebrates her first anniversary at WOL with a few thousand ghetto dwellers, more women than men, who have assembled at the Coliseum.

Before the program starts, a man walks around selling programs and souvenir pictures. The program has a large picture of Mrs. Robinson on the front page, while most inside pages carry advertisements, many of which are congratulatory messages to Mrs. Robinson. A hat is passed around for a collection toward a blind boy's college education and is finally full of quarters and dimes. Madame Vera Lee King Jones is the first emcee, introducing a hymn and a prayer by the Reverend Allen. She then announces the arrival of "that great woman" and continues her laudatory remarks while Madame Lucille Banks Robinson walks up the aisle in a white full-length gown, followed by a spotlight and accompanied by a young man in tuxedo who turns out to be her son. She turns from one side to the other to be seen by everybody, and as she reaches the stage she is crowned "the Queen of WOL". From there she takes over as emcee herself, introducing as an assistant WOL disc jockey Sunny Jim Kelsey who points out other disc jockeys from the station in the audience, has them stand up, and calls for "a big hand of applause" for each one of them.

The next person to be introduced is the wife of the pastor of a ghetto church who marches onto the stage with an entourage of women from her husband's congregation; she is crowned "Queen of Gospel Singing of the Nation's Capital". Then a number of local gospel groups appears, among them the Sensational Gospel Echoes, the Cole-manaires, and the Wings of Faith. Mrs. Robinson's Baltimore counterpart, Pauline Wells Lewis of station WSID, is introduced to congratulate her, calling her among other things "a great leader for peace". There follows more appearances of gospel groups during which Mrs. Robinson goes backstage, often to change attire—she wears about five, all flashy, full-length gowns during the evening. Between two groups she is presented with a big package, wrapped in gold paper, from her sons.

The audience reacts visibly to the gospel groups in much the same way as the audience at the Howard Theatre would to more secular groups, with clapping, stomp-ing, and some dancing. However, one of the Blind Boys of Alabama, one of the better-known groups, calls for more participation, preferably of the kind James Brown would get. This is not the place for sitting still and looking respectable, he says—"Personally I don't give much for a religion where you can't say Amen. Now I know a lot of you people say, 'I'd like to say Amen, but that's my next-door neighbor sitting next to me.' Well, let me tell you, your next-door neighbor won't be there when you come knocking at the door to heaven."

Nighthawk, the disc jockey who occupies WOL prime time on weekday evenings, is to secular soul what Madame Lucille Banks Robinson is to the sacral Sunday morning program. Nighthawk has had as a sideline to promote a beer brand in the Washington ghetto; for one thing he has gone around to more reputable bars with a representative of the brewery offering free beer to the customers. When he was due at a bar in the Winston Street neighbor-hood the proprietor passed the word about it many days in advance. Thus a considerable number of neighborhood people spent several hours drinking and playing hits on the juke box, waiting for the Nighthawk to arrive after he got off his broadcast at midnight. When he came he went around to talk to every-body, joked with them, and paid some rather straightforward compliments to the women. He left about an hour later.

Nighthawk's birthday was also celebrated as a public event, with a Saturday night Gala Cabaret:

The cabaret is held at the Masonic Temple at 10th and U Streets, Northwest. Tickets are $5.00 in advance sales at ghetto record stores, 50 cents more at the door. The event has been publicized by Nighthawk himself on WOL, and also by his disc jockey colleagues who announced that they were going. Free setups are provided—ginger ale, ice, and potato chips—but there is the customary abbreviation on the ticket to suggest that you Bring Your Own Liquor. The guests are a mixed group ranging from lower-middle class government employees via swingers in male and female ghetto fashions to a group of black power militants, including Stokely Carmichael. (Nighthawk has often mentioned him as a friend on his programs.) Nighthawk himself arrives as the tables around the dance floor begin to fill up and the latin soul band Los Latinos has already started playing. An expensive-looking coat hangs loosely over his shoulders, he wears a grey suit and has a red scarf tucked into the white shirt. On his hand is a ring with a conspicuously large stone. Later in the evening he changes suits twice, into a blue and a green one with matching ties. After greeting people at nearby

155

tables he sits down with some other disc jockeys, the white station manager of WOL, and a few people from the brewery he represents. By now the guests are doing the boogaloo and the Funky Broadway on the dance floor; there are probably a few hundred people present. Nighthawk borrows the drums in the band for a while, then takes over the stage. He thanks everybody for coming and introduces his fellow disc jockey Big Bobby Bennett who says that when he still lived in Pittsburgh he heard that WOL was the greatest station in the world and Nighthawk the greatest deejay. After introducing a man from the brewery, Nighthawk says that he is very happy to have there "a young man whose politics you may or may not agree with, but he's sure made white folks listen"; he calls Stokely Carmichael to the stage and asks for a big applause for him. Then Carmichael is made to join the disc jockeys in leading the congregation in "Happy Birthday to Nighthawk". Photographers take pictures and Carmichael writes a few autographs before going back to his table. The Stereophonics, a soul song-and-dance group in white shirts and dark trousers, perform in front of the band, and almost everybody dances to their version of "I'm a soul man", the tune which kept Sam and Dave on the hit lists for a good part of the fall. Gerome Dyson, a young vocalist in a yellow suit, follows the Stereophonics, and the floor remains crowded. By 2 a.m. some people start leaving, but others are still arriving or debating at the gates whether to go in or not.

Nighthawk's birthday party and Madame Lucille Banks Robinson's first WOL anniversary seem very much to be what Daniel Boorstin (1964) has called "pseudo-events". They are contrived public events, consciously fabricated to exploit the interest of the community for private purposes. They call attention to the services the radio station has rendered to the ghetto community and to the excellence of the station staff, but they mix these self-serving interests with entertainment which makes the occasion rewarding to community members. They also tie themselves closer to the community by acknowledging other centers of community interest, such as Stokely Carmichael and that pastor's wife, "Queen of Gospel Singing of the Nation's Capital". Whether or not all this is deliberately staged according to a detailed master plan of public relations activity, it seems fairly effective. As Boorstin notes, there is a self-fulfilling prophecy in pseudo-events. As an affair arranged by a black radio station to celebrate itself becomes understood as a public event, the ghetto dwellers are also led to think of the station as a significant community institution. Thus black radio, its programming and its personnel are not simply a faceless component of the ghetto cultural apparatus but a set of individuals and events which also take their place among the things ghetto dwellers know they have in common, the things which serve to define their community.

*The cornerstones of soul*

The shared perspective contains the ghetto dweller's reflections on the condition of his community. As we have seen, it is consciously held to be a cultural complex known only to him, and in this sense it helps draw the demarcation line between the ghetto and the outside world. Yet if we go beyond this we see how unseparable mainstream culture and society remain from the social reality of the ghetto dwellers. They feel mainstream power impinging on their lives, they see the ghetto through a mainstream screen and the mainstream through a ghetto screen. Varied as the soulful understandings may be, three themes seem to return again and again—the struggle for solidarity, the bitter-sweet mood, and the impiety toward society. These cornerstones of the ghetto-specific outlook all have a great deal to do with the mainstream.

Soul as solidarity is a reaction to the threat of a split in the community. Its internal differentiation is tied to mainstream society and culture so that individual striving for improved standing ultimately leads out of the community. Furthermore, we have noted (in chapter 2) how some "respectable" ghetto dwellers refer to others as "no good"; they are judging their compatriots on the basis of mainstream standards and disregarding that human equality which as ghetto dwellers they should understand.[18] Some of them go to the big Baptist churches which are almost like white churches and thus deny the traditional black religious experience. Storefront church preachers keep complaining about this conceit. It looks as if these people were bent on *not* telling it like it is, on disavowing that they have much in common with the rest of the black community. "These people", of course, are not always the same; a lot of people turn renegade at one time or other by espousing mainstream culture in some way that is detrimental to ghetto cohesion. The vocabulary of soul—soul brother, soul sister, soul food, and so forth—is used with all its implications of shared understandings to regain their loyalty to the community, and it is also used as a reaffirmation of their allegiance by those very persons whose ghetto loyalty may be in doubt. James Brown, after recounting his successes from the time he shined shoes in Augusta, Georgia, until the present when he owns a plane and shakes hand with the president, says, "A soul brother made it, now ain't that a groove?" But in order to make this solidarity encompass even the least privileged, it must be symbolized by those most undiluted forms of black proletarian experience which everybody can claim as his heritage, and to give it a positive valence weakness must be turned into strength. Thus poverty, oppression, and troubled relationships are interpreted as the foundation of an endurance which can only be truly appreciated by others who have passed the same way. There may be no better example of this than the ghetto use of the term "nigger". It is a repulsive term of abuse when used by white people, and ghetto dwellers themselves certainly often use it in a similar way. But many times they also use it in affectionate mockery. By using it they signalize the understanding that they are separate from the outside world. They intimate that they know all the mainstream prejudices toward the ghetto but themselves have a better understanding, since they, too, know what it means to be a "nigger". This is why black people may say "nigger", but nobody else.

In calling for solidarity on the basis of a shared perspective no outsider is expected to understand, the ghetto dwellers are also expressing their bitter-sweet view of their condition; it is a part of their understandings that life has been less than fair to them. Man is not supposed to be poor and oppressed, nor should he be hurt by the people closest to him. The comedians' jokes about poverty and the old theme of lost love in black music are assertions that what goes on is not what should go on. The ghetto dwellers have not adjusted their perspective so as to take the ghetto condition for granted as a satisfactory state of affairs. Their understanding of its human consequences differs from that of outsiders, but the standards of what life ought to be like which they apply to such problems are mainstream standards. This is how ghetto dwellers see their own community through a mainstream screen.

The impious view of the working of society is also based on the disjunction between mainstream doctrine and ghetto reality which the ghetto dweller experiences. The representatives of what should be good, right, and just in society are too often seen as corrupt, brutal cops or preachers who are actually con-men. In comparison with such examples of what happens behind the façade of the official moral order, the ghetto dwellers find rather little wrong with such community institutions as bootlegging and the numbers game— which the guardians of the outside world do not accept. So the ghetto dwellers become used to suspecting that things are not necessarily what they seem to be or what they are supposed to be; there is also the understanding that in those innocent relationships within the ghetto community which should be characterized by friendship and cooperation, there may be someone working his own game for profit and thus corrupting the situation. Piety is the sense of what properly goes with what, according to Kenneth Burke (1965:74); ghetto dwellers share their ideas of what moral arrangements ought to be with mainstream society, but their understanding of what really goes on is more likely to be impious, as they have their doubts about the efficient functioning of righteousness in their world. Here again, they apply mainstream standards to ghetto reality. But they are also bringing their knowledge of ghetto reality to bear on their judgment of the mainstream execution of morality, as they find the representatives of mainstream society certainly no less hypocritical than anyone else.

\*　\*　\*

The shared perspective of the ghetto community is a complex phenomenon with a changing structure and composition. Attempting to analyze it we are constantly faced with the danger that we depict it too statically and in terms too intellectually clearcut to represent well the vague moods of an entire community. In the summary we have tried to give in this chapter, we have particularly emphasized the significance of a ghetto-specific culture to community integration; we have also dwelt on the relationship of this culture to the influences of the outside world. In chapters 4 and 5, we noted that ghetto sex roles, specific to the community as they may be, are influenced both by mainstream cultural norms and by macrostructural influences which contradict these norms. Here we have found that this double mainstream influence, on ideals and on reality, is at work in generating ghetto culture more generally, contributing strongly to the emphases of the common understandings of the community. We will continue to examine facets of this relationship between ghetto and mainstream, as expressed within the ghetto community, in the next two chapters.

# 8
# Waiting for the Burning to Begin

Harlem 1964, Watts 1965, Chicago and Cleveland 1966 ... The list of black ghetto risings in Northern cities was growing as the study of the Winston Street neighborhood began. The events of Harlem and Watts had already been incorporated into the history of black America, the newspaper headlines about Cleveland and Chicago were only a few weeks old. More was to follow, including Newark and Detroit 1967 and—toward the end of the study— Washington, D.C., itself, in the days following the assassination of Martin Luther King in April, 1968. But by then an eruption of this kind could hardly come as a surprise. The circumstances understood to be at the basis of earlier risings had clearly been at work in Washington as well; besides, as the nation's attention moved from one violent ghetto crisis to another, people like those in the Winston Street neighborhood had also become concerned with the prospect of turmoil in their own community, its causes and its possible consequences. Although not an everyday subject of conversation for most ghetto dwellers, it seemed continuously present as a background understanding; when a verbal exchange concerning it occurred, practically everybody seemed to have pertinent experiences and opinions. There were also a number of incidents which pointed forward to more tumultuous times. The climate of large-scale trouble thus existed long before the outbreak became a fact. Here we will attempt to throw some light at grassroots conditions and events along the road to a ghetto rebellion, with an emphasis on the ghetto dwellers' own perspective toward it.

## The sharing of discontent

Ghetto dwellers have much to resent about the way the outside world treats them: poor jobs, unemployment, unfair practices on the part of many employers, high rents for unsatisfactory housing, inadequate schools and health and welfare services, arbitrary, inefficient, and sometimes brutal police work, the poor performance and sharp practices of many businesses aiming at ghetto customers, as well as a host of major and minor expressions of prejudice and discrimination which may confront a member of the black minority as he goes about his everyday social traffic in American society.[1] Although such circumstances do not hit every member of the community with equal force, they provide each ghetto dweller with some basis for discontent, and probably they all play some role in the accumulation of grievances which may finally result in a rising. However, they do not seem to be equally prominent in the collective articulation of resentment which occurs spontaneously in the ghetto, and some of them are obviously of greater significance than others for the understanding of the form of ghetto rebellion. Some of the grievances are discontinuous and more private in their character, and one may perhaps only diffusely conceive of who is responsible for them. Thus complaints may be aired now and then about the insufficiency of garbage collection, about hours spent in waiting rooms, about a job a no better qualified white person got, or about a landlord who refuses to make repairs. But there are fewer of these, and they tend to be assimilated to the general body of knowledge about the hostile, distant white world. In the Winston Street neighborhood, at least, many more conversations about grievances dwell on white-owned businesses and the police; probably this is so because these are continuously present, represented by "real people", on ghetto territory. This may make it easier for ghetto dwellers to share experiences directly and to see the relevance of one's own experience to that of others. Since merchants and policemen are also those outsiders who become most directly involved in the insurrection itself, we will pay particular attention to how ghetto dwellers define their discontent with respect to these. This obviously does not mean that they are the only objects of "real" grievances; rather, they seem to become the foci of concern toward which discontent is channeled also from other sources.[2] Thus they are particularly important in interpreting the insurrectionary mood of the ghetto in terms of social processes within the community.

As we have noted before, a great many of the business establishments in the ghetto are white-owned. Although some of these are quite modest enterprises—streetcorner groceries, carry-outs, variety stores and the like—most of the larger establishments are also among them, such as liquor stores, record stores, clothing stores, dry-cleaning operations, appliance and furniture stores, and auto dealers. Furthermore, there are the ghetto links of large supermarket and drugstore chains. The ghetto dwellers' attitude toward this white dominance behind the store fronts in their community is often one of bitterness. First of all this is based simply on the categorical relationship between blacks and whites. The people of the ghetto see that the meager resources allotted to them flow straight back to white people. It is very obvious to them that businessmen who are dependent on them for a living are doing much better than they. "See, there goes our bread, but he'll be back for more tomorrow," a streetcorner man says to his friends as they watch the owner of the liquor store across the street lock up his store and drive off in his car toward the suburb. But there is more to the resentment than this.

There is the question of prices, important all the way down the line from cars and TV sets to groceries. Since the ghetto dwellers are largely a low-income population, their desire for expensive goods—supported by TV and radio commercials, but also by the general affluence of the society surrounding them[3]—creates a demand for credit, and the businesses catering specifically to a ghetto public thus specialize in instalment-plan sales. These often make items more expensive than they would ordinarily be.[4] Quite often high-pressure sales tactics are used, and advertising and information about sales conditions—on black radio stations and elsewhere—are frequently incomplete and misleading, so that the customers in due time find out that they will have to pay much more than they originally thought. Of course, few ghetto dwellers are so aware of the technicalities of instalment buying that they can protect themselves fully against unpleasant surprises. Thus they have personal or vicarious experiences of how they or friends or neighbors have been pursued by creditors or their agents, claiming debts which the ghetto dwellers feel are morally nonexistent. And such questionable debts are incurred not only by those in the community who are least well off but also by mainstreamers with steady and reasonably satisfactory incomes whose wishes for a comfortable and respectable life may lead them, for example, to acquire expensive furniture from one of the stores advertising their credit plans on ghetto radio.

Whether he knew what he was doing or not when he entered into debt, there are times when the ghetto dweller simply cannot make the payment which is due. The creditor may then have the debt attached through a routine court action to the debtor's salary, so that the latter's income is channeled straight to the creditor. This, of course, can cause great hardship on a poverty-stricken ghetto dweller, and it can also poison his relationship to his employer. When this method of claiming debts cannot be used or for some other reason is not used, the merchandise in question may be reclaimed—and whether or not this is done in a justifiable manner, it is not likely to enhance the ghetto dweller's love for the merchants in his community. Freddy, living with his girl friend in a basement apartment, only had occasional income of his own but wanted the signs of success in street life. He made the down payment on an old Ford Thunderbird, and he and a friend of his spent days going over its engine, painting over its scratches, and cleaning it thoroughly—all a labor of love. At this time he was doing a little business in bootlegging, and as the time approached for the next instalment on the car, his apartment was raided by detectives. He was fined heavily, could not pay the car dealer, and lost the Thunderbird which was his pride. Rather understandably, he turned a little bitter. A girl swinger had a coat laid away for her in a store and had made a sizeable part of the payment as she lost her job and could not pay any more. She did not get the coat, nor was she given her money back, and she was not allowed to take something else and cheaper for what she had already paid. While she was sure the store had maltreated her, she felt she could do nothing about it.

The feeling that unfair business practices are involved is also directed toward the supermarkets and streetcorner stores catering to the ghetto dwellers' daily shopping needs. The opinion is widespread that chain stores charge more for an item in a ghetto branch than they do in more affluent areas, and that the food stuffs on sale in the ghetto are often of inferior quality. When it was reported that at least one supermarket chain hiked its prices on those days when welfare payments were made, this seemed rather generally accepted as the truth by people in the Winston Street neighborhood, although business officials denied it. One community organization posted pickets outside the stores involved, but business continued much as usual. One man had this to say:

"Sure I can stop buying my groceries in those stores. But you know, then I have to buy everything from the old man up here at the corner, and he'll charge me even more. So I'll just have to go to the one who cheats me less."

It is undoubtedly true that it is generally more expensive to shop at the streetcorner groceries. It is not very difficult to give a couple of acceptable partial reasons why this is so: the small shopkeepers must make up for their limited turnover, and the small scale of their businesses also makes it difficult for them to stock up in an economical way. Yet it is not difficult for a ghetto dweller to believe that the streetcorner grocer is simply charging as much as he can possibly get away with.

The quality of the interaction between businessmen and ghetto dwellers is also often tense in a more personal may. Probably this is partially due to simple racial prejudice on the part of the white merchants; at least many ghetto dwellers complain about unjustified rudeness on the part of store owners. However, when shopkeepers appear to behave unnecessarily brusquely they may also be influenced by their fear of pilfering and even robbery which they understand to be common problems of ghetto business.[5] This is certainly particularly likely to hit those customers whose outward appearance is not altogether "respectable": children, teenagers, or streetcorner men. But even if there is some basis for this fear it will anger a great many innocent people who find yet another reason to dislike white businessmen. This is evident as streetcorner men try to convince each other to make the visit to the liquor store with their collected funds; several of them hesitate to go because they "don't like the man in there". And when they send a child on an errand to the grocery store although they are idle themselves, one may also suspect that they want to avoid a confrontation with a disliked shopkeeper.

With the businessmen, the police are the representatives of the wider society who are most strongly in evidence on ghetto streets. According to the President's Commission on Crime in the District of Columbia (1966:165), Washington's police force is about four-fifths white, despite the large black majority in the city. Thus most of the policemen patrolling the ghetto are also white. The relationship of the people of the ghetto to these policemen is markedly ambivalent and often tinged with more hostility than respect. True, as ghetto dwellers sometimes point out, "You got to say this about them, they got a job to do". As we have noted before, the people of the ghetto feel that theirs is a dangerous environment; they are almost constantly conscious of the potential of trouble. For this reason they are highly aware of the need for law enforcement, and they have nobody but the police to turn to. If there is a violent fight in the house next door some ghetto dwellers will indeed call the police, and occasionally a streetcorner man may report an enemy just to settle a score. Thus there is no consistent policy of non-cooperation. But one of the complaints ghetto dwellers have against the police is that to a great extent it fails to protect them against the violence of the urban jungle. This laxity, they feel, is itself evidence of racial discrimination:

"The police say, 'Let the niggers cut each other up.' They don't care as long as it is not in a white neighborhood. They're just watching out for the stores."

However, the kinds of actions the police do take is probably more important in causing ghetto resentment than what they do not do. Teenagers and streetcorner men feel they are being harassed quite unnecessarily in their everyday lives at the hangouts. As we have seen, for instance, public drinking and drunkenness are among the offenses for which most arrests are made. The men who are drinking at the corner or in the back alley are constantly on guard against policemen and patrol cars; since they consider their drinking quite harmless to everybody else, they do not consider it any business of the police. It may indeed be impossible for them to find more privacy for their sociability than they do at their hangouts in public places; wives, mothers, sisters, or landladies may object to their getting together at home, and it is too expensive to drink at bars all the time. In fact, some policemen look the other way most of the time to avoid unnecessary arrests in such cases, but others seem to want to enforce the law to the letter, and the outcome is a feeling that the policemen act quite arbitrarily.

There are certainly a great many ghetto dwellers who take a much dimmer view of public drinking and drunkenness than these men do, and who would not mind if the police could actually enforce the law even more firmly in this field. Even so, they may concur in seeing the police as a source of trouble in their lives. A great many men can recall being arrested some time in their lives—if not recently, then quite often when they were young. In many of these cases they still consider the arrest to have been unjustified, and whether they do or not, they may reminisce about harsh treatment. One middle-aged man recounted a recent experience of his as follows:

"I just got out of bed and had breakfast, and then I stood here on the stairs and thought about what I should do next, you know, and I had just decided to go over across the street and see some buddies when this police car came up, and the policemen called me. 'Hey boy,' he said. So I said, 'Yeah.' And then he said, 'Get into the car.' 'What for?' I said. 'Just get into the car.' And then when we got down to the precinct I was booked as a drunk. So I said, 'Shi-it, I'm no more drunk than you are.' So they had to let me go, and I said I'd bring charges against them. Yeah, I really think I should, you know, but I won't, 'cause, see, if I do that he'll be bugging me every time he sees me, and charging me with one thing or another, and I don't want none of that. Would have been another thing if I had lived in another precinct."

Another man, complaining about his lack of exercise, said that he really should take to running around a few blocks each morning.

"But I can't, 'cause if I do that I'll probably get busted. The police won't believe that you're up to any good if they see you running, see."

Only slightly later, it did indeed happen that a man was arrested while running toward the hospital where his mother lay dying.

Some such actions on the part of the police may well be simple harassment. The use of disliked epithets—"boy", "nigger", and so forth—shows that many policemen do not bother to hide their prejudice, and some excessive use of force cannot be understood as anything but police brutality. However, it seems that the police may also behave in ways unacceptable to the ghetto dwellers— or any public—because of the understandings they have of what the ghetto situation calls for from them as professionals.[6] To the police the ghetto is a high-crime district where the dangers of police work are great and where the public is generally suspect. Any strange behavior—and what is "strange" to an outsider like a policeman need not at all be so to someone with a greater

163

knowledge of the community—should be investigated, and if an infraction against the law has occurred, anybody who happens to be seen close to the scene of the crime soon afterwards is liable to be treated as a suspect, especially if he is young or if he does not look quite "respectable". Since a person who gets arrested in a high-crime community is thought to be potentially dangerous —he may resist arrest or even carry a weapon—the policeman may anxiously show a little extra strength just in case it should be necessary. With such rather primitive and categorical notions of how to treat ghetto dwellers, the police-men are apt to make arrests which should never have been made and to leave themselves yet more open to allegations of racism and police brutality. And since their actions may hit any member of the ghetto community, even its most law-abiding people may come to resent the police, not only for what they fail to do but also for what they do. One is not always ready to give the police the benefit of a doubt; the following notes from a street incident in the Winston Street neighborhood show how quickly the tensions between police and ghetto dwellers may escalate.

It was a rather cold Friday night in November, about 8 p.m. I was talking with Carl, George, Sonny, and Lee, one of the mainstreamer men in the neighborhood, outside Rubin's grocery. Outside the carry-out across the intersection a group of teenagers were talking and laughing loudly, with a couple of them engaging in a boxing bout. Two policemen walked up to the police telephone at the corner with a young man under arrest—apparently for drunkenness, as he had some difficulty walking. Another policeman came just after them. They called the precinct station for a car, then started searching the arrestee. To the bystanders they seemed to shake him with more force than necessary; he reacted with a jerk and shouted, "Leave me alone, mother-fucker". They found no weapon on him and continued to hold him in a firm grip. More people were coming by, and many of them stopped to watch. Before the police car arrived, there were people watching from each corner of the intersection. The teenagers outside the carry-out were shouting insults at the police; a number of friends of the arrestee arrived in cars, and some got out. "We'll make sure they don't do nothing to you", one of them said. The people in my group began speculating whether this was the start of a major clash. They felt the policemen would not dare beat the man while everybody was watching but that he would probably be brutalized in the car on the way to the precinct station, then sentenced for "resisting arrest" which would serve to explain any marks on him. A couple of teenagers were threatening the policemen as daringly as was possible without yet coming to blows. Lee went over to them and said that policemen are dangerous and do not know what they are doing, so they had better not provoke them. Finally, after one of the police-men had made a new hurried call to the station, a patrol car came to take two of them and the arrestee to the station. Immediately afterwards, three police buses rushed in with lights flashing, coming to a halt at the intersection where each parked at a different corner. A number of policemen jumped out and shouted to people to leave, so as not to "hinder traffic on the sidewalks". Faced with this massive show of concern with the problems of pedestrians, everyone left.

This was obviously a routine arrest. It just so happened, however, that there were unusually many people outside for a late fall evening, and the policemen and the arrestee were highly visible to them for a rather long time. Both the policemen and the spectators seemed to overreact to each other. The ghetto people were quickly ready to interpret what they saw in terms of police brutality; the policemen feared a riot and brought in a force which may have stopped any further escalation but which to the ghetto dwellers constituted strong evidence that the police saw them all as an enemy. Thus a minor event became a basis for symmetrically schismogenetic interaction between the police and the ghetto as they progressively strengthened their showing and understanding of animosity.[7] As the spectators walked off from the scene they were talking about what might be happening at the precinct station; it was generally held that the police have turned to beating prisoners over their heads through telephone books. It is said to hurt just as badly but to leave no marks.

As the ghetto dwellers experience the behavior of white businessmen and policemen and work out interpretations of it together, they arrive at a collective definition of their grievances. They chuckle as they see a good friend and neighbor leave by the back door as the bill collector enters through the front door. They find themselves under constant surveillance from slow-moving patrol cars and feel they know what the policemen inside are thinking about them. They note that the "fresh greens" at the grocery look like they have been around for some time, and that the children they send to the store on an errand often seem to get too little change in return. And they know of instances when policemen "accidentally" shot those suspected of only minor offenses—something they can only see as gross disregard for black lives. Of course, a great deal of the interaction between the ghetto dwellers and these white outsiders in their territory flows quite smoothly. Quite possibly, too, the outsiders may be able to explain satisfactorily some of that behavior of theirs which from the ghetto dwellers' point of view is only evil. But what matters is that the people of the ghetto do in fact accumulate and share among themselves so much evidence of injuries to their interests and honor, and that they find little or no reason not to see the merchants as exploiters and the police as oppressors. Thus there is a withdrawal of legitimacy from these as community institutions; for they seem to be working against the community rather than for it. With the ghetto dwellers continuously strengthening this interpretation with new data, the foundations for rebellion against these outside powers exist long before the eruption comes.

## The tradition of being oppressed

One should not, however, understand the ghetto view of the police and the ghetto merchants only in terms of their own ability to cause resentment. They have the additional burden of being the most accessible representatives of the white world as a whole, a world by which black people have a tradition of being exploited and oppressed. It is indeed a tradition; to many ghetto dwellers the relationship to whites does not seem to have changed much in recent times, and the white problem is still defined in terms reminiscent of the racist politics of the Deep South. The typical black-and-white joke at the Howard Theatre is still about the Ku Klux Klan. Whether or not the understanding of white people's racial attitudes which this reflects remains correct today, the institutionalized segregation of ghetto dwellers prevents many of them from finding out much about the current state of white opinion at first hand. Just as black people are taught about the meaning of blackness by other blacks, they

165

learn about white people and race relations within the ghetto community rather than in face-to-face contacts with whites. White people are being typed by black people, as "crackers", "grays", "Whitey", "Mr. Charlie", "ofays", "PWT" (poor white trash), "honkies", or "blue-eyed blond devils" (a Muslim term), just as white people among themselves are typing black people. In both cases the vocabulary becomes a cultural storehouse for hostility, a part of the community's own information about its external affairs which is seldom contradicted by other sources. Perhaps the white suburbs do not all share the views of the Klan, but the unemployed streetcorner man who hardly knows any white people personally does not necessarily know. As far as he is concerned, the machinery of the society may still seem like a Klan device to keep him down, and it is not impossible to fit ghetto merchants, the police, and many fleeting contacts with other whites into such an interpretation. In his state of isolation from mainstream society, a ghetto dweller may well view institutionalized segregation as a direct expression of average white personal prejudice. Whether he is correct in this or not, the impact of this is such that he will take any not obviously prejudiced white person with whom he comes in contact to be an exception to the rule. There are shopkeepers in the ghetto who can hardly be said to be "liberals on the race question" but are yet hailed by neighborhood people as "good white people", and the moderator of one TV talk show whom a fair number of white people would certainly consider strongly conservative was believed by many Winston Street people to be a "typical white liberal".

The ghetto community can thus keep alive its traditional representation of the relationship between white and black America without being confronted with much contrary evidence. To the notion of racism as a dominant force in the wider society is added that of racketeering—this understanding is probably a Northern ghetto innovation. Many ghetto men hint in conversations to "the Syndicate" as one of the great powers in society, if not even the greatest. Some of the facts of ghetto life which cannot be easily explained in terms of racism may be blamed on large-scale white racketeering, with influences extending into government—"the Syndicate" is said to have its own congressmen. One former alcoholic threw light on his conception of the power of racketeers in this statement:

"I'd rather smoke pot than be a juicehead, you know, you can stay cool, you don't piss in your clothes, you don't get into fights with your friends, and you can have some whenever you want it and you can afford it. Look, it's these ordinary cigarettes that give you cancer and you get addicted to, and they're legal, but pot which only makes you feel good is outlawed. You know why? Because if pot was legal, all those racketeers couldn't make so much money—that's why they keep pot illegal."

Most of the talk about these racketeers is independent of most ghetto dwellers' personal experiences, and their ideas about big crime are very hazy. If the imagery about "the Syndicate" is not entirely without foundation, it certainly seems rather exaggerated. Even so, it must be taken into account as a part of many ghetto dwellers' model of black-white relations. The power imputed to racketeers constitutes a further reason for the ghetto dwellers to deny the morality of white dominance in their community.

166

*The young and the old*

If there is continuity in the tradition of oppression, its impact on the oppressed may yet be changing. There is a growing feeling that white dominance need not be accepted. A strong generational cleavage is noticeable at this point, for the younger people are clearly much more militant than the older. In the Winston Street neighborhood this shows up in how people regard the idea of black power. Hardly anyone feels that more power for black people to manage their own affairs would be a bad thing, but particularly the middle-aged and the elderly are worried that any kind of action against white dominance would hurt nobody more than it would hurt the ghetto dwellers themselves. They feel that "black power" may be taken as a licence for unruly teenagers to go around knocking down people, black and white, thus starting a white avalanche which would come to destroy ghetto lives and homes. That is, the older people still believe much more in white power than in black, and they feel that the less noise they make about the latter, the less risk is there that the former will engage in retaliation. When a well-known spokesman of a black power organization paid a visit to the neighborhood some of these older people were afraid that he would start trouble there. Afterwards they expressed their support of a bootlegger's wife who went out into the street to tell him in no uncertain terms that although she surely had no more love for white people than he did, she wanted him out of there. It may be, of course, that her action was partially motivated by her particular concern for the family business which could be harmed if police attention were drawn to the neighborhood; this was the view of some of her more cynical young neighbors.

Among the younger people, on the other hand, many more are willing to listen to the black power message and acknowledge that "it makes a lot of sense". Many of them know little or nothing about the older civil rights organizations; they are familiar with the Nation of Islam (the "Black Muslims") with which some of the streetcorner men in the neighborhood sympathize, but they are rather skeptical of it. The Muslim ideology seems notoriously unhip with its bans on pork, liquor, tobacco, dancing, flirtation, and so forth, and there is a feeling that the Muslims who were once in the front line of militant protest are accommodating themselves to co-existence with white power, despite their continuing rhetoric.[8] Besides, Elijah Muhammed gets his share of the suspicion that religious leaders are con-men. Thus for the younger generation at least, black power seems more in line with their own thinking. Although they usually continue to stay away from organized political participation, they can accept it as a rallying concept; this does not necessarily mean that they are aware of all its implications. But the black power movement gives some coherence to their own notions of what is wrong with the ghetto condition, and particularly to the discontent with white power. In so doing, it serves as a catalyst for ghetto change.

While the older people are concerned with the rebelliousness of the younger men and women, the latter feel that the preceding generations have too often been "conned by the white man" into a complacency which has taken them nowhere. The middle-aged and the elderly have been "Uncle Toms", "handkerchief heads". If there is some truth to this, there may be a good reason for it in that the generations have to a great extent lived their lives under different circumstances. More of the older people are still to a great extent black

167

Southerners. They have had their own experiences of being under constant white scrutiny in a much more personal way than is possible in the large Northern ghetto. What this meant not too long ago was made clear by John Dollard in *Caste and Class in a Southern Town* (1937); for instance, it was possible to punish by whipping those black persons who had been found to subscribe to Northern Negro newspapers. Perhaps the older ghetto generation of migrants are still more prone to "watch their step" as they begin new lives in the North. One of the streetcorner men at Winston Street clearly had this opinion about his neighbors:

"Those people around here ain't gonna do nothing they'd think a cracker wouldn't like. They're all from the Carolinas, you know—North Carolina and South Carolina. They just say 'Yes, sir', 'no sir'. They gonna shuffle forever."

The younger people "ain't gonna shuffle no more". In fact, it is questionable whether they, as born ghetto dwellers, ever had reason to shuffle very much. Harsh as the circumstances of life may be in the ghetto, black-white relationships in the North are seldom so close that the white party needs constantly to reassert its dominance, and the anonymity of the large ghetto also provides greater personal freedom for black people. It is, at least, a freedom to be relatively more militant in one's views and to be more daring in one's behavior.

*The lack of politics*

As we have noted, grievances were strongly felt and openly articulated in the Washington ghetto before the April rising. Yet most ghetto dwellers took no part in those organized political expressions which occurred. Civil rights groups and others carried on their work but seemed to draw little interest from most people in the community who agreed with what the groups did but paid little or no attention to them. The black power groups were to some extent an exception, both because they made some attempts to take their message to the streets and because mass media took a noticeable interest in them. Generally, however, there was no concerted political activity. Many people, of course, still felt it could be dangerous. They continued to look to the South for examples and had no trouble finding them. The weekend before Martin Luther King was killed a few men at a Winston Street corner were talking about the Poor People's March he was planning for Washington, D.C.; King had just participated in a march in Memphis in connection with the sanitation workers' strike, and the march had broken up in disorder. Reinhardt Ross, one of the men, was skeptical of marching:

"They don't get me to walk in one of those marches and get my head busted. So where was King when all those people were beaten up by the police? On his way to the airport! You see? On his way to the airport! That's what happens every time with those protests, the leaders run off and the people who have been dumb enough to follow them get busted. No, he ain't gonna have no march here, King ain't gonna have no march here."

More often, however, the organized political activities were simply not of a kind which most ghetto dwellers would regard as any of their business, such as public meetings. When asked if they planned to go to some meeting coming up, most people in the Winston Street neighborhood were obviously surprised at the idea, and in this they seemed to represent well the ghetto as a whole. Attendance at public meetings tended to confirm the ghetto dwellers' lack of concern with this kind of organized activity. In the fall of 1966, when the black power concept was fairly new and widely debated, in the ghetto as well as outside, the local branch of the NAACP held a public meeting to discuss it. The meeting was held at the YMCA in the middle of the ghetto and included the local SNCC representative as a main speaker, but although the meeting was well advertised, few other than the predominantly middle-class, outer-city NAACP supporters showed up. More people came to a meeting on police brutality, called by all the better-known militant black groups and personalities, centrally located in a black church and again widely publicized. The ghetto population was also clearly better represented; plainclothes policemen in the audience were pointed out and asked to leave. Yet considering the size of the Washington ghetto, attendance was still small. At neither of these two meetings was anybody from the Winston Street neighborhood present. A third meeting was held by a civic group in order to discuss urban renewal plans for a large area including Winston Street. It was advertised through leaflets distributed to all households in the area, but only one resident of the Winston Street neighborhood attended, a preacher from a storefront church who took a greater than ordinary interest in community affairs.

Another test case for ghetto activism was a plan for a May Day boycott of public schools, to protest against conditions in ghetto schools and against the reappointment of an unpopular school superintendent. This boycott was largely a failure. Few children, on Winston Street or elsewhere in the community, stayed home. In this case, however, black groups were not united behind the boycott.

Although school conditions were not talked about a great deal in everyday ghetto conversations, at least in the Winston Street neighborhood, black power and police injustice certainly were recurrent topics, and neighborhood renewal was certainly a matter of concern. The very limited number of people who went to meetings such as these seems to show, then, that organized political activity did not reach the majority of ghetto dwellers. Although groups and meetings were involved in articulating ghetto grievances, their work had very little noticeable impact on the everyday lives of the majority of ghetto dwellers. Successes which could dramatize their activity were largely lacking. Meanwhile, other ghettos showed a radical way out of muteness.

*The state of readiness*

It did not escape the ghetto dwellers of Washington that the characteristics of other Northern ghettos were similar to those of their own community, and as Watts, Detroit and others burned, this was easily seen as a forecast for Washington. The mass media certainly strengthened this view as they detailed the conditions likely to lead to an eruption and spoke grimly of long hot summers to come. Over the afternoon paper Bee Jay could comment that if there were a rising in Washington it would be really bad; he thought there were firearms in practically every house. (This was probably greatly exaggerated.) But he would go along with it, for he would always be with his people.

His friend disagreed. They could not win, and there was too much to lose. "If anything happens here I'll go and hide in the basement till it's over," he said. But although opinions were divided about what to do in case of an eruption, few doubted that there might be one coming. Now and then as someone felt poorly treated by a ghetto business, he could mutter that "a place like that ought to be burned to the ground". Mass media showed quite clearly what goes on in a rising, and further information was supplied by friends who came to visit from cities where risings had already occurred—or who were visited there by Washingtonians. While some of this evidence was clearly unfavorable, there were visitors who evinced enthusiasm about their own rebellions. Sonny ran into an old musician acquaintance who had just returned to Washington from Detroit and who told him the ghettos of the two cities were a lot alike; "you ought to do it here, too". And at the meeting against police brutality mentioned above, a young man stood up to say that he had recently arrived from Watts—"the brothers back there wonder what's going on in Washington, if you're all a bunch of Toms or something." Obviously visitors such as these gave risings a political interpretation. These were rebellions, acts of black self-assertion—not just riots, outbreaks of selfish plundering, lawlessness, and irrational violence. Although the terminology varied, the general idea was clear. It was obviously one which many ghetto dwellers could develop on their own; but if they were so inclined, ideological support from experienced outsiders would do nothing to diminish their readiness for rebellion.

The Washington ghetto dwellers did not only take note of turmoil at a distance. There were also a number of incidents involving their own community. During the 1966 Easter holidays there was a disturbance caused by black teenagers in an amusement park outside the city; reportedly those in the Winston Street neighborhood knew of it in advance. In late summer that year there was a considerable rise of tension and some violence between the police and the inhabitants of a distant ghetto area in Southeast Washington. For some time afterwards Washington newspapers focused their attention on the "breakdown of law and order" in this area, particularly on the problems of shopkeepers. Ghetto dwellers in other areas also acknowledged that there was "a lot of trouble" going on there. The next major period of crisis came the following summer. As the risings of Newark and Detroit had followed closely on each other many asked the question whether Washington was next in line. Some younger men in the Winston Street neighborhood alleged that there were newcomers to the city who were propagating the opinion that a rising would be a good thing; with the high death figures in Detroit and Newark in mind, they were themselves among those who were worried by the prospect of a repetition in their city. Therefore they very consistently argued strongly against a rising when conversations turned to this topic. During this period a number of rumors about agitators and incidents were flying and given varying credence. One very real incident occurred in the Northwestern corner of the ghetto where a young man left in charge of a delicatessen shot two youths who were allegedly trying to rob the store. Other young men in the area reputedly felt that there was something odd about the circumstances of the shooting. For some time people in this neighborhood were brooding over what had occurred, and at one point an angry crowd assembled close to the store. Apparently it was dissolved by a leader of a local civil rights group who dissuaded the people present from taking violent action. The situation was generally understood as one which could have been the starting point of general turmoil.

There came an outburst of looting and burning a rainy summer night, largely concentrated to the lower ghetto end of Seventh Street in the Northwest section of the city where there were a number of used furniture stores. Comparatively few stores were damaged, however, and there were not many arrests. Compared to what people expected could have happened, this was only a minor outbreak involving mainly a rather small number of teenage boys—it was generally believed that the rain had contributed strongly in keeping people off the streets. Those in the Winston Street neighborhood who had feared a large-scale rebellion with police and military reprisals on the model of Newark and Detroit seemed almost relieved. Many saw only a temporary respite, however; this was certainly not the expression of pent-up feelings which they thought would be as natural in Washington as it had been elsewhere. One swinger with a far-ranging network who usually appeared to have a good idea of what was going on in the community had this to say:

"I think maybe that's it for this summer, but a lot of people I know would be in that kind of thing didn't even hear about this one till it was over. The rain did a lot, you know. And then a lot of people are a little scared right now, with all those people who got killed in Newark and Detroit, and they might be ready again when they've forgot about that. Next year they could start all over again."

In late October there was a tumultuous ending to a rock-and-roll show at the Washington Coliseum which was crowded to more than capacity with an audience of 6,000 to 8,000 people, most of them young; there was a noticeable amount of gatecrashing. It was an attractive bill including the popular duo Peaches and Herb and the comedian Clay Tyson as emcee; the stars of the show and thus last to appear were the Temptations, one of the leading Motown groups. Since there had been few major musical events in the community this fall even the Coliseum which usually has many empty seats was not large enough. People were standing in the aisles, and anybody who left his seat during the show—and there are always people moving around—could not be sure to get it back. Thus there was considerable commotion throughout the show. Finally, soon after the Temptations came on stage, a crowd surged forward toward it, dancing, walking, and pushing. This is not unusual at such shows, although it is discouraged by the management. In this case, however, the people who were moving ahead pushed one of the special policemen guarding the stage area to the ground. He apparently panicked as he felt he might get trampled to death; thus he reached for his gun and fired in the air. With the kind of expectation of violence prevalent among ghetto dwellers, this started a panic. People in the hall cried in alarm, one young woman could be heard shouting, "They're shooting! No, No!", and while many fled, others joined those pushing toward the stage which was quickly vacated by the Temptations. Several people were hurt in the throng. Rufus "Catfish" Mayfield, the well-known leader of a recently formed ghetto work corps, went on stage to ask people to return to order but was greeted with hostility or indifference. Chairs and other objects were flying as it was announced that the show would not be resumed. In the next hours there was rock throwing, window breaking, and looting in the area around the Coliseum; a few police-men were injured but not many arrests were made.

The years and months preceding the insurrection of April were thus far from uneventful to the ghetto dwellers. Again and again they were reminded of the possibility of violent conflict. Apart from the incidents which became more generally known there were such neighborhood happenings as the Friday night streetcorner arrest described earlier in this chapter. If the quick response of part fear, part violence by the Coliseum audience at the Temptations show gave a glimpse of how ready many ghetto dwellers were to see danger and violence in a situation, such an incident as this fall evening arrest showed the ghetto dwellers that the police were thinking in similar terms. As the next spring approached, it was a very obvious question whether there was another long, hot, violent ghetto summer beyond it.

*The insurrection*[9]

Like most people those in the Winston Street neighborhood were used to thinking of ghetto risings as phenomena of the summer; the street scene is more lively then, so escalation comes quicker, and the summer unemployment of high school students may add to the unrest. Among young people with a higher degree of political awareness it was pointed out now and then that turmoil could very well occur any time of the year, but as April came there was no widespread expectation that anything would happen very soon. One of the first evenings of the month there was an incident at a drug store at the always restless corner of Fourteenth and U Street, but it was reportedly calmed through the intervention of black power militants. Only two days later Martin Luther King was assassinated in Memphis, and the same street corner was soon again in the midst of the action.

As the news of the Memphis shooting—and somewhat later, of King's death —came over radio and television, neighbors on Winston Street quickly told each other about it, and many of those who had telephones called friends and relatives to see if they had heard about it. They speculated about what might happen. As the black radio stations turned to religious music the disc jockeys counseled their listeners to be calm. On WOL Nighthawk asked everybody to stay off the streets; King would not have wanted anybody to take to arms. But it could hardly be avoided that crowds formed to vent their united anger. Apparently there were more of them at the corner of Fourteenth and U Streets than anywhere else. As Stokely Carmichael appeared from the SNCC office on Fourteenth Street just north of the corner, a crowd gathered around him. He went around to those businesses which were still open, asking them to close in honor of Dr. King, and they did so. In a couple of instances he advised those around him against violence, pointing to the overwhelming power of the adversary. Yet he could not contain the anger of the people on the streets whose number grew as the news of the assassination spread. Store windows started breaking and looting followed. After a while Carmichael gave up his attempt to keep the protest orderly and left the area. While he may have influenced the ghetto's contemporary ideology of discontent, he had little power over its ultimate expression. One young man who had been out on the streets this night commented a few days later:

"You know, this thing had been building up for a long time, and so when something like this happens you can't just say, 'Hey, cool it, it's dangerous.' People felt they just got to do something, you know, and I guess most people don't believe too much in marching and that kind of stuff any more."

There were few policemen in the area as looting began, and the looters apparently did not feel very constrained by their presence. (According to one report, the police were told when crowds started to assemble that a conspicuous presence on their part could only exacerbate feelings.) Soon there were also attacks on stores on other main business streets in the ghetto. According to eye witnesses euphoria was added to anger as people felt they were finally striking back. When more police arrived on the scene bottles, bricks, and other objects were thrown at them; they were still too few to confront the larger groups involved in ransacking the stores, but a heavy rain began to fall during which the number of people on the streets decreased. However, looting did not stop. One young man on upper Fourteenth Street apparently shouted a few words out of a popular James Brown hit: "We all get together, in any kind of weather..." Fires began to burn along the street, but with fewer people around, the police were slowly regaining control, partly with the use of teargas. Toward the early morning hours the community seemed largely quiet again.

This was Thursday night. On Friday morning people on Winston Street were debating what would happen that evening; ghetto streets are always lively on weekend nights, with more people than usual moving about, and people were still angry. "This ain't over yet," one of the mainstreamer men said. "It could go on a couple of more days."

He was quite right; already that morning people were throwing bricks at cars passing through the ghetto, and looting and burning began again. Some groups went downtown but looting there was rather limited—as we have noted once before, it was particularly men's fashion stores that were hit—and there was hardly any burning outside the ghetto, where most of it continued to be concentrated on the main shopping streets. Some groups seemed to concentrate on going around "opening up" stores which had closed early—that is, they broke doors and windows to leave the way in open to looters. This made it possible for a great many to join in who had qualms about taking the first step themselves. One young mother said afterwards:

"Well, you could see all the stuff lying there and all those people going in and out, and somebody was gonna take it, so I thought I could as well get some for myself."

Of course, a great many ghetto dwellers took no part in the looting. There were those who felt it safest to stay home, perhaps following what was happening on radio and television. One young man on Winston Street accounted for his weekend this way:

"I got myself a bottle of gin on Friday morning when the stores were still open, and then when I came home from work and saw all those people running around I just sat down and switched on the television. And that's what I did all the time, drinking and watching those crazy people taking care of business."

Some older people disapproved more directly of what was going on, seeing it not as a rising but as theft and destruction. This was the view a middle-aged woman expressed a few days later:

"I was really sorry to see it. Some of the people I saw should have a lot better sense. They was just stealing, that's what I think. Some of the people in them stores hadn't done nothing wrong."

As far as most of the people on the streets were concerned, however, they did not appear to think that they were doing anything immoral; rather, they were affirming an emergent community morality. It was as if goods hoarded by somebody who had no right to it were suddenly released for general consumption. Although profits were derived from looting, it could be easily understood as a political act against white oppression and exploitation. At the very least, there was little question of "theft" on the part of any individual participant, as previous ownership became simply irrelevant when the stores came temporarily under generous community control. Furthermore, the burning which often followed on looting was obviously to be seen within the framework of black-white conflict; nobody could profit directly from throwing Molotov cocktails. Even more important, the participants abided quite strictly by their definition of the ghetto moral community and generally did not harm businesses with "soul brother" or "soul sister" signs. (There were at least one "sole brother" and one "sold brother" sign—ghetto-specific culture is largely non-literate.) Any harm to ghetto dwellers' lives and properties was thus unintentional; yet it was rather extensive, as fires spread to black-owned businesses as well as to the apartments where ghetto dwellers lived above white business establishments. To the residents on the large business streets, then, the firebombing was a great danger. Fats, who had recently moved from Winston Street to a building just off Fourteenth Street where the fires were heaviest, said afterwards that if he had seen anybody trying to set fire to his building he would have shot him.

During much of the Friday the police were alone in trying to halt the rising. However, they were much too few to do so successfully. Their presence in small numbers had little effect, as their authority was not recognized. There were acts of hostility against them as well as against firemen; however, they were under orders to use their weapons only with the greatest restraint, so direct violence between ghetto dwellers and police was limited. Very few sniping incidents were reported; afterwards there were many comments to the effect that ghetto dwellers could well have responded in kind had the police started shooting. As it was, the police often seemed simply irrelevant as the looting and burning continued.

Those who went on radio and television to ask people to leave the streets did not seem to have a great influence either. On Saturday, as the rising was drawing toward an end, they were joined by "soul brother number one", James Brown; this must have been one of the few times when many young ghetto dwellers reacted to him only with derision. Otherwise the black radio stations had a very restrained coverage of what was going on in the city, as it had been claimed that the news media had helped intensify earlier risings through their reporting. One station returned repeatedly to a gospel hit by the Violinaires, "I don't know what this world is coming to", with this bewildered beginning:

> *Demonstration and protest*
> *putting brother 'gainst brother*

*juvenile delinquency*
*putting child against mother*

While this responded to the sentiments of some ghetto dwellers, others found it simply ridiculous.

In the Winston Street neighborhood, a few blocks away from ghetto business centers, there was no burning, but some of the businesses at neighborhood street corners were raided. Liquor stores were particularly heavily hurt as people swarmed in and around them on Friday afternoon. However, those neighborhood people who took part in the looting did so mainly on the principal shopping streets. Most of them were swingers and teenagers, but there were also streetcorner men and younger children.

### After the turmoil

On Friday evening the National Guard and federal troops were called into action in Washington, and through their massive presence, rather than through much use of force, they put an end to the rising. During Saturday looting and burning gradually ceased. Soldiers were standing guard outside the stores that were left, but along long stretches of the main business streets only ruins remained. While white radio stations reported that the soldiers' guns were unloaded, black radio stations said nothing about this. In the Winston Street neighborhood small boys who had been to see the military encampment at a nearby school were practicing marching, while adults stood in small groups gossiping and joking about the last few days' events. On Sunday things were returning to normal. People hurried to do their shopping at those chain stores which were still in existence and which opened for a little while to meet the needs of those customers who had not been able to do any shopping in the past days. Some neighborhood people went over to the large shopping streets to see what they looked like; there they could mix with sightseeing white suburbanites whose movie cameras, steadily aimed at the ruins, were spinning out of the windows of slow-moving cars.

First people wondered what would happen on Tuesday when Martin Luther King was buried in Atlanta; then the question arose if something might not happen again the following weekend, which was Easter holiday. Fires were set to several ghetto business establishments in the days which followed, and acute tenseness remained for some time as many were not yet convinced that the turmoil was over. There was a good laugh as somebody appeared in a new outfit he had not had before the rising, and one could hear of exchanges as well as goods for sale—some had gotten the wrong size, and there were obviously those who had taken booty not only for their own consumption. In the Winston Street neighborhood there appeared to be rather few who strongly resented the rising.[10] Nobody there had been greatly harmed by it, while those ghetto dwellers who had lost homes, belongings, and jobs may well have had another opinion. Fats, coming back to see his friends from his new home, complained that there was nowhere to go shopping in the area of upper Fourteenth Street, but even so he was only rather slightly inconvenienced. Even those, particularly among the mainstreamers, who did not approve of what had happened were usually ready to explain it in terms of ghetto grievances, although some of them then continued to propose rather superficial remedies, such as more youth workers on the recreation department payroll. (However, they thought of this as a black power program.) Others looked at the rising from a more humorous angle—looting was made to resemble trickster behavior, a familiar ghetto theme. The illegality of taking from the oppressor could be recognized, but it was a wickedness it was easy to empathize with. Younger people, in particular, looked at the rising in the most strictly political terms, expressing the hope that "they gotta do something now". Thus for some, participation in the rising, if only a matter of momentary anger at first, or fun and convenience later, may have become an act of political commitment—at least public meetings held in the months after the rising seemed to draw larger audiences than most earlier meetings.[11]

However, what would actually happen continued to be uncertain. It would probably take long before ghetto business streets were rebuilt, and it was very likely that many of the white merchants would not come back even then. A considerable number probably did not want to, and with insurance rates in black ghettos soaring, even more of them could not afford to. Perhaps this could leave niches open for black enterprises, since only their "soul brother" signs seemed to be as valuable as a lot of insurance.

As far as the police is concerned, the other focus of discontent which we discussed above, its relationship to the community continued to deteriorate in the months following the April rising. A number of incidents were quite widely talked about, and black power groups emphasized the demand for some kind of community control of the police. Undoubtedly it would help to have more black policemen, recruited from the ghetto. After all, a policeman's role is to a great extent that of an officer of the peace; if the goal of keeping the peace is best pursued by his staying off the streets, as it seems to have been in many recent critical ghetto situations, he is obviously a failure.[12] Black officers might be better able to calm feelings in the community by virtue of their skill in the interaction idiom of the ghetto dwellers, even if it is true that they are no less harsh than others if violence does erupt. It is also likely that their common-sense knowledge of ghetto life would make them more sure of themselves and thus much less vulnerable to accusations of arbitrariness and brutality. But in the current situation of conflict between the police and the community, it may not be easy to recruit ghetto dwellers to the force, as they could well come to be seen as renegades. Even if it were possible, there could come a reaction on the part of ghetto militants against attempts to manipulate the community by putting a black man on the beat. So perhaps there is no other way of restoring confidence in the police than granting some form of community control.

But after all, if demands for greater black participation in ghetto business and law enforcement were met, the problems of the relationship between the ghetto and mainstream society would still have been dealt with only in a marginal way. The questions of income and employment, for instance, would probably not be greatly influenced.[13] Because they are based within ghetto territory, shopkeepers and policemen are particularly easily touched by ghetto protest, but they are only the most accessible symbols of the whole body of ghetto grievances against the wider society. And, we must conclude, for the wider society to try to deal only with the symbols may be an unrealistic solution, since symbols could possibly be exchanged.

# 9
# Mainstream
# and Ghetto in Culture

In the preceding chapters we have identified a number of features of ghetto life and outlook which we have taken to be characteristic of this community in contrast to mainstream American society. Among the components of this ghetto-specific complex are for instance female household dominance; a ghetto-specific male role of somewhat varying expression including, among other emphases, toughness, sexual activity, and a fair amount of liquor consumption; a relatively conflict-ridden relationship between the sexes; rather intensive participation in informal social life outside the domestic domain; flexible household composition; fear of trouble in the environment; a certain amount of suspiciousness toward other persons' motives; relative closeness to religion; particular food habits; a great interest in the music of the group; and a relatively hostile view of much of white America and its representatives. By way of conclusion, we will devote this chapter to a discussion of the sense in which features such as these can be said to constitute a ghetto culture—or, more exactly as well as more clumsily, a ghetto subculture. As we have dwelt on this problem in a piecemeal way before, a perspective toward it is at least implicit in some of the earlier chapters. Here we will bring our point of view to bear on problems of cultural analysis in a more general way—problems which have engendered considerable discussion in recent years. The principal problem is simply what we shall mean by culture in such situations as that of the ghetto, and what are the implications of a cultural point of view toward ghetto life. How does ghetto culture relate to the culture of the wider society? Can anything be said about the role of this culture in the future participation of black people in American society?

The concept of culture can be stretched to various lengths and in different directions. A general anthropological notion of what it means to act according to one's culture is, loosely speaking, to follow one's inclinations as these have been developed by learning from other members of one's community. In line with this, there can be no doubt that it is an expression of ghetto culture for a ghetto dweller to like soul food and soul music. It is "natural", culturally speaking, that he should prefer James Brown while his white counterpart prefers the Beach Boys or Mantovani. Likewise, while a black person may say that chitterlings are tasty, someone from another cultural background may find that they taste like rubber. But the listing of ghetto-specific features above contains other items which have a more questionable cultural status. Is it cultural to be afraid of crime in the streets? To dislike the police? For a man to desert his family? For a woman to share her household with her mother, her brother, her children, her sister's son, and a boarder? The problem we are raising here is this: what kind of freedom of action do poor and oppressed people actually have? Or if we put it another way: is the ghetto dweller actually doing what he wants to do in cases such as these, or is he somehow constrained to acting the way he does by the nature of the situation he is in? If the latter is the case, does he actually behave in accordance with his culture?

In order to arrive at a more explicitly reasoned kind of answer to such questions, we will have to move in a rather roundabout way. Perhaps it seems like an unnecessary effort; after all, what we should mean by culture may be only a terminological quibble. But concepts are tools for thinking, and unless we know how to use them our thinking may be bad. In trying to decide how to use the culture concept in the ghetto context, then, we will also be working toward a more exact understanding of the bases of continuity and change in ghetto life.

### The culture of poverty

Questions about the relationship between culture and external constraints have been intensely debated recently, in connection with the rise to popularity of the notion of a culture of poverty. Although the discussion has partly been abstract and generalizing, it is obvious that it has drawn so much interest among American social scientists because it is directly relevant to the practical problems of poverty in the United States, including those of ghetto poverty. We will relate to this discussion here; yet we must not take it for granted that poverty is the only fact of life that is important in understanding the behavior of ghetto dwellers. True, the point has often been made by social scientists that what has tended to be seen as "typically black" is often actually "typically poor".[1] Phrasing it somewhat differently, as it appears to many ghetto dwellers: to be black means to be poor. In the preceding chapters we have given little explicit attention to the distinction between blackness and limited access to resources, as we have simply accepted the fact that they tend to coincide. But here, as we turn specifically to poverty as a determinant of behavior, we must be aware that there is a residual category of blackness, including such foundations for behavior as the African origin, the Southern background, and the subjection to racism which ghetto dwellers do not share with all other poor. These facets of blackness we will temporarily leave aside here.

The breakthrough of the culture of poverty as a catch phrase may be due to a great extent to the fact that it was used, in a rather non-technical and diluted sense, by Michael Harrington in his well-known book *The Other America* (1962). However, the current concept of a culture of poverty did not originate in a study of the American poor. Although it has had some precursors, it seems first to have been suggested by Oscar Lewis in *Five Families* (1959), a book of Mexican case studies. Lewis has continued to discuss his understanding of this subculture (for by his definition a culture of poverty is never the property of an autonomous society) more thoroughly in *The Children of Sánchez* (1961) and *La Vida* (1966), the former on Mexicans, the latter on Puerto Ricans. Since his statements have had a great influence on the debate concerning the culture of poverty, we will turn to them briefly to see what are the major points of controversy which we will have to take into account in our interpretation of the cultural side to ghetto life.

Although Lewis' studies have so far involved Latin Americans, he explicitly formulates the culture of poverty as a cross-cultural regularity transcending regional, rural-urban and national differences. Like other commentators we will have to agree that there are noteworthy parallels in the kinds of behavior which occur among the poor in different societies. We can recognize from the ghetto such items as gregariousness, informal credit among neighbors, a high incidence of alcoholism, the use of violence in settling quarrels, consensual unions, male desertion and a tendency toward matrifocal families, a cult of masculinity, and a corresponding martyr complex among women; these are traits from a list of the components of a Mexican culture of poverty (Lewis 1961:xxvi-xxvii).

This kind of culture of poverty, according to Lewis, is something which occurs particularly in a class-stratified, highly individuated capitalist society with few or none of the characteristics of a welfare state. There is in this kind of society a high rate of unemployment or underemployment for the unskilled labor force. Such labor is poorly paid, there is little formal organization of any kind for the low-income population, and the members of the dominant class stress the accumulation of wealth and the value of upward social mobility while explaining poverty as the result of inferiority or personal inadequacy (Lewis 1966:xliii-xliv). These conditions all seem rather clearly to be present in the case of the ghetto. However, we should not only note this similarity of setting. We must also take cognizance of the fact that Lewis makes the point clearly that in his view these kinds of constraints give rise to the culture of poverty—that is, his model is both cultural and macrostructural. The latter kind of constraints are the ultimate determinants of behavior; culture is defined in a conventional anthropological manner as based on learning within the community. A culture of poverty is thus a design for living within the constraints of poverty, passed down from generation to generation, thereby achieving stability and persistence (Lewis 1961:xxiv). The direct rather than ultimate origin of the modes of action encompassed by an ongoing culture of poverty is consequently the cultural repository made up of earlier poor generations.

Parenthetically we may note that Lewis seems slightly inconsistent on this point. Some commentators may wish to dispute the idea that cultural transmission is really very much at the basis of such items from Lewis' trait list as reluctance to defer gratification, the abandonment of mothers and children by their fathers, and a high tolerance for psychological pathology (Lewis 1961:xxvi-xxvii). Yet we may not be ready to dismiss this possibility. It is more difficult to take the cultural learning criterion seriously, however, when Lewis lists such features of a culture of poverty as unemployment and under-employment, low wages, a chronic shortage of cash, and living in crowded quarters. Is this really the culture of poverty, or is it the poverty itself, upon which the culture is built? Here Lewis seems to be using another notion of a culture as "a whole way of life", with no clear distinction between the culture and its environment, between causes and consequences. The holistic culture concept has a long and venerable tradition in anthropology, of course, but as a tool of dynamic analysis it is of very limited utility. It may be, however, that this notion of culture has also contributed much to the popularity of the concept of a culture of poverty; terms such as this seem often to be used only as a convenient way of subsuming a great number of modes of action under one cover. And Michael Harrington, in taking over Lewis' concept for *The Other America,* may have found the holism of the culture concept appealing as a weapon in the struggle for social reform. It implies the fact that poverty influences the entire ways of life of the American poor, and with this point clearly made one could hope for a stronger commitment to a crusade against poverty.

However, what has turned out to be most controversial as far as the culture of poverty is concerned is the emphasis on culture as modes of behavior learned within the community. Lewis has certainly not been alone in providing fuel for this debate. Other recent analyses by social scientists have also noted specifically lower-class modes of behavior, and in some cases they have been less explicit in spelling out the nature of the macrostructural concerns. Among the most noted writings of this kind are those by Walter Miller (1958, 1959), delineating a lower-class culture which to a great extent parallels Lewis' conceptualization of a culture of poverty and which thus also contains many of the modes of action and outlook which we have viewed as ghetto-specific above; the tendency toward matrifocality, the concerns with toughness and trouble, the orientation toward peer group life, the idea of "figuring out an angle" in interpersonal relations are all there, together with other familiar features. Miller, as an anthropologist, obviously uses the culture concept to convey the picture of a way of life a great deal more orderly than it appears according to the widely accepted imagery of disorganization and deviance which outside observers apply to lower-class behavior. In this sense, he contributes to depathologizing the understanding of such behavior. Yet there are obviously problems which cannot be normalized out of existence on very good grounds, and according to Miller's conceptualization these arise out of the distinctive cultural system of the lower-class community. Miller therefore suggests treating these within the community; that is, he emphasizes cultural social-work solutions to the problems of the poor.[2]

Although such ideas certainly have some relevance, many commentators have felt that they do not go far enough and that therefore they may be quite dangerous. It has been widely feared that analyses of the behavior of the poor in cultural terms, such as those of Lewis and Miller, could be turned around in such a way that by the time a concept like the culture of poverty is assimilated into the generally familiar stock of ideas about the nature of society, it could provide some spurious scientific underpinning for the timeworn belief that the poor have only themselves to blame for their condition. The idea that the life style of the poor is self-perpetuating has probably always been popular among those groups in society which are better off. By pointing particularly to non-adaptive, not to say immoral behavior among the poor, they have often been able to refuse responsibility for life at the bottom of society. If promiscuity, births out of wedlock, alcoholism, conspicuous consumption, and unemployment (defined as voluntary) are parts of a cultural heritage, it could be held that the culture of poverty causes poverty, rather than the other way around. As regrettable as such a conclusion may seem, of course, we cannot easily exclude the possibility that it has some partial validity. Oscar Lewis himself makes allowance for this as he states that once the culture of poverty comes into existence, it tends to perpetuate itself in new generations. Slum children soon absorb the values and attitudes of their sub-culture so that they may not be able later to take advantage of increased opportunities (Lewis 1966:xlv).

This idea, if given an emphasis it probably does not deserve, certainly has profound implications for American social policy. If nothing helps, why bother with a war on poverty? As the idea of a culture of poverty spread, policy-makers and others concerned with a positive program for eradicating social ills felt bound to criticize some interpretations of it. One of them, Alvin Schorr (1964:907), expressed his concern with the "corrupt use" of the concept which he felt was gaining currency both among some whose prejudices it supported and among others whom one could have expected to have a greater under-standing. According to this usage, the culture of poverty is an autonomous outlook toward the world, with obscure origins and little connection to reality.

There is another facet to this rather negative conception of a culture of poverty. Not only does it refer to a cluster of existing non-adaptive elements; it also denotes a lack of such elements as the dominant groups in society would regard as adaptive. Roach and Gursslin (1967:387 n.), in an article sharply critical of the delineation of a culture of poverty they have found widespread but largely based on conjectures, note that it is not easy to ascertain exactly what is supposed to be transmitted between generations of the poor; to a great extent it seems to be simply the absence of mainstream culture. This picture of the culture of poverty as a void also finds some support with Oscar Lewis, who notes that the poverty of culture is one of the crucial aspects of the culture of poverty (Lewis 1966:lii).

Obviously this point need not only be a part of a coldly contemptuous view of the life of the poor. It has been embodied in the concept of cultural depriva-tion, a twin term of the culture of poverty which has come to cover a great many social action programs designed to give the American poor, and not least the ghetto dwellers, valuable mainstream cultural skills. Yet one may feel somewhat uneasy with the orientation of this term as well, both because it may lead to the belief that such programmed acculturation really takes place in a cultural vacuum and because it focuses attention on changing the poor as individuals rather than on changing that system where they have been assigned places as poor.

## The adaptation of the poor

With the tendency to interpret such ideas as the culture of poverty and cultural deprivation so as to imply that the way of life of the poor is self-perpetuating, there has obviously been a new need for analyses showing both how opportuni-ties taken for granted by the majority are blocked to the poor and how the modes of action of the poor in many cases are realistic adaptations or at least understandable reactions to the particular situations they are in. The preceding chapters have given examples of this. We have seen that variations in economic constraints cause variations in behavior in the ghetto as elsewhere, so that those members of the community who are lower-middle class or reasonably satisfactorily salaried working class tend to a greater extent to be main-streamers while those in a more severely compressed economic niche form the greater number of those evincing ghetto-specific modes of behavior. True, the correlation is not perfect, in that some with more satisfactory resources behave ghetto-specifically in many ways, while others with very limited resources still manage to come rather close to a mainstreamer way of life. But even so there can be no doubt that much of what has been labeled ghetto-specific here is directly related to poverty. We have noted that the ghetto-specific male role is more in line with the economic, occupational, and educational position of many ghetto men than is the mainstreamer male role; we have established the fact that economic problems form one of the foundations of male-female conflict as generated within the ghetto household; and we have pointed out that the pooling and redistribution of limited resources are functions of both flexible household composition and informal neighborhood interaction. Certainly there may be touches to these features of ghetto life which are not directly determined by poverty, but it cannot be gainsaid that they are strongly influenced by it.

This kind of emphasis on situational constraints and on the ways in which the behavior of the poor adapt to them has been prominent in recent writings which have been more or less direct comments on the concept of a culture of poverty. Charles Valentine devotes a good part of his book *Culture and Poverty* (1968) to this theme; a paper by Louis Kriesberg (1963) explores more generally the analytic differentiation of explanations of behavior into on the one hand cultural explanations, defined as based on parental transmission of values, beliefs, and behavior patterns, and on the other hand situational explanations, based both on such social conditions as interaction patterns and on such factors as financial constraints, which Kriesberg terms non-social;[3] William Yancey (n.d.) argues similarly for a less parsimonious, more differentiated conception of the culture of poverty, in which situational explanations are established for the greater number of the modes of behavior characteristic of the poor; and Hylan Lewis (1967 b) notes the vagueness and the many uses of the culture concept, the variability of behavior in the low-income category, and the character of this behavior as a spectrum of pragmatic adjustments to stresses and deprivations.

The general trend of such comments is clearly insightful. To some students of human behavior the insights may appear trivial, but because of the prevalence of other ideas about the behavior of the poor and because of the implications for social policy it has obviously been deemed necessary to make these points with great emphasis. In contrasting situational adaptiveness, however, some commentators may have gone to unnecessary lengths. There has been a tendency to argue against the stereotyped and extreme notion of a culture of poverty in such a way as to lose sight of the merits of a more subtle kind of cultural analysis of life in poverty. The distinction set forth by Kriesberg and others between cultural and situational explanations is often not easily applied; certainly a mode of behavior can be both learned from an older generation and suited to situational constraints. Kriesberg notes that there will necessarily be large areas of such ambiguity but suggests problems to which it can be more easily applied. If the distinction is to be generally upheld, however, it becomes necessary to define "cultural" and "situational" in such a way as to make one a residual category of the other. Some writers indeed lean toward such a usage. One way of doing it involves taking note of the fact that poor people often do not practice what they preach. As we have seen there is much verbalization of mainstream ideals in the ghetto, even from those who often act ghetto-specifically in direct contradiction of these ideals. This can be interpreted to mean that the values which are culturally trans- mitted in the ghetto community are actually those of mainstream culture, while the behavior in conflict with these values is held to be situational, going against the cultural grain. Roach and Gursslin (1967:387) and Valentine (1968:118—119) are among those leaning to such a view; they take culture to constitute strong values. This conception obviously limits the cultural section of the behavior of the poor, leaving a great deal to be defined as situational. Herbert Gans (1967 b:14) goes a step further; he explicitly cuts through the Gordian knot by defining culture as what is resistant to change, and the cul- ture of poverty, consequently, as those patterns of culture which keep people poor when improved opportunities are at hand. Thus defined, the culture of poverty probably does not amount to very much, according to Gans; poor people share the aspirations of those with more adequate incomes and would soon approach these in their way of life, were their own economic opportunities improved. In this emphasis on values and aspirations shared by the poor with working-class or middle-class people Gans agrees with Hylan Lewis (1967 b:23) and Elliot Liebow (1967:222) who both feel that more attention should be paid to the fact that poor people share mainstream ideals.

It is not difficult to sympathize with such ideas. However, anthropologists may find it very hard to appreciate the innovation of defining culture as change-resistant or even the restriction of the culture concept to encompass only strong norms and aspirations. Are we really accustomed to viewing as non-cultural every kind of behavior which occurs as a matter of convenience, possibly going against some deeply cherished ideal? It is not all there is to the culture of a hunting band that it would be a good thing to live at the Zoo. It also has a culture for the ongoing constraints of everyday life, a "design for living" as the saying goes. In fact, it is only anthropological common sense that any culture is adapted to its environment—otherwise there would be nothing to call cultural ecology. Culture, then, is largely situational. If in the case of the ghetto dwellers, and the poor more generally, the constraining environment is social, rather than natural as in most traditional ecological studies in anthropology, it makes little or no difference in principle.[4] Here we must part company with some of the critics of the concept of a culture of poverty, finding that they may well fail to see just how the ways of life of the poor are cultural. Instead we will return to the original point of view of Oscar Lewis.

## The sharing of culture

An anthropologist does not have to agree with every detail of Lewis' concep- tualization of the culture of poverty in order to find his idea of modes of action as both macrostructurally influenced and culturally transmitted more congenial than the simplistic either-or notions of some of the critics of his concept. One can only attempt to stick to this view more consistently than Lewis has done, and perhaps develop it more explicitly. One part of such a more fundamentally anthropological approach to cultural analysis is to suggest a minimal definition of culturalness, in line with what is understood to be the essence of conventional usage. The basic fact of this usage, it seems, is that there are social processes of sharing of modes of behavior and outlook within the community. As we have seen, the usual emphasis is on learning through such processes; however, it also appears important to take note of the continuous community-based maintenance of such cultural features in interaction idioms. These are questions which can be analytically distinguished from questions of macrostructural constraints and adaptation, although the substantive focus of interest may be the same. To some extent the latter kinds of questions can be dealt with separately. In the analysis of behavior in terms of its cultural status they may be treated as given while interest is concentrated on the recurrent generation and maintenance of images of modes of behavior through social relationships within the community under study, in this case the ghetto. The extent to which such cultural phenomena are relevant for the understanding of ghetto behavior may well vary between different modes of action. It may be difficult, however, to determine exactly when cultural influences are significant. The difference in behavior between a person who is alone in being exposed to certain macrostructural constraints, on the one hand, and a person, on the other hand, who is influenced both by these constraints and by the behavior of others who are also affected by them cannot be easily determined unless there is an experimental situation. This means that our discussion of cultural influences on ghetto behavior will be couched to some extent in terms of mere plausibility. Perhaps this can be defended if it is felt that it contributes to our understanding of the issues involved. Besides, it is not worse in this respect than the definition of culture as change-resistant, as this kind of cultural influence cannot be isolated in a single, macrostructurally stable situation either.[5] Admittedly ours is a softer culture concept than that encompassing only strong norms which are clearly much more easily identifiable and which are more often likely to be an autonomous force in generating behavior when a more completely free choice is possible. But such a hard culture concept may simply lead us away from questions which may be interesting although difficult to answer.

One further clarification of our conception of culture as applied to the ghetto situation may be inserted here. We have recognized that the influences toward similarity of behavior through intra-community processes may be of varying strength for different modes of ghetto-specific behavior; this is to say that the degree of culturalness of the latter varies. Thus questions about culturalness had better be asked about specific modes of behavior rather than about "a whole way of life". The integration of ghetto-specific modes of behavior among themselves is a separate problem which does not influence the definition of culturalness—it is not only in the ghetto community that the existence of such over-all integration may be to some extent questionable although it is often assumed as a matter of definition.[6] Modes of action influenced by learning within the community may well be related to macrostructural or other external ultimate determinants rather than to each other while still qualifying as more or less cultural.

If we take the learning and maintenance of modes of behavior within the community as the fundamental criterion of culturalness, then, one of our problems is obviously what kinds of behavior are culturally influenced. With a hard culture concept, we would be on safe grounds taking note only of the explicit instruction which the older generation gives the young about its basic values and beliefs. As we have seen, explicit statements of this kind are often strongly mainstream-oriented in all segments of the ghetto community. Thus there would seem to be little ghetto-specific culture. As Valentine (1968:113) suggests, ghetto-specific behavior would not be cultural because ghetto dwellers do not give sufficient allegiance or emotional investment to it to care to pass it on to their children.

However, it is highly questionable whether we usually confine ourselves to such a restricted notion of cultural transmission. The role modeling which is generally held to be an important part of the transmission of sex roles is an obvious example of a process of cultural sharing where the instruction is largely accidental. With this example in mind, we must realize that any act which occurs in the presence of others has the potential of transmitting an image of itself to these others. In a most elementary sense, it is an act of cultural transmission—it is turned into such transmission, that is, if the potential recipient adds his image of the mode of action in question to his own cultural repertoire. It is then unimportant what the person evincing ghetto-specific behavior thinks about it, if he likes his own way of life or not; if others are present, he cannot choose not to communicate about it.[7]

This kind of transmission may be most readily understood as cultural if its quantity is taken into account. While cultural transmission by explicit instruction is of an intensive kind, transmission by precept as involved in role modeling is most likely to be efficient when a mode of behavior is encountered frequently and in many different persons. What has been described before as ghetto-specific modes of action, of course, are such recurrent phenomena of ghetto life. Consequently a ghetto dweller can hardly avoid familiarizing himself with them as he meets them among the people he interacts with daily in his community.

Here we may note that modes of behavior are more or less public, so that some of them are less easily transmitted through everyday life than others. Those kinds of ghetto-specific behavior with which we have been concerned in the preceding chapters, however, occur often enough and publicly enough for almost everybody to become acquainted with them. It should also be recognized that individuals can expose themselves more or less strongly to this kind of cultural transmission, by being in greater or lesser contact with others. Here Roach and Gursslin (1967:388) find reason to doubt the tenability of the idea of a culture of poverty, as the studies on which they base their critique seem to emphasize the isolation of poor people. However this may be in other groups of poor people—and there is obviously good reason not to generalize about the ways of life of all poor people everywhere—it is hardly a very valid criticism in the case of the ghetto where there is much informal interaction outside the domestic domain.

Exposure thus gives practically every ghetto dweller opportunities to familiarize himself with a range of modes of behavior and combinations of modes of behavior, from mainstream-oriented to ghetto-specific ways. It is obvious, however, that man is not a mindless cultural automaton; some of the doubts raised against the notion of a culture of poverty may be reactions against tendencies to view culture as an oppressive tradition which people can only slavishly follow. First of all, when people develop a cultural repertoire by being at the receiving end of cultural transmission, this certainly does not mean that they will put every part of it to use. Rather, the repertoire to some measure constitutes adaptive potential. While some of the cultural goods received may be situationally irrelevant, such as most of that picked up at the movies, much of that derived from school, and even some of that encountered within the ghetto community, other components of an individual's repertoire may come in more useful. This is the way in which we see culture as situationally adaptive; since most people are exposed to others who have already taken on adaptations to a roughly similar situation, much of what is culturally transmitted may be counted upon to constitute a reasonably relevant repertoire. There is no need to give either too rosy or too mechanical a picture of this. It is not at all certain that one has been exposed to detailed solutions to the very complicated kinds of situations one may be confronted with, so certainly there must always be much innovation in individual adaptations. And even if ghetto-specific culture can provide some guidelines for adaptation, there are situations which are simply so difficult that good solutions to the problems involved cannot be found. But we may guess that when for instance the readiness to change household composition or the techniques of streetcorner panhandling occur among new generations of ghetto dwellers inducted into the relevant situations, there is a measure of cultural influence involved which is helpful in adaptation.

Another problem of analysis as far as accidental cultural transmission through role modeling is involved is the question of the normative status of the modes of behavior concerned. We have rejected the hard culture concept which takes only explicit norms into account. Yet it is scarcely in line with the common-sense anthropological conception of culture to which we are trying to adhere to view as cultural a mode of action which occurs in the community but is regarded as unambiguously illegitimate by its members. That is, a person must be able to account for his behavior in acceptable moral terms in order for it to qualify as cultural. This criterion will constitute a problem in some cases of ghetto-specific behavior, as we know that according to the mainstream culture which ghetto dwellers know and tend to idealize, some ghetto-specific modes of action are to be labeled morally inappropriate. In the mainstream society outside the ghetto this labeling would probably function in a rather unambiguous way in most cases of such behavior; it would be denounced so thoroughly that there could be little doubt that it should not be taken as an appropriate model for the behavior of others.[8] Considering the ghetto dwellers' sharing of mainstream culture, would such behavior be more acceptable in their community?

Here we will again have to argue only in terms of plausibility. If we look only at the act itself, without moral judgments coming in from the side, we can probably assume that its very occurrence can be taken to indicate that at least the actor involved regards it as an appropriate mode of behavior. In the

186

absence of any information to the contrary, the prospective learner who happens to be present will thus assume that this is a permissible way of behaving. To put it another way, doing something in the presence of others is not merely doing that something but also communicating a way of doing it, and furthermore, it is a communication that it is in all probability an acceptable way of doing it.

Such ghetto-specific features as public drinking, the overt emphasis on sexuality, the lack of a steady job, and illegitimate means of income certainly do not go free of denunciations in the ghetto community. At the same time, however, they occur much more frequently there than in mainstream society. It would seem, then, that there is at least another balance between communications pro and con these kinds of behavior, since the latter serve as their own advocates. The situation is definitely more ambiguous in this community as far as their cultural status is concerned; it seems one might say that they have at least a higher degree of culturalness in the ghetto than outside.

It is important to note here that we are discussing only the effects of overt behavior. One may hypothesize, of course, that someone behaving in one of these ghetto-specific ways which are unacceptable according to mainstream norms can himself agree with the mainstream judgment of unacceptability while he yet feels utterly constrained by his circumstances to do as he does. Remaining unemployed, for instance, could easily be a case in point. As far as other people's judgments of his standards of appropriateness are concerned, however, they may draw the conclusion from his overt behavior that he regards this as permissible. It may be possible to draw a parallel here between everyday cultural processes as they occur within a community and a controversial item of anthropological methodology, the inference of values from behavior. As we have seen, those students of the life of the poor who argue in very straight terms of constraints and situational adaptation often make the point that such inferences can be wholly incorrect in a case where the actual freedom of action is extremely limited. Walter Miller is one of the scholars who have been criticized on such grounds, as he states explicitly that the "focal concerns" which he sees as the basic facts of lower-class culture are analytical constructs on the basis of overt behavior (Miller 1958:7). The criticisms may not be entirely fair, since a focal concern is not quite the same thing as a value; anyway, Miller imputes mental states to the people under study on the basis of their overt behavior. What is important to note here is that the kind of inference which anthropologists and sociologists have become sophisticated enough to start criticizing is probably a common-sense mode of establishing the values of others which everybody uses to a greater or lesser extent, and it thus becomes a fact to be taken into account in studies of culture building as it generally goes on in human communities. As far as the individual's evaluation of a mode of behavior is concerned, it is likely that the more often it occurs in his milieu, the greater will be his readiness to find it not only convenient but also morally appropriate. We can hypothesize that someone who more or less alone in his community is situationally constrained to adapt his behavior is more strongly morally constrained not to do so than are those in whose community there is a common tendency to adapt behavior along similar lines. Although the former may well be able to experiment with practical solutions to his problems, there is a stronger pressure from mainstream morality not to do so. In the latter community, on the other hand, there is, in a figure of speech, a better climate of acceptance to count on, at least as it is made to appear by the overt behavior of others. Morality, we are saying, is partially a matter of statistics. This point is obviously similar to one made by Albert Cohen, cited in chapter 4, on the collective development of adaptations; here we simply note that adaptations are also maintained collectively through a continuous traffic of messages about what are convenient and acceptable modes of action. In a way this may be judged to constitute self-perpetuating processes of a ghetto-specific culture; but on this level, at least, it is a perpetuation of a cultural freedom to act ghetto-specifically, rather than a cultural bondage. Here, too, ghetto-specific culture may be seen as at least to some extent adaptive, in that situationally suitable modes of action are not only made available as techniques but also tend to be given some measure of apparent legitimacy. This is a point one is liable to lose sight of if one makes an analysis purely in terms of an opposition between what is cultural and what is situational.

Perhaps one may say, since mainstream modes of behavior remain legitimate to ghetto dwellers, that ghetto culture, in Linton's (1936:273 ff.) terms, contains a range of alternatives. More specifically, the argument we have attempted to make explicit here is directly related to Rodman's (1963) conceptualization of a lower-class value stretch, a range of acceptable modes of behavior which, translated into our terms, can be said to include mainstream ideals as well as ghetto-specific adaptations and reactions. With such a range of acceptability in action, the deprived individual does not have to fix his attachment to a point on the scale which he is unlikely to achieve. Here, however, we are not so interested in how this stretch operates for the individual as in the kinds of social processes whereby the individual can arrive at the understanding that the stretch is stably anchored in his community. Thus far we have largely argued about likely interpretations of the morality of ghetto-specific behavior, as if no direct statements about it were made within the community. As we have seen in the preceding chapters, such verbal reflections indeed occur.

## Talk and ghetto culture

Recurrent kinds of statements about the facts and evaluations of life are obviously important in cultural sharing. We may repeat once again that many such statements in the ghetto community are in line with mainstream American culture. However, there is also a ghetto-specific public imagery in support of equally ghetto-specific modes of action to which we have given attention repeatedly in the preceding chapters. These representations constitute a third source of definitions concerning the appropriateness of ghetto-specific behavior as seen by the community, beside mainstream judgments and the prevalence of the ghetto-specific behavior itself. It is often on a different level than those two, however, in that it may be based on awareness of the existence of both of them: it is frequently an attempt to bridge the contradiction between them. A statement of this kind, then, is often what Scott and Lyman (1968:46) have termed an account: a linguistic device employed when an action is subjected to valuative inquiry. Accounts explain why mainstream norms do not apply in cases of ghetto-specific behavior, and they thereby make it unnecessary to condemn it. As Sykes and Matza (1957) have put it in another context, they are techniques of neutralization which can be used by people who are not totally immune to the demands for conformity made by the dominant social order. The accounting comments can be of a variety of types. A very simple form is only a verbal recognition of the point made above: a mode of action which occurs very frequently in the community cannot easily be judged to be completely beyond the pale. On a single act of breach of mainstream morality it can be commented that it is only one out of a multitude of such infractions occurring continuously. The typical form is: "Ain't no big thing, you know". Another kind of accounting is basically the same as that usually employed by social scientists: in the specific situation of the ghetto dweller, a mode of action which breaks mainstream norms is acceptable, or at least understandable as a consequence of victimization and frustration:

"Some people might say, why the hell don't he go out and get a job? You know why? 'Cause I can't get one."

"Look, these boys get their heads busted every time they try to do something. How do you think there can be much sense left inside?"[9]

In these cases, the accounting is clearly a kind of excuse. The mainstream norm is upheld in principle, but the circumstances provide some release for behavior which is not itself valued. Yet another major type of accounting for ghetto-specific behavior to which we have paid extensive attention is that pertaining to the ghetto-specific model of masculinity—it is "in a man" to be tough, to be highly active sexually, and to drink, and so a man cannot help behaving in these ways. This, however, is not an unambiguously excusing kind of accounting. There is also, as we have seen, a tendency to affirm this as a program for masculinity and even to ridicule fellow males when they very obviously do not conform with it. Naturally, we may have our doubts about the autonomous cultural validity even of the norms of ghetto-specific masculinity. Again, even those whose behavior is in line with it sometimes criticize it in mainstream terms. But whatever kind of manliness is most strongly internalized—and here one may guess that ghetto men may vary a great deal even when their overt behavior is similar—it seems clear that the public imagery concerning the ghetto-specific kind has such unusual strength that if a man has private doubts about his ghetto-specific male role they are at least alleviated by the affirmations of its appropriateness which he finds particularly among his peers. Liebow (1967:222), in an apparent reference to this kind of public imagery, seems to want to minimize its importance as a component of ghetto culture. Although one may readily agree with other parts of his argument, one may feel that in this area he underestimates the importance of a ghetto-specific culture for the personal adjustment of a male to his compressed niche. Here we have given particular emphasis to the social processes involved in this adjustment in the chapters on ghetto sex roles. Of course, accounting quite generally functions as such as way of adjustment, as it goes some way toward satisfying potential critics: but then manners of accounting are clearly cultural phenomena. As C. Wright Mills (1963:439—452) pointed out, in an essay on vocabularies of motive which foreshadowed the concept of accounting as used here, the ways in which a mode of action can be satisfactorily "explained" to others vary quite widely in time and space. The kinds of accounting in the ghetto exemplified above are obviously not equally acceptable in all communities. Although a social scientist may approve particularly of the "constraint" and "reaction" kinds as good ways of accounting for ghetto-specific behavior, there are clearly other communities in which ghetto dwellers marshaling such accounts would be looked upon with habitual disfavor— while the theory of natural manliness may be accepted. Fortunately, however, none of them is consistently rejected in the ghetto, even if some members of the community are less ready than others to accept them. Thus as they are more or less publicly recognized as valid bases for the evaluation of ghetto-specific behavior, such modes of accounting tend to take on a cultural status in the community.

Obviously ghetto-specific evaluations are generally based on ghetto-specific interpretations of pertinent facts. This seems to be an important point. Any attempt to define a culture only in terms of its values is no more than partial, as it fails to take into account culturally constituted meaning—that is, in line with our discussion above, any meaning significantly influenced by processes of cultural sharing in the community. Certainly meaning and value are often closely related, but a community also has conventional understandings which are not easily transformed into evaluative terms. As we have seen in preceding chapters, the public imagery of the ghetto involves much culturally constituted knowledge of this kind. There are understandings of times and places of danger, of the nature of the sexes, of the kind of behavior typical of white policemen and shopkeepers, of the functioning of bootlegging and the numbers game, of the Southern background of ghetto dwellers, and of that whole complex covered by the concept of soul. Of course a ghetto dweller can come to an individual understanding of some such facts, but to a great extent his knowledge is added to and stabilized by communications with other members of the community, and he interacts with them within this organization of shared meanings; it is in this sense it can be said to be cultural to dislike the police. Certainly the importance of this culture to the ghetto dweller's everyday life must not be underestimated. It has almost become a fad in recent years to state that the culture concept has become a fad; in the debate over the culture of poverty such statements have been made by Hylan Lewis (1967:14), Charles Valentine (1968:104—106), and Roach and Gursslin (1967:384). To some extent, of course, they may be right; but their own severe restrictions on the use of the culture concept, as discussed above, while possibly useful for purposes of social policy, may not serve our attempts to understand ghetto life very well. As Everett Hughes (quoted in Becker 1963:80) points out, wherever a group of people have some common life with a modicum of isolation from others, a common corner in society, common problems, and perhaps some common enemies, there culture grows. But with this view of the sharing of culture, we must be ready to admit that there are only some ways in which ghetto dwellers form one group, while in other ways they are divided into several. They may all share the understanding of what it means to be black in a white society; somewhat fewer are directly involved in the problems of being both black and poor; and unemployed male alcoholics are a yet smaller number who face some of their common problems in cultural processes of streetcorner mythmaking. This heterogeneity must be taken into account as we try to arrive at an outline of the distribution of shared culture in the ghetto community.

*Action and repertoires*

As we have seen, mainstream and ghetto-specific cultural items co-exist in the ghetto and are shared to varying degrees. At this point when our idea of what we should mean by culture may have emerged clearly enough, we may be able to throw some brighter light on the organization of culture in the community and its functioning in social process, by rephrasing some of the points made before and by making some new ones.[10]

By participating in social processes, every individual learns beliefs, values, and modes of action which are shared by others; of course, as we have noted, the beliefs and the values may be only inferred to be shared by others, on the basis of overt behavior. These form the individual's cultural repertoire—the items of culture which are somehow stored in him.

Among the ghetto dwellers a great many of these items are mainstream items simply because there are no ghetto-specific alternatives. For example, there can be no ghetto-specific culture pertaining to the techniques of making telephone calls or regulating the picture on a TV set. In other areas, however, ghetto-specific culture provides alternatives. It is one of the weaknesses of an unspecified use of the subculture concept that it does not give an immediate idea of how mainstream and subculture relate to one another in that community in a wider society where the subculture exists. However, the possibilities are that subcultural items are either added to mainstream items or substituted for them in an individual's repertoire. Of course, there may be in-between cases where the repertoire includes some familiarity with both alternatives (or, in some cases, a greater number) but where it is considerably more developed for one of them. Thus addition and substitution are better seen as polar opposites than as mutually exclusive categories into which all cases can be conveniently ordered. As far as ghetto dwellers' repertoires are concerned, there may be some domains in which substitution is dominant at least for a great many people. For example, most people are more knowledgeable about black music than about white, they have a definite preference for it, and they are much more involved in it in their overt behavior. But even in this case there is an awareness of the dominance of white music in the wider society, and as we have repeatedly shown before, there is much less a question of repertoire substitution in most other domains where ghetto-specific behavior occurs. Ghetto dwellers tend to have some familiarity with mainstream modes of action, although they may not know them in detail and although in many cases their inability to practice them makes them unskilled in their performance; they usually agree with mainstream norms and aspirations, although the operation of a value stretch as discussed above appears to make ghetto-specific behavior more acceptable than it is according to mainstream culture alone. It is only if one consistently underplays the power of the macrostructural constraints, the variability of behavior within the ghetto community, the exposure to the wider society, and the verbal statements of the ghetto dwellers that one can take ghetto-specific overt behavior on their part to be fully representative of their cultural repertoires.[11]

Obviously there is most likely to be an incongruity between preference and actual behavior in the case of those persons who are most severely constrained by macrostructural circumstances. However, we should note that those who are better able to live mainstream lives also develop a wider cultural repertoire than their major overt involvements might let on. Just as those constrained to act in ghetto-specific ways are exposed to mainstream culture, the mainstreamers continuously witness ghetto-specific life and thus develop familiarity with various cultural items which at least their niches in the structure of the wider society do not bid them to adopt. In terms of cultural repertoires, to be a mainstreamer in the ghetto is quite different from being a member of the mainstream society outside. This also means that ghetto dwellers irrespective of life styles tend to have relatively similar cultural repertoires, although the repertoires are used quite differently. If we permit ourselves the oversimplification of seeing ghetto-specific culture as one single bloc of cultural items, we might say that ghetto dwellers tend to be bicultural. Of course, the repertoires are not identical. Mainstreamers, as we have noted earlier, are less likely to approve of the ways in which the range of acceptable behavior is stretched, they are less attached to some collective definitions of reality, such as those concerning the battle of the sexes, and many of them are more concerned with a peaceful accommodation with the outside society. They may have greater mainstream skills and a more detailed knowledge of mainstream society and culture—such as acquired, for instance, by reading more newspapers and magazines. On the other hand, they may not have total familiarity with all the techniques of living of for instance streetcorner men who regard it as common sense to chew gum before one visits a girl friend after drinking with the peers and who often have a clear idea of how to help a friend who has an attack of *delirium tremens*. But as the sharing of the soul complex shows, mainstreamers are quite familiar with a large body of ghetto-specific culture and find it possible to identify at least parts of it as in some ways their own. While in terms of dominant overt involvements and interaction idioms ghetto culture may seem to consist in a number of small-group cultures, there is much more similarity on the level of repertoires.[12]

This kind of general cultural sharing is important in the social traffic between people of different life styles (that is, different dominant cultural involvements), as it facilitates "taking the role of the other". A mainstreamer can infer that he has some knowledge of the cultural repertoire on which a streetcorner man bases his actions and vice versa; if their maps of the distribution of culture in the community are correct they have some chance of predicting each other's behavior in different situations and can thus manage their own behavior so as to lead the other to define the situation in the way desired. If both parties are favorably disposed to a smoothly flowing interaction, that is, they will try to adjust their overt behavior so as not only to present their own preferences but also to draw on that part of their respective cultural repertoires which they regard as the most suitable response to the dominant cultural involvement of the other. They will operate in an interaction idiom drawing on their supposition that they are familiar with each others' repertoires. Often, as we have seen, this is not a way of intensifying relationships but only a means of accommodation, as in avoidance or in keeping the right amount of social distance through joking. Even so, it is clear that cultural sharing contributes to stabilizing co-existence in the community.

*The likelihood of change*

Perhaps we have now reached the stage where our interpretation of ghetto culture can be made the basis of some comments on the possibilities of change in the ghetto. Since we have dealt with ghetto culture and community as an ongoing system in this volume, such prospects have not been given much explicit attention, although surely the implications of much of what has been said must be quite clear.

The critics of the idea of a culture of poverty have been skeptical toward cultural points of view because they have felt that culture is at least too easily understood as a term used to predict stability. They have seen a cultural interpretation of poverty as based on an idea that there is a heavy hand of tradition reaching down to leave its mark on each individual. This is an essentially psychological notion of cultural stability—culture provides an individual with blinders which prevent him from seeing anything but his habitual way of life. In Thorstein Veblen's words, it is a case of trained incapacity. Oscar Lewis has given some support to this view in the statement cited above to the effect that young children cannot change after they have been socialized to the culture of poverty.

Against this it has been held that most of the behavior specific to poor people can be accounted for in macrostructural terms. Some manage to live something resembling a mainstreamer life despite their severely compressed niches and a few do not although they could, but for most of them there is a close relationship between life style and constraints. If social-work solutions are the answer to the kinds of problems posed by a presumably hard culture of poverty, constraint theory obviously suggests changes in that structure of the society which causes poverty as the only feasible way out. Above all, this would be a question of providing satisfactory employment and income. Valentine (1968), for instance, makes a convincing case for such a program.

The soft culture concept we have delineated here leans strongly toward the latter kind of interpretation. We have seen culture above all as providing adaptations and reactions to a given situation rather than as a completely autonomous determinant of behavior. Whether or not an individual will adopt a culturally suggested mode of action may be taken to depend to a great extent on its relevance to his situation. Here it may be argued, in line with the hard culture position, that relevance is to a significant degree culturally determined. While a very compressed niche makes it very clear which mainstream aspirations are situationally irrelevant so that the people involved will have to adapt their behavior away from them, the opposite is not necessarily true; that is, behavior adapted to a compressed niche does not have to be discarded when a macrostructural decompression occurs. There could be a cultural lag in that the earlier behavior is still thought to be as relevant as any. For instance, the emphasis given to the ghetto-specific model of masculinity could constitute a

193

barrier to change. Finestone (1957) suggests along such lines that although this role is originally a ghetto-specific adaptation, there is such a lag based on the role modeling of the preceding male age set. There is probably something to this view which cannot be easily dismissed. There are certainly instances when men hesitate to take jobs open to them or drift away from jobs they already have. In such cases it may be that the men have invested much of themselves in the ghetto-specific role and have some difficulty in making the transition to a role demanding skills for which they have had little preparation.[13] However, one must also note the reason given by some men that the jobs usually open to unskilled black men are simply not worth having.

In most cases when opportunities for change appear, however, it would seem doubtful that internalized ghetto-specific culture would prevent changes from taking place. It is more likely that the cultural blinders suggested by the hard culture conceptualization of poverty would exist where adaptation has consisted in substitution of adapted modes of behavior for mainstream behavior, whereas in this case, where addition to the cultural repertoire seems to dominate, people are generally quite aware of mainstream alternatives.

Despite this, it is necessary to suggest another possible basis for a lack of change, or at least a lagging change, should opportunities for mainstream-oriented behavior increase. As we noted above, when people draw on their repertoires to establish idioms for interaction with more or less specified others, they enter to some extent into the control of these others as they orient their behavior toward that of the others. This is not a case of explicitly recognized norms and sanctions. The basic fact is simply that in order to achieve efficient and satisfying interaction with significant others one is constrained not to deviate too far from the culture one shares with them, as imputed from their habitual overt behavior. This could be particularly important in the case of the peer group interaction which is so important in the lives of many males. Men may find it difficult to leave their peer groups or to make their standing in them precarious by breaking out of the interaction idiom, even if they might otherwise prefer other ways of life to which they see openings. And since compartmentalization of different domains of life may be difficult to accomplish, they may have to choose between the peer group and greater opportunities. This prospect of resistance to change is based on the social processes of cultural maintenance and may be seen as a complement to the notion of an internalized culture of poverty discussed above. Like the latter, it may explain some lag in the use of improved opportunities, but it hardly points to an insurmountable barrier to change. Even in the current situation when better opportunities seem to be rather scarce, individual men now and then leave their peer groups when they are about to change their lives. If a conspicuous large-scale reduction of macrostructural constraints were to occur it is likely that the recruitment to membership in peer groups strongly engaged in ghetto-specific modes of action, such as streetcorner drinking groups, would gradually be reduced to a trickle. In the case of a very noticeable decompression of ghetto dwellers' niches it would also appear likely that in processes of cultural sharing there would be a move away from ghetto-specific definitions and standards of appropriateness as they are now understood. Throughout this volume we have tried to see ghetto culture as something always in process—in the process of being maintained, most likely, when conditions remain stable, but quite possibly in the process of changing should new circumstances come into the picture. On the basis of our attempt at cultural analysis here, then, we cannot see at least the ghetto variety of the culture of poverty as a lasting obstacle to change.

*Prospects for black culture*

Perhaps what we have just said may be seen as a rather positive evaluation of ghetto culture. From another perspective, however, it is not complimentary at all. We have tended to see ghetto-specific modes of action as at best good adaptations to a situation one must want to get out of, at worst non-adaptive reactions with which one can only try to feel empathy. We have said little about anything that is valuable in its own right. Of course, this has much to do with the fact that we have connected our discussion to the debate over the culture of poverty. If we do not regard poverty as anything good, we can hardly expect to idealize the culture arising out of it. But black people are not just any poor people but an ethnic community existing under very special circumstances in American society. Our final comments on the culture of the ghetto will be devoted to its status as an ethnic culture, now and in the future. Although they will relate to the view developed above, there is a paradox involved. While hitherto we have seen a movement toward a mainstream way of life as desirable, we will now find that voices are raised which seem to be in opposition to such cultural assimilation. Our last focus of interest, within our general perspective toward cultural analysis, will be the problems of this black cultural nationalism: the motives behind it, the goals in front of it, and the kind of culture that meets its requirements.

Franklin Frazier (1934:194) has once written that the most conspicuous thing about the Negro is his lack of a culture. The same view is taken by Glazer and Moynihan (1963:53), rather faithful latter-day followers of Frazier's views. To them, black people are only Americans, without values and culture of their own to guard and protect, and thus without an opportunity to view themselves as other ethnic groups do. Thus they would be less likely to organize themselves to take care of their own social problems. Slightly differently, Gunnar Myrdal (1964:928—929) has written that in practically all its divergences from mainstream culture, black culture in the United States is not an independent phenomenon but a distorted development, a pathological condition, of the mainstream. He assumes, therefore, that it would be to the advantage of black people, as individuals and as a group, to become assimilated to mainstream culture.

What writers like these and others commenting in a similar vein agree upon is the absence of a readily identifiable foreign national tradition among black Americans. Thus there is no cherished alternative—there is no way to go but into the American mainstream, as it appears. But Frazier and Glazer and Moynihan carry the point too far, in our terms of what culture means. An ethnic culture does not have to be foreign, and all those who are one hundred percent American are not American in the same way. There is a black culture. largely evolved in America as a response to black American conditions, just as "black" has become a term for an ethnic group only in America. As Singer (1962) describes it, there has been an ethnogenesis on American ground.

Myrdal, has a clearer view of this fact, but in his dramatic terms he rejects the possibility that maintaining or even strengthening the separate black culture would be to the advantage of black people. Obviously there is at least some kind of a disagreement between such views and those of protagonists of cultural nationalism. Maulana Ron Karenga (1968:164) states that black people must free themselves culturally before they can succeed politically. Stokely Carmichael (1968 a:158) sees the fight for the cultural integrity of black people as one of the struggles of the black power movement. And Julius Lester (1968:84—85) suggests that white Americans have consciously attempted to commit cultural genocide ever since the days of slavery—it was impractical to let black people have a culture of their own. The nationalists clearly feel that black culture at present has too little integrity. Lester (1968:83—84) bemoans the fact that a ghetto bride wants her wedding just the way it is described in the white magazines. She walks down the aisle with a little girl walking behind, holding the train, she gets a big diamond on her finger, she has a six-tiered cake with a little white bride and groom on top, she poses for pictures in her white gown in front of her decrepit slum building, she throws her bouquet and the guests throw rice, and then she walks past the garbage cans to the car in which she and her groom drive off. It would have been better, Lester suggests, if she had had a good time in the ordinary way, drinking liquor and dancing to Aretha Franklin and James Brown.

In our terms, apparently, the integrity of black culture which nationalists desire would be a result of cultural substitution rather than cultural addition. Black culture should be alone and the ideal in its community, not at the lower end of a value stretch. What would be the purpose of such an integrity? To some degree the intent seems to be one of identity therapy. Black people, the familiar argument goes, should learn to value their ascribed selves. Their notion of beauty should not be "light, bright, and damn near white", they should not want their hair straightened and their skin bleached. In short, they should not want to be somebody else—"black is beautiful". This program seems already to have succeeded to a great extent with the younger generation. Grades of skin color do not seem to be strongly correlated with esteem any more, and the men seem to be turning away from hair processing; to the extent that it remains it probably has little to do with wanting to look more like white people. But these are matters of physical characteristics rather than of changeable culture. Should black people really value ghetto-specific culture as well? The answer to this question from nationalists seems far from unambiguous. It is one thing to speak appreciatively of black culture in general and abstract terms; it is another to point out what deserves appreciation for its own sake. Black music, of course, is one domain of culture which one does not find it hard to praise. Thus Lester speaks of James Brown and Aretha Franklin for the ghetto wedding. But what about ghetto-specific life styles in general?

In a speech to a Black Panther rally in Oakland, Stokely Carmichael (1968 b:11) suggests that in ghetto communities people are dope addicts, pimps, prostitutes, hustlers, teachers, maids, porters, preachers, gangsters. So in the schools in these communities, he suggests, one should learn to be a good maid, a good porter, a good hustler, a good pimp, a good prostitute, a good preacher. An education is supposed to prepare you to live in your community, and this is what the community is like. But this, of course, is bitter satire from Carmichael. The ghetto schools cannot function efficiently even in terms of the *status quo*—obviously it is necessary for the people of the community to take over its schools, in order to start preparing the young to change the community, so that people can live like human beings. The current lives of many ghetto dwellers are nothing to idealize. In an earlier article Carmichael (1966:8) notes that black people want to be in the white man's place; they want to be there because that is where a decent life can be had. This hardly sounds like an outright rejection of mainstream culture.

Yet we know that there are frequent criticisms leveled at the middle-class black people who have taken a white man's place and who are living that decent life. They range from Frazier's classic *Black Bourgeoisie* (1957) and Hare's *The Black Anglo-Saxons* (1965) to a song by a militant preacher, entitled "You're nothing but a laughing fool". According to the nationalist view of the world, the black middle class is typically composed of handkerchief heads. So what is wrong with achieving a decent life?

The answer seems to have slipped quite unobtrusively into one of Myrdal's formulations as cited above. Black people are not moving into mainstream society as individuals *and* as a group—they are only trickling into it one by one on white people's terms, while most of them remain in the ghettos. Of course, this is what the black power movement is against. It aims to make the entire community proceed toward a better life, and apparently cultural nationalism is to a great extent seen as a tool to be used for this purpose. To share a cherished culture, supposedly, is to have one's past, present, and future tied with strong bonds to the group. Black power is essentially a question of a cooperative mobilization of the resources of the black community in the pursuit of shared goals, and here cultural nationalists apparently agree with Glazer's and Moynihan's point that the protection of a common culture is a good basis for coming together to deal with the problems of the community. It becomes a part of the political vocabulary to idealize the culture which is generally assumed to have held the community together since times immemorial. The strategy of cultural nationalism is to ensure that resources are committed inside the community by developing loyalties to it which supersede those connecting the individual to mainstream society. If each individual sees his success in terms of his private movement toward mainstream society, as ghetto dwellers tend to do now, attachment to community goals is bound to be weak; resources will not be committed to cooperative mobilization. Black culture must be substituted for mainstream culture at strategic points and defined as so fundamentally important to black people that it will be difficult to alienate oneself from it.

What is needed is a body of culture which can serve as a symbolic basis for group cohesion while the group is in strenuous economic and political movement. This does not mean that the whole way of life has to be culturally distinct. It is enough that what there is of such group symbolism keeps people committed to the mobilization.

Of course, a rhetoric of black culture need not be given very precise content in order to have some cohesive effect in the community. In terms of the goals of black power even rather vague understandings of what culture there is to guard may serve well enough. Furthermore, there may well be complexes of black culture which black people need not give up for a better life: black music, black speech, black sociability, black fashions may serve as well as any alternatives. To some extent, then, cultural nationalists may genuinely want to save some ghetto culture for a better day. But in general there appears to be little of the kind of culture in the ghetto which may be envisaged as suitable for black power symbolism, at least not in the lives of most people and at least not for purposes of mobilization. In these cases it is unlikely that nationalists should be interested in cultural antiquarianism. In chapter 7 we noted how the concept of soul at present provides some basis for solidarity among black people, and undoubtedly it can be used to some extent to intensify commitments in a more organized fashion. But the content of soul has inherent weaknesses as a basis for a concerted movement forward. Certainly, as we have noted, some of the aesthetics involved can be idealized without much trouble, such as soul music, but otherwise the soul concept is apt to bring to mind the problems of the past and the present rather than shared greatness or the prospects of a better future. Soul is a reflection of oppression and hardship, of faithlessness from other people, of lack of control and of the battle of the sexes. There is impiety and bittersweetness, and soul is almost literally an involvement with personal feelings, a turning inward rather than toward the community. This hardly seems like a good basis for an active organization attempting to mobilize power. In fact, soul seems to have a great deal to do with the culture of poverty, although some of it derives from other areas of the black experience.[14] This is an interesting point in the light of Elizabeth Herzog's (1963) comment that one positive aspect, the sense of belonging, seems to be absent from cultures of poverty. The soul concept gives such an idea of belonging to some degree, but quite possibly not enough. This may be so also because the sense of sharing in the soulful experiences is already somewhat attenuated for a considerable number of black people who may be able to participate in them only vicariously. If the soul concept is to be an instrument of cultural symbolism for black power, then, it may have to be given new connotations.[15]

It is possible, however, that the cultural basis of mobilization need not be found in any particularly prominent attribute of current ghetto-specific culture. While the black heritage in the New World has largely been one of humiliation, there may be more for ethnic pride to seize upon further back. Thus it has been a major approach of black cultural nationalism, naturally, to focus attention on suitable parts of the African heritage—that is, on the times and places of autonomous black communities with cultural integrity. Certainly there is little left of easily identifiable africanisms which have been continuously transmitted from generation to generation throughout black American history. Most of them are probably to be found among the microcultural modes of action and outlook to which we have given little attention in this volume: in aesthetics, such as in music, in language and paralanguage, and in patterns of physical movement. These are likely to be cultural items which can be transmitted on low levels of awareness—the kinds of things Herskovits (1966:59—60), in his studies of African survivals in black America, called cultural imponderables. It may well be that some of the little nuances of behavior which ghetto dwellers sometimes identify as markers of soul are thus of African origin, but they are hardly significant enough for black power mobilization. Like most of the current ghetto-specific behavior they are very much a part of what Redfield (for instance in *Peasant Society and Culture,* 1960:41 ff.) used to call a little tradition—the everyday way of life of the common people. The shared perspectives toward Africa which the black power movement seems to want must involve a great tradition of blackness, a body of knowledge about learning and heroic deeds which can seep into the little tradition and inspire its bearers to live up to high ideals. This is why many of the cultural nationalists emphasize the teaching of Swahili, understood by them to be an African national language, although it cannot have been spoken by the West African ancestors of the black people in America and although it seems utterly impractical in their present situation. It is also the reason for the interest in the power and the glory of ancient African empires and centers of learning. These concerns may seem quite artificial to an outsider, as black people in the New World have for so long been completely cut off from such traditions. But in the words of Karenga (1968:162—166), black people do not "borrow" from Africa, they only utilize what was theirs to start with. Black people need a history, but all they need at this point, as Karenga puts it, is heroic images—the white boy has got enough dates for everybody. To develop these images black people must be their own historians.

Whether this Africa-oriented great tradition can succeed seems uncertain. It must necessarily come to clash with older and more established ideas about Africa which are much less favorable and which may be difficult to uproot, and those intellectually inclined people who could be expected to be engaged by a great tradition may reject too simplistic and idealized "heroic images". Neither can we know if it will be possible to make this tradition seem relevant to ghetto dwellers and other black people who could possibly see African names, African clothes, and African history as peripheral exoticisms. It does not seem to have had an immediate impact outside relatively small circles. In the Winston Street neighborhood, some of the younger people have started to speak vaguely about "our own culture", and streetcorner intellectuals like Bee Jay and Sonny know that black people have been robbed of their heritage; they may cite items of garbled history such as the facts that the first man to cross the Alps was Hannibal, a black man, and that the black emperor of Haiti was the only man who defeated Napoleon. But to most people Africa still seems to mean little or nothing. The real experience of black people in the New World still appears to be more in line with that original conception of Negritude which Aimé Césaire stated in his well-known lines in *Cahier d'un Retour au Pays Natal:*

> *Hurray for those who never invented anything*
> *for those who never explored anything*
> *for those who never conquered anything*
> *hurray for joy*
> *hurray for love*
> *hurray for the pain of incarnate tears!*

The sensitivity and humility of this Negritude is quite simply close to soul; it is crystal clear that the great majority of soul brothers have been in no position to invent anything, explore anything, or conquer anything which could make their names go down in history. It does not seem easy to bridge the gap between them and African emperors and to use the reputation of the latter to mobilize ghetto power.

With our understanding of culture as something which can easily change when subjected to new external influences, however, we certainly cannot predict that cultural nationalism will necessarily fail. We have seen that mainstream cultural definitions have an overwhelming impact on the ghetto despite the fact that they are rather uncomfortable to the ghetto dwellers; they have this impact because they are always conspicuously present in the environment and because they are stated with great authority through the cultural apparatus. If cultural nationalists can achieve a similar effect, by engineering on the one hand public definitions of ideals and reality which appear authoritative and relevant, on the other hand an efficient cultural apparatus of their own which distributes these definitions, they could possibly meet with greater success than they have had so far. Perhaps the African identity can serve as a basis for greater cohesion in some way after all; perhaps soul can be strengthened or reconstructed; or perhaps nationalist culture building can find other ways not yet thought of. Should they be able to use for instance schools and radio stations more directly to spread this black culture than is now possible their cultural apparatus would probably already be quite strong. Possibly other means of cultural distribution can also be expanded. To some white Americans these may be frightening prospects of blacks brainwashing blacks; to some blacks they are a wholesome antidote to centuries of white brainwashing. But here they are speculations. It is still possible that the wider structure of society will change enough so that ghetto dwellers can find better lives without collective mobilization, in which case the strategy of cultural nationalism may be irrelevant. If this does not happen, the question may be if it is possible, even with the best basis of cultural integrity, to organize enough economic and political power within the ghetto community to change its relationship to the wider society. Symbols alone may make little difference. On the basis of the present dearth of resources and the present looseness of community structure it is not easy to take the success of ghetto mobilization for granted. At present, as we have seen in the past chapters, ghetto culture and community are split many ways. People try to take care of their personal troubles, coming together in everyday life only to help each other out of immediate crises, to reflect on common problems and to try to forget them. The idea of ghetto power is to bargain with the wider society from a position of strength. If this is the road the ghetto community will have to take, it has a long and difficult way to go—unless the wider society can finally decide to come to meet it.

# Appendix:

# In the Field

How an anthropologist conducts his field work will depend on his own theoretical and methodological predispositions and on his personality but obviously also to a great extent on the field situation. Typically, an anthropologist attempts to immerse himself in a way of life which is not his own. He has a particular interest in finding out about the behavior of people in their natural social contexts; he takes a broad view of the range of phenomena which he should be ready to take into account, and he is very concerned with getting to where the action is, which he doubts that he can do unless he is accepted by people more or less on their own terms. He is one individual among other individuals whose life and outlook he is studying. They are necessarily aware that he is there, and so he becomes temporarily a part of the context within which they are acting. He is acutely conscious of the possibility that his presence may make people change what they do and say away from what is representative of their normal views and modes of behavior. While he cannot help making himself a part of the entity he is studying, the anthropologist will at least try to be an insignificant part of it as far as the influence on his data is concerned.[1] In this way, as many commentators have noted, he has quite different methodological problems from those of scientists who cannot influence the natural phenomena they are studying—astronomers, for instance—or those of for example some of his social science peers who emphasize "precise, controlled techniques of data gathering" in which the investigator establishes his dominance in a research situation which is far from natural. The anthropologist has to deal with the people in whose way of life he is interested in such a way that they give him as much access as possible to "real life" situations or their near substitutes while at the same time he attempts to minimize the possibility that he influences their behavior away from representativity. There is a need for some flexibility on his part in finding a *modus vivendi* in relation to the community under study; implicitly or explicitly, he must negotiate the most feasible research strategy with its people.

This appendix involves an attempt to discuss the major problems of the social process of field work in the Winston Street neighborhood. It should provide some idea of how the data presented in the preceding chapters were gathered; it may also explain why they were gathered in this way and why some other kinds of data were not collected. As an account of field work in a minority neighborhood of a large urban area, it shows some parallels with such earlier discussions as those of Banton (1955:111—119), Gans (1962 b:336—350), Whyte (1964:3—69), and Liebow (1967:232—256).[2] Obviously sociologists and anthropologists who are participant observers in this kind of situation tend to meet similar problems, and the ways in which they attempt to handle them do not seem very different either.

The Winston Street neighborhood was not totally unfamiliar to me as I began my work there. The Urban Language Study of the Center for Applied Linguistics had become acquainted with it through contacts with the white church group which had been involved with it, for instance in the case of the Friday night open house mentioned in chapter 2. The linguists at the project had used some neighborhood children as informants already before my work began, and the project sociologist had had interviews administered to the majority of the Winston Street households, with an adult member as the respondent. Thus it was possible to get a very enlightening briefing on many of the characteristics of the neighborhood before I approached it myself; one of the purposes of my work was to provide social and cultural background data for the project study of the black dialect.

The church and project involvements with the neighborhood meant that white people occasionally appeared in the neighborhood who were not the ordinary kinds of ghetto whites—they were not policemen, businessmen, social workers, and so forth. Naturally, these extra outsiders were quite familiar to some of the neighborhood people. However, they were not much in evidence and did not appear to influence neighborhood life significantly. Furthermore, both church work and strong Urban Language Study connections with the neighborhood—except through my own work—gradually came to cease relatively soon after my field work began. It does not seem necessary, then, to regard the Winston Street neighborhood as very atypical in terms of its people's relationships to white society, nor did the presence of other outsiders significantly affect field work.

My own introduction to neighborhood life was a very unstructured one. Since I had found that there were no suitable living quarters in the neighborhood when I arrived, I took an apartment which was approximately a five-minute walk from Winston Street. The neighborhood was thus conveniently within reach at any time of day or night, and it was possible to take neighborhood people to the apartment for occasional conversations in greater privacy than was sometimes possible in the crowded neighborhood homes. From this base, I began to take walks in the neighborhood where I did not yet have any personal contacts; I preferred not to be sponsored there by the direct involvement of any other outsider. To begin with, this was an odd experience of being "not wanted". Perhaps I was less conspicuous than I felt. In any case, I felt that a great many pairs of eyes were looking at me, and since I later came to know how people follow what happens on the neighborhood scene, I do not doubt that a lot of people really took note of my presence. However, as soon as I tried to meet someone's eyes and establish some kind of contact, I seemed to turn invisible, as at that precise moment nobody would give me any direct attention. After a few fruitless walks of this kind during which I was not yet ready to take any more abrupt steps toward contact, I came upon a gathering of streetcorner men, one of whom called out to ask if I had a match. I did not, but I stopped to ask for the time, then went on to ask if they knew much about the neighborhood. This may have been an odd question; anyway, for one reason or other, they were ready to engage in conversation, and I explained that I lived only a few blocks away, that I was Swedish, and that I was interested in the neighborhood. We sat down to talk at the street corner where a few old crates served as chairs, and as it began to get dark we shared a couple of family-size bottles of beer. I asked the men various questions about themselves and about the neighborhood—questions which I tried to keep as harmless as possible. Nevertheless, I discovered later that a great many of their answers had been misleading, and a couple of them had given me false names. On the other hand they probably found out more about me, and from my point of view this was just as important, as I got a chance to define my identity to someone in the neighborhood.

After a couple of hours of unevenly flowing conversation another man appeared and got into an argument with my new acquaintances. He was obviously quite intoxicated, and the exchange was loud. I was about to go home as he said to me, "Don't sit here with those hoodlums, I'll let you meet some friends of mine". This was Bee Jay. As we walked down Winston Street he introduced me to a few other men who were sitting on the front stairsteps we passed by. One of them said that he had seen me around before. "He's OK", Bee Jay told him. We then went into the house where he was staying as a boarder at the time. His landlord, whom we encountered in chapter 3 as Leroy, a swinger with mainstreamer leanings, was there with a number of younger men including two brothers who were also staying in the house at the time. (Later the composition of the household changed so that by the end of field work it included only Leroy, his younger sister, and her baby son.) "Guess where I found this fellow", Bee Jay said. "At the corner with Arthur and Ribs! They were getting ready to yoke him." Most of those who were in the room laughed, and Bee Jay told them what he had found out about me at the corner. Some of it was mistaken, so I gave a fuller account of myself and my purposes in the neighborhood in response to their questions. Leroy inquired into my academic background and talked a little about the problems I was likely to encounter; his major point was that to start with, I had better not ask too many questions but keep my eyes open. He made a very strong impression on me this evening and continued to do so throughout my field work. Although he does not appear much on the preceding pages, he gave me access to wide social circles and took much of his time to talk about life in the ghetto community as it appeared to him. At the same time, since he probably read more widely than most people either in or outside the ghetto, he was very concerned about the preservation of anonymity in works like this study, and clearly he was worried that some neighbors should regard him as an informer if he gave me any personal information about them which was to be published. Thus he never discussed neighborhood life except in general terms unless he was sure that I already had all the personal data involved.

This first evening, however, the conversation of the gathering soon turned to Swedish topics, particularly to the heavyweight championship fights of Ingemar Johansson. Thus my emergent identity soon seemed to be Swedish first, some-kind-of-fellow-who-wants-to-know-about-the-neighborhood-and-maybe-write-a-book-about-it second. Relatively few knew exactly what an anthropologist is or does, of course, and "finding out how people live here" seemed a quite satisfactory definition of my purpose. Already this evening a mispronunciation of my first name became stabilized, and this was the name by which I became known in the following period. When the mistake was later discovered, I identified the mispronunciation as my nickname. Possibly this was a useful accident, as white people in the ghetto are not usually familiar enough to have nicknames.

That evening Leroy, Bee Jay, and one of Leroy's brothers walked me home, pointing out that I was not particularly safe. In the following days I returned to their household every day to meet them and more of their friends and neighbors. (Generally I was in the neighborhood afternoons, evenings, and weekends, as these were the times when most people were there.) As I got to know more people, I gradually became less dependent on my first acquaintances, although they remained among my closest friends. Bee Jay never let me forget that he had probably saved me from yoking the first evening, and possibly he was right. Of the two men he said he had met me with at the corner, Ribs was described at length in the story about a knife fight by another streetcorner man in chapter 4, and Arthur decided to go to a mental hospital a couple of months later because he felt he was "going crazy". Both turned out to be "gorillas" with lengthy crime records.

From the start at the street corner, I thus followed the natural links of social networks as I was introduced to more people. In this way I became rather readily acquainted with a great number of neighborhood people, as neighbors in daily interaction do not remain unaware of each others' friends, particularly not when these are as consistently present as I was. Of course, such introductions may have been helped considerably by the village-like atmosphere of Winston Street to which we referred at the beginning of chapter 1—it seemed to be literally a neighborhood to a greater extent than most ghetto areas.[3] In the introductions, it was particularly pointed out that I was Swedish, which apparently created a special position for me, clearly separated from that of other whites; this seemed quite useful in that I was not quite so readily assimilated into the perspective of black-white conflict.

At times I was a little concerned over the clarity of my anthropological identification. Often, of course, my purposes in getting to know something about the ghetto community were mentioned in introductions. When this did not happen, however, I could not always easily determine what to do. Perhaps some of the burden in such a situation could be seen as falling on the person who makes the introduction, as he sponsors the researcher in relationships where he can expect him to carry on with his observations. But if one is uncomfortable with a concealed status, this hardly seems good enough. Here I tried to be reasonable. I would rather not interrupt the situation immediately to make an alternative presentation of myself but tried instead to make my reasons for being there clear as soon as a convenient opportunity appeared. In some cases, this opportunity never came, as I met a lot of people only very superficially once or twice—this is what happens in an urban situation where there is a large turnover of acquaintances and where one sees some of one's friends quite rarely. Generally, however, I felt that I had made the point of being a student of community life clearly enough. At the same time, I must confess to being rather pleased that Winston Street people generally seemed to interact with me much more in personal terms than on the basis of my being some kind of investigator. There seemed to be few advantages with too distinct an emphasis on the latter kind of role. Perhaps if one can build up a good case for the importance of one's research to the community where it is conducted it might be good strategy to give emphasis to the role and convince people to go out of their way to be cooperative, for their own sake. However, knowing that black people's situation is what it is despite decades of social science findings which could have been helpful, I did not feel that I could honestly claim that what I did would make much difference to the future of the community. To those relatively few who took a direct interest in the research angle of my presence, such as Leroy and some of his friends, I tried to be absolutely frank on this question; they would have to accept or reject my interest in the community on a personal basis, since I could not promise that my research would benefit their community much. I could only try to make life in the community more understandable to other outsiders and not to cause the neighborhood people any inconvenience by identifying them in writing. We had a few intensive debates about this and related matters, but apparently those who raised the issue were reasonably satisfied with my views and my behavior since we continued to be good friends.

If ghetto dwellers thus often tend to reap little advantage by interacting with researchers, it could easily be uncomfortable to them. With a more formalized researcher role I suspect that I would have been ranged more easily among the white persons of authority who dominate ghetto dwellers and, in their view, disrupt their lives: social workers, police investigators, and others. These are not usually the kind of people one talks to spontaneously or in front of whom one behaves normally, nor are they people one cares to have around much. At the beginning of my presence in the neighborhood some people asked me if I had anything to do with such categories and made it quite clear that they disliked their kind of prying. This could easily make much information either unrepresentative or unaccessible. It turned out, too, that although most of the information collected through the interviews conducted before my arrival was rather uncontroversial, there were points where Winston Street interviewees had given information which was not quite correct—for instance, fewer people actually had set meal hours and home work hours for the children, much fewer went to church regularly, and some households included members, usually men, who were not present according to the interview census data. Obviously, when people are not living up to ideals which they may hold themselves or at least impute to a researcher, they are apt to want to present themselves in a favorable light, and in some cases men prefer to avoid any kind of contact with officialdom.

In attempting to avoid such problems, I was particularly interested in observing everyday life in situations where attention did not focus on me, especially ordinary interaction sequences between ghetto dwellers, most often conversations where their interests, interpretations, and evaluations were freely expressed. Of course, these are the natural processes of cultural sharing which we have taken note of repeatedly in the preceding chapters. In such situations, particularly when the participants were people who had gotten to know me well, I had a feeling that my presence did not serve as a significant constraint on them. There were some occasions when I was apparently conspicuously quiet while everybody else was talking, but I felt I could truthfully answer any comments about this by explaining that I had always been a rather quiet person. Occasionally I tried to get natural conversations started on topics which interested me particularly. Sometimes these attempts were quite fruitful; at other times they were painfully obvious failures, in which cases one could only let conversations proceed to find more spontaneous courses. Of course, I also engaged in direct conversations with people which were consequently somewhat more like interviews, but I tried to give these the form of small talk, and they usually took place in decidedly informal settings, such as on the front staircase of a house, in a carry-out, or over a kitchen table. The results at least usually had "the ring of truth", that is, they did not seem to constitute an interaction idiom developed specifically for me, and they were generally congruent with what I could observe in other situations.

I never took notes in the presence of others in the neighborhood, and tape recording was used only in relatively few cases with children as informants. This means that the quotations from neighborhood people which appear in this volume are not likely to be quite exact; they should certainly not be made a basis of a precise linguistic analysis. However, I do not think they are very far from the original, for with a reasonably good memory which one is consciously straining to capacity I believe it is possible to reproduce even rather complex statements and exchanges with a fair degree of accuracy. Naturally, I hurried to take notes on observations of this kind as soon as I got home in order not to risk losing data or interfering too much with them.

While this kind of informality of data gathering may ensure that the information one gets is really from ordinary life and that it is not isolated from its context, it certainly has drawbacks from the point of view of hard science. All one's data on a certain topic are not strictly comparable, and if they are one is still not likely to have the quantity of data which could be collected, on certain topics and in certain communities, by door-to-door interviewing. In this kind of situation one must simply make a decision about priorities. Since I did not feel I could combine participant observation with such a line of action, I had to choose, and my interest in the realities of household and peer group life, modes of interaction, processes of culture building and the like were not of the kind which can be contained in questionnaires. Besides, of course, some of the important bases of my field work had already been established by the earlier Urban Language Study survey, so I did not have to compromise my participant observer role for example by eliciting data on household composition.[4] In general, however, I could not aim at acquiring precise quantitative data amenable to statistical analysis. The generalizations in the preceding chapters thus tend to be based on rather uncontrollable impressions of observable behavior in combination with the statements of ghetto dwellers who gave their views on the topics in question. This, of course, is not very satisfactory. However, it may represent a typical anthropological preference in a field work situation of this kind, with its alternative constraints on the researcher role.

Clearly an anthropologist engaged in participant observation is often to some extent undercommunicating, although not usually concealing, those facets of his identity which tend to separate him from other people in the community. In my case there was certainly a great deal to undercommunicate about; that is, there was little likelihood that I would ever manage not to be conspicuous wherever I was. Bee Jay suggested jokingly that I might be the real "blue-eyed blond devil" the Muslims were talking about. But at least I could try not to make my behavior seem equally out of place. I dressed informally in order not to look like those whites who are only in the ghetto "on business", and although Fats once asked if he could exchange his thirty-dollar hat for mine, my clothes were not generally anything out of the ordinary—the hat in question was from a dime store. I also tried to change my speech in the direction of the ghetto dialect, although I knew I would not be able to master its complexity very easily. Of course, I could not become like a ghetto dweller. I would not have been comfortable trying too hard to be someone else than my ordinary self, and certainly there is almost nothing as contemptible as an outsider who tries to affect the style of an in-group but who is constantly falling out of it. But at least I could hope to intimate my personal acceptance of ghetto dwellers' behavior by coming relatively close to it.

These are minor ways of trying to keep people comfortable with one's participant observation. In a community like the ghetto, this approach also makes other demands relating to the establishment and maintenance of the personal relationships which are fundamental to it. One must be ready to take part also in time-consuming activities which may be satisfying because of one's new friendships but which do not directly result in new information. While watching late shows and Saturday afternoon sports on TV, while going shopping or on a family outing to the Zoo, one is at best nursing one's chances of being present also when something more directly promising happens, in streetcorner sociability, while driving around visiting friends, or at a more or less spontaneous weekend party. Of course, one may well try to keep "wasted time" to a minimum and seek out situations with a greater potential of becoming rewarding—preferring the carry-out gathering to the TV gathering, for instance—but since the lives one hopes to participate in are repetitious, so are many of one's observations.

I tried to get a rather full view of the kinds of activities which a greater number of ghetto dwellers take part in. Thus I talked with housewives while they were preparing dinner or doing their children's laundry, shared a common bottle of wine with streetcorner men in a back alley, went drinking at ghetto bars, visited social club picnics and parties, belonged to a bowling team for a while, and engaged in various other pursuits of which the preceding chapters give evidence. As far as more public events are concerned, I visited a number of churches of varying sizes and inclinations as well as other religious meetings, attended a number of gatherings of civic concern, and frequented the Howard Theatre and other places of entertainment quite regularly. My radio at home was usually turned to some ghetto station.

Consequently I feel I got a rather strong exposure to many spheres of ghetto life. Obviously, however, my mapping of ghetto culture and community continued to have some blank spots. First of all, of course, people everywhere tend to keep some parts of their lives private. There may be more of this in an urban community than elsewhere, although compared to the lives of other city people it seems that a great many ghetto dwellers are forced by the nature of their situation to leave an unusually great part of their lives open to the public view. Furthermore, by entering into a field work situation by following natural networks, there is a danger that one does not get access to a representative sample of the community population. This is bound to be a serious question in a community which is as heterogeneous and as characterized by social cleavages as the ghetto. In my own case I became aware of several difficulties.

To start with, the Winston Street neighborhood functioned as a sample of the ghetto in two ways. As a neighborhood, it could be taken to serve as a sample of ghetto ways of neighborliness. We have noted above that it may be somewhat more village-like than most ghetto neighborhoods, with more intimacy between residents. This could tend to make it slightly unrepresentative, although more suited for anthropological participant observation than other neighborhoods would have been. However, it does not seem to be very different from other areas of the Washington, D.C., ghetto, as this rather generally has small buildings and the kind of small-town street atmosphere where people should have a better chance of getting to know each other than I would expect them to have in Harlem or in the Chicago ghetto.

In addition, the neighborhood is a sample of the ghetto population—or, as I came to see it, a starting point for the gathering of a sample. By following networks from the people I first encountered, of course, I got to know not only neighborhood people but also friends and relatives of theirs. On the other hand, there were some Winston Street people I never got to know, largely because they did not interact more than minimally with other neighborhood people and because they had not lived there long—some of them moved on while I was there. Apparently they had their social roots elsewhere.

The possibility exists here that the sample I assembled by tracing accessible relationships from the neighborhood was not representative of the ghetto population. Typical ways of ghetto life could have been left without notice, particularly because people who were poorly integrated into the neighborhood structure were not reached. As far as I could discern, however, there seemed to be nothing particularly unusual about those people who were marginal to neighborhood life. Probably they just took their sociability to other parts of the town, just as some people from outside the neighborhood were frequent visitors on Winston Street. Yet some uncertainty remains on this point.

I have a more precise conception of the problems involved in dealing with the internal ghetto cleavages which have been discussed in the preceding chapters: life style, age, and sex. To me, the difficulties of conducting participant observation among people of different life styles at the same time and in the same neighborhood in fact seemed rather small. As we have seen, networks reach readily across life style boundaries because of kinship, neighborship, and, to some extent, friendship ties. For instance, Leroy's brother Percy is a streetcorner alcoholic who associates continuously with other streetcorner men, while Leroy's closest friends are swingers and mainstreamers. Thus there was no problem involved in making contacts naturally from one end of the neighborhood field of diversity to the other. There were instances, however, when the animosity between on the one hand mainstreamers, on the other hand street families and streetcorner men, came to touch lightly on my participation. One dark evening an elderly mainstreamer lady came out to say a word or two about moral principles to a group of men she had seen drinking beneath her back window; she and I were probably equally embarrassed as she found me in the group. At a few other times mainstreamer men noted with a laugh that they had seen me with "the niggers down there in the alley". It also happened that streetcorner men or the women of street families asked with a sneer about when I had last been to see some particular mainstreamer family. In general, however, this seemed to be one point where it was useful not to be a full member of the neighborhood population. My special position as an accepted outsider apparently made it possible for me to commute between groups and life styles in a manner which may have been more problematic to an ordinary neighborhood resident; I did not have to take sides.

As far as age was concerned, I seemed able to establish rather satisfactory relationships with adults of all ages represented in the neighborhood, although I had little to do with the few old people who were there. I also had good contacts with the younger children. However, I had relatively little direct contact with the teenagers except through their families, largely because they tended to keep very much to themselves and often assembled at hangouts outside the neighborhood. Since this age set prefers not to have adults around too much and is particularly likely to be rather hostile toward curious outsiders, there seemed to be relatively poor prospects for participant observation. It would probably have demanded a concentrated effort of attention which I was not ready to make since it would have had to be taken from my other relationships in the neighborhood. It may also be noted that since adults tend to be quite concerned with "unruly teenagers", it could have proven difficult to be friendly with both categories.

The division of the ghetto community along sex lines also necessarily affected my work. The sex role is an ascribed one, and the field worker may not be able to do much about its effects on his relationships in the field. With so much of ghetto life segregated along sex lines, I was necessarily much better able to gain close friends among men and participate in their activities. The results of this are reflected in the preceding chapters where men tend to play a greater role than women. Most of the women I got to know well had some more or less close connection to the men whom I knew considerably better; they were their wives, girl friends, sisters, daughters and so forth. Thus they tended to appear rather incidental to my closer circle, and I could scarcely intensify these contacts very much as many ghetto men, including those involved as intermediary links in such cases, tend to view male-female relationships in sexual terms. Since I found that suspicions were easily generated in this area I could only take note of these constraints on my role. The ghetto is apparently one community where it is preferable to have field workers of both sexes.

The social cleavage which was bound to affect my position in the community particularly strongly, however, remained that which separated black from white. It did not ever seem wise to take for granted that I had been unconditionally accepted. Particularly some of the streetcorner men with a rather weak connection to the neighborhood continued to be suspicious of my motives for being there, although some of their peers asserted very strongly that I was quite acceptable. Thus I tried to be very careful not to do anything which could be misinterpreted, but obviously even a very innocent remark could be seen in an unexpected light. Jimmy, for instance, noted before for his hot temper, was upset when I made a complimentary remark about his new sweater and asked where he had got it.

"What the hell do you mean, where did I get it? This is my own sweater, I bought it. Why do you ask? I don't know if we can trust you."

Ribs, one of the first men I met in the neighborhood, also turned out to be very suspicious as I encountered him one evening on the street when I was speaking with Sonny and Carl. He had been away from the neighborhood almost since we first met, so at this time he had less of an idea why I was there than most people. After telling me that he did not want to have me around he threatened to cut my throat some time; at that moment a police-man walked past on his beat, and Ribs left. Sonny told me I had handled Ribs nicely, and Carl said that if Ribs wanted a fight he might lose his other eye as well. Later on, Ribs became quite friendly, once invited me for a snack at a nearby café, and told me we ought to go fishing together some time. However, we never got around to it.

Since I was careful to keep my neighborhood standing good, my relation-ships to other whites in the area became rather ambiguous. The policemen who patrolled the area could not fail to see me occasionally; as Freddy said when a police car passed by when I was with a number of men lingering at the corner, "I can hear them say, who the hell is that white fellow hanging out with all them niggers?" The businessmen also noted my presence, and I did a part of my shopping with them. Yet I never discussed why I was there with them, nor did I want to engage in too much fraternization with them since they were not very popular with neighborhood people. Of course this was rather uncomfortable interaction, but I wanted it to be quite obvious that I was not to be aligned with these other outsiders. Perhaps it was not strictly necessary to be so careful in such matters; on the other hand, I could see no very good reason for becoming more involved with other neighborhood whites.

If I was continuously aware of my possibly precarious status in the neighbor-hood, there were clearly many neighborhood people to whom my position was soon rather stably defined. To them I had become a natural part of the setting. When at some times I was away for a few days they wondered where I had been when I returned, they asked now and then if I had written anything about them yet, and they wanted to find out whether I would come back to the neighborhood some time later. When I was on vacation in Sweden after one year's acquaintance with the neighborhood I sent a few post cards which were apparently passed around, and as I returned some weeks later I felt welcomed like an old friend. By then some of the tougher streetcorner men had taken to stating occasionally that anybody who wanted to fight me would also have to fight them—an idiomatic way of affirming friendship—and those neighborhood people who had worried about my safety when I first came could smilingly assure me that I was probably rather adequately protected in the area. In general, then, it seemed to me that I could move rather comfort-ably within the network of relationships I had built up. It is difficult to deter-mine whether I could have reached a more favorable settlement—possibly one can drive a harder bargain over one's researcher niche, but in a situation like this it seems preferable to be reasonably tactful, since people have a right to ask you to get lost. When I left the neighborhood at the end of field work, after a somewhat sentimental evening in the company of friends, I was told to turn around the corner into Winston Street again some time; and although there is little reason to romanticize ghetto life, I could look back at some friendships and experiences to be nostalgic about.

# Afterword:

# *Soulside* Revisited (2004)

It is surely with pleasure, but also with some trepidation, that one finds one's first professional book about to be reissued several decades after its original publication. The research that led to *Soulside* was my first full, intensive experience of anthropological fieldwork, and "first fields" probably often leave their traces on what anthropologists go on to do afterwards. I return to *Soulside*, consequently, not only with some nostalgia, but also with a sense that it mattered to what I went on to do in later years. Yet more importantly, the question is whether, after these decades, my 1960s ethnography and interpretations could still be of any wider interest.

When *Soulside* was written, much of anthropology was still reasonably and unreflectively comfortable with the format of "the ethnographic present," a manner of representing societies as stable, somehow out of time and the passage of history. Not that I gave much thought to this as I was writing, but it seems to me now that the first thing to say about *Soulside* is that it is a document of a period—which does not necessarily mean that everything has changed since then, but that both my ethnography and my analytical concerns were rooted in a very special slice of time. When I was in the Winston Street neighborhood, within walking distance of the White House, Lyndon B. Johnson was trying to engage simultaneously in two wars: one against poverty, one in Vietnam. The American political and cultural climate was turbulent: deeply divided, but also creative. Not far from Winston Street either, the Counterculture and "flower power" had their Washington base around Dupont Circle. In the neighborhood itself, the anticipations and events that took *Soulside* out of any assumption of timelessness were those that led me to title one chapter "Waiting for the Burning to Begin." These were the days and years of violent upheavals in many American inner cities. Yet thinking about what has appealed to my nostalgia in later years, I am also struck by how many of the classics of soul music, appreciated more or less worldwide, are from the very years when I was in my first field. It was the time of James Brown, Otis Redding, Aretha Franklin, and the Supremes. The tunes I first heard at the Howard Theatre or on one of Washington's black radio stations I still hear from a local broadcaster close to my summer place in southern Sweden.

## Changing words

In some ways, *Soulside* offers distinctively 1960s ethnography. Probably what also places it in time is some of the vocabulary (unless it merely appears quaint or vaguely antiquated or, at worst, even offensive). A reader interested in the history of concepts may find a modest site to explore here.

To begin with, "African American" was not yet a preferred ethnic designation; "black" and "Afro-American" had recently come into wider use as acceptable terms, although there were still those individuals, in the neighborhood as well, who were not so aware of such changing preferences and still said "Negro" or even "colored." One of my first published articles, on the uses of the soul concept (Hannerz 1968), had "black" in the title of the manuscript I submitted to a reputable British academic journal—but the editor changed it to "Negro."

Most people will realize that such shifts in vocabulary have occurred. Other changes may be a little less conspicuous. I will note only in passing that, while three chapters in *Soulside* are largely concerned with male and female as a primary divide in the community, and especially with being and becoming male, the analytical term was still "sex role"—not yet "gender." It is perhaps more necessary to reflect briefly on my continuous use of "ghetto" (even in the subtitle of the book), and of related terms such as "ghetto dwellers" and "ghetto-specific" (the latter referring to particular modes of action).

My sense is that the respected black psychologist Kenneth B. Clark's book *Dark Ghetto* (1965) helped bring the term "ghetto" into the mainstream of American discourse on social issues. And, in its late twentieth-century American context, there was little doubt that the ghetto was black. I discuss the definitional matters involved rather elaborately in the introductory chapter. More recently, there has been a tendency to recognize a wider variety of ethnic ghettos in American and other cities, but also to define "ghetto" rather more in terms of low-income areas than in ethnic terms (although the actual areas referred to are often much the same), which seems to be an undesirable drift away from the original usage. Moreover, the term may be less widely accepted now. If in the 1960s it was an analytical term with rhetorical overtones referring to injustice and discrimination, in a more recent period some may have taken it to be stigmatizing. If we started using "ghetto" in order to get away from "slum"—and certainly not as a mere euphemism for it—in the social climate of a later period, have these two terms become synonyms?

My notion of the "ghetto-specific" also calls for some retrospective comment, as I have heard some adverse reaction to it. One colleague keeps pointing out to me, now and again, that drinking, even heavy drinking, occurs elsewhere in American society. I am aware of this (although one could argue that there may be differences in drinking styles), and still think that my brief comments on the matter, early in chapter 2, might have been sufficient to avoid misunderstandings. William Julius Wilson (1996, 52) prefers the term "ghetto-related." Perhaps that is the term I should have used, even if I am not absolutely sure that it is a way of avoiding all problems.

*Debates over poverty*

A preoccupation with particular terms and usages, however, is not the most productive way of placing *Soulside* in its time. Whatever the 1960s American "war on poverty" actually did or did not accomplish, it was a time of considerable activism, involving a multitude of actors: branches of the government, organizations at all levels, major foundations (the sociolinguistic/educational project to which I was connected in Washington was supported by the Carnegie Corporation of New York), and a great many academics of varied backgrounds and with somewhat different agendas.

The ethnographic studies of black urban life that were conducted in the period must also be understood in that context. There were indeed a number of such studies, and I have been pleased in later years to find *Soulside* identified, along with books like Elliot Liebow's *Tally's Corner* (1967), Lee Rainwater's *Behind Ghetto Walls* (1970), and—slightly later—Carol Stack's *All Our Kin* (1974), as part of a corpus of research that was central to debates over the causes and consequences of urban poverty, and that mattered in the policy arena (see e.g., Newman 1992, Wacquant 1997). It is certainly important to realize, however, that the researchers involved did not only provide research data from which others could draw policy conclusions, or which others could argue over. They—myself included—were also actively involved in the field of debate themselves. Probably this was more true of these studies than of the ethnographies of black American life that have followed in later years, in another social climate.

*Soulside* clearly identified two centerpieces of the debate. One of them was "The Moynihan Report," a government document authored by the then assistant secretary of labor Daniel Patrick Moynihan, officially titled *The Negro Family: The Case for National Action* (1965). Moynihan related the "deterioration of the Negro family," as indicated by a growing number of female-headed households, to a "tangle of pathologies." The other was the notion of a "culture of poverty," drawn from the work of the anthropologist Oscar Lewis. Lewis—who was not directly involved in research on black Americans but based his general conceptualization of the culture of poverty on his research in Mexico and Puerto Rico—was rather ambiguous in his own use of the concept. In both cases, the resulting arguments focused on the danger of "blaming the victims" of poverty and discrimination. As I put it in the concluding chapter of *Soulside*, "the idea that the life style of the poor is self-perpetuating has probably always been popular among those groups in society which are better off."

Anthropologists responded to "The Moynihan Report," as I did to a limited extent in chapter 4, by using their knowledge of comparative family structures to argue that such structures do indeed vary (rather more than Secretary Moynihan might have approved of), and that they should in any case be seen as embedded in wider networks of social relationships. Some decades later, public opinion may be more generally accepting of the different ways that households and families—including those in mainstream America—can be put together. Yet clearly the characteristics central to "The Moynihan Report" have remained matters of intense debate. The prevailing point of view among anthropologists at the time was that "the culture of poverty" was not a particularly good term: too unclearly conceptualized, too open to misuse (cf. Valentine 1968, Leacock 1971, Eames and Goode 1973). By now it is rarely used, and has entered the history of anthropology. In a recent review, Philippe Bourgois (2001, 11906) concludes that "the culture of poverty furore reminds us that academics fight so hard over so little especially when marginalized political perspectives are at stake."

Some battles go on, however, even as the fighting words change. The term "underclass" now seems to occupy much the same space as the "culture of poverty" did thirty-some years ago. There is a certain difference in that "class" is a concept that intrinsically points more strongly in the direction of a wider structure. Yet as Wilson, Quane, and Rankin (2001) summarize debates about "the underclass," these still obviously deal in large part with the issue of whether the people involved can rightly blame the structure of society or have only their own character flaws to blame for their condition. In the 1960s, there were few in public or scholarly debate who espoused the latter position, but this seems to have changed.[1] Incidentally, I am a little amused to find "underclass" incorporated into the vocabulary of political and policy debate in the United States, and spreading from there to other parts of the world. It was apparently introduced already in the early 1960s, in a book by my Swedish compatriot (and sometime neighbor in the Old Town of Stockholm) Gunnar Myrdal (1962), and understood as a striking neologism with a radical touch.[2] It gained greater currency as William Julius Wilson, the leading black American sociologist, used it in his books *The Declining Significance of Race* (1978) and *The Truly Disadvantaged* (1987). But strange things can happen to words as they travel. With a certain aplomb, Myrdal had picked up the old, somewhat disreputable and politically incorrect Swedish word *underklass*, employed mostly in bourgeois circles, particularly in the early- and mid-twentieth century, to refer to conduct lacking in good manners and knowledge of etiquette. If some American users have thus interpreted it again to mean a culture of poverty, which is much like a poverty of culture, the concept may have come around in a full circle.

*Debates over culture*

George Marcus (e.g., 1998, 233ff.) has drawn attention to the fact that there have recently been striking differences between the first research projects of some anthropologists and the

213

work they have later gone on to do. One reason for this could be that their first studies were Ph.D. dissertation projects: chosen, conducted, and written up under the watchful eyes of advisors who made sure that the apprentice anthropologists did not stick their necks out, and socialized them into the established conventions of the discipline. Later on, if there was a second (or third or fourth . . . ) project, a somewhat more experienced practitioner might have used greater professional license to take on more unconventional topics, and also conducted the research in more varied and innovative ways.

Such assumptions do not really fit with *Soulside*. My generation of anthropologists in Sweden hardly had either mentors or patrons in academic life, and although that could involve some intellectual as well as organizational risks, it entailed a kind of early freedom that might not have been regarded as either normal or desirable in more settled academic environments. I came to do my first field study in Washington, D.C., somewhat by chance. I had first been drawn to anthropology after some travel in West Africa. The opportunity to join a research project in Washington came up conveniently after increasing political violence, and eventually a civil war, made impossible the research I had planned to do in Nigeria. Engaging with my field in and around Winston Street, I adhered closely to the guidelines for ethnographic work as I understood them, and made necessary local adaptations; the appendix "In the Field" probably describes clearly enough what this entailed. With regard to other influences on *Soulside* outside the field itself, some more comments may be useful.

I sometimes wonder about the readings anthropologists bring to the field, or pick up while there, and what influence these may have on their work. My readings during and immediately after my Washington period certainly included much on poverty, and the war on poverty, and the ongoing debates over poverty. I read widely, if not always systematically, in theoretical fields that seemed relevant (which is why some items in the *Soulside* bibliography may seem a bit offbeat) and in early exemplars of urban ethnography—the Chicago classics of the 1920s and 1930s, William Whyte's *Street Corner Society* (1943), Horace Cayton and St. Clair Drake's *Black Metropolis* (1945), and Herbert Gans's *The Urban Villagers* (1962). These latter choices may not seem surprising. But then a few other books came my way, somewhat serendipitously, that were more influential than mentions of them in *Soulside* may suggest. One of them was Charles Keil's *Urban Blues* (1966), of which I picked up a review copy for sale, even before the official publication date, at Strand Bookstore in New York, as I was on my way to Washington. Another was *The Social Construction of Reality* by Peter Berger and Thomas Luckmann (1966), which was published while I was grappling with my early impressions of the field. Not quite as important but provocative was a fad book of the times, Marshall McLuhan's *Understanding Media* (1964), which did something to define and fill an intellectual void: anthropologists at the time had little to say about the media, and I was not sure what to do with the peculiarities of media use that were conspicuous in ghetto everyday life.

This trio of books probably had a part in pushing me into a view of life in the black urban community that could not be wholly contained by a dominant concern with the causes and consequences of poverty. The Berger-Luckmann book took the sociology of knowledge in a new direction (more or less), and was a pioneering effort in what has been in later years described across the human sciences as "constructionism." To me it mattered in the way it emphasized the building of shared understandings through continuous microsociological processes. Keil, embarking with *Urban Blues* on an important scholarly career in the anthropology of music, pointed out that the people of the ghetto had their own modes of expression and enjoyment. Together with these two books and in interaction with my experiences in the field, McLuhan's book also suggested to me that there was still something to be said in terms of ghetto culture.

If eventually the line I took in *Soulside* differed from that of some other ethnographers of the black ghetto at the time, it had a lot to do with my feeling that the highly partisan debate over "the culture of poverty" did not really do justice to some ordinary, if multifaceted, anthropological understandings of culture. Consequently, I labored, especially in the final chapter, painstakingly and perhaps even a bit pedantically to make clear that there was, for one thing, a *collective* adaptation to poverty—involving practical recipes, public imageries, collective representations, call them what you will (but not necessarily ideas at a strongly normative level). This was not to claim that this adaptation necessarily entailed homogeneity. Some commentators, including black anthropologists, have told me that one of the things they appreciated about *Soulside* was its emphasis on the internal diversity of the ghetto (even though my ethnographic emphasis was not on those inhabitants who were closer to the American mainstream). Although it is not among the references in *Soulside*, I had been impressed by Anthony Wallace's (1961) insistence that culture can be as much an "organization of diversity" as a "replication of uniformity"—a theme that has been recurrent in much of what I have written since. In part, ghetto culture precisely involved the habitual ways of managing the coexistence of lifestyles. I could add here that one of the useful aspects of the ghetto concept, at least in its original form, is that it draws attention to an enforced, unidimensional ethnic/racial exclusion that may entail a diversity, in the shared space, along any number of other dimensions.

My concern with the culture of the ghetto, and that of African Americans in general, also had something to do with the fact that I was, at the time, an Africanist *manqué*. (I did get back to my West African interests later.) Even though there is not much about an African heritage in *Soulside*, I was at least aware that African Americans were not merely Americans whom conditions had forced to deviate (that is, move *away*, distance themselves) from a mostly Euro-American mainstream, but a collectivity with an ever-evolving history of their own, complicatedly and only partially integrated with that of American society in general. At the time, interest in the African heritage of black Americans still tended to be influenced by Melville Herskovits's classic *The Myth of the Negro Past* (1941) and its preoccupation with the identification of cultural retentions. It seems as important, however, to have a reasonably robust historical sociology of the organizational and institutional contexts African Americans have passed through, and the resulting cultural adaptations. I have sympathized with Sidney Mintz and Richard Price's attempt to sketch this kind of history in *The Birth of African-American Culture* (1992). One may also note that a keyword of recent debate in anthropology and related disciplines—"diaspora"—was, as far as I can recall, entirely absent in the 1960s vocabulary of African American studies. Among cultural nationalists—more in the streets than in academia—there was a growing interest in recovering and reinventing an African heritage, but there was not yet an intellectually sophisticated conception of a wider, dynamic, yet durable cultural unity that transcended national boundaries, even crossed oceans: an image of a "Black Atlantic" (Gilroy 1993). With such later developments in mind, perhaps some may now see the 1960s terms of argument as a bit parochial.

Yet even if Africa and Africanisms were not directly the foci of interest, there were a number of scholars who took notions of black culture as a contemporary phenomenon seriously. In an early review of 1960s black ghetto studies that I gave as a lecture at a conference of the Nordic Association for American Studies, later published in a somewhat abbreviated form (Hannerz 1975), I drew attention to a divide between the studies more strictly concerned with socioeconomic circumstances and adaptations and those more attentive to black cultural tradition and creativity. Most sociologists and some anthropologists were on the former side. On the latter side were other anthropologists as well as folklorists, linguists, and musicologists who saw poverty as a context and source of symbolic, expressive, and communicative forms that could in themselves be considered as a part of the collective adaptation to circumstances. Keil's early work on urban bluesmen is a prime example here, as well as the work of the folklorist Roger Abrahams and the anthropologist John Szwed. The fact that I was tied to a sociolinguistic project in Washington, where I had close colleagues with a Cre-olist bent, contributed to my own research connections to the side emphasizing black cultural tradition and creativity. Apart from its stronger link to the humanities, this approach was more often comparativist, inclined to look at black life in the United States with at least a few side glances toward the people of African descent in the Caribbean and Latin America. It involved a kind of understanding of the complex black current in the flow of American cultural history that I have found to be enriched by the later work of African American literary scholars such as Houston Baker, Jr. (e.g., 1984) and Henry Louis Gates, Jr. (e.g., 1988).

In *Soulside* I attempted to bridge the gap between those two sides, trying never to ignore the toughness of life in the Winston Street neighborhood nor to disregard either the expressions of its shared understandings and internal debates.[3] At the time, it was an endeavor involving a rather clearly delimited province within the scholarly landscape. Looking back at it now, however, it occurs to me that 1960s arguments over black American culture, poverty, and "the culture of poverty" were really a significant rehearsal for the more general debate in anthropology, several decades later, over the uses of the culture concept. Black ghetto culture may have been, as anthropologists say, "good to think with," if only one tried. There was little room for what has lately been called "the cookie-cutter concept of culture," suggesting a stable mosaic of clearly bounded cultural wholes. Here was a culture with a provocative now-you-see-it, now-you-don't quality, involving ambiguities and ambivalences, with cultural boundaries that were blurred (even as social—that is, ethnic/racial—boundaries were conspicuous), a culture changing cumulatively in history while also shifting situationally. *Soulside*'s frontispiece quote about "double consciousness" from W. E. B. DuBois's *The Souls of Black Folk*, now a century old but increasingly cited in varied scholarly and critical writings, captures a fair amount of this.

Some years ago when we were getting short on storage space in our apartment in Stockholm, I decided I could no longer put off excavating a large closet where I realized a great many things had accumulated over time that perhaps no longer needed to be there.[4] Far in the back, I recognized a large box that contained my Washington field notes, by then about twenty years old. In the same box were several dense pages of more theoretical queries that I had jotted down for myself on my way home—they were on the stationery of the *M/S Kungsholm*, the passenger ship that had taken me back to Sweden. I was a bit amused, and embarrassed, as I looked at that brief summary of some theoretical issues I had identified as worth thinking more about. Those notes for myself were about culture, and the culture concept, and it seemed these were the issues I was still preoccupied with, although in other contexts. But my first field experience had already brought me to a view of culture as processual, based in interactions, anchored in structures of relationships, capable of including diversity and conflict, not divorced from power, and not necessarily clearly bounded. In the 1990s, as anthropologists scrutinized the routine uses of the culture concept in the discipline, they pointed out that to speak of culture—especially culture*s*—can become a way of underlining, even exaggerating, difference.[5] The critics find it a matter of "making other," creating distances. In a world of very real, greater interconnectedness, this could become more dangerous than ever before. In Europe, what has been described as "cultural fundamentalism" now sometimes serves as a convenient substitute for racism (cf. Stolcke 1995). Particularly for this reason, some anthropologists now try to avoid using the culture concept—indeed, to banish it from the discipline. Personally, I prefer to be a reformist, along the lines just suggested, rather than an abolitionist. The notion of culture is now just about everywhere, and if a small group of scholars were to decide at this point to remove the term from their own vocabulary, the rest of the world may not even notice. What anthropologists should do instead is to draw on another long-established facet of their thinking about culture, and use the concept primarily as a manner of emphasizing the potential of human social experience and learning. This entails a recognition of the possibility of diversity along varied dimensions, but not necessarily an assumption of static group differences.

If anthropologists feel some special responsibility for the concept of culture, and, moreover, if their scholarship on culture carries any intellectual authority outside their own academic institutions, we would do better to keep a critical eye on the varieties of culturespeak both among ourselves and in society at large—and try to blow our whistles loudly when a usage seems questionable, or even pernicious.[6] Even if the debate over "the culture of poverty" was occasioned by a colleague's rather unfortunate intellectual construct, it also soon enough became an example of such whistleblowing.

## *After* Soulside

Out of the field, after that more than week-long trip on the *M/S Kungsholm*, desk work followed. Writing *Soulside* could not be merely a matter of following established guidelines for anthropological monographs. For one thing, again, this was not a "whole culture." In retrospect, with a self-consciousness borrowed from a more recent phase in anthropology, I could perhaps claim that the organization and style were in some ways experimental. For a while I thought of subtitling it "Essays on Ghetto Culture and Community," but then I felt that describing one's doctoral thesis, which is what *Soulside* was, as a collection of essays was a bit too provocative. Nonetheless, the plural form of "Inquiries" still suggested a format that was not entirely monolithic.

After *Soulside*, in the following years, I wrote a handful of articles and book chapters relating to my Washington field experience and my understanding of the racial and ethnic scene in the United States (e.g., Hannerz 1970, 1971, 1974b, 1975, 1976). Soon, though, my interest turned to other topics. To some extent, I may have been influenced by the sense that the engagement by white outsiders (even a European like myself) in the study of black American life was, as things stood in the following period, almost inevitably controversial in moral and political terms. The perennial debate over insider and outsider perspectives in social research, and not least ethnography, could not fail to involve this area of study. There have been nuanced general discussions of such matters, from Merton (1972) to Narayan (1993), and I still optimistically believe in the value of encounters between these different points of view (as perhaps anthropologists must do). In America, of course, the tradition began with Alexis de Tocqueville. But such encounters will work best, most freely and openly, when the parties to the encounter can meet on terms of equality—as was not the case with black Americans in their disadvantaged position. I do not believe, however, that *Soulside* ever became a central target of criticism across an insider-outsider divide. And a couple of times I have been happy to learn from prominent black scholars of a later generation that the book actually was an early—and apparently acceptable—influence on their decision to move on to academic work.

In any case, the main reasons for my turning to other concerns were more a matter of pull than push. The late 1960s had seen an increasing number of anthropologists turning to research in cities, and a subdiscipline of "urban anthropology" was emerging as a more organized and recognized intellectual enterprise. I was drawn, at least partly on the basis of my Washington field experience, to thinking about what this meant in theoretical terms—a book on that topic followed several years later (Hannerz 1980). But this curiosity about the shapes of urban life could also be combined with a return to my West African interests.[7] Starting fieldwork in a town in central Nigeria in the mid-1970s, I wanted to experiment with the study of an entire urban community, rather than with a segment of it, as the ghetto neighborhood in Washington had been.

In a way, I was back to what I had intended as my first project, but by then it was importantly influenced by what I had actually done instead. In that African urban setting, from the loudspeakers of the small music shops, I heard once again the voices and beats of the Black Atlantic, soul music and reggae, as well as the new, more local tunes. I became increasingly interested in the mixed cultural forms brought into existence by the European and American influence on Africa—forms that neither received anthropological theory, nor other bodies of social-scientific thought, nor 1970s rhetoric about the shape of the world, seemed to capture particularly well. Clearly I was turning to questions of what would later be labeled "globalization." Yet for my own attempt to summarize certain important characteristics of cultural process as I saw them from the perspective of my Nigerian town, I drew on ideas introduced to me by my Creolist colleagues in the Washington sociolinguistic project (Hannerz 1987).

As I continued to explore what anthropology can do with a view toward an interconnected global ecumene, another reading encounter from my early Washington days, McLuhan's *Understanding Media,* also played at least some small part—McLuhan, after all, coined the term "the global village." Apart from suggesting interconnectedness, "the global village" may be a dubious slogan, yet McLuhan had his vision of how media technologies would affect human life. If I had first run into his sometimes odd insights and interpretations while I pondered the place of radio and television in the black community, what media meant to our understanding of the world was a central question when I turned, later in the 1990s, to a study of newsmedia foreign correspondents (Hannerz 2004). One of my last interviews for that study, with a correspondent for Radio Sweden who reported on American affairs, took me again to Washington.

After the completion of my 1960s fieldwork, I had returned several times to the Winston Street neighborhood when I was on brief visits to Washington. The first time was when *Soulside* had just been published. I mentioned this to my Winston Street friends and they congratulated me, and someone suggested another drink—but I do not believe anybody from the neighborhood ever read the book, and I suspect the largely academic style of the text would not have been to their liking. Yet then there is also the risk in ethnography of hurting or embarrassing someone, even when this is certainly not intended, and consequently I did not insist that they pay attention to the book. I am reminded of Whyte's (1955, 343) note that when his *Street Corner Society* appeared and one of his gang-member informants suggested that they should go down to the library and look at it, his most trusted friend, Doc, managed to discourage them. Perhaps one would no longer handle things this way now.

In any case, after a few years, my Winston Street visits came to an end. People continued to move in and out of the neighborhood, and I sensed that there were many people now who did not know of my past connection to the street and might wonder what this stranger was doing there. More importantly, people whom I had been close to had moved away, and were not easily tracked down, although I sensed that within a week or two they would hear through the grapevine that I had been there—without seeing them. I became increasingly uncomfortable with the fact that what was physically still my old neighborhood was no longer there in the more precise sense of networks and recurrent personal encounters, and thus I decided to stop heading for Winston Street on my not-so-frequent Washington trips. I would circle around it to get a sense of how things were changing, but not go very close. The neighborhood, nonetheless, remained on my mind, and sometimes I would dream about it. In the most brutal of these dreams, I came back to my old field site and found it replaced by a large parking lot. The understanding that "urban renewal" often meant "people removal" was of course not unusual.

But then, with some time to spare after I had met with my Swedish foreign correspondent informant, on a sunny winter afternoon after a major Washington snowstorm, I thought I might walk past Winston Street again, some thirty years after my field work there had ended. I knew I would find a rather different scene. The area as I had known it had been all black. Washington in the 1960s was a considerably less cosmopolitan city than it would become in later decades, and new immigrant groups had increasingly moved in not far from Winston Street, changing the character of some streets with their businesses. I had also heard that a certain low-intensity gentrification had been going on.

Winston Street that afternoon lay empty, just as it could have been on a winter weekday when I had been there in the past. A storefront church was in its old place. A Jamaican flag above a doorway was making some kind of statement. But many of the houses had new coats of paint, and the elaborate security arrangements indicated that other kinds of inhabitants had also made their way into the neighborhood. And the barber shop that had been favored by streetcorner men—for a haircut sometimes, but often simply as a place to get away from the cold—had been succeeded by a small travel agency specializing in exotic destinations. The Winston Street that I had known was evidently a place in the past.

*Notes*

1. See, for example, Murray (1984).
2. Gunnar Myrdal's reputation as a scholar of American race relations, I might add, played a small part in my coming to do research in Washington. When the idea of having an anthropologist on the project team came up, someone suggested that it might be interesting to invite a young Swede who was possibly available to follow in the footsteps, as it were, of Myrdal's *An American Dilemma* (1944). Myrdal's own approach, of course, had been far from ethnographic.
3. On another scale, the volume edited by Whitten and Szwed (1970) would also seem to hold a generous umbrella over the several approaches to black anthropology characteristic of the period.
4. I have described this incident in Hannerz (2001), which I also draw on in the following paragraphs.
5. For some contributions to the debate over the uses and flaws of the culture concept, see Abu-Lughod (1991), Hannerz (1996, 30–43), and Fox and King (2002).
6. On some varieties of culturespeak see Hannerz (1999).
7. Strictly speaking, my Nigerian urban study was not my second field project. Somewhat parenthetically, I had also done a brief study of politics in the Cayman Islands (Hannerz 1974a).

*References (to items not included in first edition)*

ABU-LUGHOD, LILA. 1991. Writing against culture. In *Recapturing anthropology*, ed. Richard G. Fox. Santa Fe, NM: School of American Research Press.

BAKER, HOUSTON A., JR. 1984. *Blues, ideology, and Afro-American literature.* Chicago: University of Chicago Press.

BOURGOIS, PHILIPPE. 2001. Poverty, culture of. *International Encyclopedia of the Social and Behavioral Sciences* 17:11904–7. Oxford: Elsevier Science.

CLARK, KENNETH B. 1965. *Dark ghetto.* New York: Harper and Row.

EAMES, EDWIN, and JUDITH GRANICH GOODE. 1973. *Urban poverty in a cross-cultural context*. New York: Free Press.

FOX, RICHARD G., and BARBARA J. KING, eds. 2002. *Anthropology beyond culture*. Oxford: Berg.

GATES, HENRY LOUIS, JR. 1988. *The signifying monkey*. New York: Oxford University Press.

HANNERZ, ULF. 1970. The notion of ghetto culture. In *Black Americans*, ed. John F. Szwed. New York: Basic Books.

— 1971. The study of Afro-American cultural dynamics. *Southwestern Journal of Anthropology* 27:181–200.

— 1974a. *Caymanian politics. Stockholm Studies in Social Anthropology*, no. 1. Stockholm: Department of Social Anthropology, Stockholm University.

— 1974b. Ethnicity and opportunity in urban America. In *Urban ethnicity*, ed. Abner Cohen. London: Tavistock.

— 1975. Research in the black ghetto: A review of the sixties. In *Discovering Afro-America*, eds. Roger D. Abrahams and John F. Szwed. Leiden: E. J. Brill.

— 1976. Some comments on the anthropology of ethnicity in the United States. In *Ethnicity in the Americas*, ed. Frances Henry. The Hague: Mouton.

— 1980. *Exploring the city*. New York: Columbia University Press.

— 1987. The world in creolisation. *Africa* 57:546–59.

— 1996. *Transnational connections*. London: Routledge.

— 1999. Reflections on varieties of culturespeak. *European Journal of Cultural Studies* 2:393–407.

— 2001. Thinking about culture in a global ecumene. In *Culture in the communication age*, ed. James Lull. London: Routledge.

— 2004. *Foreign news*. Chicago: University of Chicago Press.

GILROY, PAUL. 1993. *The black Atlantic*. Cambridge: Harvard University Press.

LEACOCK, ELEANOR B., ed. 1971. *The culture of poverty: A critique*. New York: Simon and Schuster.

MARCUS, GEORGE E. 1998. *Ethnography through thick and thin*. Princeton, NJ: Princeton University Press.

MERTON, ROBERT K. 1972. Insiders and outsiders: A chapter in the sociology of knowledge. *American Journal of Sociology* 78:9–47.

MINTZ, SIDNEY W., and RICHARD PRICE. 1992. *The birth of African-American culture*. Boston: Beacon Press.

MURRAY, CHARLES. 1984. *Losing ground*. New York: Basic Books.

MYRDAL, GUNNAR. 1962. *Challenges to affluence*. New York: Pantheon.

NARAYAN, KIRIN. 1993. How native is a "native" anthropologist? *American Anthropologist* 95:671–86.

NEWMAN, KATHERINE S. 1992. Culture and structure in *The truly disadvantaged*. *City & Society* 6:3–25.

RAINWATER, LEE. 1970. *Behind ghetto walls*. Chicago: Aldine.

STACK, CAROL B. 1974. *All our kin*. New York: Harper and Row.

STOLCKE, VERENA. 1995. Talking culture: New boundaries, new rhetorics of exclusion in Europe. *Current Anthropology* 36:1–13.

WACQUANT, LOÏC J. D. 1997. Three pernicious premises in the study of the American ghetto. *International Journal of Urban and Regional Research* 20:341–53.

WALLACE, ANTHONY F. C. 1961. *Culture and personality*. New York: Random House.

WHITTEN, NORMAN E., JR., and John F. Szwed, eds. 1970. *Afro-American anthropology*. New York: Free Press.

WHYTE, WILLIAM F. [1943] 1955. *Street corner society*. 2nd ed. Chicago: University of Chicago Press.

WILSON, WILLIAM JULIUS. 1978. *The declining significance of race*. Chicago: University of Chicago Press.

— 1987. *The truly disadvantaged*. Chicago: University of Chicago Press.

— 1996. *When work disappears*. New York: Knopf.

—, J. M. QUANE, and B. H. RANKIN. 2001. Underclass. *International Encyclopedia of the Social and Behavioral Sciences* 23:15945–48. Oxford: Elsevier Science.

# Notes

## Chapter 1: The Setting

1. Gans (1962 b: 4) uses these terms to describe the quality of social life in the areas concerned. The urban village is a stable, homogeneous home of immigrants to the city; the typical example is the working-class neighborhood of some European immigrant group, in Gans' case the Italian-Americans. The urban village is hardly a slum to anybody but outsiders ignorant of its way of life. The typical urban jungle is the skid row; it is the home of isolated individuals, families in disorder, criminals, and illegal services provided to the rest of the city. Whyte (1943) discusses two types of slums in similar terms. It seems that sociologists, following the pioneering work of the Chicago school of sociology, have been a little too prone to find only jungles in working-class and lower-class urban areas—there has been more imagery of disorganization than of organization. For an influential example see Zorbaugh (1929); also note the rubric "In the City of Destruction" in Frazier's (1939) book on the black family.

2. Miller (1958) also suggests trouble as a "focal concern" for lower-class communities more generally.

3. The opinion is now generally held among public officals and social scientists that the lower-class black population is grossly under-represented in the official U.S. census records because of enumeration difficulties. Particularly the unattached men are thus often officially non-existent; see Chapter 4, note 4.

4. For a recent study of the D.C. school system see the "Passow Report" which states that "education in the District is in deep and probably worsening trouble" (Passow 1967: 2).

5. The income figures mentioned here may be compared to current points of view of what constitutes poverty in the United States. In this field there is no complete agreement. (More specific information on the economics of poverty in the U.S. and on recent thinking about it can be found e.g. in Conference on Economic Progress 1962, Seligman 1965, and Ferman *et al.* 1965.) In 1964, the President's Council of Economic Advisors defined poverty as cash income of less than $3,000 for a household of two or more persons, and of less than $1,500 for a single-person household. It is clear, however, that adjustments must be made for place of residence (as living expenses vary within the nation), size of household, and stage of household life cycle. Thus, this measure has not been accepted by all, and regional modifications have been suggested. In an economic study directed by Keyserling (Conference on Economic Progress 1962) the $3,000 baseline is seen as far too low, and Keyserling instead puts it at $4,000 for households of two or more members and at $2,000 for single persons. His opinion is shared by many. Depending on whether one chooses the $3,000 or the $4,000 income as the poverty level, either about half or the majority of the Winston Street people are below the poverty level.

6. After many of the commercial establishments along these streets were raided and in a great number of cases burned during the April 1968 disturbance, the streets continued as centers of ghetto street life, although lined by ruins and boarded-up stores.

7. Further information on the demographic situation in Washington up to the 1960 census is most conveniently available in Grier's (1960) analysis of patterns of population changes in the metropolitan area.

8. Derthick's study, *City Politics of Washington, D.C.* (1962) is valuable for further knowledge of the political situation of the city, although it is now outdated in several respects. The most important recent change was the local government reform of 1967, in which the city got a commissioner, functioning as mayor, and a nine-man city council. The first mayor is a Negro, as are a majority of the council members. However, they are still presidential appointees, and they are therefore not necessarily the best possible representatives of the community. Also, their powers are still limited by the authority of the Congress.

## Chapter 2: Life Styles

1. A "basic role", according to Banton's (1965: 33 ff.) usage is one which affects conduct in a wide range of situations; it influences the allocation of other roles to the individual as well as his enactment of them. The sex role is probably the best example of a basic role in most societies.

2. Such dichotomies are more or less prominent for example in studies by Hylan Lewis (1955: 3 ff.), Drake and Cayton (1962: 519 ff.), and Jessie Bernard (1966: 27 ff.)

3. The concept of conscious model is employed here in conformity with the usage by Lévi-Strauss (1953: 526—527).

4. Those who are interested in comparing this to other categorizations of urban life ways in the United States may turn to the general paper by Gans (1962 a), the same author's study of an Italian-American community (Gans 1962 b: 28 ff.), Seeley's paper on the use of the slum (1959), and Drake's and Cayton's study of Black Chicago (1962: 519 ff.).

5. In the terms suggested by Bott (1957: 52 ff.), the mainstreamers often have a joint conjugal role-relationship, particularly in sociability—with husband and wife carrying out activities together—as opposed to a segregated conjugal role-relationship, where husband and wife tend to have separate interests and activities.

6. This seemed still to be the case during Drake's and Cayton's research in Chicago in the late thirties and early forties (Drake and Cayton 1962: 525, 612 ff.).

7. The network concept, as it is used somewhat loosely here, refers to an "egocentric" social structure, with one individual at the center and consisting of his relationships to other individuals as well as the relationships which these individuals may have to one another. The distinction between degrees of network connectedness, that is, between close-knit and loose-knit networks, was suggested by Bott (1957: 59). Other important discussions of "network" and related concepts are those by Barnes (1954, 1968), Mayer (1966), Mitchell (1966), and Boissevain (1968). It should be noted that the usage of network terminology has been rather varied. Mayer (1966) and Barnes (1968) have recently suggested that other terms should be used for "egocentric" structures, but the usage adopted here seems to have become rather well established.

8. Further comments on the functioning of gossip in the ghetto are made in Hannerz 1967.

9. It should be pointed out that "family" in "street family" should be understood to mean "residential unit with a core of members held together by kinship". To a great extent, the unit is also served by a common organization of domestic activities. The somewhat ambiguous term "family" is used here simply as the least cumbersome term available. Although the term "household" may have been more correct from some points of view, its use would more easily lead the thought

too exclusively toward domestic activities. Cf. Solien de González 1960, Bender 1967.

10. It is difficult to give a more exact figure because the proportion varies somewhat over time and in particular because it depends on how people are classified into life style categories. Without a clearcut criterion for classification, one will necessarily find cases which are on the margin of a street family life style and about which one may be in doubt as far as classification is concerned. There is a clear tendency, however, for most husbandless households to be among those which show the strongest street family characteristics in other ways.

11. "Conjugal union" is here taken to include long-term consensual unions as well as legal marriages.

12. See note 5 of this chapter on segregated conjugal role-relationships. This seems to be a common pattern of working class and lower class marriage not only among black Americans; see for instance Dennis *et al.* (1956: 180 ff.), Rainwater *et al.* (1959), Rainwater (1964), Gans (1962 b: 50 ff.), and Komarovsky (1964).

13. See note 5, chapter 1, for a discussion of the "poverty line".

14. The concept streetcorner men is used in the same sense by Liebow (1967). His description of this category appears generally valid also for the groups of men who hang out in the Winston Street neighborhood. Here and in following chapters we will discuss their relationship to other segments of the ghetto community, as well as aspects of this life style not discussed in great detail by Liebow. To some extent, some disagreement with details of Liebow's analysis will also be aired. However, those results of field work in the Winston Street neighborhood which parallel Liebow's work largely agree with his results.

15. Liebow also discusses this point (1967: 176 ff.).

## Chapter 3: Walking My Walk and Talking My Talk

1. The "career" concept as an analytical tool in sociology is discussed by Becker and Strauss (1956) and Becker (1963: 24 ff.). The "developmental cycle", as employed in recent anthropological analyses (cf. Goody 1958), is obviously a related concept, in that it also involves a small-scale diachronic perspective.

2. There are apparently rather few unmarried mothers and household heads who have a mainstreamer style of life; it is less rare among divorced, separated, and widowed women.

3. One view of the role of marriage in stabilizing individuals' conceptions and values is that of Berger and Kellner (1964). It should be noted that marriages vary in the extent to which they have such an influence, and that segregated conjugal role-relationships of the kind often found in the ghetto are likely to have only a limited effect of this kind, while peer relationships may be more influential; cf. chapter 5.

4. The concept of drift as employed in this sense is suggested by Matza (1964) in a discussion of juvenile delinquency.

5. Claude Brown's autobiography, *Manchild in the Promised Land* (1965), gives an excellent example of an unpredictably drifting life career.

6. There have been numerous anthropological discussions of joking since Radcliffe-Brown's two pioneering essays (1952). Among those which are most relevant here for comparative purposes are those by Hammond (1959; 1964) and Miller (1967). Other perspectives toward ghetto humor are discussed in chapters 5 and 7.

## Chapter 4: Male and Female

1. According to the statistics in the "Moynihan Report" (see note 3), about a quarter of the black women in American cities in general are divorced, separated,

or living apart from their husbands (United States Department of Labor 1965: 6—8).

2. Among the more important writings are those by Frazier (1939), Herskovits (1941), Henriques (1953), R. T. Smith (1956, 1963), Clarke (1957), Goode (1961), Mintz and Davenport (1961), Blake (1961), M. G. Smith (1962a, 1962b, 1966), Whitten (1965), Otterbein (1966a), and Greenfield (1966).

3. The "Moynihan Report", informally named after its main author, Daniel Patrick Moynihan, then Assistant Secretary of Labor, is officially named *The Negro Family: The Case for National Action* (United States Department of Labor 1965). It is largely a compilation of statistics and quotations from earlier research and thus contains little not already familiar to students of the social science literature on black American life. However, its particular emphases and inter-pretations, appearing in a sensitive political situation, were sufficient to cause a heated debate. One problem was that the document, although admitting the variety of black family forms, seemed to generalize broadly about "the Negro family". It also appears that Moynihan's choice of statistics was to some extent biased; he wanted to prove the point that the black family was in a bad state, particularly because it tended to be female-headed. However, Moynihan was somewhat vague on the question of what makes women dominant in ghetto families, and many critics feared that he left too much room for the interpreta-tion that it was largely the "fault" of the ghetto dwellers themselves. This was particularly serious as he tended to make female dominance the source of ghetto social problems, on the basis of social science evidence which hardly seems overwhelmingly strong. His emphasis was clearly on female dominance and its alleged consequences as aberration and pathology, not as adaptation to the given social situation. In this bias he was probably influenced by his personal attachment to mainstream family ideals; however, he also states that it is necessary for black families to conform to the norms of the American majority in order to gain acceptance (see also Moynihan 1967: 45). The point of view of the "Moynihan Report" is expressed in a rather similar way in Moynihan 1965; the public controversy is discussed in Rainwater and Yancey 1967, which includes the full text of the document and reprints of many of the important statements in the debate. Valentine (1968: 29—42) gives an anthropologist's view of the report.

4. The influence of patterns of land tenure is exemplified by Horowitz (1967), while Kunstadter (1963) and Otterbein (1965) emphasize male absenteeism as a factor contributing strongly to the occurrence of female-headed households. In a brief note, Fischer and Derbes (1966) have attempted to use demographic data in a related manner, showing that there is a negative correla-tion between the non-white male/non-white female ratio and the female-headed households/all households ratio in major U.S. cities with large black popula-tions. The correlation was based on data from the U.S. census 1960. The authors appear to conclude that a relative lack of males may account for a relatively great number of female-headed households, and they add that demographic factors should be considered more carefully in explaining the occurrence of female-headed households among black Americans. This may be warranted; however, one factor may throw a shadow of doubt on the argument. It has recently been pointed out that U.S. census figures are of notoriously uncertain reliability particularly for black men in urban areas. The 1960 census from which Fischer and Derbes draw their data is estimated to have missed one out of six non-white men in the age bracket from 20 to 39—family forming ages—while it left out only one out of thirteen non-white women in the same category (Trans-action 1968: 50—51). It appears likely that the unattached men, sometimes without any permanent residence, sometimes consciously avoiding contacts with public officials, would tend to go unenumerated particularly frequently. This

offers the possibility that where for some reason other than demographic the proportion of female-headed households is high, there is a greater number of unattached males, and therefore also a greater number of unenumerated males, than where that proportion is low. If that is the case, the cause-and-effect relationship would be the opposite of that suggested by Fischer and Derbes, as the figure for non-white males in the census data comes to stand not for existing males but for enumerated males. It should be noted that this alternative explanation is not necessarily any more valid than that of Fischer and Derbes. However, it should make it obvious that demographic explanations of the incidence of female-headed households can only be based on more reliable statistics.

5. This summation of Herskovits' point of view on black male-female unions is derived from *The Myth of the Negro Past* (1941), his major work on African influences on New World cultures.

6. Clarke (1957) and Greenfield (1966) also lean toward this perspective in their studies of other Caribbean societies. As far as black people in the United States are concerned, we have noted that there were tendencies toward this kind of interpretation in Frazier's work; although ambiguous, the "Moynihan Report" points to the correlation between household form and economic-occupational factors (United States Department of Labor 1965: 19—25). The same point is made more clearly in other studies which were more or less part of the ensuing controversy (cf. Gans 1967a; Herzog 1967; H. Lewis 1967a). One may also note the relevance to this argument of two papers by Talcott Parsons (1942, 1943).

7. The concept of niche is used here in line with the definition suggested by Barth (1963: 9): the position occupied by an individual in relation to resources, competitors and clients.

8. Liebow (1967: 57 ff.) also points this out.

9. There seems to be a definite although not often clearly recognized split between behavioral and compositional conceptions of matrifocality in recent writings. R. T. Smith (1956: 223; 1957: 70) makes it relatively clear that a household including a husband-father can be behaviorally matrifocal, while Kunstadter (1953: 56) —apparently misquoting Solien—uses a clearcut compositional definition. Boyer (1964), in commenting on Kunstadter's paper, employs a behavioral conception, while Randolph (1964), also in a comment on Kunstadter, appears to accept the compositional definition and in the process seems to cite R. T. Smith (1956) incorrectly. However, Randolph is critical of the utility of the concept along the lines suggested by Kunstadter. Solien de González (1965), in commenting on Kunstadter, Boyer, and Randolph, points out Kunstadter's misquote from her and distinguishes between "consanguineal household" with a compositional definition and "matrifocal family" with a behavioral definition. Goode (1966) states that a term such as matrifocality *ought* to have a normative definition but that "as everyone knows" it is always used compositionally, as a census category (see also Goode 1960: 27). Otterbein (1966b), in answering Goode, seems to accept this or at least does not refute it; of course, he uses largely compositional data in his own work.

10. The contradiction between the mainstream cultural model and the ghetto-specific structural position can be defined in the terms suggested by Merton in his well-known paper on "Social Structure and Anomie" as a dissociation between culturally prescribed aspirations and socially structured avenues for realizing such aspirations (Merton 1957:131—160). However, as Rodman (1963) and others have pointed out, Merton tends to assume a cultural uniformity throughout a society, taking into inadequate account the possibility of differentiated subcultures within the society which, while not necessarily denying the disjunction posited by Merton, at least complicate the picture.

11. Freilich's (1961) paper on the mating patterns of black Trinidadian peasants is

very explicitly based on such comparisons in arriving at a "heritage from slavery" conclusion.

12. Keil's *Urban Blues* (1966) is an interesting study of the contemporary blues singer's success in expressing focal concerns of the ghetto.

13. This may be compared to Norman Mailer's literary image of the black male in his essay on *The White Negro* (Mailer n.d.).

14. The notion of subterranean values has been introduced by Matza and Sykes (1961).

15. Goffman's (1959) work on the presentation of self is obviously relevant here.

16. Particularly the literature on the sociology of juvenile delinquency abounds with discussions of "toughness" which, although they are not all in total agreement, contain points which tend to be valid also for adult ghetto-specific masculinity. Cf. Cohen 1955, Miller 1958, Miller *et al.* 1961, Yablonsky 1962, Short and Strodtbeck 1965, Toby 1966.

17. See in particular papers by Rainwater (1966a; 1966b: 206—207) and Finestone (1957) but also Miller's (1958) paper on focal concerns of the lower class and Gans' (1962b: 29) comments on action-seeking among lower-class Italian-Americans.

18. This hypothesis appears to be in general agreement with the conflict-enculturation theory of game involvement set forth by Roberts, Sutton-Smith and their associates in a series of papers (Roberts *et al.* 1959; Roberts and Sutton-Smith 1962; Sutton-Smith *et al.* 1963; Roberts *et al.* 1963). Of course, that theory is considerably more detailed. A related perspective toward peer group life is applied in chapter 5.

19. This discussion is clearly related to some of Erving Goffman's work on interaction, particularly Goffman 1955. One might say that the way of concluding an exchange involves some marginal face-work in that the winner refrains from depriving the loser of face entirely; the zero-sum game is halted just short of confirmation of the outcome. With Goffman's (1967) essay on "Where the Action is" in mind, it may be added that as the outcome of a contest becomes clearly discernible, the individual's excitement over his activity becomes dulled.

20. This agrees with Rainwater's (1966a) view of the dramatic self as a medium of exchange.

21. Although it is hardly possible or necessary to make detailed references to factual or interpretive parallels here, Rainwater's (1966b) paper on black lower-class family life should be noted for its careful and illuminating discussion.

22. Liebow (1967: 72 ff.) has an extended discussion of the relationship of streetcorner men to their children.

23. This conception of culture as public imagery is inspired particularly by Goodenough (1963: 263—264) and Geertz (1966: 5—8).

24. The same point has been made previously in this volume on the subject of the dichotomous life-style model discussed in chapter 2.

25. On this point see Liebow's discussion of "manly flaws" (1967: 116 ff.).

26. It is interesting to note that this theme in public imagery seems to be a reversal of the "the good-bad girl" theme described by Wolfenstein and Leites (1950: 25 ff.) as recurrent in American films. The pessimistic imagery about women on the part of men in the black community seems rather well established, as its occurrence in black music from the old blues to contemporary soul music shows.

27. This point is reasonably similar to that made by Rodman in his application of the value stretch concept (Rodman 1963) to Caribbean illegitimacy (Rodman 1966).

## Chapter 5: Streetcorner Mythmaking

1. Sonny's claim to friendship with more famous jazz musicians is not unique. It is common among former musicians in the ghetto—and among some who only like to imagine themselves as musicians—to make casual first-name references to "Louis", "Duke" and others as if they had been their close friends.

2. For an analysis of the, maintenance and transformation of reality see Berger and Luckman (1966: 135 ff.). The development of the self in social process has long engaged the interest of sociologists who have had an ancestral figure in this field in Charles Horton Cooley (1902); for a recent systematization of interaction theory drawing partially on this perspective see McCall and Simmons (1966).

3. This is apparently what Merton and Barber (1963) would call sociological ambivalence in the restricted sense, as it refers to more or less incompatible expectations incorporated into a single role, namely the male sex role.

4. The classic statement on "presenting" is obviously Erving Goffman's *The Presentation of Self in Everyday Life* (1959).

5. Zijderveld (1968) has a parallel argument in his essay on joking.

6. Colby (1966) defines the template, in a paper on cultural patterns in narrative, as a cognitive element for producing folk tales and controlling behavior in general.

7. Statements on this point include Herskovits (1941, particularly p. 272 ff.), Crowley (1962), and Dorson (1967: 12—18).

8. This connection between the trickster and an oppressive social structure has recently been mentioned by Abrahams (1964: 68) and Hampton (1967: 58). The argument must have an early origin, as it is mentioned by Ambrose E. Gonzales, a folklorist with racist inclinations, in his collection of Gullah tales, *With Aesop along the Black Border* (1924: xi).

9. It appears possible that there was once a real Stack Lee somewhere in a Mississippi River town, perhaps Memphis. He gained his notoriety, as recounted in different versions in toasts and ballads, above all in a fight with Benny Long, or Billy Lyons. Cf. Odum and Johnson (1925: 196—198), Abrahams (1964).

10. Hampton (1967) also objects to a rigid separation of badman and trickster in black American folklore.

11. The idea of groups as cultural storage units is explored in a paper by John M. Roberts (1964).

## Chapter 6: Growing Up Male

1. Although overt lesbians are sometimes taunted for their deviance, there appears to be a rather high degree of tolerance toward them among people who know them; in general higher, probably, than toward male homosexuals. Since it is a focal concern among many ghetto dwellers to find an angle for making a profit of one kind or other, deviants are sometimes also drawn into such schemes, as this field note from a conversation between a few men shows:

The men were reminiscing as usual about past acquaintances and encounters, and somebody mentioned Martha, a woman who used to live a few blocks away and who has had a career of sexual deviations. Lee said that although one is inclined not to like "people like that", many of them are actually quite nice. Martha is now a bulldagger (lesbian), but earlier she wanted young men. Alfred, speaking about Martha: "She looked more like a man than I do ... She had a moustache ... In fact, she looked like a gorilla! Well, at this time when she wanted young fellows, you know, she wanted me, so this friend of mine was constantly bringing me to her house, 'cause that way we got free drinks. She always had a lot of whiskey at home. But then, you know, after that we had to get out of there quick!"

2. "Role embracement" is defined by Goffman (1961:106) as consisting of an admitted attachment to the role; a demonstration of role competence; and a visible investment of attention and effort.

3. Keil (1966:23) suggests that this might be the case.

4. Of course, one should be aware that role-taking in interaction with same-sex and cross-sex siblings can have an influence on sex role socialization quite generally—see for instance an analysis by Brim (1958).

5. Since it was generally impossible to elicit more than one interpretation of a jone—the most obvious one—plus a laugh, other possible meanings are not suggested here. The reader is invited to take another look for himself; too clean a mind might not be of any particular help.

6. Ayoub and Barnett (1965) have pointed to the existence of "sounding" also among white boys, but their study has been criticized on a number of points by Jackson (1966). There can apparently be little doubt that joning is far more common, and far more elaborate, in the black proletariat than in any other group. Although it has been reported widely—see for instance Dollard (1939:6—18)—there may be black communities in the United States where it is not common, or was not until comparatively recently. Sonny, the musician, reminisced as follows about an incident shortly after he arrived in Washington, D.C., from Jacksonville, Florida, in the thirties: "When I first came here this (joning) was one of the first things I heard, you know, and I wasn't used to it 'cause in Florida where I came from I had never heard it. So this boy said something about my mother, and I hit him, and so I beat him up. But then he said, 'I'll call my brother!' and he did, and so I had to fight his brother, and then they called another brother, and it turned out there were seven brothers! Ooh! And I had to fight all of them, but only one at a time, they were quite fair about that. And we fought all around the block, and I beat them all, but of course I was getting pretty tired. But then from then on we were buddies, real tight, you dig, and I got used to it myself and I got thicker skin, and so I used to be pretty good at joning myself." Sonny most likely improved on the story, of course; it is unlikely that there would have been seven brothers in appropriate ages for him to fight and defeat. Anyway, most other ghetto dwellers seem to have had joning around them when they were young, ever since they started to participate in life outside the home. Perhaps Sonny's lack of exposure had at least as much to do with the fact that he seems to have been downwardly mobile as with his Florida origins; his mother resented the kind of company he started to keep in Washington. Dollard (1939), in any case, seems to view at least the kind of joning with a sexual content as a lower-class phenomenon among black people.

7. It may be inserted at this point that although rhymed insults become less frequent in adult years, rhyming remains a valued component in verbal behavior. The first example is a streetcorner man's reply to a neighbor's question "How're you doing?", the second another man's retort to a friend's suggestion of a deal:

> "Ain't got no money honey."

> "I may be a little lazy
> but I sure ain't crazy."

The next is a storefront church preacher's announcement of a blessing service:

> "Now it's time for sanctifying
> and I'd better not be lying."

The final example is a temperature announcement from a black radio station:

"sixty-six degrees
in your hometown breeze,
baby."

8. The major trend in Dollard's explanation of "the dozens", on the other hand, takes the mother-son relationship into less account than the black-white relationship; the exchange of insults is seen as a way of releasing aggression in an oppressed group (1939: 21—23). This analysis, of course, is not specific enough as an interpretation of the form and content of joning. The view of aggression within the black community as a way of displacing dangerous aggression toward whites has also been stated in more general terms by Powdermaker (1943).

9. The concept of biculturation was coined by Polgar (1960) in a study of Mesquakie Indian boys.

10. Of course, this parallel socialization according to two sets of standards can easily cause some ambivalence for the boys, as the continued contrast between mainstream culture and the ghetto-specific situation does for adult men. To the boys, however, the ghetto-specific male role may seem to be more tangible, and more relevant for their own self-conception, than the mainstream role. Nor are they likely to feel the moral pressure of mainstream culture as strongly as those adult men may do who do not function as providers and family heads.

11. This is suggested by Whitaker (1967: 47); there is a curious paradox in this, as she acknowledges that other men than a father can serve as role models but takes into no account the possibility that they already do.

12. It should also be noted that the two perspectives are not so different as they may seem, for obviously when boys allegedly become compulsive about their masculinity they must give cultural content to their concern by modeling their own behavior on that of other men. The issues remain whether there is really a significant discontinuity of identification and whether the boys are exaggerating a "normal" notion of masculinity (that is, the outside observer's) or adopting a ghetto-specific form.

## Chapter 7: Things in Common

1. Scheff (1967: 36) suggests that it is this higher order of co-orientation—a recognition of shared recognition—which is at the basis of Durkheim's conception of the "collective consciousness", by ordering individual consciousnesses into a social structure. While the point is often left implicit in anthropological culture theory, it is made quite clearly in Goodenough's (1963: 257—265) analysis of interaction and public culture. This notion of shared understandings is probably of greater than ordinary interest in this case as the sharing is given prominence in community self-definition.

2. One might say that the ghetto dwellers have a clear understanding that their shared perspective is to a great extent a reference group phenomenon rather than something to be taken for granted as a universal in the society; see the very relevant paper by Shibutani (1955).

3. An extreme case of such normalization of an illegal business enterprise is that cited by Short and Strodtbeck (1965: 109) from a black area in Chicago: a marihuana pusher who was moving away included a note with each bag sold, explaining that she was leaving the area. She thanked patrons for past purchases, gave her new address, and asked them to stay with her as customers at the new place of business. Short and Strodtbeck also note that illegal businesses tend to be more strongly integrated into the black ghetto community than into white lower-class areas.

4. The point made is similar to that made by Frankenberg (1966: 78, 265) on illegal cock fighting in Cumberland. However, Frankenberg goes so far as to say that cock fights are held partially *in order to* express defiance against authority vested outside the community. I believe the intrinsic value of the numbers game and of bootlegging is quite enough to keep them alive in the ghetto, but a heightened awareness of conflict with the wider society is undoubtedly a *consequence* of involvement with the illegal institutions.

5. For more detailed, relatively early studies of the numbers game (also known as "policy") in Harlem and the black ghetto of Chicago, see McKay (1940: 101—116) and Drake and Cayton (1962: 470—494) respectively.

6. McCall (1963) has analyzed the symbiosis of occultism and the numbers game, with an emphasis on the profits derived by occult advisors and suppliers from applied numerology.

7. This discussion about the function of the soul concept has been carried out further in Hannerz 1968. For a view of the soul concept of black jazz musicians, see Hentoff (1961: 60—74) and Szwed (1966).

8. Keil provides a view of the variety of conceptions and referents of soul of black blues singers, disc jockeys, and listeners to a black radio station in Chicago who were asked to call in and talk about soul (Keil 1966: 166—181).

9. Hernton (1966: 3—9) is a recent black commentator on the Northern ghetto dweller as a Southerner.

10. The growth of soul awareness has meant that many black people who have moved out of the direct poverty and who were once bent on mainstream assimilation —who "wouldn't be caught dead with a water melon"—have now turned back to these dishes. One man in a "better" area on the fringe of the ghetto had this to say of his neighbors' changing tastes: "Some of those people wouldn't have touched that kind of stuff only a few years ago. Now it smells like down South all over the place when you get home in the evening. Soul food, you know." But most ghetto dwellers probably have more natural attachments to soul food and do not have to embrace it solely for the sake of symbolism. For a leading black writer's view of soul food see LeRoi Jones (1966: 101—104).

11. A particularly clear characterization of a preacher in such terms can also be found in Clarence L. Cooper's (1963) story "Yet Princes Follow". Powdermaker (1939: 162), in her description of the black community in a Mississippi town, notes that ministers are notorious violators of the seventh commandment.

12. Charles Keil's study *Urban Blues* (1966) is remarkable for its discussion of the blues singer's expression of the black experience, as well as for its comments on related subjects. However, it seems that with soul music in its current form, the ghetto taste has now moved beyond the singers which Keil discusses at greatest length.

13. Horton (1957: 576), who studied the lyrics of American popular songs as published in periodicals devoted solely to this field, found only a slightly stronger tendency for rhythm and blues lyrics than for white popular songs to concentrate on the downward course of male-female relationships. However, one might speculate whether there is any tendency to publish only certain kinds of lyrics in such periodicals; it is noteworthy that the rhythm and blues publication used was turned out by the same publisher as the white-oriented periodicals.

14. The objectivation of conventional understandings, whereby these become fixed as enduring facts of life beyond the negotiation of reality in the face-to-face situation, is discussed by Berger and Luckmann (1966).

15. See the discussion of the "cultural apparatus" concept in chapter 4; also Mills (1963: 405 ff.).

16. For a discussion of categorical relationships see Mitchell (1966: 52—54).

17. On the other hand, there are cities with one black radio station in a monopoly

position. Such stations need not go to great lengths to secure black listeners and are therefore sometimes only minimally responsive to the listeners' desires.

18. See Jayawardena 1968 for an interesting analysis of the conflict between differentiation and the ideology of human egalitarianism in low-status groups where achievement in the wider society is possible—the case of the ghetto appears to support his discussion.

## Chapter 8: Waiting for the Burning to Begin

1. The Report of the National Advisory Commission on Civil Disorders (1968) may be consulted for a more general survey of ghetto dwellers' grievances. Mainstream institutional contacts with the ghetto are discussed by Jacobs (1966).

2. Goldberg (1968: 125) notes that only certain kinds of grievances seem to call forth risings directly. While this may be true—and the police would then certainly have to be seen as an object of discontent particularly often involved— it seems questionable, as Rainwater (1967: 31) points out, if unrest would be prevented by dealing with factors which may be of a largely symptomatic nature. See also the comments at the end of this chapter.

3. In fact, some articles which could easily be seen as luxuries become necessities in a society where they are assumed to be everybody's property. The car is the best example. William Jackson, a teenager, was sitting in his mother's old station wagon, smoking cigarettes with a friend, when somehow the car caught fire. The two boys tried to extinguish the fire but failed; by the time the firemen arrived the car was destroyed, and Mrs. Jackson had to stop working. She was a domestic in a distant Maryland suburb, and the taxi fare would be too expensive, while there was no reasonably convenient public transportation. See also George's troubles as he crashed his car, in chapter 2.

4. According to the Report of the National Advisory Commission on Civil Disorders, retail outlets specializing in instalment sales to ghetto dwellers in Washington charge an average 52 percent more for furniture and appliances than other stores in the area (National Advisory Commission on Civil Disorders 1968: 276).

5. Such problems for the shopkeepers may also contribute to higher prices.

6. For a discussion of the professional ideology of ghetto policemen and other matters relating to their performance and standing in the ghetto community see Fogelson (1968).

7. Bateson (1935) defines symmetrical schismogenesis as the process whereby two parties progressively react to each other by strengthening those similar responses which indicate the conflict between them.

8. The routinization of the Nation of Islam is discussed by Parenti (1964); Essien-Udom (1962) gives a general account of the movement.

9. The brief account of the April rising which follows was compiled from personal observations, conversations with ghetto dwellers (most of them from Winston Street) and the reports of the *Washington Post* and the *Evening Star*.

10. Obviously there were tendencies toward the growth of what Tomlinson (1968) has called a "riot ideology", supporting or at least showing sympathetic understanding toward risings.

11. Black militant groups seem also to have become stronger after the risings in Watts, Newark, and Detroit.

12. For a discussion of the policeman as a peace officer see Banton (1964, particularly pp. 166—176).

13. Unless, of course, black enterprises in the ghetto expanded so as to take on a great part of the ghetto labor force.

## Chapter 9: Mainstream and Ghetto in Culture

1. In the debate over the "Moynihan Report", for example, Elizabeth Herzog (1967) and Hylan Lewis (1967a) both note the correlation between ethnicity and low income.

2. A paper by Gladwin (1961) is another well-known example of a social-work perspective. However, in a later book, Gladwin (1967) draws the problems of macrostructural constraints more directly into the picture.

3. It may be noted that Kriesberg takes the unduly restrictive view that only parental transmission is cultural. One might also dispute the view that interaction patterns should be seen as parts of situational rather than cultural explanations.

4. Of course, contemporary ecological anthropology tends to take both the natural and the social environment into account, as for instance in the case of Barth (1956). Bennett (1967: 452) has noted that a "natural environment model" may be difficult to apply to the relationship between a local community and its wider social setting because the latter is responsive to the demands of the community and therefore not as inflexible as a natural environment. In this case, however, this ecological paradigm may be more than usually applicable, as the wider social environment has been quite unresponsive to ghetto needs and demands.

5. As Gans (1967b: 24) makes clear, what is cultural according to his definition can only be established in an experimental situation.

6. As Barth (1966: 12) points out, one may well regard the integration of culture as questionable and a matter of degree. Here we may also note that Roach and Gursslin (1967: 387 n.) view the lack of completeness as a ground for rejecting an analysis of poverty in terms of culture. Since they find no descriptions of the culture of poverty including such characteristics as leadership, hierarchy of command, or task differentiation—phenomena generally present in complex cultural systems, they say—it can hardly be a culture. Of course, this view is easy to criticize. The culture of poverty, as is generally recognized, is a subculture. Thus it differs from mainstream culture only in some ways, and the poor also participate in many mainstream structures. The leadership, the division of labor, and the hierarchy of command are largely involved in the relationships of the poor to the wider society. Furthermore, of course, we must not determine cultur-alness on the basis of some preconceived notions of cultural universals.

7. This formulation draws on Watzlawick et al. (1967: 48—51).

8. The idea that standards of appropriateness are upheld by the "labeling" of deviance has been developed by Becker (1963: 8 ff.).

9. It should be noted that these remarks were made in conversations between ghetto dwellers; thus they are modes of accounting employed within the community.

10. The analysis which follows draws on Goodenough's (1963: 257—262) interac-tionist model of culture. "Cultural repertoire" as used here resembles his "private culture", while "interaction idiom" resembles his "operating culture".

11. The point that mainstream culture is alive and well in the low-income community has been clearly stated by Rainwater (1966c) and Yancey (n.d.).

12. Of course, the groups habitually exhibiting a mode of action are the primary information storage units for it. Unless others who usually keep it hidden away in their repertoires could continuously retrieve new information about it from these former groups, it is likely that the item in question would tend to be forgotten. For a view of cultures as information systems see Roberts (1964).

13. This is the view taken by Rainwater (1966a: 119—123).

14. Bennett Berger (1967) makes this point in a review of Charles Keil's *Urban Blues,* in which the content of soul is taken to be a basis of cultural revitaliza-tion.

15. Of course, such a redefinition of soul could very well take place. One may note

here, for instance, that the Impressions' soul hit "We're a winner" shows much more forward-looking optimism than most other texts.

## Appendix: In the Field

1. This is true of most anthropological research, of course, although not of action anthropology.
2. A noteworthy account of somewhat similar problems of field work in another area where the researcher faces considerable social barriers is Polsky's essay, "Research Method, Morality, and Criminology" (Polsky 1967: 117—149).
3. The Winston Street neighborhood, as seen by the people of the street and in this volume, is an "egocentric" territory—it refers to this street and its immediate environs beyond which it fades out. Although Winston Street people include neighboring streets at the periphery of their neighborhood, people on these streets certainly do not count themselves as residents of a Winston Street neigborhood. Since each street is the center of its world, neighborhoods overlap.
4. Curiously enough, no neighborhood resident mentioned these earlier interviews to me. Possibly they were connected only to the previous involvements of white outsiders rather than to me.

# References

ABRAHAMS, ROGER D., 1962. Playing the Dozens. *Journal of American Folklore,* 75: 209—220.

— 1964. *Deep Down in the Jungle.* Hatboro, Pa.: Folklore Associates.

AYOUB, MILLICENT R., and STEPHEN A. BARNETT, 1965. Ritualized Verbal Insult in White High School Culture. *Journal of American Folklore,* 78: 336—344.

BANDURA, ALBERT, and RICHARD H. WALTERS, 1963. *Social Learning and Personality Development.* New York: Holt, Rinehart and Winston.

BANTON, MICHAEL, 1955. *The Coloured Quarter.* London: Cape.

— 1964. *The Policeman in the Community.* London: Tavistock.

— 1965. *Roles.* London: Tavistock.

BARNES, J. A., 1954. Class and Committees in a Norwegian Island Parish. *Human Relations,* 7: 39—58.

— 1968. Networks and Political Process. In *Local-Level Politics.* Marc J. Swartz (ed.). Chicago: Aldine.

BARTH, FREDRIK, 1956. Ecologic Relationships of Ethnic Groups in Swat, North Pakistan. *American Anthropologist,* 58: 1079—1089.

— 1963. *The Role of the Entrepreneur in Social Change in Northern Norway.* Bergen and Oslo: Norwegian Universities Press.

— 1966. *Models of Social Organization.* London: Royal Anthropological Institute of Great Britain and Ireland, Occasional paper no. 23.

BATESON, GREGORY, 1935. Culture Contact and Schismogenesis. *Man,* 35: 178—183.

— 1942. Some Systematic Approaches to the Study of Culture and Personality. *Character and Personality,* 11: 76—82.

BECKER, HOWARD S., 1963. *Outsiders.* New York: Free Press.

BECKER, HOWARD S., and ANSELM L. STRAUSS, 1956. Careers, Personality, and Adult Socialization. *American Journal of Sociology,* 62: 253—263.

BENDER, DONALD R., 1967. A Refinement of the Concept of Household: Families, Co-residence, and Domestic Functions. *American Anthropologist,* 69: 493—504.

BENNETT, JOHN W., 1967. Microcosm-Macrocosm Relationships in North American Agrarian Society. *American Anthropologist,* 69: 441—454.

BERGER, BENNETT M., 1963. The Sociology of Leisure: Some Suggestions. In *Work and Leisure.* Erwin O. Smigel (ed.). New Haven, Conn.: College and University Press.

— Soul Searching. *Trans-action,* 4: 7: 54—57.

BERGER, PETER, and HANSFRIED KELLNER, 1964. Marriage and the Construction of Reality. *Diogenes,* 46: 1—24.

BERGER, PETER L., and THOMAS LUCKMANN, 1966. *The Social Construction of Reality.* Garden City, N.Y.: Doubleday.

BERNARD, JESSIE, 1966. *Marriage and Family among Negroes.* Englewood Cliffs, N.J.: Prentice-Hall.

BIRDWHISTELL, RAY L., 1966. The American Family: Some Perspectives. *Psychiatry,* 29: 203—212.

BLAKE, JUDITH, 1961. *Family Structure in Jamaica.* New York: Free Press.

BOISSEVAIN, JEREMY, 1968. The Place of Non-groups in the Social Sciences. *Man*, n.s., 3: 542—556.

BOORSTIN, DANIEL J., 1964. *The Image: A Guide to Pseudo-Events in America*. New York: Harper Colophon Books.

BOTT, ELIZABETH, 1957. *Family and Social Network*. London: Tavistock.

BOYER, RUTH M., 1964. The Matrifocal Family among the Mescalero: Additional Data. *American Anthropologist*, 66: 593—602.

BRIM, ORVILLE G., JR., 1958. Family Structure and Sex-Role Learning by Children. *Sociometry*, 21: 1—16.

BRODY, EUGENE B., 1961. Social Conflict and Schizophrenic Behavior in Young Adult Negro Males. *Psychiatry*, 24: 337—346.

BROWN, CLAUDE, 1965. *Manchild in the Promised Land*. New York: Macmillan.

BURKE, KENNETH, 1965. *Permanence and Change*. Indianapolis: Bobbs-Merrill.

BURTON, ROGER V., and JOHN W. M. WHITING, 1961. The Absent Father and Cross-Sex Identity. *Merrill-Palmer Quarterly*, 7: 85—95.

CARMICHAEL, STOKELY, 1966. What We Want. *New York Review of Books*, September 22: 5—8.

— 1968 a. Black Power. In *The Dialectics of Liberation*. David Cooper (ed.). Harmondsworth: Penguin.

— 1968 b. Speech at the Oakland Auditorium. *Washington Free Press*, 2: 26: 10—13.

CHARTERS, SAMUEL, 1963. *The Poetry of the Blues*. New York: Oak Publications.

CLARKE, EDITH, 1957. *My Mother Who Fathered Me*. London: Allen & Unwin.

CLOWARD, RICHARD A., and LLOYD E. OHLIN, 1960. *Delinquency and Opportunity*. New York: Free Press.

COHEN, ALBERT K., 1955. *Delinquent Boys*. Glencoe, Ill.: Free Press.

COLBY, BENJAMIN N., 1966. Cultural Patterns in Narrative. *Science*, 151: 793—798.

CONFERENCE ON ECONOMIC PROGRESS, 1962. *Poverty and Deprivation in the U.S.* Washington, D.C.: Conference on Economic Progress.

COOLEY, CHARLES H., 1902. *Human Nature and the Social Order*. New York: Scribner's.

COOPER, CLARENCE L., JR., 1963. *Black!* Evanston, Ill.: Regency Books.

CROWLEY, DANIEL J., 1962. Negro Folklore. An Africanist's View. *Texas Quarterly*, 5: 3: 65—71.

DAI, BINGHAM, 1949. Some Problems of Personality Development among Negro Children. In *Personality in Nature, Society, and Culture*. Clyde Kluckhohn and Henry A. Murray (eds.). New York: Knopf.

DENNIS, NORMAN, FERNANDO HENRIQUES, and CLIFFORD SLAUGHTER, 1956. *Coal is Our Life*. London: Eyre & Spottiswoode.

DERBYSHIRE, ROBERT L., EUGENE B. BRODY, and CARL SCHLEIFER, 1963. Family Structure of Young Adult Negro Male Mental Patients: Preliminary Observations from Urban Baltimore. *Journal of Nervous and Mental Disease*, 136: 245—251.

DERTHICK, MARTHA, 1962. *City Politics in Washington, D.C.* Cambridge, Mass., and Washington, D.C.: Joint Center for Urban Studies of the Massachusetts Institute of Technology and Harvard University/Washington Center for Metropolitan Studies.

DOLLARD, JOHN, 1937. *Caste and Class in a Southern Town*. New Haven, Conn.: Yale University Press.

— 1939. The Dozens: Dialectic of Insult. *American Imago*, 1: 3—25.

DORSON, RICHARD M., 1967. *American Negro Folktales*. New York: Fawcett Premier Books.

DOUGLAS, MARY, 1968. The Social Control of Cognition: Some Factors in Joke Perception. *Man*, n.s., 3: 361—376.

DRAKE, ST. CLAIR, 1957. Recent Trends in Research on the Negro in the United States. *International Social Science Bulletin*, 9: 475—492.

DRAKE, ST. CLAIR, and HORACE R. CAYTON, 1962. *Black Metropolis*. New York: Harper Torchbooks. (First edition 1945, Harcourt, Brace.)

ELLISON, RALPH, 1967. A Very Stern Discipline. *Harper's Magazine*, March.

ESSIEN-UDOM, E. U., 1962. *Black Nationalism*. Chicago: University of Chicago Press.

FERMAN, LOUIS A., JOYCE L. KORNBLUH, and ALAN HABER (eds.), 1965. *Poverty in America*. Ann Arbor: University of Michigan Press.

FINESTONE, HAROLD, 1957. Cats, Kicks, and Color. *Social Problems*, 5: 3—13.

FISCHER, ANN, and CHRISTINE DERBES, 1966. Further Comments on Otterbein. *American Anthropologist*, 68: 497—499.

FOGELSON, ROBERT M., 1968. From Resentment to Confrontation: The Police, the Negroes, and the Outbreak of the Nineteen-Sixties Riots. *Political Science Quarterly*, 83: 217—247.

FRANKENBERG, RONALD, 1966. *Communities in Britain*. Harmondsworth: Penguin.

FRAZIER, E. FRANKLIN, 1934. Traditions and Patterns of Negro Family Life in the United States. In *Race and Culture Contacts*. E. B. Reuter (ed.). New York: McGraw-Hill.

— 1939. *The Negro Family in the United States*. Chicago: University of Chicago Press.

— 1949. *The Negro in the United States*. New York: Macmillan.

— 1957. *Black Bourgeoisie*. Glencoe, Ill.: Free Press.

FREILICH, MORRIS, 1961. Serial Polygyny, Negro Peasants, and Model Analysis, *American Anthropologist*, 63: 955—975.

GANS, HERBERT J., 1962a. Urbanism and Suburbanism as Ways of Life: A Re-evaluation of Definitions. In *Human Behavior and Social Processes*. Arnold M. Rose (ed.). Boston: Houghton Mifflin.

— 1962b. *The Urban Villagers*. New York: Free Press.

— 1967a. The Negro Family: Reflections on the Moynihan Report. In Lee Rainwater and William L. Yancey, *The Moynihan Report and the Politics of Controversy*. Cambridge, Mass.: M.I.T. Press.

— 1967b. Poverty and Culture: Some Basic Questions About Methods of Studying Life-Styles of the Poor. Mimeographed, International Seminar on Poverty, University of Essex.

GEERTZ, CLIFFORD, 1966. Religion as a Cultural System. In *Anthropological Approaches to the Study of Religion* (ASA 3). Michael Banton (ed.). London: Tavistock.

GLADWIN, THOMAS, 1961. The Anthropologist's View of Poverty. In *The Social Welfare Forum*. New York: Columbia University Press.

— 1967. *Poverty U.S.A.* Boston: Little, Brown.

GLAZER, NATHAN, 1966. Foreword. In E. Franklin Frazier, *The Negro Family in the United States*. Chicago: University of Chicago Press.

GLAZER, NATHAN, and DANIEL PATRICK MOYNIHAN, 1963. *Beyond the Melting Pot*. Cambridge, Mass.: M.I.T. Press.

GOFFMAN, ERVING, 1955. On Face-Work. *Psychiatry*, 18: 213—231.

— 1959. *The Presentation of Self in Everyday Life*. Garden City, N.Y.: Doubleday Anchor Books.

— 1961. *Encounters*. Indianapolis: Bobbs-Merrill.

— 1967. *Interaction Ritual*. Chicago: Aldine.

GOLDBERG, LOUIS C., 1968. Ghetto Riots and Others: The Faces of Civil Disorder in 1967. *Journal of Peace Research*, 5: 116—131.

GONZALES, AMBROSE E., 1924. *With Aesop Along the Black Border*. Columbia, S.C.: The State Company.

GOODE, WILLIAM J., 1960. Illegitimacy in the Caribbean Social Structure. *American Sociological Review*, 25: 21—30.

— 1966. Note on Problems in Theory and Method: The New World. *American*

*Anthropologist,* 68: 486—492.

GOODENOUGH, WARD H., 1963. *Cooperation in Change.* New York: Russell Sage Foundation.

GOODY, JACK (ed.), 1958. *The Developmental Cycle in Domestic Groups.* London: Cambridge University Press.

GOUGH, KATHLEEN, 1968. Anthropology and Imperialism. *Monthly Review,* 19: 11: 12—27.

GREENFIELD, SIDNEY M., 1966. *English Rustics in Black Skin.* New Haven, Conn.: College and University Press.

GRIER, EUNICE S., 1961. *Understanding Washington's Changing Population.* Washington, D.C.: Washington Center for Metropolitan Studies.

GULICK, JOHN, 1963. Urban Anthropology: Its Present and Future. *Transactions of the New York Academy of Sciences,* ser. II, 25: 445—458.

HAMMOND, PETER B., 1959. The Functions of Indirection in Communication. In *Comparative Studies in Administration.* James D. Thompson, Peter B. Hammond, Robert Hawkes, Buford H. Junker, and Arthur Tuden (eds.). Pittsburgh: University of Pittsburgh Press.

— 1964. Mossi Joking. *Ethnology,* 3: 259—267.

HAMPTON, BILL R., 1967. On Identification and Negro Tricksters. *Southern Folklore Quarterly,* 31: 55—65.

HANNERZ, ULF, 1967. Gossip, Networks and Culture in a Black American Ghetto. *Ethnos,* 32: 35—60.

— 1968. The Rhetoric of Soul: Identification in Negro Society. *Race,* 9: 453—465.

HARE, NATHAN, 1965. *The Black Anglo-Saxons.* New York: Marzani & Munsell.

HARRINGTON, MICHAEL, 1962. *The Other America.* New York: Macmillan.

HAYAKAWA, S. I., 1968. Television and the American Negro. In *Sight, Sound, and Society.* David Manning White and Richard Averson (eds.). Boston: Beacon Press.

HENRIQUES, FERNANDO, 1953. *Family and Colour in Jamaica.* London: Eyre & Spottiswoode.

HENTOFF, NAT, 1961. *The Jazz Life.* New York: Dial.

HERNTON, CALVIN C., 1966. *White Papers for White Americans.* Garden City, N.Y.: Doubleday.

HERSKOVITS, MELVILLE J., 1941. *The Myth of the Negro Past.* New York: Harper.

— 1966. *The New World Negro.* Bloomington, Ind.: Indiana University Press.

HERZOG, ELIZABETH, 1963. Some Assumptions About the Poor. *Social Service Review,* 37: 391—400.

— 1967. Is There a "Breakdown" of the Negro Family? In Lee Rainwater and William L. Yancey, *The Moynihan Report and the Politics of Controversy.* Cambridge, Mass.: M.I.T. Press.

HOROWITZ, MICHAEL M., 1967. A Decision Model of Conjugal Patterns in Martinique. *Man,* n.s., 2: 445—453.

HORTON, DONALD, 1957. The Dialogue of Courtship in Popular Songs. *American Journal of Sociology,* 62: 569—578.

JACKSON, BRUCE, 1966. White Dozens and Bad Sociology. *Journal of American Folklore,* 79: 374—377.

JACOBS, PAUL, 1966. *Prelude to Riot.* New York: Random House.

JAYAWARDENA, CHANDRA, 1968. Ideology and Conflict in Lower Class Communities. *Comparative Studies in Society and History,* 10: 413—446.

JONES, LEROI, 1966. *Home: Social Essays.* New York: Morrow.

KAGAN, JEROME, 1964. Acquisition and Significance of Sex Typing and Sex Role Identity. In *Review of Child Development Research,* vol. 1. Martin L. Hoffman and Lois Wladis Hoffman (eds.). New York: Russell Sage Foundation.

KARENGA, RON, 1968. From the Quotable Karenga. In *The Black Power Revolt*. Floyd B. Barbour (ed.). Boston: Porter Sargent.

KEIL, CHARLES, 1966. *Urban Blues*. Chicago: University of Chicago Press.

KLUCKHOHN, CLYDE, 1942. Myths and Rituals: A General Theory. *Harvard Theological Review*, 35: 45—79.

KOMAROVSKY, MIRRA, 1964. *Blue Collar Marriage*. New York: Random House.

KRIESBERG, LOUIS, 1963. The Relationship between Socio-economic Rank and Behavior. *Social Problems*, 10: 334—353.

KUNSTADTER, PETER, 1963. A Survey of the Consanguine or Matrifocal Family. *American Anthropologist*, 65: 56—66.

LESTER, JULIUS, 1968. *Look Out Whitey! Black Power's Gon' Get Your Mama!* New York: Dial.

LEVI-STRAUSS, CLAUDE, 1953. Social Structure. In *Anthropology Today*. A. L. Kroeber (ed.). Chicago: University of Chicago Press.

LEWIS, HYLAN, 1955. *Blackways of Kent*. Chapel Hill, N.C.: University of North Carolina Press.

— 1967a. The Family—Resources for Change. In Lee Rainwater and William L. Yancey, *The Moynihan Report and the Politics of Controversy*. Cambridge, Mass.: M.I.T. Press.

— 1967b. *Culture, Class and Poverty*. Washington, D.C.: Cross-Tell.

LEWIS, OSCAR, 1959. *Five Families*. New York: Basic Books.

— 1961. *The Children of Sánchez*. New York: Random House.

— 1966. *La Vida*. New York: Random House.

LIEBOW, ELLIOT, 1967. *Tally's Corner*. Boston: Little, Brown.

LINTON, RALPH, 1936. *The Study of Man*. New York: Appleton-Century-Crofts.

MAILER, NORMAN, n.d. *The White Negro*. San Francisco: City Lights Books.

MALINOWSKI, BRONISLAW, 1926. *Myth in Primitive Psychology*. New York: Norton.

MATZA, DAVID, 1964. *Delinquency and Drift*. New York: Wiley.

MATZA, DAVID, and GRESHAM H. SYKES, 1961. Juvenile Delinquency and Subterranean Values. *American Sociological Review*, 26: 712—719.

MAYER, ADRIAN C., 1966. The Significance of Quasi-Groups in the Study of Complex Societies. In *The Social Anthropology of Complex Societies* (ASA 4). Michael Banton (ed.). London: Tavistock.

McCALL, GEORGE J., 1963. Symbiosis: The Case of Hoodoo and the Numbers Racket. *Social Problems*, 10: 361—371.

McCALL, GEORGE J., and J. L. SIMMONS, 1966. *Identities and Interactions*. New York: Free Press.

McKAY, CLAUDE, 1940. *Harlem: Negro Metropolis*. New York: Dutton.

McLUHAN, MARSHALL, 1965. *Understanding Media*. New York: McGraw-Hill Paperbacks.

MERTON, ROBERT K., 1957. *Social Theory and Social Structure*. Glencoe, Ill.: Free Press.

MERTON, ROBERT K., and ELINOR BARBER, 1963. Sociological Ambivalence. In *Sociological Theory, Values, and Sociocultural Change*. Edward A. Tiryakian (ed.). New York: Free Press.

MILLER, FRANK C., 1967. Humor in a Chippewa Tribal Council. *Ethnology*, 6: 263—271.

MILLER, WALTER B., 1958. Lower Class Culture as a Generating Milieu of Gang Delinquency. *Journal of Social Issues*, 14: 5—19.

— 1959. Implications of Urban Lower-Class Culture for Social Work. *Social Service Review*, 33: 219—236.

MILLER, WALTER B., HILDRED GEERTZ, and S. G. CUTTER, 1961. Aggression in a Boys' Street-Corner Group. *Psychiatry*, 24: 283—298.

MILLS, C. WRIGHT, 1963. *Power, Politics and People.* New York: Ballantine Books.

MINTZ, SIDNEY W., and WILLIAM DAVENPORT (eds.), 1961. Working Papers in Caribbean Social Organization. *Social and Economic Studies,* 10, no. 4.

MITCHELL, J. CLYDE, 1966. Theoretical Orientations in African Urban Studies. In *The Social Anthropology of Complex Societies* (ASA 4). Michael Banton (ed.). London: Tavistock.

MOYNIHAN, DANIEL P., 1965. Employment, Income, and the Ordeal of the Negro Family. *Daedalus,* 94: 745—770.

— 1967. The President & The Negro: The Moment Lost. *Commentary,* 43: 2: 31—45.

MYRDAL, GUNNAR, 1964. *An American Dilemma.* New York: McGraw-Hill Paperbacks. (First edition 1944, Harper & Row.)

NAROLL, RAOUL, and FRADA NAROLL, 1963. On Bias of Exotic Data. *Man,* 63: 24—26.

NATIONAL ADVISORY COMMISSION ON CIVIL DISORDERS, 1968. *Report of the National Advisory Commission on Civil Disorders.* New York: Bantam Books.

ODUM, HOWARD W., and GUY B. JOHNSON, 1925. *The Negro and His Songs.* Chapel Hill, N.C.: University of North Carolina Press.

OLIVER, PAUL, 1968. *Screening the Blues.* London: Cassell.

OTTERBEIN, KEITH F., 1965. Caribbean Family Organization: A Comparative Analysis. *American Anthropologist,* 67: 66—79.

— 1966a. *The Andros Islanders.* Lawrence: University of Kansas Press.

— 1966b. Otterbein's Reply to Goode. *American Anthropologist,* 68: 493—497.

PARENTI, MICHAEL, 1964. The Black Muslims: From Revolution to Institution. *Social Research,* 31: 175—194.

PARSONS, TALCOTT, 1942. Age and Sex in the Social Structure of the United States. *American Sociological Review,* 7: 604—616.

— 1943. The Kinship System of the Contemporary United States. *American Anthropologist,* 45: 22—38.

PARSONS, TALCOTT, and ROBERT F. BALES, 1955. *Family, Socialization and Interaction Process.* Glencoe, Ill.: Free Press.

PASSOW, A. HARRY, 1967. *Toward Creating a Model Urban School System: A Study of Washington, D.C., Public Schools.* New York: Columbia University Teachers College.

PETTIGREW, THOMAS F., 1964. *A Profile of the Negro American.* Princeton: Van Nostrand.

POLGAR, STEVEN, 1960. Biculturation of Mesquakie Teenage Boys. *American Anthropologist,* 62: 217—235.

POLSKY, NED, 1967. *Hustlers, Beats, and Others.* Chicago: Aldine.

POWDERMAKER, HORTENSE, 1939. *After Freedom.* New York: Viking.

— 1943. The Channeling of Negro Aggression by the Cultural Process. *American Journal of Sociology,* 48: 750—758.

PRESIDENT'S COMMISSION ON CRIME IN THE DISTRICT OF COLUMBIA, 1966. *Report of the President's Commission on Crime in the District of Columbia.* Washington, D.C.: U.S. Government Printing Office.

RADCLIFFE-BROWN, A. R., 1952. *Structure and Function in Primitive Society.* London: Cohen and West.

RAINWATER, LEE, 1964. Marital Sexuality in Four Cultures of Poverty. *Journal of Marriage and the Family,* 26: 457—466.

— 1966a. Work and Identity in the Lower Class. In *Planning for a Nation of Cities.* Sam Bass Warner, Jr. (ed.). Cambridge, Mass.: M.I.T. Press.

— 1966b. Crucible of Identity: The Negro Lower-Class Family. *Daedalus,* 95: 172—216.

— 1966c. The Problem of Lower Class Culture. Mimeographed, Washington University, St. Louis.

— 1967. Open Letter on White Justice and the Riots. *Trans-action,* 4: 9: 22—32.

RAINWATER, LEE, GERALD HANDEL, and RICHARD P. COLEMAN, 1959. *Workingman's Wife*. New York: Oceana.

RAINWATER, LEE, and WILLIAM L. YANCEY, 1967. *The Moynihan Report and the Politics of Controversy*. Cambridge, Mass.: M.I.T. Press.

RANDOLPH, RICHARD R., 1964. The "Matrifocal Family" as a Comparative Category. *American Anthropologist*, 66: 628—631.

REDFIELD, ROBERT, 1960. *The Little Community/Peasant Society and Culture*. Chicago: Phoenix Books.

RIESMAN, DAVID, ROBERT J. POTTER, and JEANNE WATSON, 1960. Sociability, Permissiveness, and Equality: A Preliminary Formulation. *Psychiatry*, 23: 323—340.

ROACH, JACK L., and ORVILLE R. GURSSLIN, 1967. An Evaluation of the Concept "Culture of Poverty". *Social Forces*, 45: 383—392.

ROBERTS, JOHN M., 1964. The Self-management of Cultures. In *Explorations in Cultural Anthropology*. Ward H. Goodenough (ed.). New York: McGraw-Hill.

ROBERTS, JOHN M., MALCOLM J. ARTH, and ROBERT R. BUSH, 1959. Games in Culture. *American Anthropologist*, 61: 597—605.

ROBERTS, JOHN M., and BRIAN SUTTON-SMITH, 1962. Child Training and Game Involvement. *Ethnology*, 1: 166—185.

ROBERTS, JOHN M., BRIAN SUTTON-SMITH, and ADAM KENDON, 1963. Strategy in Games and Folktales. *Journal of Social Psychology*, 61: 185—199.

RODMAN, HYMAN, 1963. The Lower-Class Value Stretch. *Social Forces*, 42: 205—215.

— 1966. Illegitimacy in the Caribbean Social Structure: A Reconsideration. *American Sociological Review*, 31: 673—683.

ROHRER, JOHN H., and MUNRO S. EDMONSON, 1964. *The Eighth Generation Grows Up*. New York: Harper Torchbooks. (First published 1960 as *The Eighth Generation* by Harper.)

SCHEFF, THOMAS J., 1967. Toward a Sociological Model of Consensus. *American Sociological Review*, 32: 32—46.

SCHORR, ALVIN L., 1964. The Nonculture of Poverty. *American Journal of Orthopsychiatry*, 34: 907—912.

SCOTT, MARVIN B., and STANFORD LYMAN, 1968. Accounts. *American Sociological Review*, 33: 46—62.

SEELEY, JOHN R., 1959. The Slum: Its Nature, Use, and Users. *Journal of the American Institute of Planners*, 25: 7—14.

SELIGMAN, BEN B., 1965. *Poverty as a Public Issue*. New York: Free Press.

SHIBUTANI, TAMOTSU, 1955. Reference Groups as Perspectives. *American Journal of Sociology*, 60: 562—569.

SHORT, JAMES F., and FRED L. STRODTBECK, 1965. *Group Process and Gang Delinquency*. Chicago: University of Chicago Press.

SIMMEL, GEORG, 1950. *The Sociology of Georg Simmel*. Kurt H. Wolff (ed.). Glencoe, Ill.: Free Press.

SINGER, L., 1962. Ethnogenesis and Negro-Americans Today. *Social Research*, 29: 419—432.

SMITH, M. G., 1962a. *West Indian Family Structure*. Seattle: University of Washington Press.

— 1962b. *Kinship and Community in Carriacou*. New Haven, Conn.: Yale University Press.

— 1966. Introduction. In Edith Clarke, *My Mother Who Fathered Me*. London: Allen & Unwin.

SMITH, RAYMOND T., 1956. *The Negro Family in British Guiana*. London: Routledge & Kegan Paul.

— 1957. The Family in the Caribbean. In *Caribbean Studies: A Symposium*. Vera Rubin (ed.). Seattle: University of Washington Press.

— 1963. Culture and Social Structure in the Caribbean: Some Recent Work on

Family and Kinship Studies. *Comparative Studies in Society and History,* 6: 24—46.

SMYTHE, HUGH H., and L. CHASE, 1958. Current Research on the Negro: A Critique. *Sociology and Social Research,* 42: 199—202.

SOLIEN DE GONZALEZ, NANCIE L., 1960. Household and Family in the Caribbean: Some Definitions and Concepts. *Social and Economic Studies,* 9: 101—106.

— 1965. The Consanguineal Household and Matrifocality. *American Anthropologist,* 67: 1541—1549.

STEWARD, JULIAN H., 1950. *Area Research.* New York: Social Science Research Council.

SUTTON-SMITH, BRIAN, JOHN M. ROBERTS, and ROBERT M. KOZELKA, 1963. Game Involvement in Adults. *Journal of Social Psychology,* 60: 15—30.

SYKES, GRESHAM M., and DAVID MATZA, 1957. Techniques of Neutralization: A Theory of Delinquency. *American Sociological Review,* 22: 664—670.

SZWED, JOHN F., 1966. Musical Style and Racial Conflict. *Phylon,* 27: 358—366.

TOBY, JACKSON, 1966. Violence and the Masculine Ideal: Some Qualitative Data. *Annals of the American Academy of Political and Social Science,* 364: 19—27.

TOMLINSON, T. M., 1968. The Development of a Riot Ideology among Urban Negroes. *American Behavioral Scientist,* 11: 4: 27—31.

TRANS-ACTION, 1968. The Census—What's Wrong With It, What Can Be Done. *Trans-action,* 5: 6: 49—56.

UNITED STATES DEPARTMENT OF LABOR, 1965. *The Negro Family: The Case for National Action.* Washington, D.C.: U.S. Department of Labor.

VALENTINE, CHARLES A., 1968. *Culture and Poverty.* Chicago: University of Chicago Press.

WATSON, JEANNE, 1958. A Formal Analysis of Sociable Interaction. *Sociometry,* 21: 269—280.

WATSON, JEANNE, and ROBERT J. POTTER, 1962. An Analytic Unit for the Study of Interaction. *Human Relations,* 15: 245—263.

WATZLAWICK, PAUL, JANET HELMICK BEAVIN, and DON D. JACKSON, 1967. *Pragmatics of Human Communication.* New York: Norton.

WHITAKER, BARBARA, 1967. Breakdown in the Negro Family: Myth or Reality? *New South,* 22: 4: 37—47.

WHITTEN, NORMAN E., JR., 1965. *Class, Kinship, and Power in an Ecuadorian Town.* Stanford, Calif.: Stanford University Press.

WHYTE, WILLIAM F., 1943. Social Organization in the Slums. *American Sociological Review,* 8: 34—39.

— 1964. The Slum: On the Evolution of Street Corner Society. In *Reflections on Community Studies.* Arthur J. Vidich, Joseph Bensman, and Maurice R. Stein (eds.). New York: Wiley.

WIRTH, LOUIS, 1928. *The Ghetto.* Chicago: University of Chicago Press.

WOLFENSTEIN, MARTHA, and NATHAN LEITES, 1950. *Movies.* Glencoe, Ill.: Free Press.

YABLONSKY, LEWIS, 1962. *The Violent Gang.* New York: Macmillan.

YANCEY, WILLIAM L., n.d. The Culture of Poverty: Not So Much Parsimony. Mimeographed, Washington University, St. Louis.

ZIJDERVELD, ANTON C., 1968. Jokes and Their Relation to Social Reality. *Social Research,* 35: 286—311.

ZORBAUGH, HARVEY F., 1929. *The Gold Coast and the Slum.* Chicago: University of Chicago Press.

# Index